CRIMINAL JUSTICE ILLUMINATED

Understanding Organized Crime

Stephen L. Mallory, PhD
Associate Professor of Legal Studies
University of Mississippi
Oxford, Mississippi

JONES AND BARTLETT PUBLISHERS
Sudbury, Massachusetts
BOSTON   TORONTO   LONDON   SINGAPORE

Jones and Bartlett Publishers
World Headquarters
40 Tall Pine Drive
Sudbury, MA 01776
978-443-5000
info@jbpub.com
www.jbpub.com

Jones and Bartlett Publishers Canada
6339 Ormindale Way
Mississauga, Ontario L5V 1J2
Canada

Jones and Bartlett Publishers International
Barb House, Barb Mews
London W6 7PA
United Kingdom

Jones and Bartlett's books and products are available through most bookstores and online booksellers. To contact Jones and Bartlett Publishers directly, call 800-832-0034, fax 978-443-8000, or visit our website www.jbpub.com.

> Substantial discounts on bulk quantities of Jones and Bartlett's publications are available to corporations, professional associations, and other qualified organizations. For details and specific discount information, contact the special sales department at Jones and Bartlett via the above contact information or send an email to specialsales@jbpub.com.

Production Credits
Chief Executive Officer: Clayton E. Jones
Chief Operating Officer: Donald W. Jones, Jr.
President, Higher Education and Professional Publishing: Robert W. Holland, Jr.
V.P., Sales and Marketing: William J. Kane
V.P., Production and Design: Anne Spencer
V.P., Manufacturing and Inventory Control: Therese Connell
Publisher, Public Safety Group: Kimberly Brophy
Acquisitions Editor: Jeremy Spiegel
Associate Managing Editor: Janet Morris
Production Supervisor: Jenny L. Corriveau
Photo Research Manager/Photographer: Kimberly Potvin
Director of Marketing: Alisha Weisman
Interior Design: Anne Spencer
Cover Design: Anne Spencer
Composition: Auburn Associates, Inc.
Cover Images: © Roberto Borea/AP Photos
Chapter Opener Image: © Masterfile
Text Printing and Binding: Malloy
Cover Printing: Malloy

Copyright 2007 by Jones and Bartlett Publishers, Inc.

All rights reserved. No part of the material protected by this copyright notice may be reproduced or utilized in any form, electronic or mechanical, including photocopying, recording, or by any information storage and retrieval system, without written permission from the copyright owner.

Library of Congress Cataloging-in-Publication Data

Mallory, Stephen L.
  Understanding organized crime / Stephen L. Mallory.
    p. cm.
  Includes bibliographical references and index.
  ISBN-13: 978-0-7637-4108-2
  ISBN-10: 0-7637-4108-6
 1. Organized crime. I. Title.
  HV6441.M38 2007
  364.106—dc22
6048   2006018229
Printed in the United States of America
11 10 09 08 07   10 9 8 7 6 5 4 3 2 1

Contents

Introduction xi
Acknowledgements xiii

1 An Introduction to Organized Crime 1

Defining Organized Crime as Part of the Process of Investigation 1
  A Working Definition for Organized Crime 2
  Definitions of Organized Crime 3
Investigation Definitions 4
Organized Crime as Defined by Laws, Agencies, and Governments 5
  International Perspective 6
  United States Federal Definitions 6
  A Synthesis of Definitions 8
  Other Approaches to Defining Organized Crime 9
Conclusions 10

2 Evolution of Organized Crime and the Impact on Investigative Strategies and Law Enforcement 14

Introduction 14
Origins of Organized Crime in the United States 16
  Colonial Piracy 16
  Rise of Robber Barons and Crime Families 17
  Immigrant Crime Groups and Political Machines 17
New Impetus for Expansion of Organized Crime in the United States 20
  Anti-Crime Legislation and the Growth of Organized Criminal Groups 21
Development of Organized Crime in the South 22
  Illegal Whiskey 23
Modern Development 25
  Commissions and Task Forces 25
Corporate and Political Corruption: The Major Contribution to Organized Crime Growth and Power 26
Future Impact on Law Enforcement Efforts 27

3 Theories on the Continued Existence of Organized Crime 32

Introduction 32
Theories 34
  Alien Conspiracy Theory 34

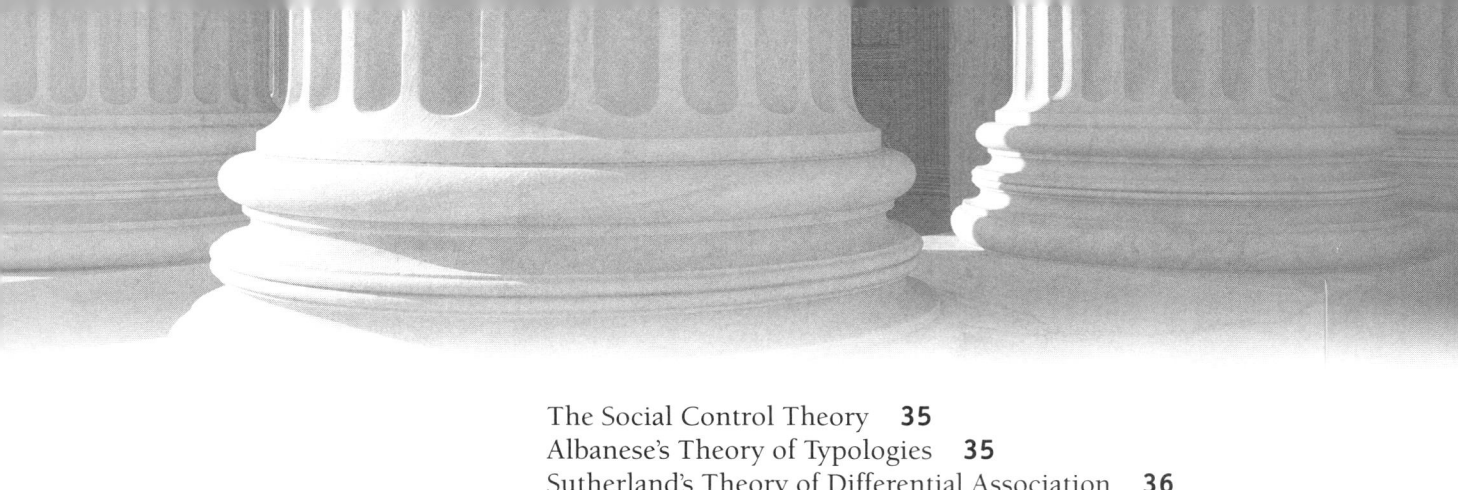

  The Social Control Theory 35
  Albanese's Theory of Typologies 35
  Sutherland's Theory of Differential Association 36
  Durkheim and Morton's Strain Theory and Anomie 36
  Beccaria and Lombroso's Classical Theories 37
  Biological Theories 37
Summary of the Theoretical Approach 37
Theories Related to Law Enforcement Efforts 38
  Enterprise Theory 39
  Hierarchical and Local-Ethnic Models 40
  Deterrence Theory 40
  Other Models 41
Beyond Theory 41
Combining Theory and Other Explanations 42
Conclusions 45

4 Colombian Drug Cartels 49

Introduction 49
Historical Perspective 49
The Medellín Cartel 52
  Operations 52
The Cali Cartel 53
  Operations 53
Decline of the Major Cartels 56
Current Activities 57
  "Baby" Cartels 58
  FARC 58
  Paramilitary Groups 58
  Plan Colombia 59
Conclusions 60

5 Mexican Drug Trafficking Organizations (DTOs) 63

Introduction 63
Historical Perspective 63
Development and Expansion 64
Mexican Drug Violence and DTO Competition 65
The Four Major Cartels 66
  Tijuana Cartel (Arellano Felix Organization) 66
  Gulf Cartel 67

    Sinaloa Cartel   **67**
    Juárez Cartel   **67**
    Subsidiary Groups   **68**
Current Activity   **69**
Drug Policies: Impact and Consequences   **70**
Conclusions   **71**

6   The Russian Mafia   73

Introduction   **73**
Historical Perspective   **73**
Structure and Organization   **76**
Activities and Methods of Operation   **78**
    Theft, Kidnapping, and Murder   **78**
    Cybercrime   **79**
    Extending Their Reach   **80**
Investigative Strategies   **85**
Conclusions   **87**

7   The Italian-American Mafia   90

Introduction   **90**
Historical Perspective   **91**
    Overview   **91**
    Immigration Years: The Black Hand   **92**
    Violation of Omerta   **94**
    The FBI and the Mafia   **94**
New York   **95**
    Arnold Rothstein   **95**
    Charles "Lucky" Luciano   **96**
    The Commission   **96**
    The Five Families of New York   **98**
Chicago   **99**
    Las Vegas and Sam Giancana   **100**
The American Mafia Today   **102**
Structure and Organization   **103**
    Membership   **105**
    Initiation   **106**
Activities and Methods of Operation   **107**
    Provision of Illicit Services and Goods   **107**

Investigative Strategies **109**
   Exposure: Informants and Witnesses **109**
   Sting Operations **110**
   Government Oversight **111**
   Grand Juries and Legislation **111**
Conclusions **112**

8   The Yakuza   114

Introduction **114**
Historical Perspective **115**
   Early Criminal Groups **115**
   The Industrial Age through Post-World War II **116**
   Yamaguchi-Gumi Crime Group **117**
   Yakuza Today **118**
Structure and Organization **120**
   Membership **120**
   Code of Conduct and Oaths **120**
Activities and Methods of Operation **123**
   Business Acquisition **123**
   Protection and Extortion **123**
   Gambling **123**
   Narcotics Trafficking **124**
   Pornography **124**
   Weapons and Smuggling **125**
   Money Laundering **125**
Investigative Strategies **126**
   Laws and Statutes **126**
   Special Task Forces **127**
   Follow the Money **127**
Conclusions **128**

9   Triads and Tongs   132

Introduction **132**
Historical Perspective **132**
   The Fighting Shaolin Monks **134**
   Chinese Rebellions Through the Revolution **135**
   Global Dispersal of the Triads **136**
Structure **137**

    Membership   137
    Tongs   140
  Activities and Methods of Operations   141
    Violence and Intimidation   144
    Turf Wars   144
    Business Investments   145
  Investigative Strategies   146
    Cultural and Language Barriers   146
    Surveillance and Sting Operations   146
  Conclusions   147

10 American Outlaw Motorcycle Gangs   150

  Introduction   150
  Historical Perspective   151
    Post-World War II   151
    1970 to Today   154
  The Big Four   154
    Hells Angels   155
    Outlaws   156
    Bandidos   156
    Pagans   157
  Other OMGs   160
    Grim Reapers   161
  Structure   162
    Membership   162
    Retirement By-Laws   167
  Activities and Methods of Operation   168
  Networks   168
  Investigative Strategies   169
    Intelligence   169
    Laws and Statutes   170
    Grand Juries   171
  Conclusions   172

11 Hispanic and African-American Gangs   174

  Introduction   174
  Historical Perspective   175
  Hispanic/Latino Gangs   175

    Gang Communication: Language, Graffiti, Hand Signals, and Dress **176**
        Clicas **176**
    Gang Culture **177**
    Gang Structure **178**
        Members **178**
    Major Gangs **179**
        Bloods and Crips **179**
        Jeff Fort and the Black P. Stone Nation **180**
        Larry Hoover and the Gangster Disciples **181**
    Historical Black Figures of Organized Crime **182**
        Frank Lucas **182**
        Frank Matthews **183**
        Leroy Barnes **183**
        Charles Lucas **183**
    Other Black Criminal Organizations **183**
        Nigerian Organized Crime **183**
        Jamaican Organized Crime **184**
    Prison Gangs **184**
    Investigative Strategies and Laws **185**
    Conclusions **186**

12 **Major Statutes, Legislation, and Methods of Organized Crime Investigations** **188**

    Introduction **188**
    The Hobbs Act and Extortion **189**
    RICO **190**
    Property Forfeiture **192**
    Violations of the Internal Revenue Code **193**
    Money Laundering Laws **194**
        The Money Laundering Cycle **196**
    Controlled Substances Acts **197**
    Conspiracy Statutes **197**
        Conspiracy Case Development **199**
        Continuing Criminal Enterprise Statute **200**
        The Kingpin Act **200**
        Regulation and Monitoring of Business and Labor **200**
        Electronic Surveillance **201**
        Investigative Grand Juries **202**

Other Statutes Frequently Used During Organized Crime
   Investigations   **203**
Conclusions   **203**

13   The Intelligence Function in Organized Crime —— 207

Introduction   **207**
Current Assessment of Organized Crime in the United States   **208**
   Organized Crime's Connection to Terrorist Groups   **208**
   Legislation   **209**
Intelligence   **209**
   Historical Perspective   **210**
   Evaluation of Information   **211**
   Sources of Intelligence   **212**
   Application of Analytical Models to Organized
      Crime Investigations   **213**
Conclusions   **217**

14   Where Do We Go From Here? —— 221

Law Enforcement Response   **221**

Introduction

With the current emphasis on terrorism, it is apparent that the assets of the U.S. Federal Government are being shifted to the enforcement efforts of antiterrorism and counterterrorism measures. This effort is placing more of the burden of the investigation of organized crime on state and local law enforcement. Although this emphasis on terrorism is both necessary and important, the enormous negative impact of organized crime on our society will not diminish, and the current trend of alliances between these criminal syndicates will demand innovative strategies and increased investigative efforts and resources. This book addresses the concept of organized crime and the various types of knowledge investigators need to effectively cope with the organizations that dominate the criminal world.

An investigation of an organized or syndicated crime group is perhaps the most complex and time-consuming effort an investigator is likely to encounter during his or her career. Facing an organization that is located in numerous jurisdictions, states, and/or countries, which commands unlimited resources and large memberships, the task of case development is very difficult at best. When the element of corruption is added to the equation, the investigation is often compromised in situations that become both frustrating and dangerous for the witnesses, informants, victims, and officers involved in the case.

Investigative techniques that have been effective in the past can be applied to each criminal enterprise with some success. Certainly, there are unique characteristics of each criminal organization that may call for specific enforcement techniques, but the majority of enforcement measures will be effective strategies to combat most of these groups and their activities. Law enforcement must continue to develop innovative tactics to address this type of criminal activity as well as build international cooperation to meet the challenge of global alliances and the growing complexity these organizations present.

The theme of corruption is paramount. Clearly, these criminal organizations cannot exist without corruption of not only police, but of many government officials as well as a variety of private citizens and businesses. The abilities of organized crime members to take advantage of financial systems that are cloaked in secrecy, supply the public's demand for illicit goods and services, and continue to create criminal opportunities that are extremely profitable are three common traits that serve to describe the organized crime groups.

Some organized groups originated as people forming alliances for good causes, such as protection and security from powerful foes. However, as with many enterprises, greed and power became the prime motivators fueling the formation of criminal syndicates. Although many writers and academics point to prohibitions of narcotics and alcohol as the origins of organized crime, it is my experience that power and greed are the root causes of this type of criminal behavior,

with prohibitions only serving as the impetus for their growth and success. Many of these groups have existed for decades and continue to evolve into more complex and diverse organizations. Leaders and bosses of these organizations typically began their career as petty criminals who escalated into the positions of authority because of their greed, cunning, ruthlessness, and lust for power. They are street-smart and often intelligent. But in the end, it is the public's demand for illicit goods and services, corruption, and the black markets that support the existence of these groups. Effective investigation can and does deter organized crime activity, but it will continue to exist as long as public support and market demand remain.

This book was written in an effort to increase the success of the criminal investigator. It is the informed criminal investigator who can apply the evolution, theories, structure, methods of operation, law, and investigative techniques to develop effective strategies to eliminate criminal enterprises. The reader will have a better understanding of the opposition as well as insights into their thought processes and operations. *Understanding Organized Crime* provides tools for the investigator to develop the critical thinking skills essential to deal with these powerful and continually evolving adversaries.

Acknowledgements

Reviewers

Stephen Brodt
Ball State University
Muncie, Indiana

David Licate
University of Akron
Akron, Ohio

Jerome Randall
University of Central Florida
Orlando, Florida

Contributors

Special thanks to the following people for their contributions to the text:

Thomas Barker
Eastern Kentucky University
Richmond, Kentucky

Stephen Brodt
Ball State University
Muncie, Indiana

An Introduction to Organized Crime

Chapter Objectives

After completing this chapter, readers should be able to:

- Describe the differences between organized and disorganized crime.
- Explain why defining organized crime is important to law enforcement.
- Compare the United States definitions of organized crime with those of other countries.
- Discuss state and federal legislation that address organized crime.

■ Defining Organized Crime as Part of the Process of Investigation

What is organized or syndicated crime? Why is it important for the criminal investigator to identify a target as organized crime? These questions must be answered before successful strategies, laws, and techniques can be developed for use in any successful investigation of a group of individuals engaged in criminal activity.

During the years when J. Edgar Hoover was the FBI Director (1924–1972), Americans debated whether organized crime actually existed. Later, organized crime became synonymous with the American Mafia. But the true nature and scope of organized crime is the insidious dynamic between those using ruthless methods (including corruption and murder) to increase their profits and an insatiable public hungry to purchase illegal goods and services.

Organized crime can be defined by the members and the activities of a group. There are many crimes in which organized crime might be involved, but what separates individual crime from crimes committed by groups of people is the term *organized* or *organization*. Organization has been described as a group of people who cooperate to accomplish objectives or goals. Max Weber, known as the "father of sociology," examined the elements of an organization. Weber (1947) lists rules, specialization and specialized training, a division of labor, a hierarchy of authority, and continuity or routinization as the parts of a structure necessary for the efficient function of bureaucracies.

Organized crime has incorporated many successful principles of legitimate business organizations including:

- A unit of command: a superior to whom one is directly responsible
- The principle of definition: clearly defining authority and responsibility
- The span of control: a limited number of people controlled by a supervisor
- The principle of objective: defining the purpose of the organization or what business is undertaken (i.e., drugs, murder for hire, extortion, gambling, etc.)
- Insulation and need-to-know principle: personnel have contact only with their immediate boss and peers
- Pyramidal structure: orders flow down the hierarchical chart and important decisions are made at the top
- Principle of specialization: members of organized crime are experts in a single job function
- Rules: omerta (vow of silence, never talking to police) and the process of becoming a member of an organized crime group

As with legitimate organizations, no two organized crime groups are exactly alike. Each group evolves in its own manner. Crime organizations require supervision and management to implement strategies that accomplish the goal of profit. Personnel administration is critical to organized crime just as it is to legitimate business organizations. Crime organizations remain bureaucratic with an autocratic leadership that employs punishment for failure, and monetary reward and promotion for success. Many organized crime members also are motivated by esteem, power, and recognition.

A Working Definition for Organized Crime

The 1986 President's Commission on Organized Crime concluded that a working definition must contain characteristics of both the activities and the group. Many countries and states include the structure of the group in their definition. The term *working definition* is useful to the investigator. Many police departments as well as state and federal agencies have dedicated resources to the investigation of organized crime. For the investigator, these resources are essential to the success of an organized crime investigation.

Resources such as manpower, money, equipment, and time are major considerations in an organized crime investigation. Classifying, identifying, or defining a group as a crime organization usually requires an extensive investment by the agency or department, a task often made more difficult by scarce resources. Once a group is declared as organized crime by a law enforcement entity, multi-agency and federal support is probable. The original case officer/agent may lose much control over the direction of the case or even be directed to go back to his or her normal duties, and allow the major case squad or agency to take charge of the case. Ideally, the supervisors would allow the originating officer or agent to be a part of the investigative team. But because special equipment and technology (such as electronic eavesdropping, remote sensing, and night or low-light vision equipment) are very expensive, these tasks will most likely be achieved by major case squads or federal or state agencies. Money is certainly the major factor in informant development, overtime pay, and special vehicles. These investigations may continue for years and require large numbers of officers and staff. It is easy to understand why organized crime investigations are not used for small support unit operations with limited resources. Therefore, the investigator must understand thoroughly and meticulously articulate why a group is an organized crime organization in order to obtain the resources needed for a successful investigation.

Definitions of Organized Crime

The definition of organized crime varies from agency to agency, from federal to state, and from state to state. An investigator must be sure to use the same definition used by the jurisdiction or agency in which the case is worked. Each element of the statute or definition must be articulated clearly to ensure the necessary resources and investigative support from the proper agencies are obtained. Defining organized crime accurately also will result in determining solutions for unique problems arising from a long-term and complex investigation. These cases often require long-sitting grand juries, informant protection, special prosecutors, extensive undercover operations, and extraordinary surveillance techniques.

It is important for investigators and resource allocators to agree upon a definition of organized crime when distinguishing between it and other criminal activity. A well-defined problem can link an initial investigation to the current evolution of organized crime. This may be a transnational or even international criminal organization requiring international cooperation and assistance. The proper definition refers to acts that are both *mala in se* and *mala prohibita*, and includes detailed information about how these became organized. The investigator must have an understanding of not only the academic definition, but also the legal definition.

However, finding a comprehensive definition is difficult and requires the investigator to synthesize definitions from both academia and the legal community. There are differences in world perceptions of organized crime (Albanese, Das, and Verma, 2003). If investigations are conducted outside the United States, knowing the other country's legal and academic definitions of organized crime is essential for obtaining assistance from the foreign government.

The advantages of synthesizing definitions of organized crime are as follows:
- Develops strategies and techniques for effective investigation
- Gains appropriate resource allocation to complete a long-term investigation
- Obtains cooperation and assistance regionally, nationally, and internationally
- Increases the investigator's understanding of the particular criminal group
- Prepares the investigator to address the sophistication, activities, and structures of organized crime
- Increases the understanding of the motivations that drive those involved in both case strategy and the judicial process

- Copes with the ever-present aspect of corruption
- Develops proactive solutions to prevent organized crime from becoming involved or controlling legal enterprises
- Predicts future organized crime trends and activities

Definitions provide understanding and often lead to effective solutions. The investigator who can synthesize numerous and diverse definitions becomes more effective because of the deep knowledge of the magnitude and complexity of the target: organized crime.

■ Investigation Definitions

The investigator can use a variety of terms to define organized crime. While these terms are similar in some respects, each provides a different insight into what it means to the investigator.

Consortium has been defined as "the union of fortunes, or the joining of several persons as parties to one action" (*Black's Law Dictionary*, 1990). A broader definition is "an agreement among or the combination of groups to undertake an enterprise beyond the resources of any one member" (*Webster's Dictionary*, 1983).

Cartel is "a combination of producers to control, monopolize, and restrict competition of the sale and price of a particular product or service" (*Black's Law Dictionary*, 1990).

Syndicate refers to an association of individuals who wish to carry out a business transaction, usually financial in nature. The risk of any single investor is diminished because of this partnership.

Organization also refers to two or more persons forming an association to conduct business. Individuals organize to function as a whole to become more effective and efficient.

A **gang** is "a company of persons who act in concert for criminal purposes (*Black's Law Dictionary*, 1990). Gangs are organized entrepreneurs who reinvest profits into the gang. They are structured organizations that market their illicit goods and services to make huge profits (Taylor, 1990). Other authors view gangs as disorganized individuals who form alliances to make money for each member (Fagan, Kelly, & Chin, 1989). Gangs have been described by law enforcement as an organized group with a recognized leader and a less powerful under-command. Their activities are viewed as criminal and a threat to society. Street-gang mentality includes what is often referred to as the "Three R's": Reputation, Respect, and Retaliation. (Note that the Three R's are characteristics found in almost all organized crime groups.) The Texas penal code defines a gang as, "Three or more persons having a common identifying sign or symbol or an identifiable leadership who continually or regularly associate in the commission of criminal activities" (*Texas Statutes and Codes Annotated*). Some street gangs have reached a level where they could be classified as organized crime, but this classification is debated even today.

Complex criminal groups may be classified as organized crime, syndicated crime, cartel, consortium, or gangs. How each group is classified is still debated.

One author refers to the "Bloods" or the "Disciple Nation" as a gang, while another refers to them as organized crime. The most important point for the criminal investigator to know is the specific definition that the resource allocators employ to make their decisions.

■ Organized Crime as Defined by Laws, Agencies, and Governments

Organized crime is defined differently depending on the perspectives of the legal profession, academia, government commissions, and other writers. Though some definitions are similar, there is no consensus of what defines a group as an organized crime group. In fact, there is no agreement that organized crime can be fully defined at all. Attempts by the legal community include the following:

> *Organized crime means the unlawful activities of the members of a highly organized, disciplined association engaged in supplying illegal goods and services including, but not limited to, gambling, prostitution, loan-sharking, narcotics, labor racketeering and other activities of members of organizations. (Omnibus Crime Control and Safe Streets Act, 1968)*

The FBI describes organized crime as a continuing criminal conspiracy with an organized structure that it is successful because of its use of fear, corruption, and violence. The motivation is greed (Bill McMath, FBI, personal communication 8/2/2001). This definition is very similar to that given by the President's Commission on Organized Crime in 1986. The FBI considers the following groups to be organized crime, and they are top priority targets for FBI agents:

1. La Cosa Nostra
2. The Russian Mafia
3. The Mexican drug cartels
4. The South American drug cartels
5. Asian organized crime groups
6. Major national gangs ("Bloods", "Crips", biker gangs, and so on)

The Racketeering Influenced and Corrupt Organizations (RICO) statute describes acts of organized crime as, "acquiring or receiving income from a pattern of racketeering through a criminal enterprise" (18 U.S.C. 1961). There are federal and state RICO statutes that include both civil and criminal remedies. Congress passed the federal RICO statute in 1970 as Title IX of the Organized Crime Control Act of 1970 (Public Law 91-452).

Conspiracy to violate RICO is included in both the federal statute as well as many state statutes. *Conspiracy*, the agreement between two or more people to commit a criminal violation, helps to describe the operation of criminal groups such as organized crime. Investigators must understand the concept of conspiracy and be able to apply the conspiracy statutes for organized crime to be effectively addressed.

Two other laws that help to define organized crime activities are the Continuing Criminal Enterprise statute and the Money Laundering Control Act of 1986 (U.S. Codes 21 and 18). The Continuing Criminal Enterprise (CCE) statute was part of the Comprehensive Drug Abuse Prevention and Control Act of 1970, and is directed at any person who "occupies a position of organizer, supervisor, or any other position of management" in a narcotic-producing or distribution enterprise such as organized crime. The Money Laundering Control Act created two new offenses that are common to organized crime during attempts to conceal the origin of illicit funds. These offenses were codified in 18 U.S.C. 1956 and 1957. Any investigator who wants to define organized crime must have a clear understanding of the activities described in both the CCE and the Money Laundering Control Act. These tools are discussed in the law enforcement strategies section for each of the criminal groups in Chapters 4 through 11.

International Perspective

Authors such as Albanese, Das, and Verma (2003) discuss the consensus of international perspective on the common features of organized crime. These include:
- Planned criminal activity for profit
- A conspiracy of a continuing enterprise formed around social, ethnic, or business relationships; or around a certain product or opportunity
- Use of violence, threats, and intimidation to achieve goals
- The use of corruption to protect its interest and avoid arrest and prosecution

These features help investigators to recognize organized crime, and are a common bond and starting place for international cooperation.

The Treaty of Mutual Assistance in Criminal Matters of 1973 illustrates an international definition of organized crime. This definition refers to organized crime as, "an association of individuals for periods of time for profit by both illegal and legal means." Although the word *corruption* is not used in the treaty, protection from prosecution is mentioned. The method of operation is described as being methodical and systematic.

Louise Shelley (1995), director of the Transnational Crime and Corruption Center (TraCCC) at the American University's School of International Service in Washington, D.C., includes three characteristics to define transnational organized crime groups:
- Based in one state
- Commit crimes in several countries when opportunities arise
- Conduct illicit activities with low risk of arrest or detection

In describing organized crime, Shelley refers to the mobility and versatility of these groups and writes that there is no prototypical crime cartel. Although their activities and structures vary, all have engaged in money laundering to conceal their enormous profits. Shelley views the corrupting influence over both law enforcement and governments to be a threat to the stability of governments and nations.

United States Federal Definitions

Many investigations in the United States use the definitions provided in both state and federal RICO statutes (1970). G. Robert Blakey, known as "the father of RICO," described organized crime as a political term. Organized crime is characteristic of an enterprise with a continuing criminal conspiracy that is motivated by profit from illicit activities demanded by the public. Violence, threats, and corruption ensure its continual existence.

Academics, law enforcement personnel, and state governments often replace the term organized crime with *illegal enterprise*. The California Penal Code defines organized crime as, "a crime of conspiratorial nature that seeks to supply illegal goods." It describes organized crime as an activity of planning and coordination of individual efforts of illegal activities for profits, and includes crime committed by criminal street gangs (*Deering's California Codes Annotated*, 2003). Arizona and Maryland refer to organized crime in their statutes (*Annotated Code of Maryland*, 2003; *Arizona Revised Statutes*, 2003). Delaware provides funding to combat organized crime under their Special Law Enforcement Assistance Fund (*Delaware Code Annotated*, 2003). Maryland lists characteristics that define organized crime as (*Annotated Codes of Maryland*):

- Criminal activity for significant income
- Combination or conspiracy
- Violating criminal laws relating to prostitution, drugs, corruption, extortion, counterfeiting, loan sharking and gambling

New Mexico statutes describe organized crime as supplying illegal goods and services for a profit by members of a structured and disciplined organization (*New Mexico Statutes Annotated*, 2003).

The New York legislature recognized the difficulty in precisely defining organized crime, but passed the Organized Crime Control Act, which includes a charge of enterprise corruption. New York also created a statewide organized crime task force to conduct investigations and to prosecute organized activities. The statute defines organized crime and gives power to issue subpoenas, obtain warrants, and to investigate organized crime activity. New York describes organized crime as, "an efficient and disciplined organizational structure that is very complex and diversified in its activity. It uses corruption as a means to protect and expand its operations. Organized crime consists of intricate statewide and nationwide conspiracies that have extended life spans. Organized crime must be addressed by a concerted, concentrated investigative, and prosecutorial effort to break the structure and power" (*New York Consolidated Law Service*, 2003). By creating the task force and addressing organized crime by statute, New York has brought together considerable resources to address this type of criminal activity.

Texas Statutes and Codes (2003) contain language concerning organized crime in their Penal Code Title 11, Chapter 71. The code requires a person or persons who intend to establish, maintain, or participate in a combination of or gain profits from a combination of a variety of illegal activities such as gambling, promotion of prostitution, sale of a controlled substance, murder, arson, and robbery, among others, to be characterized as organized crime.

One attempt to measure organized crime in Western Europe reached a consensus that eleven characteristics were common to organized crime. To meet the criteria of being defined as organized crime, the group had to exhibit at least six of the eleven characteristics. Conspiracy, serious criminal acts, and the motivation of profit and/or power were considered to be essential factors for a group to be classified as organized crime. Other characteristics include (Van der Heijden, 1996):

- Influence on politics, public administration, the judiciary, and the media (corruption)
- Money laundering activity
- Business-like structure
- Use of violence and intimidation
- International activity
- Specialization
- Continuity
- Employing discipline and control

Dobovšek (1996) also concluded that a definition of organized crime was impossible, but that characteristics that describe organized crime activity were useful. Organized crime was described as "quick development and changing of the forms" in response to the environment. Dobovšek specified the traits of organized crime as professionalism, organization, unlimited financial means, and enormous corruption potential. Organized crime varies from country to country because of differences in geographic, economic, and social factors of each country. The variety of definitions by each country leads to problems with measuring organized crime activity and obtaining international cooperation.

Donald Cressey (1969), a consultant to the 1967 President's Commission Task Force on Organized Crime, wrote that the positions of corruptor, corrupted, and enforcer were essential to the activities of organized crime. He used such terms as division of labor, coordinated activities, and rules involved in criminal operation. Other U.S. government committees and commissions have also contributed to defining organized crime and its activities and players.

The Kefauver Committee identified the syndicated nature of organized crime and described an organized hierarchy with centralized direction and use of violence and corruption to achieve organized goals of profit. The Committee described the Mafia as a secret conspiracy that was ruthless and very successful. The President's Task Force on Crime of 1967 and 1976 and the 1986 President's Commission on Organized Crime expanded the definition and knowledge of organized crime.

A Synthesis of Definitions

Definitions incorporate a range from five to more than ten characteristics. Kenny and Finckenauer (1995) list twelve characteristics that are a synthesis of the studies of Hagan (1983) and Maltz (1976, 1985). Albanese (1996) lists eleven characteristics similar to those of Kenny and Finckenauer. Howard Abadinsky (1985) proposed two different models of organized crime, the bureaucratic/corporate model and the patrimonial/patron-client model. There are six to eight attributes of organized crime according to Abadinsky's work.

The characteristics of organized crime described in the scholarly work above can be found in the reports of U.S. government and European task forces, committees, commissions, and a variety of organizations. These attributes include:

- Has non-ideological in motives
- Exhibits continuity over long periods of time; perpetual in nature

- Uses tactical and strategic or long-term planning to reach the goals of organized crime
- Governed by rules and codes of secrecy
- Seeks to monopolize products and services
- Has an organized hierarchy
- Uses force and intimidation
- Restricts membership
- Provides illegal goods and services as demanded by the public
- Obtains enormous profits by criminal means
- Employs corruption for immunity and control
- Creates a division of labor with job specialization
- Engages in money laundering
- Invests profits in legal enterprises and seeks to control these businesses
- Exhibits an ability to adapt to changes in supply and demand, law enforcement, and competition
- Operates internationally
- Engages in more than one illicit activity (diversity in business)
- Uses legal businesses as fronts for illegal activity

[Margin note: Combination of OC Definitions]

Other Approaches to Defining Organized Crime

When examining the numerous definitions of organized crime, it was found that some countries divide organized crime groups into traditional organized crime (such as Italian Mafia and American La Cosa Nostra, Yakuza, etc.), drug-specific organized crime (South American cartels), and entrepreneurial organized crime (Russian, Ukrainian, West African, and so on). Other types of classifications include the terms *transnational*, *international*, and *amalgamation*. *Amalgamation* is based on factors such as geography or territory, ethnicity, product, or service as a commodity or a sociopolitical cause.

Another approach to the classification of major criminal groups is viewing them as *organizing* crime rather than *organized* crime. This concept by Brodeur (1996) views these organizations as continuously changing or fluid rather than a single bureaucratic enterprise. The groups are constantly evolving around a variety of activities and alliances. These alliances are dependent on a symbiotic relationship with society and—if unchecked—form a global threat.

Organized crime has become both transnational and international because of its ability to be opportunistic with products and services as well as alliances with other criminal and non-criminal groups. Prohibition of drugs has made organized crime the most powerful criminal groups in history. Santino (1988) defines the Mafia as, "a financial Mafia employing the tactic of investing in legitimate markets and institutions to gain enormous wealth and power." International rules ensure secrecy and tax havens, which allow money to be circulated through trust companies, stocks, and other financial innovations.

The President's Commission on Organized Crime reached the same conclusion as Santino's conception of organized crime. It reported that drug trafficking was the major source of income and it required complex money laundering operations. The Commission concluded that organized crime consists of three essential components:

- Criminal groups that are structured using corruption, violence, and intimidation to gain wealth and power
- Corrupt public officials and businessmen who act as protectors ensuring continuity and insulating the group from civil and criminal action by the government
- Social support including use of illegal services and products and specialists who facilitate organized crime activity

Unlike its predecessors, this Commission identified a number of organized entities in addition to La Cosa Nostra that included the Colombian cartels, Yakuza, Russian Mafia, outlaw motorcycle gangs, and others. The Commission viewed these as emerging groups that met the definition of organized crime. History has proven both Santino's and the Commission's concepts to be correct. Organized crime evolves and continues to form alliances and new groups to expand their control over the market of a product or service.

Conclusions

Clearly, there is much debate about what organized crime means. There are many different types of organized crime, just as organized crime groups are not limited to La Cosa Nostra (LCN). Investigators of these and other criminal groups must understand and be capable of presenting the elements that are used by both the prosecutor of the case and the agency or department that can supply the needed resources for a successful investigation. In defining organized crime primarily as a criminal conspiracy, the investigator has only to include the legal requirements of a criminal conspiracy in the definition. This allows for those such as LCN, Yakuza, the Russian Mafia, Militant Groups, Triads, and other specified groups to be legally declared a criminal organization. Membership in one of these groups would mean that the person is guilty of a criminal conspiracy simply by belonging to the group. LCN has been classified as a racketeering enterprise; thus, all members are guilty of RICO violations. By declaring a group as a criminal enterprise, a *prima facia* case for the existence of a conspiracy has been established. This allows all members to be prosecuted for the crimes of all involved in the conspiracy, and allows the prosecutor to employ rules of evidence and testimony such as hearsay in the trial. This is a very innovative strategy to prosecute every member of entire organizations.

As discussed in this chapter, the criteria needed to classify an organization or group as organized crime varies not only between jurisdictions, but also between agencies, states, and countries. Some countries have yet to define organized crime. Definitions are crucial because they provide information for effective laws, investigations, and prosecutions. In addition, these definitions enhance efforts to prevent the formation of new organized crime groups and the unholy alliances formed between numerous organized crime groups worldwide. The creation of measures used against organized crime must begin with an understanding of what organized crime is and how it functions.

Sun Tzu, the 5th century Chinese general and author of *The Art of War*, had this to say about an enemy and victory:

> *If you know the enemy and know yourself, you need not fear the result of a hundred battles. If you know yourself but not the enemy, for every victory gained you will also suffer a defeat. If you know neither the enemy nor yourself, you will succumb in every battle.*

In our case, the enemy is organized crime. You as a potentially successful investigator must first define the problem before attempting to address a phenomenon as complex and constantly evolving as organized crime.

DISCUSSION QUESTIONS

1. How would you define organized crime? What distinguishes it from disorganized crime?
2. Why is defining organized crime important to law enforcement? Prosecutors?
3. Discuss United States Commissions' findings with regard to organized crime.
4. Of the 18 characteristics discussed in this chapter, which do you consider the most important? Why?
5. How do the United States definitions and those of other countries differ and how are they alike?
6. List and discuss state and federal legislation that address definitions of organized crime (i.e. conspiracy laws, RICO, money laundering, etc.).

REFERENCES

Abadinsky, H. (1985). *Organized Crime* (2nd ed.). Chicago: Nelson-Hall.
Albanese, J. (1996). *Organized Crime in America* (3rd ed.). Cincinnati, OH: Anderson.
Albanese, J. S., Das, D. K., & Verma, A. (Eds.). (2003). *Organized Crime: World Perspectives.* Upper Saddle River, NJ: Prentice Hall.
Annotated Code of Maryland. Retrieved July 22, 2003 from: http://www.lib.umd.edu/guides/MDAnnCodes.html
Arizona Revised Statutes. Retrieved July 22, 2003 from LexisNexis Academic: http://lynx.lib.usm.edu:2147/universe/printdoc
Black's Law Dictionary. (1990). St. Paul, MN: West Publishing.
Brodeur, J. P. (1996, September). *Organized Crime: Trends in the Literature.* Paper presented at the meeting of The Forum on Organized Crime, Ottawa, Canada.
Cressey, D. (1969). *Theft of a Nation: The Structure and Operations of Organized Crime in America.* New York: Harper.
Deering's California Codes Annotated. Retrieved July 22, 2003 from LexisNexis Academic: http://lynx.lib.usm.edu:2147/universe/printdoc
Delaware Code Annotated. Retrieved July 22, 2003 from LexisNexis Academic: http://lynx.lib.usm.edu:2147/universe/printdoc
Dobovšek, B. (1996). Organized Crime – Can We Unify the Definition. In: *Policing in Central and Eastern Europe: Comparing Firsthand Knowledge with Experience from the West.* Retrieved June 3, 2006 from http://www.ncjrs.org/policing/org323.htm
Fagan, J., Kelly, R., & Chin, K. L. (1989). *Patterns of Organized Crime Activities in Asian Businesses in the New York Area.* Newark, NJ: Rutgers University School of Criminal Justice.
Hagan, F. (1983). The Organized Crime Continuum: A Further Specification of a New Conceptual Model. *Criminal Justice Review, 8,* 52–57.
Kenny, D., & Finckenauer, J. (1995). *Organized Crime in America.* Belmont, CA: Wadsworth.

Maltz, M. (1976). On Defining organized crime. *Crime and Delinquency, 22*, 338–346.

Maltz, M. (1985). Toward defining organized crime. In: H. Alexander and G. Caiden (Eds.). The Politics and Economics of Organized Crime. Lexington, MA: Lexington Books.

McMath, B., FBI; personal communication, 8/2/2001.

Money Laundering Control Act of 1986. (Pub. L. 99-570).

New Mexico Statutes Annotated. Retrieved July 22, 2003 from LexisNexis Academic: hppt://lynx.lib.usm.edu:2147/universe/printdoc

New York Consolidated Law Service. Retrieved July 22, 2003 from LexisNexis Academic: http://lynx.lib.usm.edu:2147/universe/printdoc

Omnibus Crime Control and Safe Streets Act of 1968. (Pub. L. 42 U.S.C. §3789d).

Organized Control Act of 1970 (Pub. L. 91-452, Stat. 922).

Racketeer Influenced Corrupt Organizations Act of 1970 (Pub. L. 91-452, Stat. 922).

Santino, U. (1988). The Financial Mafia: The Illegal Accumulation of Wealth and the Financial-Industrial Complex. *Contemporary Crises 12(3)*, 203–243.

Shelley, L. I. (1995). Transnational Organized Crime. *Journal of International Affairs, 48(2)*, 485.

Taylor, C. (1990). *Dangerous Society.* East Lansing, MI: Michigan State University Press.

Texas Statutes and Codes Annotated by LexisNexis. Retrieved July 22, 2003 from LexisNexis Academic: http://lynx.lib.usm.edu:2147/universe/printdoc

United States Code 18 U.S.C. 1956.

United States Code 18 U.S.C. 1957.

United States Code 18 U.S.C. 1961.

United States Code 18 U.S.C. 1961–1965.

United States Code 18 U.S.C. 1962.

United States Code 18 U.S.C. 1963.

United States Code 18 U.S.C. 1964.

United States Code 18 U.S.C. 1965.

United States Code 18 U.S.C. 2510–2520.

United States Code 21 U.S.C. 846.

United States Code 21 U.S.C. 848.

Van der Heijden, T. (1996). Measuring Organized Crime in Western Europe. In *Policing in Central and Eastern Europe: Comparing Firsthand Knowledge with Experience from the West.* Retrieved June 3, 2006 from http://www.ncjrs.org/policing/mea313.htm

Weber, M. (1947). *The Theory of Social and Economic Organization* (A. M. Henderson & T. Parsons, Trans.). New York: Oxford University Press.

Webster's Ninth New Collegiate Dictionary. (1983). Springfield, MA: Merriam Webster, Inc.

2 Evolution of Organized Crime and the Impact on Investigative Strategies and Law Enforcement

"Choose as a guide one who you will admire more when you see him act than when you hear him speak."

–Lociuc Annaeus Seneca, philosopher (3 bce–ad 65)

Chapter Objectives
After completing this chapter, readers should be able to:
- Recognize how American organized crime has become more transnational.
- Discuss the impetus to evolution of organized crime in the United States and identify the first organized crime groups in America.
- Understand the common threads between early organized crime in America and current organized crime groups.
- Discuss the impact of organized crime on the U.S. government, society, U.S. business, and law enforcement.

Introduction

The origin of organized crime in America is debated among academics, law enforcement professionals, and historians. Many believe that organized crime in

America began with the pirates (Kenny & Finckenauer, 1995). Others point to the New York and Chicago gangs of the 1920s as the beginning of organized crime in America (Albanese, 1996; Peterson, 1952). Abadinsky (2003) writes about the "Robber Barons" who were replaced by the Irish, Jewish, and Italian criminal gangs. Currently, these enterprises are being replaced with "nontraditional enterprises" of Asians, Russians, Africans, Hispanics, outlaw biker gangs, and other emerging groups.

Regardless of the origin of organized crime, its impact on American law enforcement has been substantial. The downside is the extensive capability of these organizations to corrupt law enforcement, making corruption an integral characteristic of organized crime. Upsides include the trend of modernizing law enforcement in terms of training, selection, technology, and the ability to network internationally and globally.

Today, nearly all of the approximately 200 nations of the world are experiencing some form of organized crime, which is evolving toward transnational crime as operational links between these groups strengthen. Shadow governments control much of the businesses and economy of the developed and most powerful nations, including the United States. One example is the Japanese group, the Yakuza, who were estimated to reap $10 billion in 1988 through smuggling American guns into Japan, controlling the crystal methamphetamine market in Hawaii and the mainland, and making heavy inroads in the lucrative pornography and prostitution industries.

Law enforcement and governments have been threatened by organized crime activity. This resulted in the United Nations Convention Against Transnational Organized Crime in 2000. International measures were developed, signed by 147 countries, and ratified by 40 countries. These documents are a commitment by nations to adopt a number of measures against organized crime, such as money laundering, extradition laws, mutual legal assistance, and some standards for the law enforcement effort. The United Nations is providing assistance to countries to develop measures to combat organized crime.

In the post-September 11, 2001 terrorist attack era in the United States, the highest political priority of Congress and the President is to address the threats of terrorism from groups such as Al Qaeda. Another priority is corporate (or *white collar*) crime, best illustrated by the 2001 Enron and 2002 WorldCom scandals. While these forms of criminal activity justify a considerable effort and expenditures of resources, there is concern among many in law enforcement that the issue of organized crime is taking a back seat in terms of resources and investigative activity. However, there are data showing that enforcement activities against both terrorism and white collar crime have an additional impact on organized crime activity. A hardening of borders prevents some smuggling activity, financial investigations have uncovered organized crime activity, and law enforcement have discovered weapons trafficking by organized crime groups that has a connection to terrorism.

Efforts against terrorism may evolve into one against organized crime groups as well. Alliances between terrorist and organized crime groups are a trend predicted by some in the U.S. intelligence community to escalate for two reasons: greed of the organized crime groups and the need for weapons by terrorist groups.

Although there has been much distrust and competition between the major organized crime groups such as La Cosa Nostra (LCN; American Mafia), Yakuza, and Russian Mafia, this has not prevented alliances between these groups to reap huge profits from drugs, arms trafficking, and other criminal activities.

■ Origins of Organized Crime in the United States

Colonial Piracy

Organized crime in the United States did not begin during the Prohibition era of the 1920s, but with the pirates of the colonial period (Browning & Gerassi, 1980). If the characteristics of organized crime explained in Chapter 1 are compared to the actions and character of the pirates of colonial America (hierarchy and structure, non-ideological, violent, restricted membership, huge profits from criminal activity, continuity and supplying public demand, and above all, corruption), then pirates indeed can be considered the earliest form of organized crime in America.

Piracy was the result of the British rulers employing a number of seafaring buccaneers to attack and disrupt Spanish shipping to defend the American Colonies. The pirates, who were referred to as *privateers* (because their pay came from the plunder and goods of the Spanish ships they captured), soon began to attack ships other than Spanish and form alliances with corrupt governors of the colonies. Many pirates became famous; Captain William Kidd, Bartholomew Roberts ("Black Bart"), and Edward Teach ("Blackbeard") are a few. These pirates established rules of conduct and recruited men with skills needed to carry out their attacks on shipping.

Pirates were initially perceived by the colonists as gentlemen or Robin Hood type bandits. As such, privateers were honored guests of the colonists and governors with whom they traded. Colonists bought goods from the pirates and offered them refuge and protection. Pirates sold the luxury items to the colonists at a fraction of their cost, much like "hot goods" are purchased by the public today from fences or other criminals. Like later criminals such as Al Capone in Chicago and Pablo Escobar in South America, pirates ingratiated themselves with the colonist and government officials. At the peak of piracy in America, around 1720, an estimated 2,000 pirates controlled many of the shipping lanes off the eastern seaboard.

Piracy, like the illicit drug trade today, flourished because of the demand by the colonists. Pirates became the best customers of the colonist's goods and services. The colonist did not seem to care if the pirates were bringing stolen goods and corrupting their new government. But when the colonists began to export their goods, they also became victims of attacks on shipping. Soon they withdrew their support from the pirates. In addition, colonists replaced corrupt officials with those who could not be corrupted. America had become more commercial with a number of industries thriving. When piracy began to die, another enterprise began to flourish: smuggling. Smuggling survives today with its influx of arms, drugs, humans, and body parts. Pirates used corruption and mercantile demand to support their illegal activities. This trend of American organized crime was set in early colonial America through the cooperation of the pirates with the public, government, and legitimate business enterprises, and it forms the future vector of organized criminal activities.

Although piracy has ended along the U.S. coastlines, modern piracy is common today off the coasts of Southeast Asia and Africa (Gallant, 1999). Like the pirates in colonial America, corruption continues to play a role in the success of modern piracy. These modern networks obtain shipping routes and schedules from corrupt sources to plan their action. They are extremely successful and violent, often disposing their bounty through other organized crime groups. Losses to legitimate companies and nations amount to millions of dollars and an ever-increasing number of deaths of crewmembers. Environmental damage to the seas and coastlines often results from abandoned ships that were carrying hazardous material.

Rise of Robber Barons and Crime Families

As the piracy era ended in America, criminal groups were disorganized for a few years, during which time disproportionate wealth became the trend. By the mid-1700s, crime had become a major problem in major cities. Before the 1920s (when the LCN became powerful), a number of American businessmen began to monopolize the American economy by violent and corrupt means. The Vanderbilts, Rockefellers, Carnegies, Standfords, and others used the law, private police, military, and even the National Guard to gain financial and political control. These groups of ruthless businessmen in the Industrial Age were referred to as the *Robber Barons* (Browning and Gerassi, 1980; Klepper, Gunther, Baik, Barth & Gibson, 1998). This ruthless business activity is very similar to the newly discovered corporate crime the United States is experiencing in this decade (such as the Enron and WorldCom scandals). In writing about corporate corruption, Clinard (1990) concluded that organized criminals and corporate criminals are very similar because both influence law and employ corruption to achieve power and profits. Clinard's examples included the 1986 Union Carbide disaster in Bhopal, India; the selling of illegal pharmaceuticals, pesticides, and medical devices to third world countries; exploitation of land for agribusiness and lumbering operations in underdeveloped countries; and exploitation of workers to produce products for these corporations. Much of what these corporations are doing in those countries would be illegal in the United States. As Sutherland and Cressey (1960) pointed out as early as 1949, a large number of violations by corporations are a type of organized crime. Until recently, most of these corporate criminals were unidentified or not prosecuted, and remained in their powerful positions. These Robber Barons of America were the quasi-forerunners to the enterprises of LCN and the present nontraditional groups such as the Russian, Mexican, and Colombian drug-trafficking organizations (**Figure 2-1**).

Immigrant Crime Groups and Political Machines

By the 19th century, major population growth had occurred in cities such as New Orleans, New York, and Chicago. Although the evolution of organized crime had many similarities in both urban and rural, north and south, and east and west in the United States, each area had some unique characteristics in development

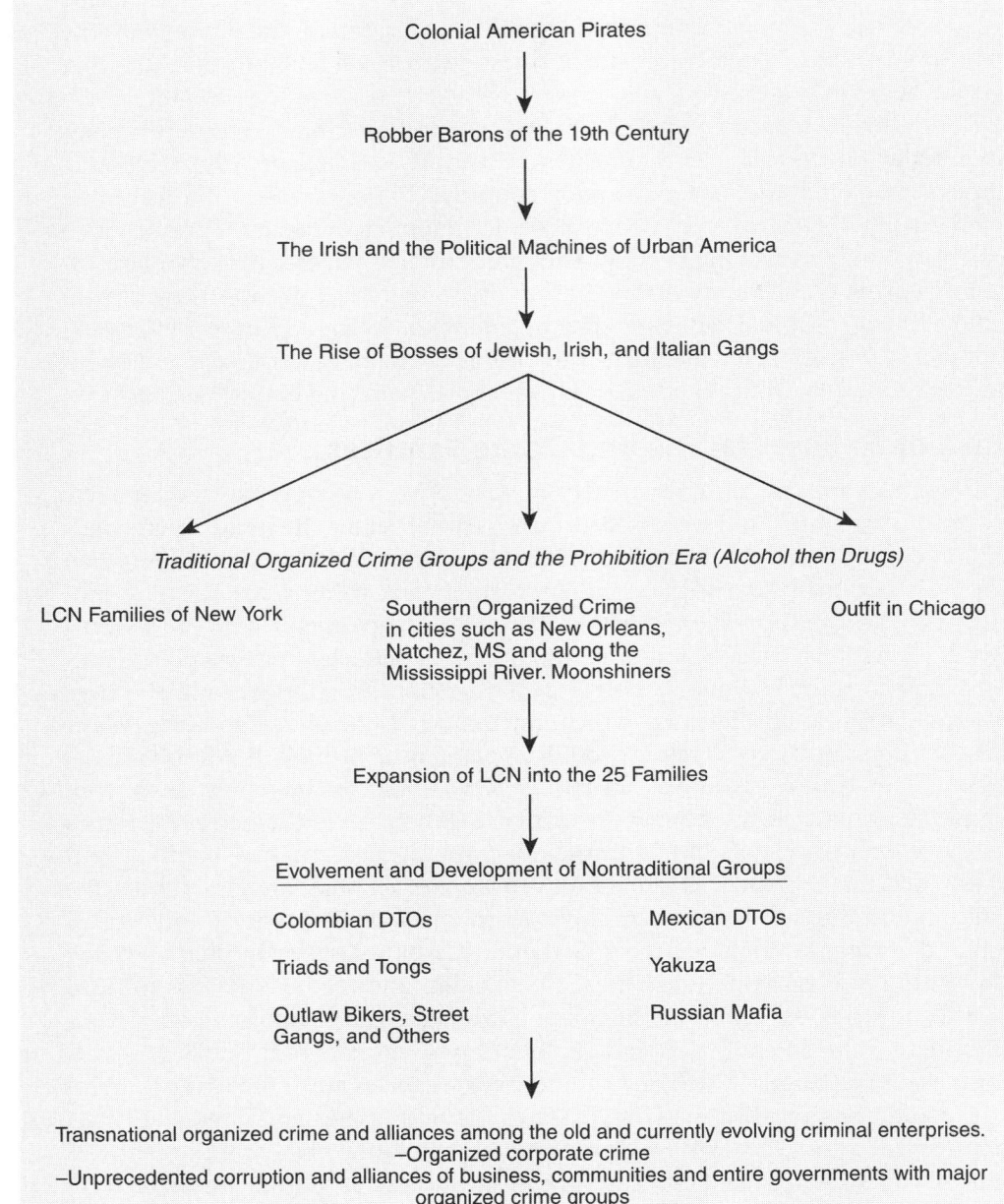

Figure 2-1 Historical Evolution of Organized Crime in the United States

of particular organized crime entities. Even before the prohibitions of alcohol and illicit drugs, organized crime had begun to develop in America. Rapid and massive immigration into cities like New York resulted in tremendous overcrowding and unemployment. To survive, the unemployed began to commit criminal acts and then form gangs for power and profits. Politics became the means to obtain power and money for many immigrants. The vote became a commodity that could be controlled by the alliance of gangs and political organizations. These so-called *political machines* gained control of not only the gangs but also of the police, courts, prosecutors, and the government. Immigrant groups such as the Irish, the Jews, and the Italians became involved in organized crime, as did non-immigrants such as African Americans (Joselit, 1983).

The first massive immigrant group to come to the United States was the Irish, who were enticed by economic opportunities that America offered in the early 1700s. Most were farmers who settled in eastern and midwestern cities. Living in poverty and denied access to education, their first jobs were as laborers. During the potato famine in Ireland of the 1840s, more than 250,000 Irish Catholics entered the United States, and by the 1950s the number of Irish immigrants approached nearly two million. The Irish established their own neighborhoods and with their large ethnic vote established the corrupt political machine, which allowed them to control both the legal and illegal enterprises of the cities.

Two of the most notorious of these political machines were the Tammany Hall Machine in New York and the Pendergast Machine in Kansas City. The Tammany Hall Machine controlled the gangs, jobs, and gamblers of New York. This alliance between the politicians, gangs, and gamblers led to the rise of such characters as William March Tweed ("Boss Tweed"). Tweed and other bosses who followed him (such as "Big Tim" Sullivan) stole millions from the city and government by fraud, bid-rigging, overpricing goods and services, and kickbacks. Municipal graft was a way of life for the people who ran these powerful machines. The machines operated "wide open" cities where gambling and vice were protected and encouraged, and relationships between the criminals and machine bosses were symbiotic. Gang violence ensured the vote and in turn gang members were protected by the corrupt government controlled by the machines.

Gang leaders became wealthy and powerful men in early America, and many became powerful bosses of the LCN in a number of cities. Al Capone was a member of the Five Points gang in New York before moving to Chicago. Gangs performed legal and illegal activities for the machines, including distributing campaign material, garnering repeat voters, and assaulting rival campaign workers. The politicians controlled the police and courts, which allowed for protection of the gang members who helped the politicians stay in office. Kansas City's Thomas Pendergast ran the political machine and employed gangsters to ensure survival of the machine just as Tweed did in New York. The 1800s was the era when gangs in major cities of the United States became more organized and entrenched in politics. The Five Points and Eastman gangs of New York, the Purple Gang of Detroit, and the gamblers of Chicago were the beginning of the criminal organizations such as LCN in the United States (Browning & Gerassi, 1980; Peterson, 1952).

New Impetus for Expansion of Organized Crime in the United States

As criminal groups became large organizations allied with the political machines, the stimulus for growth was market-driven. These huge markets required an infrastructure able to import, distribute, protect, and monopolize the organization's products and services. Gambling, prostitution, labor racketeering, and loan sharking had contributed to the growth of organized crime in the early years. Now, two new prohibitions would be the impetus to unprecedented growth of these criminal groups. The Harrison Narcotics Act of 1914 was the first major step of drug enforcement. It established a tax and regulations for the manufacture and distribution of narcotics as well as licenses for pharmacists and physicians who prescribed them. At the time, patent medicines, many of which contained opium and/or hard liquor and herbs, were unregulated "cures" for a variety of ailments and were marketed especially for women who would never dream of drinking an alcoholic beverage. With over 500,000 opiate addicts in the United States, a huge market opportunity for organized crime existed. The United States drug rings suddenly became nationally organized crime groups. (These drug rings preceded the alcohol-Prohibition era gangs.) There were reports of corruption of large police departments because of the enormous profits from drug operations. Before the 1920s, large drug rings existed that were both highly organized and international. Not only were opiates a major product of organized crime profits, but cocaine was a highly profitable product as well. (Until the 1920s, it was an ingredient of the soft drink Coca-Cola.) As the profits soared from the illicit drug trade and distribution, the corruption of politicians, law enforcement, and businessmen grew.

The prohibition of alcohol era from 1920 to 1933 provided yet another market opportunity for expansion of organized crime in America. In New York, the early gang era was ending and the political machines were evolving into the next phase of the alliance of politicians, gamblers, gangs, and the criminal world.

Men like Arnold Rothstein brought about the Jewish influence. Rothstein is credited with creating the modern bureaucratic structure of an organized crime group. He was an effective administrator from 1914 until 1928, and transformed criminal activity by using specialization, administrative hierarchy, and methods of operation that were similar to those of a successful legitimate business. He is known as the original "Don," because he brought bootlegging and narcotics trafficking into the modern era of organized crime. Much of his illegal profits were invested into legitimate enterprises. He engaged in labor racketeering as well as a variety of legal and illegal business ventures such as real estate, the garment industry, securities, insurance, bail bonding as well as smuggling, bootlegging, gambling, narcotics trafficking, and strikebreaking for hire. Rothstein was the role model for the rise of organized crime bosses in other ethnic groups including the Italian LCN. Like many organized crime bosses throughout history, Rothstein was shot and killed by an unidentified assailant. The organized crime figures who followed him continued to expand organized crime activity in New York (Joselit, 1983).

Other cities, such as Chicago, were also experiencing an evolution in organized crime. After Big Michael McDonald came characters such as Mont Tennes, James Colosimo, and Johnny Terrio, who was an original New York Five Pointer. Eventually, the infamous Al Capone, also a New York Five Pointer, became the boss of organized crime in Chicago, known as the "Outfit."

Anti-Crime Legislation and the Growth of Organized Criminal Groups

Another impetus to the continued growth and expansion of organized crime in America was the proliferation of drug control legislation. After the Harrison Narcotics Act, public opinion changed to reflect a perceived threat from drug addiction, particularly for the youth of America. The fear of dangerous Chinese and black drug addicts added to public support for drug laws (King, 1972). Repeal of prohibition of alcohol in 1933 left the LCN and other criminal enterprises without the profits of bootlegging they counted on for growth. Drug trafficking became a more important source of income for organized crime. Organized crime bosses such as Meyer Lansky, Lucky Luciano, and Arnold Rothstein became heavily involved in the illicit heroin market. Because other LCN bosses such as Joseph Bonanno, Tony Accardo, and Frank Costello were initially opposed to involvement in drug trafficking, their hesitation allowed for the new faces of organized crime to begin their own rise to power.

The Depression, the Korean Conflict and Vietnam War, and the 1960s social climate produced ideal conditions for illicit drugs. Albert Anastasia, Vito Genovese, and many others became wealthy as a result of drug trafficking. However, the new generation of organized crime, such as the Mexican drug trafficking organizations (DTOs), Colombian DTOs, the Tongs and Triads, among others, also have become major players in the world of criminal enterprises because of their ability to supply illicit drugs to America and the world. Heroin from Mexico, The Golden Triangle (Burma, Thailand, and Laos), and The Golden Cresent (Pakistan, Iran, and Afghanistan) arrived on American shores, providing enormous profits to LCN and other organized crime enterprises. Cocaine from Colombia, Peru, and Bolivia produced new billionaires and a new generation of organized crime organizations. Marijuana, clandestine drugs such as ecstasy (methamphetamine), PCP (phencyclidine), and LSD (lysergic acid diethylamide), and diverted pharmaceuticals drugs became a lucrative money market for organized crime.

The Uniform Narcotic Drug Act of 1932 was passed by Congress as a complement to the Harrison Narcotics Act and became a model for statutes in the United States. Other acts, such as the 1937 Marijuana Tax, were passed to stop the illegal use of marijuana. By 1951, penalties began to be more severe for violations of drug laws. Today, the federal government and all states have a Controlled Substance Act that lists drugs with penalties for the sale, possession, and delivery, and a variety of laws regarding conspiracy and assets forfeiture for violation of drug laws. With these laws in place, the price of illicit drugs has soared, as have the profits for organized crime.

The latest organized crime organization to enter the drug trafficking business is probably the Russian Mafia. Partnered with the Colombians, they have established operations in areas such as Miami, Florida, to smuggle cocaine from South America to Russia. Oleg Kirillov, a leader of a Russian group, has been identified as having a number of operations in the United States that are involved in the cocaine smuggling business.

Some would argue that we should deal with drug prohibition the same way we dealt with alcohol prohibition (Nadelmann, 1989). However, America currently has drugs that are restricted and legal. Pharmaceuticals account for more than 40 percent of addictions and are still providing profits for organized crime groups. According to estimates, if some drugs were legalized, the number of addicts would increase as much as 20-fold. Given the correlation between drug use and crime, the results would be devastating for our society.

■ Development of Organized Crime in the South

Southern organized crime often is described as the *Dixie Mafia*. The question of whether a Dixie Mafia exists and if it is defined as organized crime is debatable. However, it is clear that some form of criminal organization and planning involving corruption has operated in a number of southern states, especially the Mississippi Gulf Coast. This network of individuals has been, and continues to be, involved in numerous crimes. The impact of this activity on law enforcement has been mixed. The public image is tarnished when a sheriff and former mayor are found guilty of criminal activity. The public may become more apathetic on the one hand and more demanding of action against corruption on the other. More oversight by federal authority of local law enforcement has been instituted, but corruption is difficult to discover and requires lengthy investigations and expenditure of resources that should be directed at criminals who do not wear badges. The enormous profits of drug trafficking have been too tempting for many in law enforcement whose salaries cannot come close to matching that of "the bad guys." Although law enforcement has become more professional and high tech, corruption remains an avenue for organized crime to continue to operate in the south.

Unlike the LCN, which is a structured organization with a hierarchal command, the Dixie Mafia was a loose knit group of professional or traveling criminals who formed partnerships based on enterprises or geographic location to execute a variety of criminal activities. This group was active in the states of Texas, Mississippi, Louisiana, Tennessee, Arkansas, Kentucky, and possibly other states. The group had no central bosses or commission (as does the American Mafia), but formed subgroups as needed to carry out specific crimes or operations. The most powerful criminals knew whom to contact to contract a murder, arson, transport of guns or dope, or for any specialty required to achieve the objective of the criminal activity. Members were involved in a variety of criminal activities that included gambling, bootlegging, prostitution, drug trafficking, murder, arson, theft, and fraud. Each member frequently specialized in one criminal activity.

Some of the organized crime in southern states, specifically prostitution, gambling, and drug distribution, was assisted by corrupt law enforcement officials.

Much of this activity took place in coastal bars and gambling halls (*joints*) that operated 24 hours a day in violation of numerous statues and regulations.

Intelligence indicated that the Mississippi Gulf Coast was wide open to a variety of criminal activity somewhat like Chicago and New York during the Prohibition era. It was obvious that local officials did little to engage the criminal activity by members of the Dixie Mafia. A recent example of the exploits of the Dixie Mafia was the trial of former mayor of Biloxi, Pete Halat in 1997. Halat and members of the Dixie Mafia were involved in an extortion scam operated from Angola Prison in Louisiana. Members of the group were convicted in the murder of Biloxi Circuit Court Judge Vincent Sherry and his wife Margaret. Mike Gillich, Jr. and a number of alleged members of the Dixie Mafia were convicted on a variety of charges surrounding the murder of the Sherrys.

Illegal Whiskey

Although many in academia attribute the development of organized crime to the Prohibition era, the smuggling and production of illegal whiskey in America began during colonial America. Known by many names such as *shine*, *hooch*, *rock gut*, *white lightning*, and *corn liquor*, illegal whiskey has existed in America since the founding of the country. John Hancock was the owner of a sloop named the *Liberty* that was seized by British customs agents in 1768 for smuggling rum and spirits to avoid taxes owed to the British government.

To pay off the debts incurred in the American Revolution, the fledgling United States government placed a tax on whiskey and other distilled spirits, and the American moonshiner was born. Scotch-Irish farmers were among the first to produce illegal whiskey in the northeastern states. The whiskey riots of 1794 in Pittsburgh, Pennsylvania marked America's first resistance to taxes and began its tradition of rebellion to federal authority or oversight. President Washington led a militia to stop the rebellion with little bloodshed. However, because of this political pressure, moonshiners began to migrate to the southern states and western areas such as Kentucky and the Appalachian Mountain region, which shortly became the capitol of American moonshine (Miller, 1991).

The first prohibition of alcohol was not the 18th Amendment. Early prohibition occurred in Georgia in 1733 and continued for nine years. The results were illegal alcohol stills and smuggling of illegal whiskey by boats (similar to methods used in the 1980s to smuggle drugs into America). Moonshiners manufactured whiskey and bootleggers sold their product. The second prohibitions were probably in Maine in 1851, where whiskey consumption had reached 5 gallons per capita per year. Crime associated with alcohol soared and included abuse of spouses and children. The price for alcohol rose to $5.00 per gallon. By 1917, about half the U.S. states had enacted prohibition laws. Then in 1920, the 18th Amendment was passed, nationally banning the manufacture, sale, and transport of alcohol. Many citizens became lawbreakers for the first time. Fisherman became smugglers. Farmers operated stills that percolated homemade hooch. Hip flasks and semi-secret bars known as *speakeasies* became normalized among the citizenry. Criminals and gang members did not lose the opportunities for gaining enormous profits.

While national prohibition did reduce overall alcohol consumption, it also sparked the growth of corruption of law enforcement, business, and politicians along with the establishment of powerful organized crime families. Due to national prohibition, 800 million gallons per year of illegal whiskey entered the market. Almost anyone could make $500.00 a day in the illegal business, but it was risky. Many deaths were attributed to whisky produced or smuggled into America because of a lack of quality control and inspection. In 1920, there were 1,000 deaths from the consumption of illegal whiskey.

Smugglers were innovative at developing routes and methods that avoided detection. Boat builders became part of the business as they built fast boats with secret compartments that were suitable for smuggling illegal alcohol. Even a World War I German U-boat was used to deliver the product to American shores. People were willing to risk jail or even death to enjoy the profits, adventure, and excitement produced by this dangerous game. The U.S. Coast Guard battled the smugglers with frequent gun battles and chases.

Perhaps the most serious impact of prohibition was the formation of organized crime groups such as the Purple Gang of Detroit, Michigan. Cooperation between gang members resulted in organized crime. When Canada legalized the production of whiskey for importation, a massive amount of smuggling across the Detroit River into Michigan began. The use of airplanes, boats, vehicles, and the development of sophisticated secret compartments were the result of the smuggling phenomena. Not satisfied with their individual profits, criminal groups began to monopolize the illegal alcohol market by highjacking other smuggler's loads and violent takeovers of the transportation and distilleries. The Purple Gang supplied liquor to such organized crime figures as Chicago's Al Capone. Prohibition bankrolled organized crime and became the impetus to its growth.

Even with the repeal of the 18th Amendment by the 21st Amendment, the U.S. Congress continued to tax liquor. This produced—and continues to produce—moonshiners such as Junior Johnson, who later became a famous racecar driver. The creation of the National Association for Stock Car Auto Racing (NASCAR) in 1947 is attributed to the so-called *ridge runners* and *blockaders* who developed fast cars to outrun the *revenuers* who were trying to arrest them for hauling illegal whiskey. Family operations had stills and produced spirits, which were then transported to distribution sites in vehicles with supercharged engines and large load capacity. These drivers became legends in U.S. history.

Whiskey organizations included those who financed the operation, transportation specialists, distillers, distribution, and security. The 18th Amendment resulted in a huge market for moonshine and—like the LCN—moonshiners in the south used corruption and sometimes violence to ensure their operations continued to profit. From 1950 to 1965, the U.S. government reported the production of over a billion gallons of illegal whiskey that produced a loss of $12 billion in federal and state taxes (Miller, 1991; Woodiwiss, 1988).

Illegal distillers were common in the states of Mississippi, Tennessee, Georgia, Kentucky, Missouri, Arkansas, Alabama, North and South Carolina, and West Virginia. The Appalachian region became infamous for its production of illegal whiskey and selling whiskey without a license. The average still produced around 80 gallons a week, which meant an income of approximately $100 a week. It was common knowledge that the sheriff or chief mostly overlooked the illegal alcohol trade. Some took payoffs to allow the whiskey operations to do business.

Moonshining was usually a family business that traditionally was passed down from one generation to the next. In most southern towns, the public knew where to buy illegal whiskey and knew who was producing it. Both white and black people were involved in the manufacture and selling of whiskey.

From the perspective of the blockaders of the mountains of the south to rural towns and big cities like New Orleans or Atlanta, moonshining is an organized activity that is part of the historical development of crime in the south. Like illegal drugs, it was an impetus to the growth and expansion of organized crime activity. Today's moonshiners may operate stills capable of producing up to $40,000.00 a month in profits. Despite the fact that the ATF (Department of Alcohol, Tobacco, and Firearms) agents often find illegal whiskies that contain poisons that can be very dangerous for human consumption, there is a large public demand for the product.

Modern Development

Organized crime has many activities that contribute to its growth and expansion in addition to drug trafficking and bootlegging. These groups have derived much power and profit from business racketeering, gambling, labor racketeering, and a variety of white collar and fraud crimes. LCN remains a major player in the evolution of organized crime in America. It learned much from its Jewish and Irish gang predecessors, and improved the concepts of diversity, corruption, and integrating their operations into legitimate business.

The rise of the American Mafia, who many refer to as La Cosa Nostra (LCN), is discussed in depth in Chapter 7. Powerful families in New York (such as Luciano, Columbo, Gambino, Luchesse, and Bonnano), Chicago (Al Capone, Sam Giancana, John Torrio, and Joseph Aiuppa), the New Orleans family (Carlos Marcello), and families in at least 22 other major cities established the American Mafia as a lasting presence in American organized crime. The rise of LCN covers much of the history of organized crime in America up until nontraditional groups began their rise to power in the 1970s.

Commissions and Task Forces

Much of what is known about organized crime in America comes from a number of governmental commissions that investigated organized crime in America. As early as 1915, the Chicago Commission made inquiries into what was called *institutional crime*. Later, the Wickersham Committee of 1931 examined the impact of prohibition on organized crime growth and power. In 1950, The Kefauver Committee concluded that there was a nationwide syndicate known as the Mafia that controlled much of lucrative crime in major cities. Described as "muscle and murder," the Mafia was involved in criminal interstate commerce. The McClellan Committee recorded the testimony of Joseph Valachi (a low-level organized crime "made" man who gave questionable testimony before Congress in 1963; he was the first member of the LCN to confirm its existence). The Oyster Bay Conferences from 1965 to 1966 assembled a number of experts to examine organized crime as a criminal enterprise. President Lyndon Johnson established the President's Commission on Law Enforcement and Administration of Justice in 1965. It examined the activities of organized crime, how the groups were organized, and identified some members of these organized crime groups. Influenced by the Kefauver and McClellan hearings, the 1967 President's Committee concluded that organized crime was a national threat motivated by money and power, and the result of intricate conspiracies. In 1976, the National Task Force on Organized Crime recognized a lack of knowledge and understanding of organized crime, and added groups other than LCN to the list of organized crime activity.

In 1983, President Reagan created yet another commission to analyze organized crime on a regional basis to determine the extent of LCN and emerging organized crime groups. His President's Commission on Organized Crime classified other groups as organized crime and concluded that drug trafficking was the largest source of income for organized crime in America. Groups identified as organized crime included outlaw biker gangs, a number of prison gangs, Colombian cartels, Cuban Marielitos, Russian groups, and the Japanese Yakuza. Although the Yakuza was considered the largest group by this commission and other organized crime groups poised a serious threat during the last 20 years (1966–1986), LCN remained the most powerful and extensive group operating in the United States. The LCN recognized the importance of corruption in its ability to continue to extend its power and influence while amassing large profits. Some states such as New York, Pennsylvania, and Florida have examined organized crime activity over the past century and determined that organized crime is dynamic, and that corruption plays a vital role in the existence of these criminal enterprises.

■ Corporate and Political Corruption: The Major Contribution to Organized Crime Growth and Power

Corruption is not confined to organized groups. Corporate scandals, the Robber Barons' methods, and political corruption all share one similarity with organized crime: their common use of corruption. From price fixing, toxic waste dumping, and illegal campaign contributions to criminal violations by executives in companies such as Enron and WorldCom, corporate corruption may have been an impetus to methods employed by modern organized crime.

The connection between the underworld (organized crime and others) and the upper world (corporate America and politicians) has a long history, beginning with the pirates and continuing with the political machines of the 1860s and today's complex political system. This symbiotic relationship between organized crime and the political system is well documented. Beginning in the 1960s, organized crime members have contributed $2 billion annually to a variety of public officials (King, 1969). But this is not unique to the United States. The Japanese government and the Yakuza are almost indistinguishable, as are: the Cali cartel and the Colombian President, Ernesto Samper; Mexican presidents and

Mexican DTOs; and the Russian Mafia and government officials in Moscow and other major cities in the former Soviet Union countries.

In the United States, senators, mayors, police chiefs, governors, and prosecutors are prime targets for corruption by organized crime. This can be found in yesterday's and today's headlines.

Other U.S. presidents have reported connections to LCN as well. Richard Nixon's campaign manager in his race for the California Congress, Murray Choitner, was a well-known Mob lawyer. Nixon had friends who were friends of Meyer Lansky, and Nixon obtained the endorsement of the teamsters (Moldea, 1978, 1982). Even the popular President Reagan's administration had connections to organized crime members who included Reagan's friends Senator Paul Laxalt, Jackie Presser (Teamster Union president), and Raymond Donovan (Reagan-appointed Secretary of Labor), all of whom had connections to known LCN figures. Many of Reagan's appointments were determined to have connections to organized crime (Moldea, 1978, 1982).

The executive levels of the Governor's office in some states have been reported to have Mob connections. Two governors of Louisiana were convicted of felonies and had alleged connections to Carlos Marcello. Louisiana political boss Huey P. Long was alleged to have approved and accepted money for allowing Frank Costello, a New York Mob boss, to bring slot machines to New Orleans.

LCN is not the only organized crime group that employs corruption as a means to an end. Mexican DTOs, Colombian DTOs, outlaw bikers, and most all organized crime groups have corrupted politicians, law enforcement, and legitimate businesses to maintain and protect their lucrative enterprises. Without exception, when organized crime activity has been detected in any jurisdiction or area, political or corporate corruption has been revealed. The connection to licit business allows organized crime members to safely invest their illegal proceeds and form symbiotic relationships similar to that between organized crime and politicians.

Organized crime has become transnational and international, as groups form alliances wherever or with whomever to achieve power and wealth. It has become a global enterprise and is so intermingled in the socioeconomic and political process that it is difficult to separate these entities. This evolution presents a formable challenge for American law enforcement.

■ Future Impact on Law Enforcement Efforts

The growing disparity between organized crime and law enforcement resources has put law enforcement at a distinct disadvantage. The enormous profits and power of organized crime allows them to employ the finest support. Attorneys, financial advisors, and experts in technology and methodology allow organized crime to maintain highly effective and efficient operations. The expansion of the size and number of organized crime groups now operating in the United States stretches law enforcement resources to the point of limited success.

Add to this mix the threat of terrorism, which demands resources, diverting investigators and agencies away from their focus on organized crime, and it's clear that fewer resources exist to combat this growing threat. Many agencies have begun to connect terrorism to drug trafficking, as it may be the major source of income for terrorists and is a definitive organized crime mainstay. This has allowed some agencies to battle both terrorism and organized crime with added resources. However, it is apparent that Homeland Security has become the political and economic priority for United States law enforcement.

The impact of corruption has resulted in a lack of sharing information between many law enforcement entities out of fear of compromising major cases and danger to informants and law enforcement personal. Federal agencies were not sharing information after the terrorist events of September 11, 2001. Task forces are reluctant to provide or share information with local or state members who might be represented on, or assigned to these federal task forces. Corruption scandals also have required extensive scrutiny and resources dedicated to internal investigations at the state, local, and federal level of employees of these agencies who themselves investigate organized crime activity and are watching the people who are watching members of organized crime. Temptation combined with greed has compromised a number of organized crime investigations.

There is an upside. The growth and evolution of organized crime has forced improved intelligence gathering, enforcement techniques, and strategies. Law enforcement strategies are improving intelligence-gathering capabilities and are becoming more proactive. The creation of task and strike forces focused on organized crime activity has resulted in the arrest and conviction of many traditional and nontraditional organized crime members.

Another positive impact has been the creation of more effective crime control legislation, both at the state and federal level. RICO, money laundering acts, chemical diversion acts, asset forfeiture, improved physical and electronic surveillance, conspiracy and Continuing Criminal Enterprise statutes, drug control legislation, and most recently the Patriot Act have allowed law enforcement to become a serious threat to organized crime activity.

The recent creation of multi-jurisdictional task and strike forces has resulted in increased cooperation between agencies and all levels of law enforcement. Task forces offer advanced training and additional resources dedicated to law enforcement. These resources are not limited to money. The technology and equipment provided to these task forces has led to increased efficiency and effectiveness of law enforcement in general. The techniques and technology applied by the task forces often carry over to member agencies that employ these advanced technology and strategies to develop other criminal investigations.

The overall impact on law enforcement of the growth and evolution of organized crime in the United States has been the development of strategies, technology, training, education, and improved law and statutes to address such a dynamic phenomenon as organized crime. This has resulted in a more professional and effective law enforcement community at the local, state, and federal levels.

Although there is increased cooperation among state, local, and federal agencies, law enforcement has not arrived at the level of cooperation needed to reverse the growth of organized crime activity that is impacting the United States profoundly. Additional resources along with highly experienced, educated, and trained personnel are required to check the deeply integrated growth into the political and economic structures of our country.

Organized crime is continuing to evolve, and its growth or demise will depend on how the United States, as a culture and a people, along with the law enforcement efforts, choose to deal with this threat. Examining the evolution of organized crime, and the mistakes and successes of the past may result in more effective legislation and better efforts to address the growing complexity of organized crime. History is a great teacher.

DISCUSSION QUESTIONS

1. How has American organized crime become more transnational? What strategies are needed to address this trend?
2. What do you believe was the impetus to evolution of organized crime in the United States? Who were the first organized crime groups in America?
3. What are the common threads between early organized crime in America and the current organized crime groups?
4. What parts did Lansky, Rothstein, Luciano, and Marcello play in the development of organized crime in America?
5. Is there or was there a "Dixie Mafia"? Who are/were these people?
6. Discuss the impact of organized crime on the U.S. government, society, U.S. business, and law enforcement.
7. What can be learned from past efforts, including enforcement and legislation, to improve modern efforts to address organized crime?

REFERENCES

Abadinsky, H. (2003). *Organized Crime.* Belmont, CA: Wadsworth/Thompson Learning.

Albanase, J. (1996). *Organized Crime in America.* Cincinnati, OH: Anderson Publishing.

Browning, F., & Gerassi, J. (1980). *The American Way of Crime.* New York: G.P. Putnam's and Sons.

Clinard, M. (1990). *Corporate Corruption: The Abuse of Power.* New York: Praeger.

Gallant, T. W. (1999). Brigandage, piracy, capitalism, and state formation: transnational crime from a historical world systems perspective. In: J. McC Heymand, (Ed.). *From States and Illegal Practices.* New York: Berg Publishers.

Joselit, J. (1983). *Our Gang: Jewish Crime and the New York Community, 1900–1940.* Bloomington, IN: Indiana University Press.

Kenny, D., & Finckenauer, J. (1995). *Organized Crime in America.* Belmont, CA: Wadsworth Publishing Company.

King, R. (1969). *Gambling and Organized Crime.* Washington, DC: Public Affairs Press.

King, R. (1972). *The Drug Hang-Up: America's Fifty Year Folly.* Springfield, IL: Charles C. Thomas.

Klepper, M., Gunther, R., Baik, J., Barth, L., & Gibson, C. (1998). The American Heritage 40. *American Heritage,* October, 56–60.

Lardner, J., & Repetto, T. (2000). *NYPD: A City and Its Police.* New York: Henry Holt.

Miller, W. R. (1991). *Revenuers and Moonshiners.* Chapel Hill: University of North Carolina Press.

Moldea, D. E. (1978). *The Hoffa Wars: Teamsters, Rebels, Politicians, and the Mob.* New York: Paddington.

Moldea, D. E. (1982). Reagan administration officials closely linked with organized crime. *Organized Crime Digest, February,* 6–10.

Nadelmann, E. (1989). Drug prohibition in the United States: cost, consequences and alternatives. *Science, 245,* 939–937.

Peterson, V. F. (1952). *Barbarians in Our Midst: A History of Chicago Crime and Politics.* Boston: Little, Brown and Company.

Sutherland, E., & Cressey, D. (1960). *Principles of Criminology* (6th ed.). New York: Lippincott.

Woodiwiss, M. (1988). *Crime, Crusades and Corruption: Prohibition in the United States, 1900–1987.* Totowa, NJ: Barnes and Noble Books.

3

Theories on the Continued Existence of Organized Crime

"The first to present his cure seems right, till another comes forward and questions him."

—Proverbs 18:17

Chapter Objectives

After completing this chapter, readers should be able to:

- Recognize the impact of globalization on organized crime.
- Explain specific theories or explanations that apply to the different organized crime groups.
- Understand why some law enforcement professionals believe that enterprise theory is the most valuable contribution of the explanations of organized crime.
- Discuss how public demand for illegal products and services can be reduced, and how illegal markets can be disrupted.

■ Introduction

Many investigators have not been enthusiastic about studying and understanding theory. What they want is concrete application and a discussion of what works. However, applications of theories can assist the investigation. Theory provides a systematic view of a phenomenon and helps to explain the phenomenon (Kerlinger & Lee, 2000). Theories help by describing all that is known about a concept (such as organized crime) and, thus, suggest what can be done to control its activities.

One of the purposes of research is to predict future events and developments. As past events and behaviors are analyzed, they become strong predictors of future actions. A theory must consist of certain sets of interrelated concepts that define the problem and specify a means of measurement. In the case of organized crime, this relates to measuring the types of crimes of organized groups that are interrelated. These measurements stimulate further research and planning, help to distinguish between organized and disorganized crime, and suggest strategies for complex investigations to use that will deter the existence and expansions of organized criminal activities.

From a practitioner approach, the continuity of organized crime should be examined in a social context. Organized crime groups operate in complex economic markets and are impacted by the legal system, politics, and the community environment where they do business. The investigator must not only target criminal activity, but also focus on the institutionalization of organized crime into the political and economic arena of society. Corruption and the politics of big business are targets for effective enforcement of organized crime activity. Investigators must develop an understanding of how organized crime groups emerge, determine the cycle of profit from their activities, and how they survive against enforcement efforts.

Not only do investigators need to understand the motivation of individuals to become members of organized crime groups, they need extensive knowledge of corporate crime as well as political and economic corruption. Efforts need to focus on market assessments, production, and conditions in society that spawn organized criminal activity. Law enforcement's lack of strong alliances to regulatory agencies and inadequate funding of these agencies has allowed organized crime to continue to form legitimate business partners who allow banks, corporations, and other business entities to assist these criminals in creating fortunes. Through those fortunes, organized crime groups gain power in society, the business world, and even our government. These groups grow when prohibitions are implemented. There will always be prohibitions in society and organized crime groups will profit from supplying black market goods and services demanded by the public and unavailable in legitimate markets. Increased oversight and public education would likely result in market disruption of these criminal organizations. Supply and demand of illegal services must be priorities of strategies for reducing the growth of organized crime. A focus on white-collar criminal activity is necessary before the connection between organized crime and political and business entities can be reduced or eliminated entirely.

Another practical approach involves examining the specific characteristics of criminal operations as well as those who depend on them for their survival. The number of safe havens is growing where organized crime members are protected because of corruption and collusion with governments. The number of locations throughout the world where money can be laundered also contributes to the growth and continuity of organized crime. Increases in the number of alliances between organized crime groups help their survival, as do the lack of accurate and timely intelligence and the non-cooperation of international law enforcement.

The level of sophistication of major organized crime groups is the most important factor in their ability to continue to dominate both criminal and non-criminal enterprises. Organized crime groups have an ability to adapt to changing markets and new technologies. Law enforcement is playing catch up when it comes to resources, technology, and inter-agency cooperation.

Many of the major organized crime groups have some form of *guanxi*, a concept that has existed for generations. This concept requires a binding and reciprocal obligation between members of organized crime groups that creates an enterprise that protects itself through trust and a code of silence. This code of silence is also termed *omerta* by La Costra Nostra (LCN, the American Mafia).

■ Theories

Bell (1953) uses the "queer ladder of mobility" to explain organized crime as a means of finding wealth and power through expedient means such as gambling and/or illicit goods and services. This theory does not attribute organized crime membership to frustration or blocked opportunity, but to greed.

Ianni's (1973) view on organized crime as ethnic succession is that every new immigrant population in the United States encounters blocked opportunities and obstacles in achieving respect, power, and wealth. In response, many resort to organized crime activity to achieve their dreams or goals. This theory helps explain the ever-changing face of organized crime in America; with each new wave of immigrants, new organized crime groups emerge to present a challenge for law enforcement.

Most criminological theories deal with characteristics of individual behavior and some connection to social problems. Are causes of organized crime different from individual or disorganized crime? After reviewing a number of theories, it becomes clear that no single theory can explain the existence of all the various organized crime groups. Each theory provides insight on why organized crime exists. As discussed in Chapter 1, corruption, political involvement, illegal markets, and influx of new cultures and immigrants all contribute to the existence and the extent of the growth and stability of organized crime groups.

Alien Conspiracy Theory

One of the most common theories found in many texts is the *Alien Conspiracy Theory*. Many authors refer to the members of the Sicilian Mafia who transplanted their criminal culture when they migrated to the United States. More recently, this theory has been supported by methods used by the Russian Mafia as they established operations in the United States after the breakup of the former Soviet Union. There is also evidence that many organized crime groups organized themselves around ethnic backgrounds (Abadinsky, 1985). However, as explained in Chapter 2, organized crime in America began with the pirates and profiteers, and continued with the Jews and Irish long before other ethnic groups immigrated (Kenny and Finckenauer, 1995). Certainly, while this theory has some merit, it falls short of explaining the rise of other groups, such as outlaw motorcycle groups and the rise of black organized crime groups.

The question remains: Why do most men choose not to become organized crime criminals?

The Social Control Theory

The *Social Control Theory* proposes that it is the community, family, and bond with society that prevents entry into a life of crime. Fear of punishment, shame or embarrassment, and psychological restraints such as conscience (described as the "super ego" by Freudian Theory) are a few reasons why not everyone who has the opportunity will engage in criminal activity. Wilson and Herrnstein (1985) illustrated the personal decision in terms of considering both the rewards and punishment as a result of committing a crime. Becoming a member of a criminal group creates more opportunity for rewards, and the group encourages the type of criminal behavior that requires structure or organization to reap as much gain as possible. The group seeks low risk with much reward activities and, thus, moves toward syndicated criminal activity. Gottfredson and Hirschi (1990) believe that self-control is an underlying cause of criminal activity. The criminal is opportunistic and impulsive, which is the result of poor family monitoring and correction. Greed, anger, lust, and peer pressure are common characteristics of many organized crime members.

Albanese's Theory of Typologies

Albanese (1996) explains crime and possible organized crime in terms of the typologies of positivism, classicism, structural, and ethical explanations. The positive approach explains organized crime as caused by social and economic factors that include: poor neighborhoods and role models, lack of opportunity to achieve the "American Dream," dysfunctional families, and even genetics. The positivist sees change in the conditions as a means to prevent criminal behavior.

The classical view is the tendency of people to consider pleasure and pain as guides to their decision to commit criminal acts. Individuals choose to become organized crime members because it offers maximum pleasure and short-term gratification with little risk of apprehension and punishment. The classical school suggests that the certainty of arrest and other painful consequences will prevent individuals from becoming members of organized crime.

The structural approach concerns the political and economic conditions of society. It suggests that individual gain is the most important goal and that success equals assets and money. Structuralists believe that arbitrary laws create criminal activity, so what is needed to prevent criminal activity is equitable distribution of power and wealth. They attribute criminal activity to class conflict. Capitalism creates both the desire to obtain success and the blocked opportunities to success. The ruling class creates laws and policies to simultaneously protect themselves and control the working class to maintain the status quo. Conflicts between the upper and lower classes result in more prohibitions and acts that are prohibited, which in turn creates more crime. A differing theory of this aspect of the structural view is that many organized crime groups emerged to protect themselves from the upper or ruling class and governments (Triads, Yakuza, Sicilian Mafia). Organized crime has developed in countries with both weak and strong governments. Not all people take advantage of prohibitions and commit criminal acts for profit and power.

The ethical perspective views crime as a moral failure, where self-interest is the driving force of existence. The ethical view asks two questions: Why are most people not criminals and what deters them from belonging to an organized crime enterprise? Their response to these questions is that values or virtues of morality prevent people from harming other human beings. The protection of human dignity and human rights is important to good people. Most people are taught right from wrong and have a method for making ethical decisions.

Sutherland's Theory of Differential Association

When a group of people shares common values and associate in a common environment, behavior is learned. This behavior can be criminal when the group a person belongs to has a tradition of organized crime activity. Sutherland (1973) wrote that criminal behavior is part of knowledge passed on during intimate personal group contact, such as gangs or cliques. The group rationalizes criminal behavior and develops a lack of respect for law and law enforcement. This type of association can vary in intensity and duration, and results in a criminal lifestyle that may produce a member of an organized crime group. This theory has been referred to as *differential association* and *cultural transmission* (Sutherland & Cressey, 1960). Those authors propose that the development and recruitment of organized crime members occurs frequently when the environment has considerable crime; there is frequent contact between upcoming youth and organized crime members who are role models and mentors; and a community has little respect for the law. Cultural transmission involves passing down criminal values from generation to generation.

This ecological explanation of criminal behavior is similar to today's "hot spot" theory, where most crimes occur in the same location repeatedly perpetrated by the same people. The proximity of wealthy "targets" to those living in lower income areas produces feelings of anger and frustration in poor youths who are deprived of opportunities for success, so the targets become a means for them to obtain wealth.

Durkheim and Morton's Strain Theory and Anomie

Durkheim (1964) and Merton (1964) wrote of an American society and culture that produced strain. They described the American dream as obtaining wealth and power, which equates to success. When a group or individual cannot obtain this success by legal means, they resort to illegal means. *Differential opportunity* is a term associated with this type of strain that is supported by socioeconomic stratification of people into lower, middle, and upper classes (Abadinsky, 2003). This *anomie* occurs when people cannot obtain the "American dream" of success because there is not equal opportunity to climb the ladder of success. Organized crime members act with what Merton (1957) refers to as *innovation*, which is defined as success by organized, planned, and strategic activity, or employing the characteristics discussed in Chapter 1.

Anomie, cultural transmission, and the concept of cultural conflict add to the understanding of why organized crime exists. Cultures and subcultures (alien conspiracy and ethnic succession) were brought to America by immigrants or they have developed here (outlaw biker groups). Sellin (1938) described *culture conflict*, where crime was the result of different cultures having different norms of what to believe or value. Because America is a country of many cultures with many different values, there are also many conflicts. Activities and products that may have been acceptable in the country of origin may not be legal or culturally acceptable in their new homeland. People then become involved in organized crime activity to obtain these now illegal services and goods.

Beccaria and Lombroso's Classical Theories

Most of the above theories were developed from the classical school of Marches e de Beccaria (1735–1794) (Beccaria, 1819) and the positive school associated with Cesare Lombroso (1836–1909). The classical theory often is referred to as *rational choice*, where people are free to make choices based on their values and logic. This theory resulted in harsh and immediate punishment to prevent offenders from making a choice to commit criminal activity again. Their motto was that punishment should fit the crime. The thinking is that before committing a crime, people weigh the risks of getting caught and being punished against the rewards of getting away with the crime. But members of organized crime groups believe that the organization can prevent them from being caught or can use corruption to reduce the risk of apprehension and punishment. Jeremy Bentham (1748–1832) measured the degree of good or bad of an act by proportion to affect the greatest happiness for the greatest number (Ferm, 1956).

Positivism examined criminal behavior in terms of internal or external influences. The poor economy, bad associates, poor family supervision, lack of positive role models, peer pressure, unequal opportunities such as inability to attend college or find a good job, all are factors that the positivists attribute to the propensity toward criminal activity. Blocked opportunity and criminal association do explain much of criminal activity; however, most people who are exposed to all of the above conditions rise above criminal activity and become successful noncriminals. These so-called *utilitarians* assumed that people exercised free will in seeking pleasure and avoiding pain. Lombroso placed more emphasis on the individual and environmental influences on individual behavior.

Biological Theories

Another group of individuals proposed explanations for criminal behavior that are based on biology. These factors range from research in endocrinology, physical and physiological characteristics (redheaded men), mental deficiency, and morphological characteristics. However, there is much criticism of this approach (Hooten, 1939).

■ Summary of the Theoretical Approach

Three identified theoretical approaches to explain criminal activities are environmental, individualistic, and genetics/biological. Much of what today is termed *profiling* originated from psychoanalytical theories that conceptualized mental deficiency as an additional explanation of criminal activity. Goddard (1923) wrote that at least half of all criminals suffer from some form of mental deficiency. The

Freudian explanation is that the super ego, id, and ego are the unconscious world of inner feelings that become the source of mental conflict and results in criminal activity. Certainly, the study of psychoanalytic theory can help the investigator "get into the mind" of a criminal and help develop a plan for intervention and arrest.

Some believe that organized crime exists solely because of prohibitions, such as with drugs, prostitution, and gambling. But although illicit drugs are the mainstay of most organized crime groups, many continue to profit from legal enterprises, such as waste management, the garment industry, and labor racketeering. The Russians, Chinese, and the Yakuza extort millions from companies and individuals in legitimate businesses.

Organized crime will find a means to obtain enormous profits and power no matter what is decriminalized, made illegal, or legalized. Organized criminal groups are a part of the political and economic systems of every nation and, as such, will continue to develop schemes to take advantage of their political and economic links. As long as the risks are acceptable and the profits large, organized crime will continue to exist in our complex global environment. Removing the criminal statutes for drug trafficking and other crimes will not eliminate organized crime activity.

Theories Related to Law Enforcement Efforts

Albanese (1996) believes that organized crime should be defined by its activities. His more recent typology of organized crime includes the activity or provision of illicit goods and services (gambling, sex, drugs, and human trafficking) and infiltration or abuse of legitimate business (Albanese, 1996). According to Albanese, three kinds of factors explain the existence of organized crime: opportunity factors, the criminal environment, and special access or skills.

Opportunity factors include economic, governmental, law enforcement, and social or technological changes. Economic factors include poverty, poor standards of living, or demand for an illicit product with adequate supply available. Government conditions include weak governments that cannot effectively address organized crime or may have inadequate laws or regulations to deal with the complex nature of organized crime. Law enforcement factors include the level of training, corruption, and the degree of government interference. Internal control leads to weaknesses that include the failure to monitor an agent's activity or evaluate training. The level of professionalism contributes to the ability or inability for organized crime to be successful. Social and technological changes such as globalization (travel and unlimited communication) also affect organized crime activity. The ability to supervise an organized crime group operation from a long distance or to easily transfer money allows organized crime to flourish.

Special skills may be needed to exploit opportunities. Computer expertise, smuggling expertise, management skills, and other technological abilities permit organized crime to grow and become more efficient and effective, the same way as legitimate enterprises. Countries where education and training levels are high offer organized crime these skills and knowledge.

Criminal environment issues include whether organized black markets exist in the country, prior existence of organized groups, and the presence of gangs. If the country or jurisdiction has a history of frequent and serious criminal activity, then the presence of organized crime is more likely.

Albanese developed a risk assessment tool based on the above explanations of organized crime. Seventeen factors (among them risk factors of economic, government, law enforcement, criminal history, social and technology changes, and harm) and measurement methods are utilized to determine specific illicit activities in a particular locality to predict the existence and extent of organized crime activity (Finckenauer & Schrock, 2004).

Enterprise Theory

The enterprise theory is probably of more interest to the investigator for its practicality. This theory explains organized crime activity as the result of unfilled goods and services to a demanding public. For example, when the number of people who use illegal drugs in the United States is examined, it is evident that a huge market exists. The Office of Drug Control Policy estimated that about 3% of the population (about 4.5 million persons) were dependent on illicit drugs. This is also true of gambling, prostitution, and stolen goods. Prohibition and the Controlled Substance Act produced a market whereby large profits could be made by providing illegal services and goods that had once been legal, and now were in high demand. The law of supply and demand results in an enterprise that uses corruption, violence, planning, and organization, combined with the other characteristics of organized crime described in Chapter 1 to control and expand the market for these illicit goods and services. This results in a single supplier who can control the price and reap huge profits. Organized crime and transnational criminal organizations continue to evolve by networking between organized crime groups and structures that adapt to a globalization of markets.

Although drug trafficking remains a mainstay of organized crime groups, new markets of illicit activity are emerging. Among these growing criminal enterprises are the trafficking in human body parts, biological and nuclear materials, trafficking of women and children for the sex industry, smuggling of humans, cyber crime, and a wide variety of crimes of fraud.

Enterprise theory describes organized crime activity as being well planned and executed with the primary objective of profit and other goals, such as power and political influence. The organized crime group involves itself in both licit and illicit activities to meet demands by willing consumers. This theory suggests that the structure of organized crime groups is flexible and often has a decentralized leadership or leadership by a cartel/committee. McFeely (2001) concluded that enterprise theory leads to a proactive investigative strategy that is an effective approach for destroying an organized crime group.

The enterprise theory of investigation (ETI) is effective against organized crime groups, which are highly diverse in their criminal activities. Organized crime groups nearly always invest their profits into legitimate businesses that often serve as a front for such activities as money laundering, fencing operations, and warehouses for contraband. This type of investigation attempts to identify all members of an organized crime group and develop prosecutable cases on all members.

The primary target is the money trail or financial operations of the group. By seizing the money and assets of the group, their ability to continue operating is destroyed. Seizure of legitimate businesses of organized crime groups cripples their ability to develop corruption opportunities targeted at both government officials and business executives, which are fundamental for the expansion of their criminal enterprises.

Because organized crime has an identified leadership structure, the application of conspiracy statutes is very effective when prosecuting these individuals. Enterprise theory describes organized crime members as members of a group whose structure and membership are identified, and are an internal threat to a country. The integration of illegal funds into legitimate business amounts to a national threat for organized crime to control large corporations and the political process.

Hierarchical and Local-Ethnic Models

Albanese (1996) presented three models (paradigms) of organized crime, but admitted that, due to its dynamic nature, their use is limited to understanding the activities of organized crime. The hierarchical model describes the structure of organized crime as a family with ranks from boss to soldiers, where the boss supervises the activities and is in control of the group members' behavior. A commission of bosses exists that handles disputes between "families" and it approves certain aspects of the organized crime organization of families. The American Mafia exemplifies this model. The local or ethnic model of organized crime is bound together by cultural or ethnic ties. Activities are controlled by individuals rather than by a single boss. Partnerships form around choices to work on a particular project or in a specific area. This model suggests that there is no national commission that oversees all groups.

The difference between the hierarchical and the ethnic/local models is how the individual relationships are structured. As previously discussed, the enterprise model defines economic relationships rather than personal relationships as forming the organized activity and structure. These activities are similar to legitimate business, are not ethnically exclusive or violent, and center on market opportunities. Albanese (1996) gives the example of cooperation between the Italians, Greeks, Irish, Jews, and African-American criminal groups. One current example is the cooperation between the Colombian drug cartels and the Mexican drug cartels and black, Dominican, and Jamaican criminal groups or gangs.

These models offer strategies for enforcement efforts. The hierarchical and local/ethnic models describe how organized crime groups are structured. The enterprise model provides insight into how the activities are organized and carried out. The primary goal of organized crime is power and profit, and according to the enterprise model, all criminal groups share these goals.

Deterrence Theory

The assumption that organized crime groups and members consider the risk of arrest and punishment gives rise to the Deterrence Theory. This theory concludes that crime can be prevented by the threat of punishment. But Wilson (1975) wrote that most crimes are committed by a small number of people who are habitual offenders. Like others in law enforcement, Wilson views the severity and surety of punishment as elements not considered by organized crime members because of the leniency of the courts and lack of resources to investigate and arrest major violators.

Other Models

Abadinsky (2003) offers two models to describe the structure of organized crime groups. The first is the *bureaucratic/corporate model*, where efficiency is the prime factor for large operations or activities; this model follows the characteristics of Weber's and Taylor's models described in Chapter 1. When activities continue to expand, the bureaucratic structure becomes necessary to control the enterprise with rules, hierarchy, specialization, and means of communication. Colombian cartels and the outlaw biker groups are examples of this type of structure.

The *patrimonial/patron-client model* is based on bonds that tie the organization together. The patron provides aid and protection while the client becomes a loyal member who is respected. The emphasis is on traditions such as rituals and personal relationships. This model offers the advantage of continuity when the leader is incapacitated, as a patron will assume the position. The patron-client model is less centralized and has less control over subordinates than the bureaucratic model. Albini (1971) and Abadinsky (2003) characterize the American Mafia as a patron-client group whose structure is a hierarchy and bureaucratic, but its activities are patron-client models that operate as independent crews who are entrepreneurs. The Mafia's goal is to conduct criminal activity for profit, while the outlaw biker's goal is to promote their lifestyle, which includes criminal activity.

The patron-client model requires a more complex law enforcement effort because of its decentralized activities and large number of social networks whose members are not connected to each other. The bureaucratic model is more susceptible to law enforcement efforts because of its rigid chain of command, communication structure, and heavy involvement of the leaders in the criminal activity; the leaders give orders and oversee operations directly. The patron is often uninvolved in the actual criminal activity and only provides information on targets for the client to rob or steal.

■ Beyond Theory

Organized crime will continue to exist because these organizations are extremely dynamic and resilient, and they can re-form even after effective law enforcement and intervention strategies. LCN is not finished in the United States despite the arrest of most of the crime family bosses. These organizations are network-based, which allows them to ally with both powerful political and economic structures and other powerful organized crime groups to continue to survive and prosper. Organized crime remains part of the local culture and depends on corruption and market demand. They take advantage of technological advances and the new era of global trade and communication. Their current connection to multinational business and corporations is unprecedented and provides additional evidence of their resiliency. This durable characteristic comes from years of survival with violence, corruption, and successful recruitment lending to the survival—not demise—of organized crime.

The increased emphasis on fighting terrorism and decreased emphasis on organized crime investigation can only help organized crime. Funding task forces, research, regulatory agencies, and intelligence operations is crucial to plan successful strategic and tactical interventions. The United States government will never be able to provide the employment, security, and goods and services demanded by the public. Thus, the enormous profits earned by organized crime groups will continue to be a driving motivator for criminal enterprises to exist. These profits are invested into both the political arena and the economy, which gives organized crime groups more power and influence than the government, and allows them to become "shadow governments."

The question of international cooperation remains an uncertainty. Are organized crime groups too powerful and political to allow governments to fully cooperate and aggressively pursue strategies for dealing with or even eliminating these groups? If not, then organized crime groups are certain to attempt to extend their activity and become even more powerful. Will countries address the problem of corruption or will governments continue to allow bribery and apathy to continue? If corruption is necessary for organized crime to continue, the answers to these questions already have been answered, because organized crime activity is expanding and becoming more embedded into our society.

Globalization along with economic interdependence has provided still another reason why organized crime has expanded. Agreements such as the North American Free Trade Agreement (NAFTA), liberal immigration policies, and growing transnational networks have provided organized crime with opportunities that are equal to drug and alcohol prohibitions. The emergence of the international banking systems that have little oversight or control has allowed organized crime to move money undetected to and from anywhere in the world instantaneously. Extensive advances in technology have given rise to communication systems that allow organized crime members and leaders to communicate without detection from any location around the world.

The rising trend of rural crime now presents organized crime groups with opportunities and markets in addition to the large urban areas. Because rural areas are often not provided the same levels of resources and enforcement as that of major urban areas, professional law enforcement in rural America is not prepared to deal with the sophistication of organized crime activity.

The world is becoming smaller through globalization and networks and many benefits result from this process. However, this interdependence is counterbalanced by the rapid growth and longevity of organized crime.

■ Combining Theory and Other Explanations

Smith (1980) wrote that *conspiracy* is the only way that people engage in organized crime. Conspiracy answers the question of how the activity is planned and executed. None of the theories or models fully explains organized crime. A comprehensive theory is needed that contains elements of all those discussed in this chapter. There is a trend for immediate gratification in today's society. There will always be a condition of anomie—the "haves" and the "have nots." Society's preoccupation with success (power and wealth) is a powerful force that drives some people to criminal activity when they are deprived of these goals. Albini (1971) found that criminal patrons exchange information, are connected with corrupt government officials, and that these networks are in a constant state of change with the roles of patrons and clients fluctuating. These networks exist because of a demand by society. Society has accepted and embraced this relationship with organized crime groups, prohibition, the drug trade, gambling, and prostitution.

Then there is the reality of environmental and role model influences where youths begin their criminal career as specialists in theft, drug trafficking, or arson, and later become a member of an organized crime group due to their expertise. Flashy cars, expensive jewelry, and large rolls of money help organized crime members appear as success stories for recruiting young people into their organization (Cressy, 1969).

Ethnicity serves as a variable, but is only part of the equation. American Mafia membership, Yakuza, or certain black gangs require certain ethnic backgrounds. Kenny and Finckenauer (1995) summarize that conspiracy is the *how*, ethnicity is often the *who*, and illicit enterprise to supply demand is the *what* that, all combined, produce organized crime. An example of ethnic succession was when the Irish were replaced by the Italians who, some in law enforcement say, are now being replaced by the African-American, Russian, Hispanic, and Asian groups.

These emerging groups are in an American environment where in the last decade there has been a reduction of major industries, resulting in fewer good paying jobs for low skilled and uneducated workers. This has resulted in a growth of the lower class, which, in the case of gang members, makes a living in the criminal world. Examples are groups such as The Disciple Nation, The Crips, Vice Lord Nation, Bloods, and many others. Nigerian criminal groups have evolved as major drug suppliers to many of these street gangs.

Crime has become a way of life for many of these Americans. The socialization function helps explain community acceptance in many localities. Many studies by researchers such as Albanese (1996), Potter and Lyman (2004), and Abadinsky (2003) have reported a criminal–community relationship where criminal groups are not considered very different from legitimate enterprises. This relationship leads to successful recruitment and support for organized crime groups.

However, poverty, limited opportunities, and lower socioeconomic backgrounds do not explain why the great majority of people with a low income do not become members of organized crime. Merton (1964) and Durkheim's (1964) anomie concept provides some clarity on this matter. Merton (1957) and Abadinsky's (2003) conclusion is that organized crime is an adaptation to anomie by innovation (illegal means to obtain the American dream of success), such as long-termed, strategic planning and other characteristics of organized crime activity. Durkheim's research reached the same conclusion.

However, this theory does not explain why the wealthy become members of criminal groups. Many in organized crime groups explain that they are just providing what the public desires and demands. This is summarized in their beliefs that "only suckers work" and that laws are made to control the working class.

What is the relevance of all this theory? If an explanation of why organized crime exists can be developed, then a comprehensive plan of action by the government and law enforcement can also be developed.

Still another approach would be to determine why most people do not enter criminal organizations. Certainly, most people fear the threat of apprehension and punishment. Social control theory also helps explain why most do not choose criminal careers. Many who do choose criminal careers could be diagnosed with antisocial personality disorder or possess psychological traits that predisposed them to criminal careers (i.e., sociopathic personality disorder). Criminologists believe that crime is the result of individual personality and social conditions or social disorganization. Organized crime may be described more as criminal cooperation with the "legitimate" world than groups or individuals engaged in criminal activities. Conspiracy is an accurate description of organized crime activity. Co-conspirators are the people who demand the goods and services provided by organized crime. There does not appear to be any real possibility of completely removing organized crime from the world or more specifically from the United States because of the demand for its existence due to human weaknesses.

Perhaps a deeper understanding of these theories may provide a better explanation of organized crime activity and answer the question of why individuals become organized crime members. However, it seems that the enterprise theory gives the investigator more suggestions for investigative techniques.

Although there have been successful law enforcement efforts, such as the demise of both the Cali and Medellín cartels and arrests of many LCN and other members of organized crime groups, the removal of large groups or bosses has not eliminated organized crime in any country. Other groups or bosses always replace the ones who have been removed.

Market demand remains a determining factor in the continued existence of organized crime. The failure to effectively address corruption, develop accurate and timely intelligence, and reduce public demand for illicit goods and services ensures the survival of organized crime. Unless governments can disrupt the relationship organized crime has with the political and economic elements of society, organized crime groups will continue to expand into new markets and governments, ensuring their survival. Criminal intelligence in part consists of identifying members, structures, methods of recruitment, retention, methods of operations, motives, areas of activity, types of services and goods provided by the group, and how money and assets are handled.

Theories help with assimilating this information and can help make predictions of future growth and development of organized crime. Immediate gratification, greed, and power are motives that make organized crime both successful and vulnerable. Organized crime is a career pattern that offers much opportunity for tracing its participant's activities and assets. The investigator must understand that the activities of organized crime groups are flexible networks that change with market demands and opportunity. Organized crime groups are often loosely structured and fragmented with no single group exercising complete control over activities such as drug trafficking, gambling, or prostitution. This does not make them any less a threat and often results in conflicts that produce extraordinary crime rates in categories such as murder. Ianni's (1972) view was that organized crime groups are ethnic social systems. Haller (1990) described organized crime groups as small-scale business partnerships. Again, there's no consensus.

What is evident from these studies is that organized crime requires public participation and corruption to achieve either enterprise status or power. Block (1983) defined enterprise syndicates as forming to distribute large amounts of illicit goods and services that require a large number of members, hierarchy, centralization and division of labor. Power syndicates were involved in extreme violence to control other enterprise syndicates. These power syndicates often had no division of labor and were loosely structured, flexible associations. These power associations did not last for any long periods of time, in contrast to enterprise groups that were long-lived organizations.

■ Conclusions

The investigator must identify the group operating in their jurisdiction and determine which of the theories do not apply. Perhaps a comprehensive theory could be developed for an individual organized crime group, but to date there is no "one theory fits all." Understanding and prediction should be the investigator's goals when examining theory and organized crime. Both theories and common sense help explain why organized crime activity exists and why individuals choose to belong to these groups. So far, enforcement and policies have failed to take the profit out of organized crime activity. It appears that some people who choose a criminal career join an organized crime group for a better assurance of success and power, extraordinary wealth, peer pressure, role model influences, and recruitment efforts of these criminal enterprises.

The investigator can benefit from examining the "why" of organized crime groups to better develop plans of intervention, market disruption, arrest, and prosecution. Individuals who belong to organized crime groups tend to support each other and continue the group's purposes, just as bureaucracies tend to support bureaucratic characteristics. These actions and mindsets tend to keep the members doing what the group has always done to continue their organized activity.

Organized crime's survival depends on two elements: corruption and public demand. Although structure, individual motive, and conspiracy are important elements of organized crime, it is the exploitation of human weakness and weak governments that ensures the continuity of organized crime groups. Arrest and prosecution of members of organized crime groups will not eliminate these criminal enterprises. There will always be an ambitious recruit or member waiting to take the place of the arrested leader. These organizations are too dynamic to be destroyed by law enforcement efforts alone. Public demand drives the illicit markets that organized crime groups depend on for profit. Groups such as the Yakuza and Triads have existed for hundreds of years and will continue to exist because they are not only shadow governments, but are necessary to supply the public's insatiable desire for illicit goods and services. The trend for organized crime groups to invest in legitimate companies and businesses allows them both political power and control of corporations that are an integral part of society or part of the political economic system. There is a high probability that businesses benefiting from partnerships with organized crime groups will continue to resist measures that would lead to effective enforcement. Strict regulation and monitoring of corporate America may be difficult to implement due to the many benefits, including power and profit, these business and corporate entities receive from organized crime activity and partnerships. These explanations may say more about why organized crime will continue to exist than do the traditional theories of crime. Certainly, there is a need for additional research about why organized crime exists and continues to be a national threat to society.

DISCUSSION QUESTIONS

1. Why are theories important in addressing organized crime?
2. What particular theories do you think explain organized crime and why?
3. What has been the impact of globalization on organized crime?
4. What specific theories or explanations apply to the different organized crime groups and why?
5. Why do people become members of organized crime?
6. Why do some in law enforcement believe that enterprise theory is the most valuable contribution of the explanations of organized crime?
7. How can public demand for illegal products and services be reduced? How can these illegal markets be disrupted?

REFERENCES

Abadinsky, H. (1985). *Organized Crime*. Belmont, GA: Wadsworth/Thompson Learning.

Abadinsky, H. (2003). *Organized Crime*, (2nd ed.). Chicago: Nelson-Hall.

Albanese, J. (1989). *Organized Crime in America,* Cincinnati, OH: Anderson Publishing.

Albanese, J. (1996). *Organized Crime in America*, (2nd ed.). Cincinnati, OH: Anderson Publishing.

Albini, J. L. (1971). *The American Mafia: Genesis of a Legend*. New York: Appleton-Century-Crofts.

Beccaria, C. (1819). *An Essay on Crime and Punishment*. Philadelphia: P. H. Nicklin.

Bell. D. (1953). Crime as an American Way of Life. *Antioch Review, 13 Summer,* 130–150.

Block, A. (1983). *East Side – West Side: Organizing Crime in New York, 1930–1950*. New Brunswick, NJ: Transaction Publishers.

Cressy, D. (1969). *Theft of a Nation: The Structure and Operations of Organized Crime*. New York: Harper and Row.

Durkheim, E. (1964). *The Rules of Sociological Method (1985)*. New York: Harper and Row.

Ferm, B. (Ed.). (1956). *Encyclopedia of Morals*. New York: Philosophical Library.

Finckenauer, J. O., & Schrock, J. L. (2004). *The Prediction and Control of Organized Crime: The Experience of Post-Soviet Ukraine*. New Brunswick, NJ: Transaction Publishers.

Goddard, H. H. (1923). *Feeblemindedness: Its Causes and Consequences*. New York: MacMillan.

Gottfredson, M., & Hirschi, T. (1990). *A General Theory of Crime*. Stanford, CA: Stanford University Press.

Haller, M. (1990). Illegal Enterprise: A Theoretical and Historical Interpretation. *Criminology, 28(2),* 207–236.

Hooten, E. (1939). *The American Criminal: An Anthropological Study.* Cambridge, MA: Harvard University Press.

Ianni, F. (1972). *A Family Business.* New York: Russell Sage Foundation.

Ianni, F. A. (1973). *Ethnic Succession in Organized Crime.* Washington, DC: U.S. Government Printing Office.

Kenny, D., & Finckenauer, J. (1995). *Organized Crime in America.* Belmont, CA: Wadsworth.

Kerlinger, F., & Lee, H. (2000). *Foundations of Behavioral Research,* (4th ed.). New York: Harcourt College Publisher, Inc.

McFeely, R. A. (2001). Enterprise Theory of Investigation. *FBI Law Enforcement Bulletin, May* 19.

Merton, R. (1964). M. Clinard (Ed.) *Anomie and Deviant Behavior.* New York: Free Press.

Merton, R. K. (1957). *Social Theory and Social Structure.* Glencoe, IL: The Free Press.

Potter, W., & Lyman, M. (2004). *Organized Crime,* (3rd ed.). Upper Saddle River, New Jersey: Prentice Hall.

Sellin, T. (1938). *Culture, Conflict and Crime.* New York: Social Science Research Council.

Smith, D. (1980). Paragons, Pariahs, and Privateers: A Spectrum-Based Theory of Enterprise. *Crime and Delinquency, 26(3),* 375.

Sutherland, E. H. (1973). K. Schnessler (Ed.). *Edwin H. Sutherland: On Analyzing Crime.* Chicago: University of Chicago Press.

Sutherland, E., & Cressey, D. (1960). *Principles of Criminology,* (6th ed.). New York: Lippincott.

Wilson, J. Q. (1975). *Thinking About Crime.* New York: Basic Books.

Wilson, J., & Herrnstein, R. (1985). *Crime and Human Nature.* New York: Simon and Schuster.

Colombian Drug Cartels

4

"Example moves the world more than doctrine."
—Henry Miller, author (1891–1980)

Chapter Objectives

After completing this chapter, readers should be able to:
- Describe the major drug trafficking organizations of Colombia.
- Discuss the organization and growth of the Medellín and Cali cartels and their methods of operation.
- Describe how the efforts of law enforcement led to the decline of the Medellín and Cali cartels.
- Explain the significant aspects of the U.S. policy, "Plan Colombia."

Introduction

During the last two decades of the twentieth century, drug trafficking became a staple of organized crime in the Americas. As profits from the smuggling of marijuana, heroin, and, subsequently, cocaine across national borders multiplied, organizations devoted to supplying the demand for these substances grew in size, scope, and sophistication. Until recently, the primary destination for smuggled drugs was the United States. The major players in this process were the Medellín and Cali cartels of Colombia and a variety of Mexican drug trafficking groups who eventually became partners with the Colombians and have now become powerful in their own right.

Historical Perspective

Colombia's role in the international proliferation of drugs is rooted in its politics, and the policies designed to minimize drug production and distribution within and across its borders (Ramirez, Clemencia, Stanton, & Walsh, 2005). The civil war, La Violenca (1947–1953), created divisions that have had an impact until the present time. A force that emerged from this internal conflict was leftist guerillas. U.S. Presidents Kennedy and Johnson feared that this group would set in motion the type of upheaval that had occurred in Cuba, which resulted in a communist state. With this in mind, support for the military and subsequently for paramilitary groups became part of U.S. policy toward Colombia in the 1960s.

The threat posed by leftist guerillas has been a constant concern of U.S. policymakers during subsequent presidential administrations. The control these groups have had over prime coca-producing territory has enabled the United States to link drug control issues to the counterinsurgency campaign. This was important because it provided a rationale for the support of "Plan Colombia," a formal policy still supported financially by the United States. Success in combating the drug traffickers would have to be limited to a by-product of anti-guerilla efforts. One significant aspect of Plan Colombia is that the Colombian military now receives more money than the police, a change from prior years and an indication that the balance of power is shifting.

As the 1970s began, Colombian drug entrepreneurs had made marijuana their drug of choice. Elsewhere, heroin attracted the lion's share of enforcement activity. In 2003, according to freelance journalist Ron Chepesiuk, this caused the DEA to neglect the emerging popularity of cocaine, which was becoming associated with a glamorous life style. Colombians were able to capitalize on cocaine's comeback because they had been shadowing Cuban criminals, learning the cocaine production process (Chepesiuk, 2003).

As the 1970s progressed into the 1980s, Colombia became, as Chepesiuk coined, "the linchpin of the Latin American drug trade" (Chepesiuk, 2003). Several factors contributed to this newfound prominence. Initially, access to coca leaves was provided by Colombia's neighbors, Peru and Bolivia, where large quantities of the plants or bushes were grown. However, as Bagley states, by the 1990s, Colombia had become the "premier coca-cultivating country in the world, producing more coca leaf than both Peru and Bolivia combined" (Bagley, 2001:1). The last half of the decade was a period of dramatic increase in the amount of land devoted to coca leaf cultivation.

With the ample supply of coca leaves available, Colombia solidified its position as the world's major refiner and supplier of cocaine hydrochloride. Clandestine laboratories in Peru, Bolivia, and Colombia produced hundreds of tons of pure cocaine.

Smuggling the finished product into the United States was facilitated by Colombia's proximity to the U.S. border and the fact that Colombia has both Caribbean and Pacific coasts (**Figure 4-1**). Colombia's historical affinity for smuggling provided an atmosphere that was conducive to making drug trafficking just another facet of a national tradition (Chepesiuk, 2003). In addition, the money to be made in trafficking drugs was very attractive in a country experiencing a high poverty rate and an unstable economy. Initially, the Colombians did their own smuggling using the Caribbean as the main route and the United States as the primary destination.

Necessary changes in trafficking patterns were brought about by the U.S. government's move to stem the flow of drugs into the country (Chepesiuk, 2003).

Figure 4-1 The Caribbean and Pacific Coasts of Colombia

Central America and Mexico became logistical destinations for the airlift of drugs destined for U.S. drug customers. Shipments were transported to northern Mexico and then flown across the southwestern border of the United States. Mexican traffickers became more directly involved in the business and by the early 1990s were major players. Cocaine was added to the list of drugs finding their way along the so-called *Mexican drug highway*. Entrance across the United States border has been facilitated by driven vehicles and couriers, called *mules*, who transport small quantities. Passage of the North American Free Trade Agreement (NAFTA) has increased border traffic making detection of illicit drugs far more difficult. Commercial vehicles of all types, including tractor-trailer units, are now used to haul drugs in large quantities.

During the 1990s, as the Mexican drug groups became increasingly involved in the diversified cocaine trade, Colombian cartels switched their focus to heroin trafficking. Home-grown opium is processed locally and then transformed from opium gum to morphine to heroin. Movement to the United States is directed by the smaller cartels and syndicates that also have replaced the larger, more notorious groups that were formally synonymous with Colombian drug dealing. Discussion of the participants in the Colombian drug scene from the 1970s to the present follows.

■ The Medellín Cartel

The Medellín Cartel was the first of the major Colombian drug groups to emerge. This organization was the most powerful cartel for more than 12 years, and its power transcended national boundaries. The organization employed producers, murderers, chemists, attorneys, government officials, accountants, transportation experts, and a variety of distributors throughout the world. Cartel leaders became major landowners with powerful political influence. The Medellín cartel increased its efficiency through alliances with such groups as the traditional American La Cosa Nostra.

This loosely knit group of drug dealers joined forces for the purpose of achieving common goals with fewer liabilities than operating individually. The leaders of this tough group became known as the Hoodlums ("Los Hampones") and included Pablo Escobar, Carlos Lehder, the Ochoa brothers, and Jose Gacha.

As the boss of the Medellín cartel, Escobar was considered by many to be the "godfather of cocaine." The son of a schoolteacher and a farmer, he chose the criminal life. He ingratiated himself not only with the people of his native country, but also with officials of the governments of both the United States and Colombia while building his cocaine empire. He simultaneously built schools, churches, and housing while corrupting government officials with bribes and intimidating them with threats of violence.

Escobar began as a petty thief, became a gang member, excelled as a paid murderer, and rose to become boss of a major organization with a personal net worth estimated at between two and four billion dollars. While building his empire, he established a large following among Colombians because of his physical and financial support of Colombian soccer. Escobar was so politically powerful that when the Colombian government, under U.S. pressure, finally agreed to deal with him, he was able to dictate his own terms of incarceration. He continued to run his enterprises while imprisoned.

Although Escobar captured more headlines because of his public persona and violent style, Lehder was perhaps more important to the success of the Medellín group. Lehder established an airlift that involved flying cocaine shipments from Colombia to an island in the Bahamas where refueling took place before the planes continued to the United States. This process served as a model for other similar operations during the 1970s and 1980s.

Operations

The Medellín group's backgrounds were reflected in the way they conducted their drug business (Chepesiuk, 2003). Violence was the primary tool for dealing with discord. Much of this activity was engineered by Escobar. During the 1980s, the cartel planted bombs that killed 63 people in one incident. In 1989, the cartel blew up a commercial aircraft, killing a large number of people because they believed an informant/witness was aboard. They killed 30 of Colombia's judges, a state police officer, a presidential candidate, and a minister of justice as well as hundreds of police officers and innocent bystanders. Bounties were placed on police officers and hundreds were killed. Innocent bystanders in the wrong place at the wrong time routinely paid for it with their lives. The violence intimidated the government to such extremes that Colombia gave in to the cartels, refusing for years to extradite members to the United States for trial. Members lived in fortified homes protected by armed guards and elaborate surveillance equipment.

For a time, Medellín leaders even attempted to become a part of Colombia's political system. This effort had limited success before they reverted to the most extreme form of narco-terrorism: the murder of anyone who stood in their way.

The Cali Cartel

The second cartel to have an impact on the international drug scene, the Cali cartel developed a stronger presence than the Medellin group. Its founders were the Rodríguez brothers, Gilberto and Miguel, and Jose Santacruz. Ron Chepesiuk, author of the definitive work about this group, *Drug Lords: The Rise and Fall of the Cali Cartel*, states that the backgrounds of these individuals were unclear (Chepesiuk, 2003:22). Whatever their origins, the skills of the three men blended together to create an effective and powerful organization. The fourth member of the directorate was Pacho Herrera, whose initial focus was the New York market and who would later be the major player in establishing alliances with Mexican traffickers.

Operations

The approach taken by the Cali leaders was in stark contrast to the flamboyant style of Escobar and his Medellín partners. Avoiding media and legal attention and promoting a professional image were preferable to the violent stance adopted by the notorious Medellín group. However, Cali members were ruthless when murder served their purpose.

Despite their different philosophies, the two cartels were able to co-exist well into the mid-1980s. This lack of friction was due at least in part to the rapidly expanding drug market and the profits that came from supplying the demand.

The Cali cartel took numerous steps to ensure that its operations could continue without legal interruption. Security and intelligence were given high priority. Telephone calls were monitored and taxi drivers kept track of visitors (Chepesiuk, 2003).

The city of Cali quickly became the cartel's town. Chepesiuk likens the leaders' control to that of feudal barons controlling large estates in medieval times (Chepesiuk, 2003). Like the policy of earlier drug leaders, economic development was launched in a variety of areas, which created jobs, provided a way to launder drug money, and led to acceptance of Cali members by the local populace.

The cartel's control also extended to the media. Their lawyers threatened lawsuits when anything negative appeared in the press. Media employees were paid to generate favorable publicity.

Chepesiuk (2003:71) states unequivocally that the Cali cartel was solidly entrenched by the mid 1980s: "Its members felt untouchable; they *were* untouchable." This growth was aided by the preoccupation of Colombian authorities with the Medellín cartel, which they perceived as being more dangerous (Chepesiuk).

The Cali cartel grew into a multinational corporation by the early 1990s and became the model for multinational crime. Both the marketplace and corresponding personnel expanded in a dramatic fashion. Perhaps the most important step that the Cali cartel took in the early 1990s was to develop operations in a number of Latin American and Caribbean countries. Ties forged with Mexican traffickers would prove to be the most significant alliance, which proved to be highly profitable for both parties. The most notorious of these partnerships was formed with Amando Carrillo Fuentes, the so-called "Lord of the Skies" who originated the concept of using jets to fly cocaine from Colombia to Mexico (Chepesiuk, 2003).

After ties between Mexican traffickers and the Cali group were established, Colombian cocaine increasingly came into the United States via the Mexican pipeline while the Caribbean connection became less important. Mexican cartels would become major operatives in the Cali's Mexican presence. In the late 1990s, because of U.S. interdiction along the United States-Mexican border, the Caribbean countries returned to prominence as links in the drug trade (Bagley, 2001). More recently, as the Mexican cartels have grown stronger, trafficking across the U.S. border has regained its prominence.

Markets in the other parts of the world would eventually be established by the cartel. A Mafia-Cali alliance developed. The possibilities for further European business were heightened by the collapse of communism, dissolution of the Soviet Union, and the eliminating of European trade barriers. Organized crime syndicates wasted no time making international contracts.

The success of the Cali cartel can be attributed to a variety of factors, but the scale and attention to detail of the organization were perhaps most important (Chepesiuk, 2003). Operations were directed from the "home office" in Cali, which approved all customers before a drug sale occurred. Cells operating within specific geographic areas were responsive to policies and decisions made in Cali. Cell managers supervised 25 to 50 employees whose duties reflected a division of labor that included transportation, distribution, support, and accounting. Cell managers were responsible to regional managers who in turn reported to the Cali office. **Figure 4-2** shows the organization chart of the Cali cartel.

This network of managerial and support personnel numbered in the thousands. Their operations were strictly wholesale. Cali members were not involved in retail sales as those were handled by street traffickers.

Actually, the management model developed by the cartel resembled those found in fast food chains (Chepesiuk, 2003). Vacations and financial incentives were provided to maintain commitment to the organization. U.S. workers were transferred between cities and were expected to maintain the daily routines of typical Americans. Discipline for misbehavior was reinforced by potential threats of violence to family and relatives.

The major difference between Cali units and fast food franchises was the isolation of cells. This organization was not dealt a major blow when individual cells were shut down by the criminal justice system.

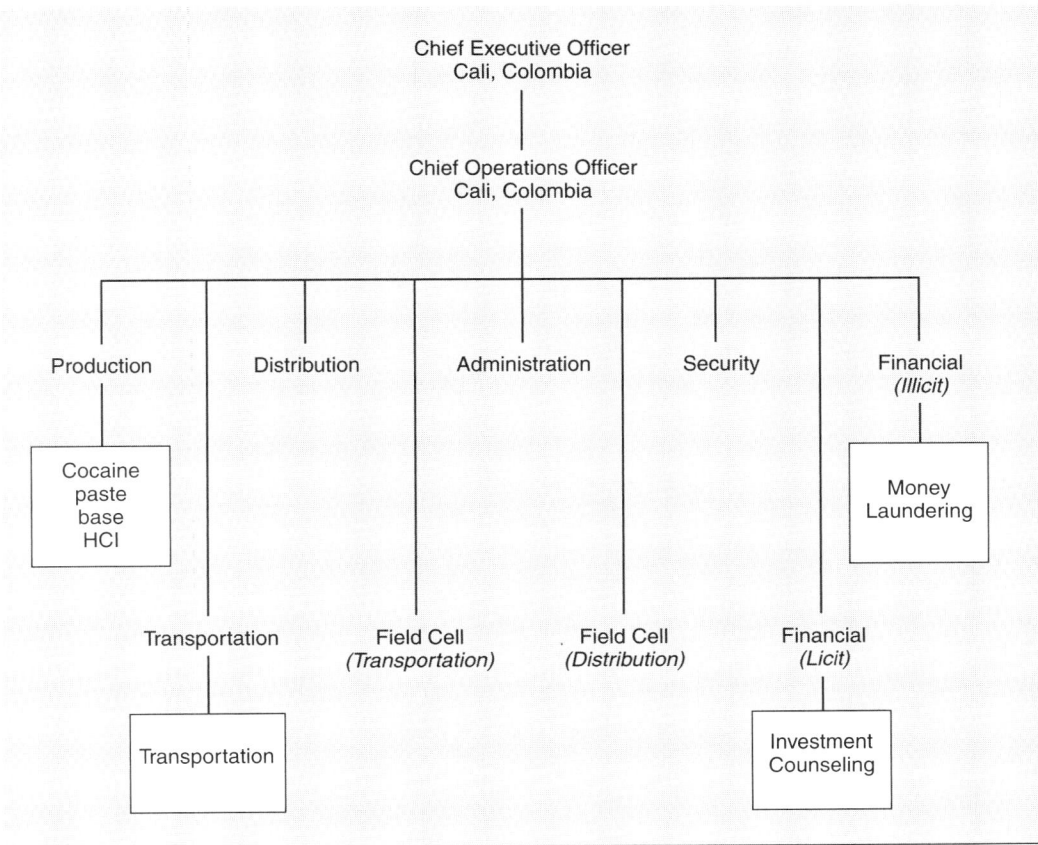

Figure 4-2 Cali Cartel Organization Chart

Movement of cocaine inside U.S. borders was facilitated by trains, vehicles, planes, and the postal service. In addition, a variety of boats, including cargo ships, fishing vessels, and cigarette boats, were used to carry the drug.

During the 1980s, the Cali cartel became a major player in the United States drug market. The income generated here was "dirty money" and by necessity then had to be "laundered" so that it could be used to finance the many operations of the trafficking business back in Colombia. *Money laundering* is a process whereby money earned illegally is made to appear to have a legitimate origin. While laundering is a useful tool for many organized crime activities, it is particularly valuable for drug traffickers given the large amounts of cash involved. The purpose of this action is to avoid prosecution and a number of other legal consequences such as taxation.

The Cali cartel graduated from the simple laundering methods used in the 1970s. By the 1980s, a series of more sophisticated techniques became necessary as financial restrictions were strengthened. Wiring money directly to Colombia, using businesses as fronts, became more difficult as all transactions of $10,000 or more were required to be filed with the U.S. government. Subsequently, so-called "smurfs," innocent-looking individuals were used to purchase money orders under $10,000 that were then either deposited into several bank accounts or wired out of the country. This system proved to be unsatisfactory, so the same large planes that transported cocaine to the United States returned with large amounts of cash on board.

The cartel constantly looked for ways to improve its laundering techniques in order to keep out of the reach of law enforcement. One of the most notable and innovative of these strategies was the Black Market Peso Exchange initiated in the mid-1980s. In this alternative to the traditional financial system, brokers used a variety of methods to convert dollars to pesos. This enabled the Cali group to steer clear of legitimate financial institutions. Billions of dollars were laundered every year by the Cali group and other drug traffickers (Chepesiuk, 2003). This system still exists and has become an important element of the Colombian economy.

Despite the Cali cartel's success in "washing" large amounts of money, international law enforcement began to adopt measures that significantly impacted money laundering (Chepesiuk, 2003). These included the "Kingpin Strategy," which targeted the higher echelon traffickers. The DEA created "Operation Green Ice" under the kingpin program, a successful sting program that enticed traffickers to launder money through a company created by the Agency. Another successful venture, Dinero, used a full service bank established specifically for Cali leaders to clean their money.

■ Decline of the Major Cartels

Although the Medellín and Cali cartels coexisted somewhat peacefully for several years, their relationship began to sour for several reasons. By 1990, the Cali cartel had become the dominant force in the U.S. cocaine market, a situation that did not please Pablo Escobar. Escobar had been at war with the Colombian government since at least 1986, and became convinced that governmental agencies were in collusion with the Cali cartel. His forces engaged in a variety of terrorist acts designed to solidify his position. Some of these activities were directed at politicians and others targeted members of the Cali group. The Calis responded in kind and kidnappings, bombings, and shootings became common.

After several more rounds of bloodshed, Escobar surrendered in June 1991 as the Ochoa brothers had done before him. He did so because he was promised that he would not be extradited to the United States. Escobar was allowed to build his own jail, dubbed "The Cathedral," a facility that cost five million dollars. Amid luxurious surroundings, he continued to run his cocaine empire. His jailors allowed him to leave and return at will and to have an unlimited number of visitors. He waged a terror campaign against those he believed did not adequately support him. Escobar allegedly killed two of his employees whom he believed had cheated him.

During his stay at The Cathedral, Escobar's enemies attacked his associates relentlessly. Escobar eventually feared for his safety and sneaked out of his fortress estate in July, 1993. This embarrassed the Colombia government and a manhunt was undertaken for the purpose of putting him in a real penal facility. It was spearheaded by the vigilante group, "Los Pepes" (those persecuted by Pablo Escobar). Information supplied at least partly by the Cali cartel led to Escobar's being shot and killed on December 2, 1993 after an 18-month search. He was only 44 years old. The Calis were immediately crowned as the "New Kings of Cocaine," a somewhat misleading title because they had been the "kings" for several years.

During the time that law enforcement officials were focused on Escobar, attention was still being paid to Cali. Despite its earlier international successes, the cartel would find that the ensuing years would be difficult. As discussed earlier, their money laundering activities were coming under increasing scrutiny from the DEA and other agencies. The structure of the organization and its chain of command were proving to be problematic. Because the home office in Cali made most of the decisions, dependence on electronic communication was a necessity. Micro-management from afar was prone to the technological and legal advances that the DEA and other agencies were making with tapping into transactions and conversations (Chepesiuk, 2003).

The other major problem that developed for the Cali group was one of its own making. As the organization grew, it relied on the same methods for sending its product to market (Chepesiuk, 2003). For example, the vehicles of preference were large boats and frequently cocaine was hidden in shipments of coffee, frozen vegetables, and other products. The Cali group also preferred to use a transfer point rather than shipping drugs directly from Colombia to the United States or some other destination.

After years of frustration and hard work, the efforts of law enforcement began to get significant results. The combination of improved investigative techniques, luck, and Cali greed would prove to be the end of Colombia's slide toward "narco-democracy." The proverbial "nails in the coffin" were the sanctions applied by the Office of Foreign Assets Control (OFAC). This agency used information gathered by the DEA, FBI, and other law enforcement agencies to create a stranglehold that squeezed the economic life out of the cartel.

Because of the slowly turning wheels of justice, the end came gradually for the leaders of the Cali cartel. Arrests and imprisonment occurred during 1995 to 1996. A brief respite for Gilberto Rodríguez occurred in November 2002 when he was released from a Colombian prison by a judge who cited his participation in a work-study program. Eventually, however, Gilberto and his brother Miguel were extradited to the United States and plead guilty to drug trafficking and money laundering charges. On September 26, 2006, the brothers were sentenced and imprisoned, forfeiting several billion dollars in fines, businesses, and assets. U.S. Attorney General Alberto Gonzales commented on the sentencing, stating that it was, "the final fatal blow to the powerful Cali cartel" (Eggen, 2006:A08).

■ Current Activities

The takedown of the Cali cartel was perhaps the DEA's finest hour (Chepesiuk, 2003). Defeat of the multinational monolith left a giant hole in the Colombian drug scene. However, demand for illegal drugs did not disappear. In fact, even before the "last hurrah" of the Cali godfathers, a multitude of trafficking organizations were jockeying for position in the contest to see which ones would become primary suppliers for the world's drug cravings.

The Norte del Valle cartel reputedly has been the most powerful drug coalition of any size following the Medellín-Cali years. One of its leaders, Diego Montoya Sanchez, is on the FBI's "Ten Most Wanted Fugitives" list alongside Osama bin Laden. This drug gang had ties to the Cali group and has operated in Cali territory. In 2004, violent infighting among factions occurred and hundreds were killed. This produced three divisions, reflecting discord within the cartel. These three syndicates now operate separately from one another. Arrests of several major figures since 2004 have weakened these groups and their future is now less viable given the uncertainties of the drug trade (El Espectador 2004). The remaining elements rely on Mexican syndicates to handle cocaine smuggling and wholesaling.

"Baby" Cartels

Another development in the post-Cali era has been the emergence of baby cartels, the so-called "cartelitos" or "traquetos." These smaller groups do not have the problems of scale that plagued the Cali group (Chepesiuk, 2003). They use the latest technology, alliances formed during the Cali reign, and face-to-face meetings to further their interests. They have also become a force in the trafficking of heroin that is home-grown in the central area of Colombia where the climate and terrain are ideal (Chepesiuk). Colombian heroin has dominated the East Coast market in the United States for the past several years.

There is now agreement among authorities that Mexicans are playing a major role in the Colombian drug trade. John Walters, Director of the White House Office of National Drug Control Policy ("Drug Czar"), stated that, "the Mexicans have taken over and are running the organized crime, and getting the bulk of the money" (Harman, 2005:1). Carlos Medina, deputy director of the National Narcotics Directorate, said emphatically that, "the Colombians have a weak position with respect to the power of the Mexican mafias" (Notimex News Agency, 2006a:1). Production is still in the hands of the Colombians but Mexicans are now moving into control of transport to the United States and subsequent distribution (Harman, 2005:1).

FARC

Two groups that have emerged as players in the post-Cali period have histories that reflect their contrasting orientations. The older and larger of the two, the Revolutionary Armed Forces of Colombia (FARC), developed largely as a reaction to exclusion from the political process. It is the principal guerilla organization in Colombia and still engages in violent activity against the Colombian government. FARC has profited from the drug business by taxing coca growers and performing various services for traffickers such as protecting crops, laboratories, and air ships. There is little evidence to support FARC's involvement in trafficking itself. FARC earns a sizeable amount of money from "traditional" guerilla fare such as kidnapping, extortion, etc. (Bagley, 2001).

Paramilitary Groups

Paramilitary groups formed in opposition to the leftist, anti-government FARC. These organizations were originally created to support the military's anti-guerilla campaign and were compatible with U.S. policy (Ramirez et al., 2005). In the 1980s, they grew quickly in response to guerilla activity that forced landowners to relinquish their estates. Drug traffickers obtained the land and partnered with the military and gentry to form private armies. These paramilitary units were the antidote to the fears about marginalization harbored by the military and local elites.

By the mid-1990s, the fortunes of the paramilitary groups improved (Ramirez, et. al., 2005). First, they united under the banner of the United Self-Defense Forces of Colombia (Autodefensas Unidas de Colombia; AUC). Second, they began to compete with FARC for control of coca-producing regions. Subsequently, they began to tax the drug trade and now earn a substantial part of their income in this manner.

Plan Colombia

Ties among the military, paramilitary groups, the police, and drug traffickers have become a routine part of the narcopolitical atmosphere. Recent U.S. aid to Colombia largely has been earmarked for the military to strengthen anti-guerilla activities (Bagley, 2001). In 2000, Washington stipulated that much of that year's aid appropriation was to be used in southern Colombia, which is FARC territory (Bagley). This suggests that U.S. policy continues to revolve around the political objective of controlling leftist elements with anti-narcotic strategy being a secondary consideration.

Since its creation, Plan Colombia has received $4.7 billion from the United States (Harman, 2006b). A measure of success has been recently achieved. Colombia is now freer from the civil disorder that plagued its recent past. Tensions between leftist and rightist groups seem to be easing. Large-scale coalitions no longer dominate the drug market. Growth of coca and production of cocaine have been hampered in some areas and many drug traffickers have been caught and either imprisoned or extradited to the United States.

Despite these achievements, Colombia is still the top producer of cocaine in the world, amounting to 776 metric tons in 2005 (National Narcotics Directorate data as quoted in Harman, 2006a). The flow of product continues northward purveyed by the remnants of the Norte del Valle coalition and the cartelitos. The failure of the fumigation campaign, directed by U.S. government agencies, illustrates the frustration associated with finding effective strategies. Aerial eradication using U.S. pilots to spray coca leaves with a variation of the herbicide Roundup® resulted in a record-breaking number of acres of coca being destroyed in 2005 (Harman, 2006a). Despite this destruction, coca cultivation actually increased by 8% according to a United Nations agency (Harman, 2006a). Improved growing techniques and the spread of cultivation to two-thirds of the country's provinces have produced more coca leaves. This geographical expansion also has led to more agencies interfacing with drugs, creating an increased potential for corruption (Harman, 2006a).

As early as the 1920s, it was evident that conventional law enforcement efforts were no match for the complexity of organized crime. Although undercover operations and physical surveillance continue to be used today, it is increasingly difficult to place an agent in an organization at a level where he or she can gather direct evidence on the top management. Cartel leaders, such as regional directors or family heads, do not personally conduct drug transactions, nor do they get involved in the actual operation of the enterprise. However, informants offer an avenue that is much more effective and efficient. Informants may be cartel members or close associates who can offer information and/or testimony on the structure, membership, and operation of the organization. High-ranking members of the cartels and knowledgeable associates provide information, and their testimony can lead to convictions of major cartel leaders.

Conclusions

The gains and losses associated with Plan Colombia suggest that its future and the future of Colombia itself are uncertain. The social fabric of the country is stretched dangerously thin by the social phenomena linked to drug trafficking and the battle against it. Violence, corruption, and displacement of rural residents by both FARC and paramilitaries are still major problems despite the infusion of U.S. aid.

The primary role played by the military is problematic and raises renewed questions about its loyalties. On May 22, 2006, 11 members of an elite Colombian police narcotics unit trained by the DEA were massacred by Colombian soldiers in Jamundí, a city in the middle of Norte del Valle territory. An Army spokesman described the incident as a tragic case of "friendly fire." Others alleged that the soldiers "were doing the bidding of a drug trafficker" (Harman, 2006b). Electronic evidence supports the latter conclusion. Bruce Bagley, a leading expert on Colombian politics and drug trafficking, states that, "Jamundí is the tip of the iceberg" (Harman, 2006c). He asserts that it is indicative of the failure to develop a professional military and the tendency to ignore questions about corruption and the realities of failed policies.

In late September 2006, the U.S. Senate Appropriations Committee refused to approve this year's funding already earmarked for Plan Colombia by the State Department. The agency had taken this action three days after the massacre without mentioning the incident. Senate approval is dependent on receiving satisfactory explanations for Jamundí and other questionable events.

The re-election of President Alvano Uribe, the U.S.'s conservative ally, in May 2006 suggests that more intrigue of the type surrounding Jamundí may be forthcoming. The central role of the military in U.S.-supported Plan Colombia promises an even stronger military presence and less pretense about human rights. In addition, the hand-in-glove relationship between the military, the police, and drug traffickers discussed earlier continues to be a debilitating element in Colombia's experiment in democracy and its failure to mount an effective anti-narcotic strategy.

One sign of a more positive future was the 2005 action of 2000 members of the paramilitary group, United Self Defense Forces. These individuals turned in their weapons and were granted amnesty and give a monthly stipend by the government.

Conversely, Brazilian police reported in April 2005 that FARC had established a drug trafficking network on the Brazilian/Colombian border (Notimex News

Agency, 2006b). This operation is thought to be critical to the achievement of FARC's ultimate ambition: the creation of New Colombia, a political entity independent of the present-day state. A supply line has transported a variety of items into Brazilian territory including: portable x-ray machines, food, tool kits, and insecticide equipment. Stolen explosives and cocaine laboratories reflect FARC activity in the border area and other remote locations. Red Command, a Brazilian criminal organization, has sold weapons to FARC. Investigations indicate that purchases of arms and ammunition also have been made from Paraguayan cartels. Cocaine is the currency used in these transactions.

If these movements and transactions are a valid indicator of trafficking activity in these and adjoining areas, then the adage "the more things change, the more they remain the same" applies to the Colombian drug scene. Shifts in location, changes in group structure and dynamics, and rearrangement of the players have all taken place during the past 15 years. What has remained steadfast is the world's demand for cocaine and other drugs and the quest by various groups to supply that demand.

DISCUSSION QUESTIONS

1. How did the cartels of Colombia begin and why did they begin? What has led to their success?
2. Explain the typical structure of Colombian cartels. How have these cartels changed since the fall of the Medellín and Cali cartels?
3. What have been the most effective efforts against drug cartels?
4. If you were appointed Director of the DEA, what changes would you make to improve the law enforcement response against drug trafficking organizations?

REFERENCES

Bagley, B. (2001). Drug Trafficking, Political Violence, and U.S. Policy in Colombia in the 1990's. (Unpublished paper provided to the author).

Chepesiuk, R. (2003). *Drug Lords: The Rise and Fall of the Cali Cartel*. Wrea Green, UK: Milo Books.

Chicago Tribune. (September 9, 2006). "Police: Colombian drug trafficker held." Retrieved October 9, 2006 from http://infoweb.newsbank.com

Eggen, D. (September 27, 2006). "With guilty pleas, Cali cartel finished, U.S. says." *The Washington Post*. Retrieved September 27, 2006 from http://www.washingtonpost.com

El Espectador. (July 11, 2004). "Colombian drug lord's arrest could mark end of Norte del Valle turf war—weekly." Retrieved October 9, 2006 from http://infoweb.newsbank.com

Harman, D. (August 16, 2005). "Mexicans take over drug trade to U.S." Retrieved October 9, 2006 from http://www.csmonitor.com

Harman, D. (September 28, 2006a). "Plan Colombia: Big gains, but cocaine still flows." *Christian Science Monitor*. Retrieved October 9, 2006 from http://www.csmonitor.com

Harman, D. (September 27, 2006b). "The war on drugs: Ambushed in Jamundí." *Christian Science Monitor*. Retrieved October 9, 2006 from http://www.csmonitor.com

Notimex News Agency. (July 16, 2006a). "Mexican drug gangs funding Colombian mafias, says Colombian official." Retrieved October 17, 2006 from http://infoweb.newsbank.com

Notimex News Agency. (May 16, 2006b). "Colombian drug trafficking networks expanding operations in Brazil." Retrieved October 23, 2006 from http://infoweb.newsbank.com

The Orlando Sentinel. (July 2006). "Colombia catches suspect facing U.S. drug charges." Retrieved October 9, 2006 from http://infoweb.newsbank.com

Ramirez, L., Clemencia, M., Stanton, K., & Walsh, J. (2005). "Colombia: A Vicious Circle of Drugs and War." In: C. Youngers and E. Rosen (Eds.), *Drugs and Democracy in Latin America: Its Impact on Latin America and the Caribbean*. Boulder, CO: Lynne Rienner, pp. 99–142.

Mexican Drug Trafficking Organizations (DTOs)

"Leaders make things possible. Exceptional leaders make them inevitable."
—Lance Morrow, Boston area journalist and author of *Evil: An Investigation*

Chapter Objectives

After completing this chapter, readers should be able to:
- Describe the current major DTOs and why they are so successful.
- Understand the basic structure of the Mexican DTOs.
- Discuss the Mexican DTOs' activities and methods of operation.

Introduction

The evolution of Mexican drug cartels dates back to the early years of smuggling whiskey into American. By the turn of the 19th century, the southwestern U.S. border was a major site for illegal smuggling. During the 1930s, marijuana replaced alcohol as the smuggler's choice. Around the time of World War II, heroin became a major smuggling enterprise.

Historical Perspective

After the war, the major route for heroin into the United States was the "French Connection" from Turkey to France and then to the East Coast. As law enforcement applied pressure to this enterprise, part of the U.S. market began to be supplied by the Herrera family whose home ground was the state of Durango. The Herreras were a family unit who were low profile traffickers smuggling "Mexican brown" heroin across the border to Chicago and then to the East Coast.

In the 1980s, the U.S. War on Drugs would provide Mexican groups with more opportunities in the drug market. Law enforcement focus on the Caribbean and Florida, major routes for Colombian cocaine, led the Cali cartel to seek new avenues through Mexico to the United States. Mexico had a long tradition of production and trafficking of marijuana and heroin (Freeman & Sierra, 2005). Crops grown in the southwestern and southern areas were routed into the United States along well-established networks. These networks became more sophisticated as Mexican groups added cocaine and methamphetamines (meth) to their wares and became major players in the U.S. drug market.

■ Development and Expansion

Mexican drug trafficking is driven by the demand for drugs in the United States and other countries of the world. By a United Nations estimate, the U.S. market alone is a "$142 billion a year business" (Harman, 2005). Freeman suggests that the Mexican drug scene is a product of two intertwined segments of U.S. policy. The first is U.S. prohibition of drugs (heroin, cocaine, marijuana) for which there is a strong demand. The resultant black market generates violence as a byproduct and encourages the corruption of agencies/institutions that bear responsibility for enforcing the law.

The second segment of U.S. policy that is problematic because of drug prohibition is the failure by the U.S. government to shrink the demand for the banned substances. As an example, cocaine use has recently risen in the U.S. (Freeman, 2006).

Since 1999, Mexican drug trafficking has undergone some major changes and, concurrently, has expanded at a significant rate. These developments can be attributed to several factors. First, Mexico's 2000-mile-long porous border with the United States, traditionally a magnet for drug trafficking, became even more susceptible to smuggling contraband because of economic priorities. Passage of the North American Free Trade Agreement (NAFTA) was designed to promote free trade. It has succeeded in one sense as Mexico is now the second largest U.S. trading partner (Freeman & Sierra, 2005). However, because the United States also seeks to prevent the flow of illicit drugs, our country is simultaneously and paradoxically trying to create what is in effect "a borderless economy and a barricaded border" (Freeman & Sierra, 2005:265). The odds of achieving the latter have been reduced by the escalation of commercial vehicle traffic, with the potential of actually finding contraband becoming the proverbial "needle in the haystack" (Library of Congress, 2003).

Second, Mexican Drug Trafficking Organizations (DTOs) became an even more important element in the transport of Colombian cocaine to the United States. The decline in Colombian dominance over the process and subsequent change in the balance of power has led to Mexican DTOs financing the Colombian "cartelitos" that formed in the absence of the Medellín and Cali cartels (Nortimex, 2006).

Third, the election of Vicente Fox as Mexican president in 2000 created a hostile political atmosphere for drug trafficking. Previous administrations had benefited from the DTO's bribes and had protected smuggling operations. Having run on a "war without mercy" political platform against organized crime, Fox's anti-crime directives resulted in the killing and or jailing of numerous drug kingpins and interrupted the normal routines that had corrupted agencies at every level of government (Library of Congress, 2003). These actions, while productive in one sense, were also unsettling because they "altered the balance of power among Mexico's four major drug trafficking organizations" (Freeman, 2006:2). In turn, this has set off a particularly violent phase in Mexico's drug war, as a brutal struggle of each against all has ensued that is reminiscent of the battle between bootlegging factions in Chicago during the Prohibition era. The goal of each drug group is to attain dominance over its rivals in order to control trafficking through the most desirable smuggling routes.

By virtue of its attack on the kingpins of Mexican drug trafficking, the Fox administration has created opportunities for what the president calls, "second-level players." Bruce Bagley, a noted expert on drug trafficking, states that the drug industry has been "restructured, new, smaller groups now fight over turf that used to be dominated by the big boys" (Hall, 2006). As Mexico is now more democratic, so is the drug trade.

Mexican Drug Violence and DTO Competition

The war on and about drugs reached new heights in 2005 and 2006. Over 2000 murders have occurred since the beginning of 2005, most of them unsolved (Freeman, 2006). Drug trade violence has spread to tourist areas like Acapulco and Cancun as well as remote areas far removed from traditional smuggling routes.

A substantial amount of the current epidemic of violence can be attributed to the struggle among DTOs to gain control of key trafficking routes. Grisly murders, decapitations, and mummified corpses haunt the front pages of Mexico's newspapers. Nowhere is the violence more intense than in Nuevo Laredo, sister city to Laredo, Texas. The competition is especially fierce because Nuevo Laredo is "the most important launching point for illegal drugs entering the United States" (Freeman, 2006:3). An estimated 6000 trucks a day cross the border into Laredo, Texas and carry 40% of all Mexican imports (Freeman). These smugglers then use the interstate system to penetrate the United States. Nuevo Laredo became the murder capital of Mexico during 2005 and early 2006 (Freeman).

The Gulf and Sinaloa cartels have clashed over control of trafficking through Nuevo Laredo for several years. Both groups have used special enforcer units to spearhead their activities. Intimidation, murder, bribery, and manipulation of press coverage are among the variety of tactics employed by these deadly rivals.

The atmosphere in Nuevo Laredo has steadily deteriorated during the past two years. "Paralyzed by fear" aptly describes the demeanor of public officials (Freeman, 2006). Murders of journalists and policemen, shootouts on city streets, and the ineffectiveness of federal troops and police have created an aura of helplessness in the populace. As many as 40 U.S. citizens have disappeared recently in and around the city (Freeman). In August 2005, the U.S. Consulate in Nuevo Laredo was closed for a week after a downtown skirmish between rival traffickers who used bazookas, high-powered rifles, and rocket-propelled grenades (Harman, 2005).

■ The Four Major Cartels

Currently, there are four major drug cartels, as shown in this Latin America map, **Figure 5-1** (Freeman, 2006:13). Although each has a base of operation, their tentacles reach over the whole of Mexico from the northern border with the United States to the remote hamlets bordering Central America.

Tijuana Cartel (Arellano Felix Organization)

The Tijuana cartel (Arellano Felix Organization; AFO) has been a major trafficking network since the mid-1980s. Using fees and tolls to permit other Mexican groups to operate in its territory during the 1990s, the AFO developed ties to organized crime groups in South America and to Russian organized crime. It developed a unique internal security mechanism to guard against possible disloyalty within AFO and its business partners. Serious setbacks because of murders and arrests occurred in 2002 and again in 2006 when Javier Arellano Felix was cap-

Figure 5-1 The Major Drug Cartels of Mexico: Sinaloa (Culiscán and Mazatlán), Gulf (Reynosa and Matamoros), Tijuana, and Juárez

tured. In addition, Francisco Rafael Arellano Felix was extradited to the United States in September 2005, the first major drug lord to be sent north. Although most of the seven Arellano Felix brothers have been arrested or killed, the organization still transports cocaine and marijuana into the United States (Carl, 2006).

Gulf Cartel

The Gulf cartel is based in two northern Mexico states but has operations in eight additional states. Its leader, Osiel Cardenas, was arrested in March 2003 but, like other kingpins, still leads the organization from inside prison walls. In 2002, he made an important major move when he persuaded a group of federal soldiers to leave the military and become his "enforcers" and security detail. These individuals were "likely trained at Fort Bragg and Fort Benning in the mid-to-late 1990s as part of a U.S. program to train and equip Mexican soldiers for anti-drug operations…" (Freeman, 2006:3). This training has enabled the *Zetas*, as they are known, to operate with a high degree of efficiency for Cardenas. He used them to gain control of the drug trade in Nuevo Laredo. After his arrest, the Sinaloa cartel vied for dominance but Cardenas was able to stave them off, largely because of the Zetas' presence.

Sinaloa Cartel

Sinaloa traditionally has been associated with the production of opium and marijuana, and this state has produced a number of Mexico's most celebrated drug lords. This group has experienced a recent resurgence after being weakened by a battle with the Tijuana cartel. It has maintained ties with the Juárez cartel (CFO) over the years.

Sinaloa's current leader is Joaquin Guzman, known as "El Chapo." He escaped from federal prison in 2001 and remains at large while directing the cartel. This group has waged war against the Gulf cartel for supremacy in Nuevo Laredo. Edgar "La Barbie" Valdez, Guzman's associate, developed a Zeta-like group of enforcers, the *Negros*, to specifically counter the activities of the Zetas (Freeman, 2006).

Juárez Cartel

Discussion of the Juárez cartel and, for that matter, Mexican DTOs in their entirety would be incomplete without elaborating on the saga of Amando Carrillo Fuentes, which parallels the rise and growth of Mexican drug organizations. Carrillo grew up in the 1950s in Sinaloa, a state known as "Jurassic Park" because of its "monster" drug dealers and operations. He learned the drug trade from his uncle who was a veteran drug trafficker. His experience included membership in the Federal Police where he earned the title, Director of Federal Security.

In the mid-1980s, the Cali cartel responded to the U.S. War on Drugs by initiating relationships with Mexican drug trafficking organizations. When the Caribbean route to the United States became problematic the U.S.-Mexican border became a useful alternative. Mexico offered a "2000 mile expanse of the border that offered unlimited smuggling possibilities, experienced smugglers eager to collaborate, and a ready-made infrastructure to meet its needs" (Chepesiuk, 2003).

One of the first Colombian-Mexican partnerships involved Carillo and Albert Ochoa-Soto. They worked together in an early Carillo venture that took place in

Ojinaga, a rural town near the U.S. border that offered undetected crossings (Chepesiuk, 2003). They maintained close ties as Carrillo gradually became a major player in the Mexican drug scene.

Carrillo took advantage of the opportunities that arose, eventually becoming the prime connection between the Cali cartel and Mexican DTOs. Miguel Rodríguez became a business associate of Carrillo's and employed him to transport cocaine into the United States.

Carrillo took charge of the Juárez cartel by ordering the murder of his predecessor. He was able to sustain his position by three methods: (1) keeping a variety of officials on his payroll; (2) building an image as an Escobar-like community benefactor; and (3) orchestrating the murder of hundreds of enemies and opponents. A low profile kept Carrillo out of the public eye, perhaps providing him with whatever protection anonymity enables.

Carrillo used technology, such as beepers, fax machines, and night vision equipment to make his organization efficient. Counter-surveillance methods were employed to monitor the activities of U.S. agents. Innovation and versatility marked Carrillo's reign. The essence of his management style is captured by veteran journalist Tracey Eaton. "He ran his operation much like a corporation and got into profit sharing before it became fashionable. He bribed Mexican police chiefs and politicians. He also has the touch of Tony Soprano of the TV series, the Sopranos, in that he could go from polite gentleman to ruthless thug in a minute" (Chepesiuk, 2003.109).

As 1997 approached, Carrillo-Fuentes began to sense that law enforcement was closing in and his enemies both within and outside his cartel were becoming bolder. In July 1997, in the midst of surgery to alter his appearance, he died. Speculation about the cause, either a heart attack or drug overdose, differs; the Mexican government ruled that it was homicide.

In the wake of Carrillo's death, a deadly struggle developed over the control of the Juárez cartel. Amando's brother Vicente is the current boss and has ties with a number of regional drug barons (Library of Congress, 2003). The CFO remains a powerful force in Mexican drug circles and is worthy of its designation as a "polydrug" organization because it deals in cocaine, heroin, marijuana, and methamphetamines.

The sophistication Amando Carrillo Fuentes brought to the cartel remains. Cell organization, multifaceted leadership, and a money-laundering network give this organization stability and power. The north-central Mexico base of the CFO enables its leaders to micro-manage the shipment of tons of drugs into the United States. Recently the cartel's operations have expanded to include Cancun and Yucatan.

Subsidiary Groups

Each of the four major organizations works with a variety of mid-sized drug smuggling groups. While regionally-based, these groups often have connections to organizations in other Mexican states and frequently do business with international contacts. They have been linked to a number of incidents since 2000 involving murder and seizures of large quantities of drugs and money. Many of the leaders of these organizations are wanted by Mexican authorities but have remained at large for several years.

Beyond the more visible drug organizations are a number of small, corporate-style trafficking groups that may become the prototype of the future (Library of Congress, 2003). These emulate the cartelitos that have developed in Colombia in the post-cartel years. Mexican President Vincente Fox attributes their emergence to the crackdown on the larger cartels in Mexico. Bruce Bagley describes the result as the "atomization of the industry," with new players in the game. The presence of these new faces promises to provide more complication in an already layered and overlapping multitude of drug organizations. Bagley and Jorge Chabat, a Mexican drug trade expert, suggest that these new players will resort to violence and brutality to eliminate their rivals (Harman, 2004).

A number of other, more specialized gangs operate on Mexico's northern border with the United States (Library of Congress, 2003). These groups are often linked to the larger DTOs and provide drug smuggling services for contraband going across the border. Rivalries between these gangs have resulted in numerous assassinations.

Current Activity

Events during the last two to three years indicate that the Mexican drug scene is still changing and that Mexican traffickers are now in control of areas and activities that they formerly either shared with others or played a subsidiary role. A case in point is the Mexicans' success in taking over aspects of cocaine and heroin trafficking from the Colombian cartels. The latter, often now in smaller units (cartelitos), still control production, but Mexican DTOs are vying with each other for control of the conveying of drugs into the United States and subsequent distribution here. This new Mexican dominance has fostered the violence described elsewhere in this chapter.

One recent report by the Bureau for International Narcotics and Law Enforcement Affairs outlined the extent of current Mexican control over the United States drug market. (1) Mexican traffickers supplied 90% of the cocaine sold in the United States in 2004. (2) Mexico is the number two supplier of heroin and the largest foreign source of marijuana. (3) Mexico is now the leading supplier of methamphetamines (Harman, 2005). A DEA agent states that the Mexican version of "ice" in crystalline form is increasingly popular in the United States (Harman).

Meth labs have been emerging in Mexico in response to the crackdown on "backyard" meth labs in the United States. A significant portion of the drug sold in the country (65%) is being manufactured in Mexico or in Mexican-run labs in California (Harman, 2005). The past three years have seen significant increases in the seizure of Mexican-made methamphetamines. In addition, the restrictions placed on pseudoephedrine sales in the United States have led to the increased importation of that key meth ingredient into Mexico from factories worldwide.

A recent newspaper article about a seizure of Mexican meth in Greenwood, an Indianapolis suburb, verifies the major role played by Mexican drug traffickers in supplying the United States market (Bird, 2006). The shipment, worth

$300,000, was smuggled from Mexico to Arizona by a predominately Hispanic organization and then transported to Indiana. Greenwood police noted that "ice" was only one of several drugs dealt by Mexican DTOs. The large volume of truck traffic into the United States makes border seizures difficult and ensures that sizeable amounts of drugs will reach their destinations in various areas of the United States.

Another important development in the Mexican drug scene has been the Russian mafia's collaboration or penetration of various DTOs (Hayward, 2003). Opportunities for this activity were provided by the weakening of some of these drug gangs as a result of arrests and deaths. Russian mobsters have given advice and laundered money. Bruce Bagley points out that Russian drug "thugs" maintain a low profile but, at the same time, are "the bloodiest human beings you can imagine" (Hayward).

The war on the major Mexican cartels by the Fox administration and the subsequent emergence of smaller cartelitos have given the Russians a chance to make inroads into the drug arena. They provide the smaller groups with assistance in protection, transportation, and money laundering.

■ Drug Policies: Impact and Consequences

The increase in drug trafficking by Mexican cartels has prompted U.S. policies designed to aid Mexico's counter-drug efforts. Some of these policies are similar to those employed in Colombia and have had the same effects in Mexico. The Mexican military, with support from the United States, has assumed an increasing role in drug control efforts. This has had the effect of strengthening the military's position in the Mexican government and making it a more autonomous force. Fox's appointment of a former brigadier general and military prosecutor has led to closer ties between the military and Mexico's equivalent of the U.S. Department of Justice. It is not coincidental that the military's share of drug-related arrests and cocaine seizures has increased dramatically since the mid-1990s (Freeman & Sierra, 2005).

The increased responsibility of the Mexican military for government counter-drug activities, notwithstanding any effect on drug traffic, has had some notable consequences. One is the continuation of human rights violations that have characterized Mexican politics for decades (Freeman & Sierra, 2005). Mexican soldiers have committed a variety of acts—including torture, rape, and murder—in their capacity as drug control agents. A second is the opportunity for corruption provided by the exposure to drug trafficking. Drug-related crimes have become common among military personnel during the last decade.

President Fox's counter-drug campaign has been hailed as a success by various U.S. and Mexican officials, including the president himself. Fox contends that the increased violence is a sign of the program's success and that drug gangs are challenging each other as well as the authorities (Freeman, 2006). Arrests of cartel kingpins have been impressive. Fox recently said that Mexico was willing to extradite "all of those who have pending matters with U.S. Justice" (*Orlando Sentinel*, 2006).

Yet, despite these positive signs, a closer examination suggests a different outlook. Although the most attention has been given to the arrest of cartel kingpins, most of those convicted on drug charges by the Fox administration have been indigenous people who transport drugs simply to survive. Incarceration of these individuals presumably has a minimal effect on drug smuggling volume. Furthermore, the deaths and arrests of major traffickers have impacted the flow of drugs across the U.S.-Mexican border very little because rival traffickers or "newbies" quickly replace the departed.

As discussed earlier, the crackdown on drug trafficking by the Fox administration may have made a complicated situation even more complicated. Weakening the larger organizations produced more instability that was then exploited by newly-formed groups eager to grab a share of the drug trade profits. The increase in the number of players has ratcheted up the level of drug-related violence, a consequence of the illegal drug market.

Conclusions

As Mexico's new president, Felipe Calderon takes office, there are several reasons for pessimism regarding Mexico's role in drug trafficking. Some of these have been discussed above. They include the demand for illegal drugs, the multitude of elusive groups vying for a share of the smuggling profits, the corruption that pervades every level of Mexico's political and legal institutions, and the fear generated by drug-related violence. As Freeman and Sierra (2005) point out, these conditions are compounded by the extreme poverty of millions of Mexicans. Cultivation of drugs and involvement in their production and transportation is a means of survival for some and a means of mobility for others (Freeman & Sierra). The presence of these factors suggests that there will continue to be a thriving business in illicit drugs and continued futility in battling drug entrepreneurs and their allies.

DISCUSSION QUESTIONS

1. Discuss the development of the Mexican DTOs. What are the current major DTOs and why are they so successful?
2. How are the Mexican DTOs structured? Is this structure susceptible to enforcement efforts? How and why?
3. What characteristics of Mexican DTOs are the characteristics of organized crime discussed in Chapter 1?
4. Discuss the Mexican DTOs' activities and methods of operation. What are the most successful law enforcement strategies against the Mexican DTOs?
5. How are the Mexican DTOs different from other organized crime groups?

REFERENCES

Bird, P. (October 24, 2006). "Imported meth: State's new scourge?" Indianapolis, IN: *The Indianapolis Star.* pp. A1 & A6.

Carl, T. (September 17, 2006). "Drug Lord Suspect Extradited." *The Miami Herald.* Retrieved September 22, 2006 from http://infoweb.newsbank.com

Chepesiuk, R. (2003). *Drug Lords: The Rise and Fall of the Cali Cartel.* Wrea Green, UK: Milo Books.

Freeman, L. (2006). *State of Siege: Drug-Related Violence and Corruption in Mexico-Unintended Consequences of the War on Drugs.* Washington, DC: Washington Office on Latin America.

Freeman, L., & Sierra, J. L. (2005). Mexico: The Militarization Trap. In: Coletta Youngers & Eileen Rosen (Eds.). *Drugs and Democracy in Latin America: Its Impact on Latin America and the Caribbean* (pp. 263–302). Boulder, CO: Lynne Rienner Publishers.

Hall, K. G. (March 12, 2006). "Mexican drug traffickers' violence spreads inward." *The Philadelphia Inquirer.* Retrieved October 17, 2006 from http://infoweb.newbank.com

Harman, D. (December 13, 2004). "Drug 'cartelitos' hit Mexico resorts—17 Mexican drug agents were picked up last week for alleged involvement in drug trafficking in Cancun." *The Christian Science Monitor.* Retrieved October 17, 2006 from http://infoweb.newsbank.com

Harman, D. (August 16, 2005). "Mexicans take over drug trade to US." Ciudad Juárez, Mexico. *The Christian Science Monitor.* Retrieved October 9, 2006 from http://www.csmonitor.com

Hayward, S. (August 11, 2003). "Russian Mafia Worms Way Into Mexican Drug Cartels." *The Miami Herald.* Retrieved October 17, 2006 from http://infoweb.newsbank.com

Library of Congress, Federal Research Division. (February 2003). "Organized Crime and Terrorist Activity in Mexico, 1999–2002," Washington, D.C.

Notimex News Agency. (July 9, 2006). Mexican drug gangs funding Colombian mafias. Retrieved October 17, 2006 from http://infoweb.newsbank.com

The Orlando Sentinel. (September 20, 2006). "Mexican leader vows to send drug lords to U.S." Retrieved September 22, 2006 from http://infoweb.newsbank.com

The Russian Mafia

6

"Act locally, but think globally."
–René Dubos, French-born American microbiologist (1901–1982)

Chapter Objectives
After completing this chapter, readers should be able to:
- Discuss the origins of Russian organized crime and how they differ from other organized crime groups.
- Describe the structure of the "Russian Mafia."
- Understand the unique challenges to U.S. law enforcement that Russian organized crime groups present.
- Discuss the various criminal activities of Russian organized crime.
- Explain why Russian organized crime groups are considered a serious threat to the United States.

■ Introduction

The former Soviet Union is the birthplace of the sophisticated and violent criminal group called the *organizatsiya*. Now operating in the United States, this group is considered a national threat by the FBI and other law enforcement agencies.

■ Historical Perspective

Understanding criminality in the former Soviet Union is key to understanding Russian organized crime. Until the 1980s, the Communist Party held absolute power. Members of the Party had close associations with the black market. At the time of the breakup of the Soviet Union in 1991, an estimated 700 criminal gangs operated in Soviet block countries. Organized along both ethnic and family lines, these groups often were controlled by a leader known as the *Vory V. Zakone* ("thief-in-law"); (Handleman, 1993). Viewed as protectors of the poor and peasants, they robbed government entities or officials and then divided the profits among the group (Handleman, 1995). These thieves outlasted both the czars and the Communist Party and were publicly perceived as rebels. They became folk heroes and their outlaw culture continued even as both Lenin and Stalin tried to wipe them out, sending many to the *gulags* (Soviet slave labor camps). While in prison, they tattooed themselves, and these tattoos became symbols of status like a business card. Tattoos offered a picture of the inmate's criminal history; the more tattoos, the more convictions.

During World War II, many betrayed the thieves' code and fought in the Soviet army against Hitler. When the war ended, the government sent most of them back to the gulags where they were either killed or became "bitches" for the prison administration. The few who survived became a new breed of criminal after their release from prison and partnered with corrupt government officials. There was rapid growth in crime and corruption with a flourishing black market of goods and services. In an attempt to build a Utopia, a process of negative selection, and mass human rights abuses resulted in an ethnic and social conflict that produced the growth of Mafia-type organized crime resulting in an extremely violent country (Abramkin, 1996).

Modern organized crime in the former Soviet Union has evolved from four centers of criminality: Russian criminal elite (*Vory V. Zacone*), the *nomenklatura* (those holding powerful positions or jobs), ethnic groups, and regional criminal groups. The Vory V. Zakone developed in the gulag prison system in a similar fashion as the U.S. organized crime groups such as the Mexican Mafia, Black Guerilla family, La Nuestra familia, and other prison gangs. Russian gangs developed in order to survive against other groups and to gain power or privileges while in prison. The Vory are highly structured with established rules. Known as "The Thieves' Code," these rules include:

- Members cannot have a family (no wife or children) but can have a lover.
- They forsake all relatives.
- Members cannot have a legitimate job.
- They must assist other thieves.
- Never reveal information about thieves' activities, identities, or locations.
- Make good on promises to other thieves.
- Do not gamble if you cannot afford to pay.
- Teach young thieves the trade.
- Do not help the authorities or testify in court.
- Members cannot serve in the military.
- Do not cooperate with law enforcement.
- Carry out punishment to any rule-offending thief.
- Participate in an inquiry to settle disputes between thieves.
- Do not lose the ability to reason by using drugs or alcohol.

There are 18 rules called the *Voroskoy Zakon* that have been reported by law enforcement to control behavior of the gangs in addition to following orders of the boss. As in the U.S. prisons, Russian prison officials have to deal with these gangs to maintain peace and order. Once gang leaders and members emerged from prison, many began relationships with government officials and these alliances became part of organized crime in Russia.

Another group of criminals was formed from corrupt Communist officials and business leaders who were the power elite of the country, or *nomenklatura*. A "gray" or illegal economy developed where corruption ruled.

A third source of criminal activity consists of ethnic groups, such as the Chechens, Armenians, and Georgians. Formed along ethnic lines, these groups are extremely violent and very loyal to the gang. This group is intergenerational where succession and ethnic traditions pass from one generation to the next.

The largest criminal groups are formed by geographic regions of the former Soviet Union, according to a specific criminal activity, shared experiences, or bonding to a particular leader. These groups control much of the power within their regions, and are similar to gangs in the United States with membership in certain clubs or in control of a specific geographic region.

Due to the enormous black market, organized crime in the former Soviet Union became very powerful. Many experts believed that as much as two thirds of the economy was controlled by organized crime. In 1997, The Center for Strategic and International Studies on Russian Organized Crime estimated that 40% of private business, 60% of state owned enterprises, and more than half of the country's banks were under control of organized crime. Organized crime had corrupted officials at all levels of the bureaucracy, developed crime bosses, and taken over large legal enterprises through violence and intimidation. A Russian prosecutor reported over 6,000 cases of military corruption in one year. What the Russian Mafia has done in the former Soviet Union has become a goal for these criminal enterprises in the United States. The economic "crises" has resulted in a large number of Russians earning as little as $11 a day. Many go into crime not to have a lush lifestyle but to survive.

After the breakup of the Soviet Union, even more gangs emerged. In 1991, a thieves' world meeting occurred just outside of Moscow where the most powerful organized crime leaders planned specific actions and structured their operations to take the most lucrative advantage of the fall of the Union. The U.S. market potential was discussed and it was decided that someone needed to go to the United States to develop and organize operations.

The Russian Mafia (also known as the Red Mafia) exploited the new unstable governments in the former Soviet Union in a similar fashion as the Sicilian Mafia did in Sicily. As much as 30% of earnings were extorted from nearly every business operating in Russia. But, unlike other organized crime groups, these Russian criminal groups did not invest back into the economy. Instead, they placed billions of dollars in personal Swiss bank accounts. The Red Mafia has become the most diverse organized crime group in the world. They have operations in as many as 60 foreign countries and offshore islands, and continue to exploit unstable governments.

Russia became a free enterprise without rules. Over 1,400 murders were reported in Moscow in 1993; these included journalists, businessmen, and their families. Eighty percent of Russian businesses paid protection to criminal groups. By the 1990s, there was massive institutional corruption with over 6,000 organized crime groups in operation in the former Soviet Union (Center for Strategic and International Studies, 1997).

Educated and creative, The Russian Mafia was very well suited for international operations. Although the former Soviet Union remains the center for their operations, the United States began to experience Russian organized crime in the 1970s and 1980s. Due to the U.S. policy of expanding immigration, 200,000 Russian immigrants came to the United States during this period, many of whom had criminal records. The Jackson-Vanik Amendment allowed Soviet Jews visas to trade in the United States, and it is estimated that 2,000 criminals came into our country during this period. With advanced degrees, they presented a new challenge for U.S. law enforcement, which had to cope with their unique mixture of sophistication and extreme violence. The Russians are considered by most law enforcement agencies to be the most violent of all organized crime groups.

The majority of the Russian immigrants settled in southern Brooklyn, New York, in an area called Brighton Beach. It is believed that the Soviet government deliberately released criminals who were sent to the United States, while others from Odessa smuggled themselves out of the country via Israel or various cities, and then later immigrated. However they got to the United States, the Red Mafia had arrived with a new challenge for U.S. law enforcement (Kelly, Chin, & Schatzberg, 1994). Brighton Beach became known as "Little Odessa" (Odessa was a Soviet center for the black market).

In 1996, the FBI estimated that over 30% of Russia's 6,000 gangs operated in at least 30 of the U.S. states. There was at least one incident in Mississippi where the Russians were involved in a casino scam operation. This criminal enterprise has expanded from Russia to Brighton Beach, and on to a large number of cities, with the Odessa Mafia group/gang being the prominent group operating in the United States (Macho, 1997).

■ Structure and Organization

Over 200 of Russia's gangs are considered global entities or conglomerates. Because these groups are so diverse, it is difficult to characterize their organizational structure, which is debatable at best. Finckenauer and Waring (1998) wrote that the structure is not like that of other groups such as La Cosa Nostra (LCN).

Figure 6-1 illustrates the parallel structure of the Russian Mafia and traditional organized crime (Lindberg & Markovic, 2001).

The networks do not appear to be highly centralized nor are they dominated by a small number of leaders, as is the structure of the Yakuza, LCN, or drug cartels. A typical boss controls four specialized cells through a brigadier and two under-bosses or spies. The structure of a boss, called a *Pakhan*, controls four cells through a brigadier with enforcers at the bottom of the structure (Financial Crimes Enforcement Network, 1996).

Criminal groups are divided into four levels (**Figure 6-2**). The elite group consists of management, organization, and ideologists who develop plans and strategies for operation. The second tier is called the support group; they plan a specific crime for a specialized group or choose who carries out the operation. The third group is charged with security and intelligence. The last group is the working group, comprised of individuals who actually carry out the crime (Kelly, Chin, & Schatzberg, 1994).

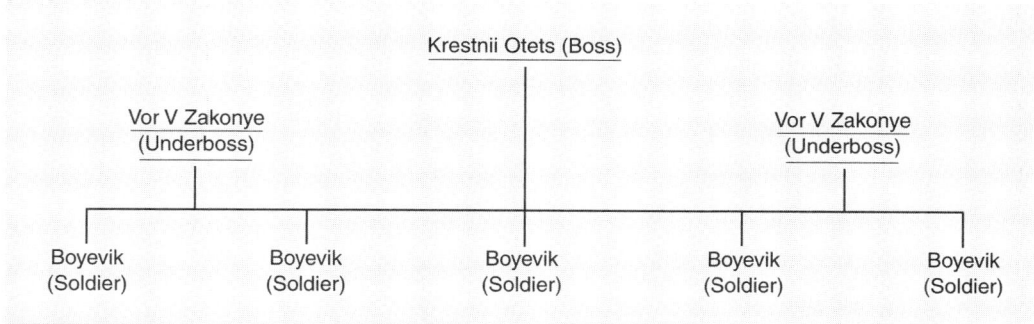

Figure 6-1 The Parallel Structure of the Russian Mafia and Traditional Organized Crime

The *nomenklatura* were once considered the most worthy communist party members. Today, their members are very sophisticated, highly educated, and employ modern technology in their criminal operations. Many are degreed in economics, physics, or engineering. Often they are former KGB (Soviet Security Agency, incorporating both intelligence and secret police) officials or agents and are involved in exploiting financial institutions in Russia and abroad. They also are involved in the illegal export of Russia's natural resources. Extortion is a specialty of this group.

The most potent threat to the United States may be from the group of former state officials and KGB agents. The investigator who identifies members of the Russian Mafia belonging to this group should be prepared to face the same tactics that were used in Russia. Enforcers known as *Kryshas* are extremely violent as well as cunning, and are often employed to protect a company from other criminal organizations. In 1995, over 400 Ministry of Internal Affairs (MVD) officers were killed while many others were bribed by criminal organizations in Russia.

Russian groups in the United States are ad hoc teams that came together for a specific criminal opportunity. These teams are flexible and project oriented. Their structure is described as being similar to many modern legitimate organizations that are more horizontal than vertical. Members had been acquaintances in their home country of the former Soviet Union and now are professional entrepreneurial criminal groups. These groups have powerful leaders, but one individual does not monopolize the leadership. While similar to criminal groups that operate in the former Soviet Union, they are evolving criminal organizations whose structures can change (Finckenauer & Waring, 2001).

Abadinsky (2003) concluded that most Russian groups operating in the United States are fluid, each varying from 5 to 20 members. He compares them to the ICE Sicilians (Zips) groups (discussed further in Chapter 7) because of the similarity of their loose structure. Groups are formed around regional backgrounds or a specific enterprise and members may be of Armenian, Chechen, Georgian, Latvian, or Ukrainian origin. Structure does vary among groups. For example, the Chechens are highly structured with hierarchy composed of relationships formed from families or clans, similar to that of the Sicilians. They have a code of silence like the LCN's *omerta*, and most often recruit from within their families.

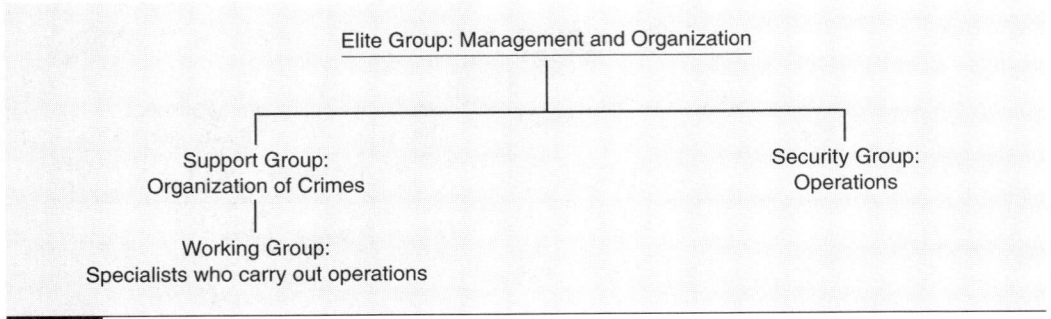

Figure 6-2 The Four Separate Levels of Russian Crime Groups

A clear line of authority exists from the leader to the lowest member (Abadinsky, 2003; *Columbia Daily News*, 2002).

Other groups form around criminal opportunity with a structure necessary to carry out the operation. After completion of the operation, the structure may dissolve and another formed to take on another criminal operation. Groups may also form around a dominant individual. Whatever the structure, Russian organized groups include an amalgamation of thieves-in-law, corrupt officials, and businessmen working as criminal syndicates to reap huge profits from a wide variety of criminal enterprises. The investigator must identify the structure and leadership of groups operating within his jurisdiction to be able to develop strategies for attacking this particular leadership as well as the group's assets and methods of operation. The structure of Russian organized crime groups is likely to be fluid and dynamic.

Because of changing markets, geographic locations of activity, and enforcement strategies, this educated and experienced criminal group changes when necessary to continue earning enormous profits while avoiding arrest and prosecution. It is difficult for law enforcement to identify leaders and structures because membership and leadership shift often from gang to gang. Apprehension of even identified leaders and members is difficult.

■ Activities and Methods of Operation

It is essential for the investigator to examine past and present activity of organized groups in cities such as Moscow, where as many as eight major criminal groups operate. Other crime groups are active in other major cities such as St. Petersburg and Odessa.

Theft, Kidnapping, and Murder

Russian groups operate in any market or enterprise that offers profits, power, or both. Extortion, drug trafficking, prostitution, forgery, art theft, and auto theft are among the many criminal activities of Russian organized crime groups. A group located in Northern California consists of Ukraine and Western Russians who specialize in auto thefts and "chop shops," selling both parts and automobiles.

The group has also expanded into narcotics, extortion, and prostitution, employing violence to succeed in their operations. In 2002, prosecutors in California indicted leaders of Russian criminal groups for kidnapping and murdering Soviet immigrants involved in an extortion scheme. Victims included: chief of Matador Communications, Georgy Safiev; film producer, Nikolai Kharabadze; president of Advanced Mobile Technologies, Alexander Umansky; financial clerk, Margarita Peckler; and Meyer Muskalel, director of a home building company. These victims, all of whom were wealthy, were kidnapped for ransom, and were forced to call relatives or business partners for the money.

The Odessa Mafia headquarters in Brighton Beach is highly structured with satellite operations located in several major cities in the United States. Money laundering, fraud, loan sharking, murder, and narcotics are the group's areas of specialization.

An Armenian group operates in the Hollywood area of Los Angeles with an estimated 450 members. They are involved in fuel frauds, extortion, credit card fraud, and narcotics. Members also have been convicted of kidnapping and attempted murder. Many groups make huge profits from rackets in Russia dealing with anything from narcotics to illegal exports of resources, such as tin, aluminum, bronze, and other natural resources, including weapons-grade uranium (Frankel, 1995). These profits are entering countries such as the United States at a rate of more than one billion dollars a month, and once laundered, returned to Russia.

Complex fuel frauds have cost the U.S. government over two billion dollars in lost tax revenue between 1990 and 1995. The fraud involves the creation of a fictitious company or companies that exist in name only (a so-called *burn company* existing for the purpose of hiding the true identity of the owners), which alter the fuel chemistry or fraudulently sell low-grade fuel as premium, rig fuel pumps to cheat customers, and not pay taxes on the fuel. Called a *daisy chain*, these strategies transfer fuel a number of times and create a massive paper trail until it is sold to the burn company, which disappears without a trace soon afterwards with the organized crime group pocketing as much as 50 cents a gallon in federal and state taxes. The fuel is sold below market prices, which forces legitimate fuel companies out of business. These groups use bombing, kidnapping, assault, and murder to ensure that the competition is eliminated or the company is turned over to the organized crime group.

In 1995, 13 members and the leader of a Russian-Armenian group known as the *Mikaelian Organization* were convicted of multiple acts of mail and wire fraud, money laundering, extortion, and narcotics trafficking charges. This group had gained control of the independent diesel fuel wholesale and retail gas stations throughout Southern California, pocketing 42 cents per gallon by not paying federal and state taxes.

Cybercrime

Russian organized crime groups also have been involved in telecommunication fraud, including cloning cellular phones, which cost billions in lost revenues. The FBI, Interpol, and other British and Australian authorities have investigated Russian cybercriminals who are targeting bookmakers and online betting. When the bookmakers refuse their demands for ransom, the Russian Mafia shuts down these networks. In 2004, Russian Mafia attacks in Alice Springs, Australia crashed Telstra's online gambling network for five hours in an attempt to extort protection money. The Russian organized crime group can bring these booking operations to a standstill by hacking into their systems (O'Brian, 2004).

Extending Their Reach

Medical and insurance fraud is committed by means of staged auto accidents, resulting in billions in false medical billing. Auto theft rings, money laundering, and murder are common with this type of Russian organized crime activity. Intelligence indicates that alliances with LCN and the Colombians have allowed the Russians to become heavily involved in narcotics distribution in areas of New York, California, and other states. A 1993 seizure of 800 kilos of cocaine and the arrest of Russian organized crime members indicated that distribution was being conducted in Detroit, Los Angeles, and New York.

The 1991 RICO indictment of Boris Goldberg as head of a criminal enterprise is further evidence of Russian organized crime activity in the United States. Goldberg was indicted for an enterprise involving cocaine trafficking, armed robbery, extortion, attempted murder, weapons charges, and fraud. Members of the Russian mafia have associated themselves with the Mexican DTOs (see Chapter 5). Mexican authorities have reported Russian penetration of DTOs in the cities of Tijuana, Mexico and Baja and San Diego, California.

In 2001, Steven Casteel, Director of Intelligence for the DEA, reported Russian organizations laundering Mexican DTO drug money for a fee of 30% or more in addition to approval to operate in the DTOs' area. Casteel believed that the Russian infiltration of Mexican DTOs is consistent with globalization of organized crime. Much of the Russian money laundering occurs in offshore sites and countries such as Haiti, Russia, Puerto Rico, Cuba, and the Dominican Republic. An April 2001 seizure of 13 tons of cocaine near Acapulco and the arrest of 10 Russian and Ukrainian crew confirm the involvement of the Russian mafia in the Mexican DTOs' operations (Hayward, 2003).

Pirated music and computer crime also are attributed to Russian organized crime involvement. As many as 40 companies in 20 U.S. states have been the victims of Russian hackers, who target trade secrets, customer databases, and credit card information (Lorek, 2001). An estimated 95% of the music assets sold in Russia are illegal, and $310 million a year in U.S. losses has been reported (Manjoo, 2000).

Undercover operations by U.S. Customs confirmed that Russian organized crime groups working with corrupt government officials and businesses were involved in illegal weapons' trafficking. In one incident, two Lithuanians were arrested after a two-year (1995–1997) undercover operation. The sting agents used the cover story of working for Colombian drug traffickers when attempting to purchase shoulder surface-to-air missiles. They were negotiating with the Lithuanians to buy 40 missiles for $1.3 million and nuclear weapons in a deal to follow the missiles' purchase. A Bulgarian state-owned company was alleged to have agreed to sell the missiles to the undercover agents. The Minister of Defense of Lithuania signed false documents to allow the shipment to appear legal when loaded aboard a cargo ship to Puerto Rico, where the agents would receive delivery (Lungren, 1996). The following incidents from California Attorney General reports are evidence that Russian organized crime groups were expanding their narcotics operations:

- On March 4, 1993, a Russian émigré was arrested for petty theft. The Burbank Police Department recovered two kilos of cocaine and $2,200 in cash from the émigré's vehicle. It was later learned that the émigré was also involved in shipping stolen vehicles to Russia.
- On May 1, 1993, a Russian émigré was arrested for immigration violations. Information from the Immigration and Naturalization Service indicates that the émigré was involved in smuggling cocaine from the United States to Russia through his import/export business in Southern California. This émigré had spent 13 years in a Russian prison.
- In February 1995, Tracey Hill, believed to be a courier for a Russian organized crime group, was arrested in Redding, California, for possession of 18 kilos of cocaine. Hill was en route to Vancouver, B.C., from the Los Angeles area.
- On May 4, 1995, seven kilos of heroin were seized from a member of an Armenian organized crime group based in the Glendale area. The heroin came from the Middle East and was intended for distribution in the United States (Lungren, 1996).

Semion Mogilevich

In May 1995, Czech police raided a meeting of Russian Mafia bosses in Prague. "The owner of the restaurant, Semion Mogilevich, also owns a chain of companies called ARIGON with headquarters at St. Helier on the island of Jersey with branches in Prague, Moscow, Kiev, Budapest, Los Angeles, Philadelphia, New York, and Johannesburg" (Miroslev, 2001).

Money laundering operations by this college-educated, Ukrainian-born Jew were discovered when more than $6 billion and possibly even $10 billion were laundered through the Bank of New York in 1999. The transactions were said to have begun in October of 1998. "U.S. investigators suspect that government officials and politically connected businessmen who had access to billions in International Monetary Fund loans to Russia, may have cooperated with the Mafia to spirit huge transfers out of the country" (Mendellhall, 2001). The Bank of New York failure is the largest in U.S. history to date.

Mogilevich, reported to be the leader of a Russian organized crime group of over 250 members, was declared an undesirable and cannot enter the United States, but despite that impediment, he runs a company in Philadelphia. Known as the "Brainy Don" because of his economics degree and viewed by the FBI as the most powerful mobster in the world, Mogilevich is considered a grave threat to the stability of Israel and Eastern Europe. "According to the FBI and Israeli Intelligence, he rules over arms-trafficking, money laundering, drug running, and art smuggling Red Mafia. . . .He is expected to have more than $100 million to spend with a guaranteed backup source of revenue according to British officials. Part of the cash is being laundered through a very willing London Bank" ("Russian", 2001). "It is estimated that foreign companies pay up to 20% of their profits to the Mafia as the on going price of doing business in Russia" (Lindberg & Markovic,

2001). This definitely affects the willingness of foreign investors to consider Russia as a potential location for their businesses.

Gwen McClure, the FBI agent who led Interpol's organized crime division, said, "They have enough money to corrupt and destabilize entire countries" (Krane, 1999). Experts estimate that $100 billion had been laundered by 1994, $200 billion by 1996 and $300 billion by 1999 (Idea House, 2001).

It is clear that Russian organized crime groups are rapidly becoming the most threatening in organized crime today.

Other Bank Fraud Schemes

Caribbean Banks are also eager to get involved in fraud. "Billions of dollars are believed to be flowing through such offshore bank havens as Antigua, Aruba, the Cayman Islands and St. Marten" (Farah, 1996). The Caribbean governments have made it very easy to own and operate a bank here and the Russian Mafia is using it to their advantage. "In some Caribbean nations, money laundering is not even a crime" (Farah). The government requires secrecy on all depositor and transaction information. It seems the Russian Mafia has indeed found a haven in the Caribbean. Other organized crime groups—the Colombian and Mexican cartels—have also used the Caribbean banks.

The European Union Bank located in Antigua was chartered as an offshore subsidiary of Menatep, a large Russian bank. Its sole shareholder was Alexander Konanykhine (Farah, 1996). It is alleged that Konanykhine siphoned millions out of Russia through this Caribbean Internet bank. For the last decade, he has been in a U.S. prison on charges of violating conditions of his visa; his 2003 deportation to Moscow was blocked by U.S. courts. He is wanted in Russia for allegedly embezzling $8.1 million from the Exchange Bank in Moscow in 1992.

The Russian Mafia has infiltrated Canada as well and has been found primarily in Ontario, British Columbia, and Quebec. These Russian Mafia groups have been involved in the manufacture and use of counterfeit currency and false identification documents, and have organized shoplifting and large-scale theft of consumer goods that are shipped to Russia and elsewhere. A Canadian car can be stolen and shipped to Russia and sold for twice its Canadian value.

Vyacheslav K. Ivankov

One case that may be a valuable case study for the investigator is the story of Vyacheslav K. Ivankov. This notorious Vladivostok Russian crime boss was born in the 1940s in Georgia (Soviet Union), grew up in Moscow, and was known for his political stand against communism. His family had suffered under both the Lenin and Stalin regimes. Ivankov was not a member of a street gang but excelled in amateur wrestling and became a popular champion. First put in prison after a bar fight for allegedly defending a woman's honor, Ivankov began a long association with the criminal element in the Soviet Union. By the 1970s, the black market in Russia was thriving. Ivankov formed a criminal gang and frequently impersonated a police officer to rob other criminal groups. Arrested and sentenced to 14 years, Ivankov, by then known as Yaponchik ("Little Jap"), became a high-ranking *Vory V. Zakonye* ("thief-in-law"). Like other crime bosses, such as Luciano, Gotti, and Escobar, Ivankov conducted his criminal business from prison. After his early release from the gulag in 1991, he again began to prey on other criminal groups, such as the Chechens. Known for his violence, including murder and torture, he became a target for both gang rivals and Russian law enforcement. During the summit meeting in Moscow of crime bosses, leaders of the Vory allegedly decided to send Ivankov to the United States to take control of Russian organized crime in North America. Despite having a prison record and countless files bearing witness to his criminal past, he was able to gain a visa and enter the United States.

Ivankov established his organization in Brighton Beach, allegedly to direct movies. Ivankov was a very intelligent individual with extensive experience in many rackets along with a propensity for violence and torture. Many in U.S. law enforcement describe Ivankov as a typical Russian organized crime boss, an intelligent thug, unlike an LCN boss. Ivankov was probably not a "Godfather," but certainly was a high-ranking Russian mobster. He became a feared gangster in the United States and established a number of front companies. Allegedly, his organization was involved in prostitution, narcotics, money laundering, and a variety of other violent criminal activities. He paid a U.S. citizen $15,000 to marry him in order to gain U.S. citizenship. Eventually, his operations extended to New York, Miami, Los Angeles, Denver, Boston, and San Francisco, and he traveled extensively outside the U.S. border to Russia and other countries.

The reign of Ivankov ended in 1995 when two Russian immigrant businessmen reported an extortion scam. Alexander Volkov and Vladimir Voloshin, whose investment advisory firm (Summit International Corporation) served Russian émigrés, had been kidnapped and forced to agree to pay $3.5 million in extortion money. Voloshin's father was beaten to death in a Moscow train station during the extortion attempt. Ivankov was personally involved in plotting the extortion and threatening the two businessmen. However, the two businessmen had gone to the FBI, who used electronic surveillance to record much of the extortion attempt; the case was terminated early due to life-threatening situations. Ivankov was arrested with 8 members of his reputed 100-member gang in the United States for the extortion scam. He served ten years in a maximum-security prison for his crime. In 2004, Ivankov was released to Russian authorities to face murder charges in Moscow stemming from the 1992 shooting deaths of two Turkish citizens in a Moscow restaurant. (Ivankov had been on probation in Russia when he fled to the U.S. in 1992.)

While Ivankov's legacy remains a role model for young Russians in both Moscow and the United States, many in law enforcement believe that these criminals are not the real power. The most serious threats are from the former KGB and other state officials of Russia.

Links with Other Organized Crime Groups

In 2000, the television network MSNBC reported an alliance of Russian organized crime with FARC (Revolutionary Armed Forces of Colombia). Using Russian IL-76 cargo aircraft, the smugglers load planes with arms and ammunition and fly out of airstrips in Russia and the Ukraine, with stops in Amman, Jordan to refuel. With the assistance of corrupt officials in Jordan, the planes are passed through customs and travel to airstrips in Colombia to air drop their cargo, where members of FARC are waiting. The aircraft returns to Amman with huge shipments (up to 40,000 kilos of cocaine) of drugs, where part of the load is used to pay the middlemen in Amman. The remaining cocaine is flown back to Russia for distribution there and in Europe or the Persian Gulf area. This alliance is a national threat to the Colombian government because of the unlimited supply of sophisticated weapons to FARC's 16th Front under the leadership of Tomas Medina Caracas, also known as Negro Acacio. The impact on the United States is obvious. As FARC becomes more powerful, they are able to import more drugs into America with alliances with LCN, Russian organized crime groups, and others. The resources of these combined organized crime groups are an unprecedented challenge to U.S. law enforcement.

Diversity and innovation are hallmarks of Russian organized crime groups. In 1998, a warehouse in New Jersey was raided and 55-gallon drums containing alcohol were seized. Six companies, including McCormick Distilling in the United States, were the subjects of the investigation. The drums were labeled as "industrial solvent" and the liquor inside was dyed blue to resemble solvent. The drums were being shipped to Russia as solvent to avoid paying the customs duty. Once in Russia, the dye was removed and the alcohol bottled and sold as vodka. Because Russian consumption of alcohol is 6 to 12 gallons per capita per year, this is a lucrative market. This huge operation resulted in enormous profit for Russian organized crime groups that were in alliance with elements of American business.

DEA and Canadian law enforcement have reported that the Russian groups are also involved with Mexican organized crime groups in the production of methamphetamine. Russian groups have smuggled large amounts of R-11 Freon, which is used for extracting meth from the chemical solution. The Russians have also supplied weapons to the areas of Ensenada and Baja, California, and Norte, Mexico.

In yet another undercover operation, DEA agents arrested Ludwig Fainberg (a.k.a. "Tarzan") for arms trafficking. In 1984, he was living in "Little Odessa" (Brighton Beach) and became known as a "torch" man (arsonist) for the LCN around New York. By 1990 he had moved to Miami, Florida and opened Porkey's, a strip club known to be a frequent meeting place of Russian and Colombian organized crime members. Here, Fainberg established himself as an international dealer in the sex trade industry, buying women in Russia and Eastern Europe and then importing them to the United States. In 1993, he purchased six helicopters, and negotiations to purchase a nuclear submarine for $60 million were underway when a DEA sting operation halted the transaction. Fainberg was arrested by DEA and later cooperated, giving evidence against major Colombian drug traffickers; he served only 30 months in jail before being deported to Israel. A year later, he was doing business in Canada and in 2003 the Canadian government deported him to Israel.

This case was successful because of extensive undercover operations, informants, and electronic surveillance. It demonstrates that global arms trafficking is a major operation for Russian organized crime groups and that law enforcement can be successful.

Russian organized crime groups involve themselves in professional sports (fixing of the 2002 Olympic figure skating competitions) and have been implicated in fixing amateur sports as well. But there are other examples. There are reported cases of embezzlement of funds from the Central Red Army Sports Club. The president of the Russian Ice Hockey Federation was murdered in April 1997. Another major sports club, Moscow Sporteak, lost its director general in June 1997 in a contract murder. Three professional hockey players may have been targeted for extortion by the Russian Mafia. U.S. sports groups are not innocent in this type of activity. "Over $10 million in 'transfer fees' were paid to Russian hockey clubs by the National Hockey League in an effort to sign Russian talent." Their criminal activity has extended into many more competitive sports as well (including bodybuilding and weight lifting) (CSIS, 1997).

These Russian organized crime groups come to the United States with years of experience in manipulating government systems as well as financial institutions, and they have a history of extreme violence and torture. The diversity of activities demands that investigators must become knowledgeable in many areas of criminal activity to effectively deal with Russian organized crime.

Investigative Strategies

Russian organized crime groups present a new challenge for U.S. law enforcement. A comprehensive knowledge of their activities and prison terms in the former Soviet Union, methods of operation, and identifying the members and their associates are necessary to build a strategy for the U.S. enforcement effort. The close relationship with banking and business, and the use of *Kryshas* (enforcers who use violence) are likely to be repeated frequently in the United States by Russian organized crime groups. Cooperation with the source country is paramount to successfully dealing with these sophisticated groups. Countries where these groups operate must share accurate, timely, and complete intelligence. Members frequently operate in seven or eight countries simultaneously. Corruption must be addressed before information is shared, otherwise any efforts or strategies will fail. The problems of intelligence sharing and collection, communication between law enforcement in several countries, and the legal definitions of organized crime and other criminal activities combined with jurisdiction questions are significant obstacles to overcome. The case studies presented in this chapter are evidence of the present diversity and complexity of these groups in their U.S. operations.

Crime prevention officials and organizations in the United States must act quickly to prevent expansion of criminal operation of Russian organized crime groups before they become more entrenched. Task forces dedicated to Russian organized crime are necessary to focus on such a national threat. Their alliances coupled with their ability to engage in diverse criminal activities—from drugs to weapons of mass destruction to complex financial crimes—requires every resource, technology, and expertise law enforcement has in its arsenal. The 1996 case where four Russians were charged in New York for conspiring to defraud 24 Russian companies, including a charity to establish aid to victims of the Chernobyl Nuclear Disaster of over $10 million, is further evidence that the task force concept is effective (Freeh, 1996).

Implementation of appropriate training for both U.S. and foreign law enforcement is a strategy that will result not only in expertise in addressing organized crime, but closer relationships and networks between the many countries impacted by these groups. Creation of the International Enforcement Academy in Budapest (in 1995), as well as offering courses and training, supplements more established entities such as the National FBI Academy in the United States in providing state-of-the-art training for law enforcement personnel worldwide.

The International Crime Control strategy, initiated in 1998, establishes eight goals, including countering international financial crime and high tech or computer-related crime. The strategy also includes the establishment of new legislative provisions. The Organized Crime Strike Force Unit under the Criminal Division of the U.S. Attorney's Office has placed state, local, and federal offices under one roof, which combines resources, expertise, and intelligence. There are currently over 250 pending investigations targeting Russian organized crime enterprises (Finckenauer, 2001).

Because of their activities in the last decade, Russian organized crime groups require that law enforcement efforts focus on financial institutions. This includes being knowledgeable about statutes, regulations, methods of investigation, and international banking to effectively address the level of sophistication of Russian criminal activity. The Money Laundering Acts of 1986 and 1994, Currency and Foreign Transactions Reporting Acts, and other legislation that can result in arrest and prosecution of criminal organizations should be required training for any investigator who is responsible for Russian crime investigation.

The diverse nature of Russian organized crime criminal activity lends itself to violation of conspiracy and RICO laws. The predicate acts under RICO are commonly used for Russian group members operating in the United States and abroad. These complex organizations call for complex statutes and long-term investigations that require the entire arsenal of law enforcement tools and strategies. Both U.S. and international task forces must be created to address this level of criminal sophistication.

Investigators must be prepared to deal with a Russian community that does not cooperate because of intimidation and fear produced by numerous murders, assaults, and threats. Murders of government officials, businessmen, police, and even journalists should be expected. An example is the Moscow murder of Paul Klebnikov, a 41-year-old *Forbes* editor who wrote about millions being stolen by corrupt officials and Russian organized crime. The alleged murderers were subsequently acquitted.

Investigators must be cognizant of the corruption potential when dealing with organized crime groups from Russia. As many as 1500 officials have been under investigation for corruption in Russia. The element of addressing and identifying corruption will likely be part of the strategy for Russian organized crime groups operating in the United States.

Undercover operations and informants can be effective but also present an enormous risk of injury or death. Carefully planned operations with maximum security must be part of every operation where undercover agents or informants are employed. Investigators must develop a high level of expertise in handling and protecting informants. Witness protection must be available to those in the

Russian communities who do cooperate. In New York, the majority of Russian refugees are Jewish, as most Russian organized crime members are Jewish. The New York Police Department has few Russian-speaking police and even fewer reliable Russian émigré informants. These citizens fear not only for themselves but for their families who live in both the United States and the former Soviet Union. Protection is required for the cooperating Russian witnesses and family members here and abroad.

Conclusions

As with dealing with other organized crime organizations, alliances with law enforcement around the world are necessary to deal with Russian organized crime. International databases, training, innovative strategies and laws, global communication systems between law enforcement agencies, and cutting edge technologies, such as electronic surveillance and tracking, are needed to effectively combat their sophisticated levels of crime. Investigative grand juries are essential for these types of long-term sophisticated investigations. Immunity and protection for those who cooperate with authorities will likely result in additional cooperation from the U.S. Russian community. U.S. law enforcement must meet the challenge presented by Russian organized crime with not only federal efforts, but state and local as well.

Much of what is written about Russian organized crime groups is often debated. The need for more accurate and complete intelligence regarding their structure, methods of operation, activities, and a database of membership is crucial to the development of effective enforcement strategies. What is certain is that these groups are expanding their operations here and throughout the world, as they are forming alliances with many other organized crime groups. U.S. law enforcement must meet this challenge with its own alliances of law enforcement that includes government agencies, the business community, and community members where Russian organized members live and work.

As pointed out by the work edited by Finckenauer and Schrock (2004), the face of Russian organized crime is changing. It is a blend of the "Thieves' World" (an online gaming program based on a science fiction novel) and the highly educated entrepreneurs of the Russian states. Although internal conflicts exist among the various groups, the quality of management of the Russian clans ensures their success and expansion into other countries.

DISCUSSION QUESTIONS

1. What are the origins of Russian organized crime and how are they different from other organized crime groups?
2. What is the structure of the "Russian Mafia?"
3. What additional unique challenges to U.S. law enforcement do Russian organized crime groups present?
4. Why should investigators study the history of men like Ivankov?
5. Discuss the different criminal activities of Russian organized crime. Include the reported criminal alliances between Russian organized crime groups and other organized crime groups.
6. Why are Russian organized crime groups considered a serious threat to the United States, and how can American law enforcement respond?

REFERENCES

Abadinsky, H. (2003). *Organized Crime*, (7th ed.). Belmont, CA: Wadsworth/Thompson Publishing.

Abramkin, V. (1996). *In Search of a Solution: Crime, Criminal Policy, and Prison Facilities in the Former Soviet Union*. Moscow: Human Rights Publishers.

Center for Strategic and International Studies. (1997). Task Force Report. Global Org. Retrieved April 20, 2004 from http://www.CSIS.org

Columbia Daily News. (2002). "Organized Crime Task Force." Retrieved July 20, 2003 from http://www.CSIS.org

Farah, D. (1996, Oct 7). "Russian Crime Finds Haven in Caribbean." *Washington Post* Foreign Service; p. A15.

Financial Crimes Enforcement Network. (1996).

Finckenauer, J. (2001) "Russian Organized Crime in the United States." United Nations Activities. 2001. Retrieved November 24, 2006 from the National Institute of Justice, International: http://www.ojp.usdoj.gov/nij/international/russian.html

Finckenauer, J., & Schrock, J. R. (Eds.). (2004). *The Prediction and Control of Organized Crime, The Experience of Post-Soviet Ukraine*. New Brunswick, NJ: Transaction Publishers.

Finckenauer, J., & Waring, E. (1998). *Russian Mafia in America*. Boston: Northeastern University Press.

Finckenauer, J. O., & Waring, E. (2001). Challenging the Russian Mafia Mystique. *National Institute of Justice Journal*, April: 2–7.

Frankel, B. (1995, Sept 14). "Extortion Now the Least of its Activities." *USA Today*; p. 1A.

Freeh, L. (1996, April 30). *Hearing on Russian Organized Crime. Testimony before the House Committee on International Relations*. Retrieved November 24, 2006 from http://www.fas.org/irp/congress/1996_hr/h960430f.htm

Handelman, S. (1993, Jan 24). "Why Capitalism and the Mafia Mean Business." *New York Times Magazine*; pp. 12–15.

Handelman, S. (1995). *Comrade Criminal*. New Haven, CT: Yale University Press.

Hayward, S. (2003, Aug 11). "Russian Mafia Worms Way into Mexican Drug Cartels." *Knight Ridder News Service*. Retrieved June 15, 2006 from http://www.cdi.org/russia/johnson/7285-14.cfm

Idea House. (2001). *Russian Organized Crime is Big Business*. Dallas, TX: National Center for Policy Analysis.

Kelly, R. J., Chin, K-L., & Schatzberg, R. (1994). *Handbook of Organized Crime in the United States*. Westport, CT: Greenwood Press.

Krane, J. (1999, March 17). "Russian Mobsters Kick Down the World's Doors." *APB News*.

Lindberg, R., & Markovic, V. (2001). *Organized Crime Outlook in the New Russia*. Schaumburg, IL: Search International. Retrieved June 14, 2006 from http://www.search-international.com/Articles/crime/russiacrime.htm

Lorek, L. (2001, July 16). "Russian Mafia Threatens Net." *Interactive Week*.

Lungren, D. (1996, March). *Russian Organized Crime. State of California, Office of the Attorney General*. Retrieved June 15, 2006 from http://www.fas.org/irp/world/para/docs/rusorg1.htm

Macho, S. (1997). FBI Director Warns Russian Organized Crime Threatens U.S. National Security. *ERRI Daily Intelligence Report*. Chicago: Emergency Response and Research Institute. Retrieved June 14, 2006 from http://www.emergency.com/rusn-mob.htm

Manjoo, F. (2000). Russian Pirate, Rule the CD's. Wired News.com. Waltham, MA: Lycos, Inc. Retrieved July 15, 2002 from http://www.wired.com/news/culture/0,1284,39234,00.html

Mendellhall, P. (2001, Aug 31). "Russian Crime Creeps into Kremlin." MSNBC News. New York: NBC News.

Miroslev, A. (2001). "The Network of International Organized Crime in the Czech Republic." Institute of International Relations.

O'Brien, N. (2004, Sept 7). "Russian Mafia Crashed Telstra." *The Weekend Australian*. Retrieved June 13, 2006 from http://www.theaustralian.news.com.au/printpage/0,5942,10687986,00.html

"Russia." http://11members.tripod.com/orgcrime/rusorder.htm.2001

"Russian mafia still terrorizes California." (August 18, 2004). *Pravda: News and Analysis On-Line Publication*. Retrieved July 24, 2003 from http://english.pravda.ru/printed.html?news_id=13811

7 The Italian-American Mafia

"There are no problems we cannot solve together, and very few we can solve by ourselves."

–Lyndon B. Johnson, 36th U.S. President

Chapter Objectives

After completing this chapter, readers should be able to:

- Understand why the Mafia has been able to survive so long under intense pressure from law enforcement.
- Explain how the American Mafia is different than other organized crime groups.
- Discuss the history of the Mafia in America.
- Describe the structure of the Mafia and how it is susceptible to law enforcement efforts.
- Explain how law enforcement has been successful against Mafia operations.

■ Introduction

Although the "new organized crime" composed of the Russian/Eastern European crime groups, Mexican and Colombian drug trafficking organizations, the Japanese Yakuza, Chinese triads, and a variety of gangs have supplanted much of the organized criminal activity, it was once dominated by Italian organized crime groups known as the Mafia. Currently, the American Mafia is somewhat dormant but is not altogether gone. In fact, many of the above organized crime groups are allied with or pay tribute to Mafia members.

Known by many other names, including La Cosa Nostra (LCN), Mob, outfit, the office, and the family, among others, Italian criminal organizations have been in America since the 1850s. Italian organized crime groups became very active during the Prohibition years of the 1920s, consolidated their power in the 1930s, and evolved into established criminal organizations known as the Mafia and Cosa Nostra in the 1950s and 1960s.

The first official mention of an Italian-American crime organization known as *Mafia* occurred in the 1950 Kefauver Hearings, and the term *Cosa Nostra* was first used by gangster Joe Valachi in 1963 while testifying before the U.S. Senate Subcommittee on Investigations (Albanese, 2004:115–133). However, the first admission by Italian-American crime figures that the Mafia actually existed came in the 1987 "Commission" trial when leaders of the five New York City Mafia families—Gambino, Genovese, Lucchese, Columbo, and Bonnano—admitted that the Mafia existed and that they were members.

The Mafia is one of the few criminal organizations in America that has bridged the gap between the legitimate upper-world and the criminal underworld. It repeatedly has demonstrated its power and innovation by corrupting both law enforcement and the American political system. It has controlled many labor unions and major businesses through monopoly, violence, intimidation, and corruption. The Mafia remains the only organized crime group to accomplish such extensive power and control in America.

The sagas of the Mob and politicians remain one of the most debated crime topics in America. Due to extreme pressure from law enforcement, the Mafia has evolved into even a more secret organization, making the identification of Mob bosses more difficult. Their trend toward becoming legitimate has advanced over the decades as well. Federal prosecutions in the 1980s, 1990s, and early 2000s have resulted in the Mafia becoming more of an underground operation and even dormant in many areas of America. The current state of the Mafia is "down but not out."

Historical Perspective

Overview

The origins of the American Mafia as well as other Italian organized crime groups (Sicilian Mafia, the Camorra, the Ndragheta, and Nuova Sacra Corona Unita) are all connected to the culture of southern Italy and the island of Sicily. For centuries, Sicily was invaded and ruled by a series of "outsiders." These foreign rulers were viewed as unfair because they established laws that rigidly controlled the peasants. The "mafia" was organized to protect the elite landowners and their property when the weak "outsider" governments failed to maintain order. Landowners hired small armies of Sicilians called *com pagnediarm* to oversee and protect their property. Because many of these protectors were recruited from the local criminal elements, there was a natural progression toward unifying tactics for profit and forming alliances with other criminals. This led to the development of a lifestyle known as "mafioso." Even the Catholic Church sanctioned these brutal protectors, and thus they were known as *Ndragheta* (Society of Men of Honor) for their services to the church and community. The more powerful leaders of these gangs began to collect a "tribute" for "protection" from both landowners and peasants.

By the time Italy became unified, these protection organizations had become a very powerful political force in Sicily. Considerable debate remains about the development of organized crime in Sicily. The *gabelloti* (peasant entrepreneurs who were the estate managers for large landowners) were the bridge between peasants, the weak governments, and the landlords. Over time they become very powerful and violent because there was no police force or military. Each village had its own *cosa* (a group of gabelloti) but there was no centrally organized leadership; collectively, the many groups of village gabelloti became referred to as the *Mafia*. This system became one of patron–client, with the gabelloti providing land and jobs to peasants in return for their support and tribute (Blok, 1974).

It appears that no single organization controlled Italian crime. Criminal groups also emerged in other regions of Italy, such as the Camorra, Ndragheta, and the Nuova Sacra Covona Unita. Some groups were more structured than others and they developed for different reasons. As Italians immigrated, the loose system of these criminal groups gradually became established in the United States and other countries worldwide.

The current American Mafia continues to rely on many of their old traditions while maintaining an ability to adapt to the changing markets and social conditions. Visible but not omnipresent, the Mafia has cannily survived over a century and remains a serious challenge to American law enforcement. The essence of their success is their ability to form alliances between business people, politicians, and other criminal groups to take advantage of criminal opportunities for profit.

Immigration Years: The Black Hand

Italian crime groups known as *Mafia*, after the Sicilian protective groups, spawned in the major U.S. cities during the 1850s, when there was massive Italian immigration. New Orleans is believed to be the first city where the Mafia from the old world settled among Italian immigrants. Italian government anti-Mafia campaigns had pressured many Sicilian Mafia members to migrate along side of about 80% from Italy's rural south and approximately 20% from Sicily. First known as the *Black Hand* because of their inked handprint signature on a few crime scenes, Sicilian gangs formed to continue the same types of criminal activities that had existed in Italy for decades. Each gang was engaged in the traditional crimes of extortion, gambling, and kidnapping, and each operated independently under a leader or boss. Groups known as Black Hand in the New York criminal gangs soon spread to other major cities such as Chicago.

One of the most extraordinary events connected to the Black Hand group based in New Orleans was the murder of the Chief of Police, David Hennessey in 1890. Control of the Italian vote in New Orleans was hotly contested between the Provenzano crime family and the gang led by Anthony and Charles Matranga. Hennessey went on record for his disdain for Italians. A later series of murders allegedly committed by Italians prompted Hennessey to investigate. At the time, Hennessey was reported to align with the Provenzano faction and began a campaign to remove the Matranga faction.

Hennessey publicly announced that he would expose the Italian criminal organizations in a special hearing. But shortly before he could testify, he was assassinated on October 15, 1890. After the arrest and trial of several Italians for his murder, all of whom were found not guilty, a crowd gathered in downtown New Orleans and broke into the jail where other Italians were being held for Hennessey's murder. The Mob lynched eleven people, some of whom were not connected to the Hennessey case (Gambino, 2000). Despite the fact that no evidence existed of a large secret Italian Mafia, the press created a moral panic, establishing the impression of a dangerous Mafia organization already embedded in the United States. This myth quickly became accepted in the minds of the American public despite the fact that most Italian émigrés and Italian Americans were law-abiding citizens. There remains no evidence that the Black Hand was the first stage of the Mafia in America.

A significantly early development of the Mafia was the formation of criminal gangs in New York and Chicago, who began to establish ties with Italian gangsters in other cities. The climate for the evolution of crime was ripe in most major cites because of the severe overcrowding, rampant crime, disproportionate wealth, gang activity, corruption of public officials, and widespread gambling and prostitution. There also were alliances among politicians, gamblers, gangsters, and businesses.

Like many other immigrant groups arriving in the United States, Italian immigrants spoke little English and tended to settle in pocket communities with other Italians. When these Italians became victims of a crime, they were often ignored by U.S. police and politicians. Authorities were suspicious of the people who did not speak their language or understand American culture. As a result, those in the Italian community often turned to local gangsters for protection and their form of rough justice.

By 1829, well-organized gangs began to emerge such as the Five Points, Plug Uglies, Forty Thieves, and many others (Asbury, 1928). By the late 1800s, gangs had strongly infiltrated politics and businesses, and new leaders such as William "Boss" Tweed in New York and Michael McDonald in Chicago emerged as powerful crime bosses. Long before Prohibition, drug trafficking networks in cities such as Philadelphia, led by men such as "Dopey" Bennie Fein, were doing business with the Italian-American crime groups.

The Prohibition era, which extended from the early 1920s into the early 1930s, was an important period of growth in income and power for the Mafia. Although the 18th Amendment did result in reduction of alcohol consumption (an annual consumption of less than one gallon per capita), substantial demand by the public prevailed and alcoholic drink prices increased, allowing the Mob to reap huge profits. The Mafia profited and expanded their corruption efforts to infiltrate and control government officials and police. Over time, the Mafia became a more efficient and effective criminal organization, growing in both numbers and in power. During the Prohibition years, the subverted politicians and businessmen helped them to become entrenched in the economic and political systems of America.

Each city and family has its unique story. Organized crime groups in each city also evolved differently. Many of the established operations in smaller cities were simply an expansion of the powerful Mafia families from the larger cities such as New York, Chicago, New Orleans, and Philadelphia. However, once established in smaller cities, these groups had a great deal of independence from their sponsoring family. Boston, Buffalo, Detroit, Las Vegas, Los Angeles, and New Orleans all have their own horror stories of assassinations, murders, corruption, and takeovers by Mafia organizations.

Violation of Omerta

One reason for the secrecy among Mafia members was their strict vow of *omerta* (discussed in detail in the **Structure and Organization** section). Members swore that names and activities were never revealed and violators were tortured and/or murdered.

From 1950 to 1951, Senator Carey Estes Kefauver chaired the Special Committee on Organized Crime in Interstate Commerce known as the *Kefauver Hearings*. The Committee investigated corruption and organized crime in the United States by interviewing hundreds of witnesses in 14 states. These were also the first televised hearings of a congressional committee. Americans were fascinated by the secret dealings of the underworld and a criminal organization known as the Mafia. But despite the testimony and publicity surrounding the Mafia criminal organization, many Americans concluded that there was no valid evidence for this secret organization in the United States and that the findings of the special Senate committee were dramatized.

It was the Apalachin incident in 1957, where Italian-American crime bosses had convened a meeting in upstate New York, that provided further corroboration of an Italian-American crime organization known as the Mafia. Among those arrested were Vito Genovese, Carlo Gambino, Paul Castellano, and Joseph Profaci, all of whom were bosses or high-ranking Mafia members (see **The FBI and the Mafia**).

The next confirmation of an American Mafia came in 1963. The first Mafia turncoat, Joseph Valachi, testified before a U.S. Senate subcommittee and said that there was a structured crime organization known as La Cosa Nostra. However, no supporting evidence was found by the Senate subcommittee to support such a nationwide crime organization. In 1980, another Mafia turncoat, Jimmy Fratianno, testified that there was an Italian-American crime organization known as the Mafia or Cosa Nostra (Albanese, 2004). The highest ranking Mafia turncoat, Salvatore "The Bull" Gravano, provided similar testimony in the 1992 trial of John Gotti, Jr.

More than 100 Mafia members have testified in court about its members and operations, many of whom are currently in the federal witness protection program. The trials of the 1980s and 1990s finally put an end to the debate concerning the existence of the Mafia and its Commission to settle disputes between crime families. The defense in the 1986 "Commission trial" conceded to the existence of both the Mafia (a.k.a. La Cosa Nostra) and the Commission. This trial resulted in the sentence of 100 years for the leaders of the five families of New York City (except for Paul Castellano, who was murdered by John Gotti, Jr. during the trial).

The FBI and the Mafia

The FBI did not recognize the existence of the Mafia until 1957, when an enormous underworld conference was busted in Apalachin, New York (Lyman & Potter, 2006:32–33). A local cop noticed the extra traffic and out-of-state license plates, and upon discovering the meeting called in the FBI. Over 60 mobsters were arrested in the largest roundup of Mafia in U.S. history to date.

Some believe that J. Edgar Hoover (FBI director for 50 years) purposely diverted law enforcement attention away from these criminal groups to preserve his passion for racehorse betting, as his tips came indirectly from Mafia bookies who fixed the races. Others point to the unusual relationship between Hoover and his second-in-command, Clyde Tolson. Alleged Mafia photos circulated in the 1970s showed Hoover and Tolson together in drag. Still others subscribe to the theory that if the extent of Italian organized crime had been exposed to the U.S. public, it would have tarnished the shining image of the FBI and its famous director. Hoover also may have believed that the organizations were too rich and powerful to take out. For whatever reason(s), what is true is that agents were directed away from investigating organized crime and towards easier targets (except for brief periods of time) until Hoover's death.

New York

Arnold Rothstein

It is ironic that an orthodox Jew, Arnold Rothstein ("The Brain"), is considered the first chief ("Don") of an American organized crime group. In the mid-1920s, Rothstein was the first to form a criminal organization that supplied illegal goods and services (Lyman & Potter, 2006). His main contribution was providing organization to the gang's formal structure and hierarchy. This included specialization, a clear chain of command, and defined operating procedures, ideas similar to those of Max Weber (theory of bureaucracy) and Fredrick W. Taylor (theory of efficient operations). Rothstein was the impetus to the next generation of organized crime and many of his lieutenants grew in power to rank among the most famous gangsters of the 1930s to the 1960s.

One Rothstein protégé was Frank Costello, a Calabrian émigré who much later became boss of the Luciano family after Luciano went to prison in 1935. Costello expanded Mafia operations into other cities such as New Orleans where the primary Italian-Americans gangs were Neapolitans and Calabrians and smaller groups of Sicilians. Despite being similar in many respects, differences between these crime groups and perceived territory violations led to the Castellammarse Wars (discussed later in this chapter). The Wars ended with the formation of the Commission to prevent such disputes in the future.

Rothstein's organization grew in power. In addition to gambling and prostitution rackets, he expanded into narcotics, which became an enormous source of illegal income. Another of Rothstein's men was Jack "Legs" Diamond. Diamond and his brother Eddie were in the business of hijacking and later became associated with mobsters such as Dutch Schultz, Charles Luciano, and "Little Augie" Orgen. Other Rothstein protégés included Lepke Buchalter and Jacob "Gurrah" Shapiro. These two along with Orgen were in the pavement business. As has happened frequently in criminal organizations, the Orgen and Diamond factions became enemies over turf and illegal enterprises. Orgen was killed and

Buchalter was executed for his crimes in 1944. Schultz was murdered by Luciano, who was to be the next major player in the history of the American Mafia. Rothstein was shot and killed in 1928 for reasons yet unknown, although it was speculated that he was killed for supporting the Diamond brothers in their attack on Schultz and his partner, Joey Noel.

Charles "Lucky" Luciano

Although Rothstein often is described as the founder of American organized crime, another of his protégés, Charles "Lucky" Luciano (born as Salvatore Lucania) is credited with the creation of today's American Mafia. Known for his leadership ability, Luciano appeared as a dapper and charismatic lady's man, but he was also a ruthless, cold-blooded killer.

Luciano's story is a valuable lesson for understanding modern organized crime. His family emigrated from western Sicily in 1907 when he was 14 to a Jewish community in New York City. By age 14, Luciano had dropped out of high school, and by age 18 he had been charged with possession of heroin and was a suspect in a number of murders.

After serving six months of a one-year sentence, Luciano was released from prison and joined the Five Points gang. Luciano's criminal career can be best described as being in the right place—New York—at the right time—Prohibition. He was known for his ability to work with anyone, regardless of their ethnicity. While a teenager, he had formed close friendships with fellow minor hoodlums, Benjamin "Bugsy" Segal and Meyer Lansky, both of whom were Jewish. Learning about the structure of organization and the inside nature of criminal activities from Rothstein helped make Luciano an important figure in U.S. Mafia history.

In 1927, Giueppe "Joe the Boss" Masseria asked Luciano to become a major player in Masseria's faction against the Sicilian group led by Salvatore Maranzano. Each group had invaded the other's territory and tensions had escalated. Around 1930, a vicious battle known as the *Castellammarse Wars* erupted between the two groups. Over 60 men were killed during this intensely brutal rivalry for control of criminal activities and profits. The Masseria group was losing the war despite having major players such as Luciano, Schultz, Frank Costello, Vito Genovese, Al Capone, Meyer Lansky, and others. Maranzano approached Luciano about coming over to his side and betraying Masseria. When Luciano refused, he was beaten and left for dead.

In April 1931, after deciding to betray Masseria, Luciano switched factions. He and Genovese arranged for Masseria to meet them at a restaurant on Coney Island, New York. "Joe the Boss" Masserina was shot and killed and Marazano declared himself "Boss of Bosses." However, after making Luciano his powerful ally, Maranzano decided that he could not trust Luciano or Luciano's allies. But with information from Meyer Lansky, Luciano turned the tables on Maranzano and sent a hit squad posing as police to kill the last "Boss of Bosses" of the Mafia. After the hit, Luciano became the most powerful Italian organized crime boss in New York and probably the United States.

The Commission

Luciano knew that gang war was bad for business, so he negotiated with other Italian crime leaders and formed what became known as *the Commission* in

1931. This body would handle disputes and act as a semi-governing body for the U.S. branch of the Mafia. Charter members included Joseph Bonanno, Joseph Profaci, Thomas Gagliano, Vincent Margano, and himself from New York City, Stefano Maggaddino from Buffalo, and Frank Nitti from Chicago. (This body continues to exist but the representation has changed to involve more cities and bosses.) With peace between the Mob families, the American Mafia became the most powerful organized crime group in the world. Luciano led a very public and glamorous lifestyle, including ownership of an apartment in the Waldorf Towers.

Although the new American Mafia had abandoned many of the traditional Sicilian customs, it kept the strategies of violence, corruption, omerta, and monopolizing the rackets. Luciano was chairman of the board of *Murder Inc.*, the enforcement arm of the Commission. Those on the Commission assigned territories, adjudicated disputes, and carried out internal discipline. The now-consolidated American Mafia had surpassed both the Irish and Jewish crime groups under Luciano's and the Commission's leadership.

Luciano's extravagant lifestyle made him a target of New York prosecutor Thomas Dewey and his staff, and multiple investigations into his criminal activities began in the early 1930s. Finally, Dewey was able to convict Luciano of running a prostitution racket and Luciano was sentenced to 30 to 50 years. While an inmate in the dreary Dannemora prison, Luciano was treated special. The warden allowed secret visits as well as phone calls from friends and family, allowing him to continue running his organized crime empire. His two partners left New York, with Lansky moving to Florida and Segal to Hollywood.

In 1942, Mob and government interests narrowed to confluence when members of the United States Naval Intelligence, anticipating interference of the U.S. shipping industry by Nazi saboteurs, arrived for a secret meeting with Luciano at Dannemora prison. Through Lansky, they approached Luciano with a request for the Mob to provide protection and intelligence for the United States on the international shipping docks. After agreeing to help, Luciano was transferred to the "country club" Great Meadow Prison, where he continued to confer with his Mob connections as well as gain access to alcohol and the comforts of women.

Luciano again was visited secretly by Navy Intelligence while he was in Great Meadows Prison, when they asked him to help negotiate with his Sicilian Mafia contacts to aid U.S. Allied Forces with the 1943 invasion of Italy. In return for his cooperation, Luciano was pardoned in 1946 by then New York Governor Dewey, who, after prosecuting Luciano years earlier, had gained a successful political career. Subsequently, Luciano was extradited to Italy and not allowed to return to the United States. Simultaneously, he was issued a Cuban passport, and in that same year left Italy for Havana where he called a summit of Mob bosses in December 1947. Among the attendees were Gambino, Albert Anastasia, Costello, and Lansky.

They discussed establishing an international narcotics operation, the hit (assassination) on Segal for his failure in Las Vegas, and other Mob enterprises such as gambling and prostitution. The DEA had discovered Luciano's activities in Cuba and arranged for his expulsion back to Palermo, Italy. In 1957, Luciano again arranged for a summit in Palermo in an attempt to establish an international drug trafficking operation. At the time, most of the narcotics already were processed in Italy before being smuggled into the United States for distribution. That meeting resulted in the cooperation between the Sicilian and American Mafias for narcotics distribution in the United States, a contract that continues today. For Luciano's negotiation, in addition to profits, he received a $25,000 a month tribute from the American Mafia as a demonstration of respect.

Similar to other organized crime bosses, Luciano developed a reputation for charity and became extremely popular with the public, often being asked for his autograph by both Americans and Europeans. Eventually, however, Luciano became alienated from other Mafia bosses and groups because they began to resent his larger share of the profit. Additionally, he wanted to make a movie about his life, a project not approved by the other organized crime bosses. Some believe that the same Commission he had established took out a contract on him. Luciano died of a heart attack in 1962 at the age of 64 and is buried in Queens, New York.

Charles "Lucky" Luciano was a gangster genius whose contributions of structure and diplomatic ability to negotiate with other crime bosses formed an international criminal organization, the legacies of which continue today. Identification and prosecution of leaders such as Luciano negatively impacted the American Mafia and remains a priority of organized crime investigations.

The Five Families of New York

In addition to the Luciano-Genovese family, four other powerful crime families emerged in New York: Luchesse, Columbo, Gambino, and the Bonanno families. These Mafia families were among the most powerful in America, and all have had representatives on the Commission from its beginning to the present day.

Another major figure in the evolution of the Mafia in America was Joseph Bonanno. Born in 1905 in Sicily from a reputable and wealthy family, his story differs from those of Luciano, Capone, Costello, and others. His family immigrated to America but returned home in 1911. After the death of his mother, Bonanno returned to New York in 1924 during the Prohibition years. Because his family was connected to the Mob in Sicily, he arrived in America with good references. Marzanno, impressed with his ability for administration and seeing profit opportunities, became his mentor and put him in charge of the bootlegging operation.

Bonanno and Luciano made peace after the Castellammarse Wars, and Bonanno became boss at the age of 26. He assisted in the formation and was a charter member of the 1931 Mafia Commission. Bonanno approved the Carmine Galante arrangement with the French and Sicilian crime groups for a lucrative international narcotics operation between America, Sicily, and France.

Bonanno's cousin, Stefano Maggaddino, established a crime family in Buffalo, New York. However, there was bad blood between Bonanno and his cousin that eventually led to the removal of Bonanno as boss of his New York family. Bonanno's son became a "made man" (see **Membership** later in this chapter) in 1941 and married a Profaci, which united two powerful New York families.

At the age of 52, Bonanno met with the Sicilian Mob in 1957 to form a strong alliance that exists today. As early as the 1930s, Bonanno had become extremely wealthy and owned a number of legitimate businesses that included the Brunswick Laundry, Morgan Coke Company, and a hotel in New Jersey. Bonanno successfully ran the powerful family for four decades, an unusual tenure for a Mafia boss.

In 1963, Joseph Valachi's chilling testimony during a Senate hearing exposed Joe Bonanno as the family head. In 1968, after two years of family wars (the *Banana Wars*), Bonanno retreated to Arizona after a failed attempt to murder the top bosses of rival families in New York. Joseph Massina inherited the position of boss in 1989 and still ran the family from prison following his racketeering conviction. Bonanno also flouted omerta when publishing his autobiography (*Honor Thy Father* by Gay Talese; 1971) and produced a movie about his life in the Mob (*Bonnano: Godfather's Story;* 1999). At his death at age 93, he was the last of the charter members of the Commission.

Bonanno's contributions to the American Mafia's success included narcotics connections and his leading the Mob into legitimate business investments. It is interesting to note that prosecutor Rudolph Giuliani successfully used Bonanno's book as evidence in the trial of Mafia members. Much of Bonanno's later problems arose from trying to make his son Bill succeed him as boss while ignoring other prominent and productive members. Bonanno only served about 18 months in prison during his entire career as a Mafia member and boss.

Due to extensive prosecution and convictions of many bosses and members of the American Mafia, the current identification of members, bosses, and active families is difficult. Major families that are active today do include the five families of New York, but they have been weakened considerably. The Carlo Gambino family remains the largest criminal group, with an estimated 300 made members and 2000 to 3000 associates. John Gotti, Jr.'s son, John III and uncle Peter Gotti were bosses after John Jr. was sent to prison in 1992. The Vito Genovese family, headed by Vincent "The Chin" Gigante of Greenwich Village may be the second largest, with around 150 to 200 made men and 1200 associates. Dominick "Quiet Don" Cirillo took over after Gigante went to prison in 1997. The Gretano Lucchese family has been under government scrutiny with bosses Anthony "Ducks" Corallo and Salvatore Santoro convicted. Corallo has since died and was succeeded by Vittorio Amuso, who is now in prison as well. At last report, Joe DeFede was the acting boss. The Joseph Colombo family boss was Andrew Russo and had been weakened by turf wars and government prosecution. The Joseph Bonanno family has suffered demise following the 1968 plan by Bonanno to murder top bosses of their families. Joseph Massina is the last reported boss.

■ Chicago

Unlike New York, with its traditional five bosses and five families, most major cities have only one boss. In Chicago, Johnny Torrio was considered the Arnold Rothstein of organized crime. Exceptionally intelligent, Torrio began as a member and leader of New York's James Street Boys, who were associates with Paul Kelly's Five Points Gang. Chicago gangs evolved somewhat like those in New York, from "king of the gamblers" Michael McDonald, to Al Capone, to Sam Giancana, to today's Outfit, where it is difficult to identify the boss.

Like New York, Chicago had its wars and Mob violence. From 1923 to 1926, nearly 400 murders were connected to the Mob. The Torrio-Capone versus the Dion-O'Banion Organizations (later the Hymie Weiss organization) left a history of murder and violence that Chicago has yet to repeat. The Capone faction eventually killed Weiss and O'Banion. Today's Outfit is much smaller and far less visible than that of the Capone years, and yet remnants of the old Mob are found in satellite cities such as Cicero. For the most part, the Outfit has moved into competitive business strategies and away from violence and intimidation. Chicago is characterized as more of a cooperative operation with other ethnic groups, unlike the New York families who keep much of their business in the blood family.

Gangs in cities such as Chicago, where organized crime had evolved from gangsters such as "Big Jim" Colosimo to John Torrio, Hymie Weiss, and Al Capone, were not considered a federal problem in the early years.

During the 1940s, bosses such as Tony Accardo brought rock solid discipline to the Chicago conflict between the warring Italian-American crime groups. Before Accardo, Al Capone, Frank Nitti, and Paul Ricca had been the bosses of the Outfit. Although Accardo was tough like Capone, he learned from what he considered operational mistakes. In his opinion, too much publicity brought too much attention to the Mob. Accardo's philosophy was to be a parasite without disturbing the host. He allowed Sam Giancana, a gangster who started as a driver for the bosses and rose quickly to power because of his willingness to commit murder, to take over the policy and numbers operations from the Jones brothers (Edward, George, and McKissack), who were kings of the policy rackets in the so-called *Black Belt* located in south Chicago. The transition (turf battle) resulted in a number of murders and much violence, but it turned out to be very profitable for the Chicago Outfit.

After the repeal of Prohibition, the American Mafia looked for other means of illegal and legal income. Gambling, narcotics, and Las Vegas enterprises replaced bootlegging. By the mid-1950s, the Chicago crime group moved part of its operation to Las Vegas.

Las Vegas and Sam Giancana

The Flamingo was the first casino operated for the American Mafia. Skimming money from casino profits before reporting it to the IRS provided yet another substantial source of income for the Mob. In 1957, Accardo remained in control while Giancana became the operational boss and also assumed the flashy public lifestyle of Capone. At the same time, the Appalachin meeting had been an embarrassment to the FBI, and the agency had begun to engage their considerable resources to interrupting Mob business, including illegal wiretaps and bugs.

The 1960 Presidential election is a major source of debate about the power of the American Mafia. Mafia members believed that they and the Richard Daly (then mayor of Chicago) political machine delivered the election at the request of Joseph Kennedy (father of John F. Kennedy). In return, Mafia leaders expected favors from the Kennedy family, but after John's brother Robert was named Attorney General, the government went after the Mob with a vengeance.

Giancana was under intense surveillance and made history when he successfully sued the FBI, which then was forced to curtail their surveillance of his movements. Whether Mafia members were actually involved in the assassination of President John F. Kennedy is still debated. Giancana's actions brought much unwelcome heat and allegations onto the Chicago Mob. Giancana served a year in jail for contempt when he refused to testify after being guaranteed transactual immunity.

Giancana also was known for his romance with Phyllis McGuire (of the McGuire Sisters singing group), his association with singer/movie star Frank Sinatra, and the girlfriend he shared with President John F. Kennedy, Judith Exner. The secret arrangement between the Giancana Outfit and the CIA to assassinate Fidel Castro again focused a lot of attention onto Chicago organized crime. Relationships between members of the Mob and the U.S. government during the Kennedy years are obscure, and few still living know if any agreements actually existed between these crime groups and the Kennedys.

Forced into exile in Mexico by Accardo, Giancana returned in 1975 and was killed on orders from Accardo. Mob trials in the 1980s ended Accardo's nearly 40-year rule of the Chicago Outfit. Although he was not convicted, many of his associates were convicted and sentenced to long prison terms (Roemer, 1995). At the age of 86, he was one of the few bosses who died of natural causes.

Today, the Chicago Outfit is now smaller, with 50 to 200 made members and multi-ethnic crews, unlike other Mafia families. The last reported boss is Joseph "The Clown" Lombardo, who after being a fugitive from justice for nearly a year, was captured and sentenced in January 2006.

Philadelphia and Atlantic City

It is believed that the Philadelphia/Atlantic City family was organized by a Sicilian, Salvatore Sabella, who was boss from 1911 until 1927. Philadelphia was not dominated by the Mafia Commission, but it did have ties to Meyer Lansky, Bugsy Siegel, and others during the early years. Angelo Bruno (1927–1946) was integral to the American Mafia's development in Philadelphia. In the early years, the "Boo-Boo" Hoff and Nig Rosen syndicate was a loose confederation of bootleggers and gamblers that had a strong connection to Lansky. This confederation operated in several states including New York, New Jersey, Delaware, Maryland, and Pennsylvania. Bruno was the successor to Rosen's syndicate and was a Commission member until his murder in 1980. Bruno's successor, Philip Testa, was killed in a bomb blast; afterwards, Nicodemo "Little Nicky" Scarfo took control. Other bosses included Frank "Flowers" D'Alfonso and John Stanfa.

New Orleans The Marcello family of New Orleans has played a significant part in the American Mafia's history. Three bosses or families preceded Carlos Marcello; these included Antonio and Carlo Matranga. who controlled the docks, freight lines, and the fruit and vegetable markets in the early years. The Matranga brothers were from Palermo, Sicily and established probably the first Mafia family crime group in America in New Orleans.

By 1953, Marcello had become a seasoned criminal who had amassed substantial business enterprises, both legitimate and criminal. His early career included a 1930s bank robbery for which he served four years of a twelve-year sentence in Angola. By age 25, he was a *made man* in the Mafia (see **Structure** section). He was convicted in 1938 for selling marijuana and served only nine months. Marcello's club, The Brown Bomber, was known for drugs, gambling, and prostitutes. Governor Huey Long was believed to have introduced Marcello to Frank Costello. In 1947, during a meeting in New Orleans that included Tom Rizzuto,

Nick Grifazzi, Frank Lombardino, Anthony Carolla, and Joe Capro, Carlos Marcello became the undisputed boss of the New Orleans family. His organization involved bribery and corruption of government, including judges, police, sheriffs, and even a congressman.

Marcello's alleged involvement in the assassinations of Martin Luther King, Jr. and both Robert and President Jack Kennedy are still debated today. After his death in 1993, Anthony Carolla became boss and Frank Gagliano became underboss.

Prosecutors and law enforcement describe the New Orleans Mafia since the death of Carlos Marcello as dormant but not out. Marcello's organization had few disputes, unlike those in Chicago and New York. There was more autonomy of activities among family and associates, and the organization was even less structured than other Mafia families. Marcello had the power to approve a made man without Commission approval. His underboss was his brother, Joe Jr. and his caporegimes (lieutenants) were Norfio Pecora and Joe Poretto. Other brothers who helped run the family businesses were Peter, Vincent, and Pascal. Like other Mafia families, Carlos "The Little Big Man" Marcello owned motels, restaurants, and other businesses that were fronts as well as legitimate enterprises. His organization spanned the states of Louisiana, Mississippi, Texas, and parts of California, as well as Mexico and the Caribbean. He had ties to presidents, judges, the Dixie Mafia, and sheriffs (including Leroy Hobbs in Mississippi) as well as other Mafia families. His structure and power allowed him to manipulate politics, crime, and business throughout his empire. Philadelphia and Atlantic City may have interests in New Orleans and still have leadership that is somewhat active under Ralph Natale. Again, a 1989 conviction of Nicodemo Scarfo and others has lead to the alleged decline of this family's activities.

■ The American Mafia Today

Some American Mafia organizations established alliances with other ethnic groups while other groups kept their organizations primarily ethnic Italian operations. Cities such as New York and Chicago experienced tremendous violence during their evolution, while others such as New Orleans had little violence attributed to their struggle for power and control among factions. It is more difficult to identify today's Mafia bosses in the major cities.

The modern American Mafia has evolved beyond the traditional crimes of extortion, narcotic trafficking, gambling, and vice. It now has acquired a number of legitimate businesses and deeply infiltrated both government and political environments. The American Mafia has become a far more complex and sophisticated organization in order to continue to be as successful as it has been in the past. It is impossible to explore the history of the Mafia in all of the cities in which it exists. However, it would be prudent for any investigator to study the history of the Mafia in their respective jurisdiction to better understand the development of such a successful criminal enterprise.

What the American Mafia is today is still influenced by its past. This includes how they recruit, operate, and survive, continually adapting to changing law enforcement methods. Will the Mafia acquire shares of multinational corporations, become major players in the elections and appointments of government leaders, develop information systems capable of obtaining critical intelligence and technology, manipulate databases to their advantage, form global alliances that are more powerful than any ever encountered by law enforcement, and develop global money laundering operations that are almost impossible to detect? If they haven't already, these are the likely Mafia objectives in the near future.

Structure and Organization

The American Mafia membership is a subculture with its own rules and values for the purpose of profit sharing from legal and illegal activities. The organization's hierarchy insulates the bosses from arrest and prosecution. The so-called *Honored Society* of the Mafia has a hierarchical chain of command much like a legitimate business corporation. Most Mafia families are comprised of a boss, underboss, and consigliere (councelor). **Figure 7-1** shows the typical organization chart of a Mafia family.

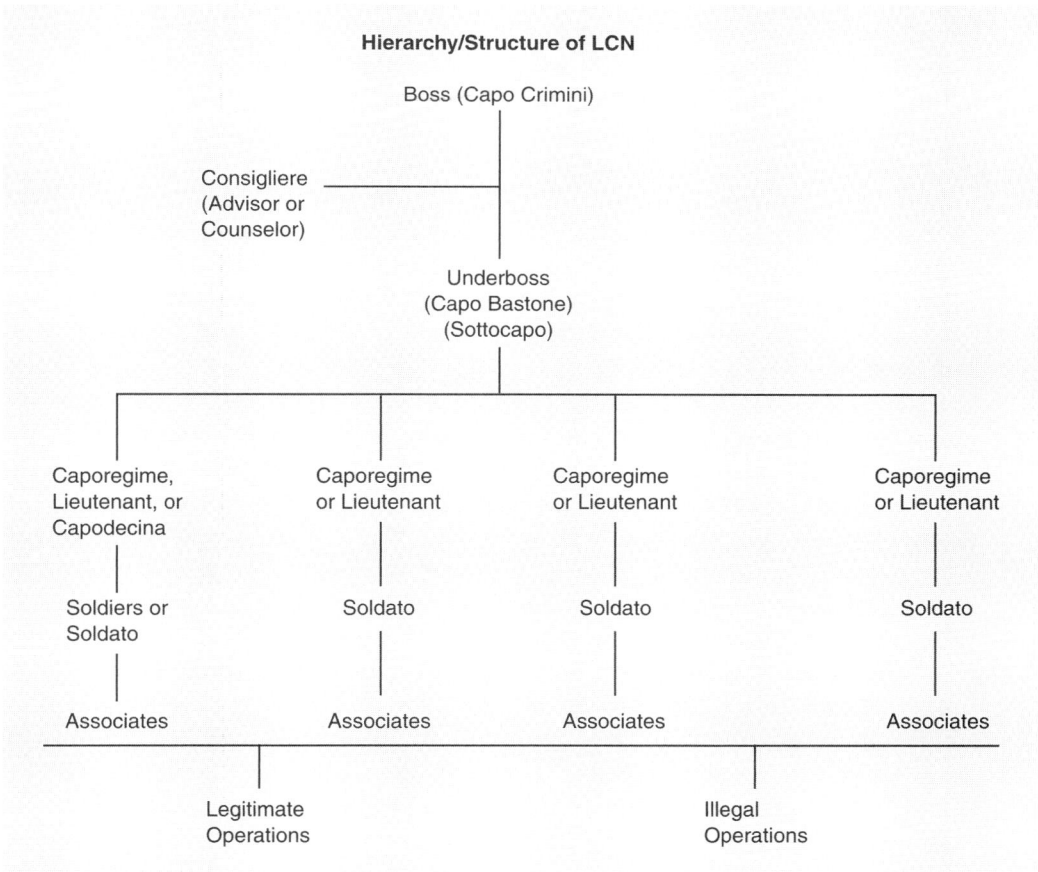

Figure 7-1 Hierarchy of a Mafia Family

Associates (*Giovane D'Honore*) are not "made" members (see **Membership** section) but made members direct their activities. Each *caporegime* oversees a "crew" of soldiers, who are made men and associates. The *consigliere* is an older member who has extensive expertise (and sometimes is an attorney). He advises the boss and also serves as a liaison between soldiers and administration. He may be a constable who serves as a financial advisor. A *piciotto* is a low ranking soldier who serves as enforcer (*hit man*). The made man is also called a foot soldier (*sgarrista*) and carries out the orders of the caporegime or lieutenant.

Each family has its own territory or type of activity that it operates exclusively. The Commission is the national organization believed to comprise the bosses of the five families of New York and Chicago, Buffalo, Detroit, and Philadelphia. This composition has changed over the years and continues to evolve with power shifts within the American Mafia crime organization. The Commission plays a coordinating and mediating role between families, settling disputes and approving hits, and assigned areas of activity for each family. The Commission also approves new membership and manages joint operations between American Mafia families and other organized crime entities such as the Sicilian Mafia. This structure allows for replacement of any position by having someone in the next level below ready to take over the vacant position. The organization may have specialty crews who operate such activities as gambling, narcotics, or loan sharking for the family. Other crews may be responsible for all activity within a specific area of a city or state. Most crews act independently of other crews. The Chicago outfit may not use the same titles as other Mafia families.

Although all Mafia families have bosses, each city is organized in a different way. New York has five separate families and Chicago has the Outfit, which consists of separate street crews, each with a specific geographic area. Families are the basic unit of the organization, but the name changes from area to area. In Chicago, it is the "Outfit"; in New York, it is the Family (*borgata*); in New England, it is the "Office." Respect and loyalty are expected and betrayal of omerta results in death. Members are referred to as "friends of ours" and associates are "friends of mine."

The family's crime operations are put into action by crews of made members and associates under the direction of a *caporegime*. The daily routine of a crew member consists of violence, treachery, and also boredom. The member works in one crew and checks in with his caporegime, letting him know what they are doing to score. Each score or operation must be approved. Crews usually work alone and only occasionally know other crew members and their activities. Members rarely use their real names. Most conversations are face to face, and rarely does a crew member know of any family activity beyond that of his crew.

The structure of the Mafia has allowed it to form what some term a *shadow government* within a government. Members and associates at the bottom may be independent entrepreneurs but pass part of their earnings up the chain of command to be shared with bosses. Through bosses and the Commission, the administration acts as a government regulating and controlling the overall operation, including dividing up areas of operation by families or crews, settling disputes, approving new members, and enforcing rules. With characteristics of both a corporation and government, the structure of the American Mafia along with extensive application of corruption has allowed the organization to survive in America for over a century. The structure of the American Mafia has avoided the turf wars that have erupted in the old country between the Sicilians and other Italians. By the 1930s, the American Mafia determined that the traditional *vendetta* (blood feud) was bad for business. When Luciano and others established the Commission in 1931, the ruling body prevented many all out wars between families by having "sit-downs" to settle disputes and solve problems. Although members are not normally paid a salary by a family organization, the family connections allow members to establish lucrative operations.

Membership

As is true for most crime organizations, membership is exclusive, often based on ethnicity, familial relationships, and/or past criminal activities. Exclusive membership adds to a sense of trust among members, which is a basic element necessary for criminal networks to come together and perpetuate (Von Lampe, 2003). There must a boundary between those who are members and "outsiders." A man does not petition for membership. A prospective member is "selected" by the other members and must undergo a series of "tests" to prove his worthiness. There are clear boundaries between members and outsiders as well as specific rules (codes of behavior) supported by oaths or affirmations at initiation that must be followed by members. The rules are enforced by a strict discipline system with death for violations.

The American Mafia is no different. Each Mafia family consists of a number of *made men* who are often referred to as *wise guys* or *goodfellows*. To become a made man, you must be a male of Italian decent on your father's side. In the old tradition, a member had to have committed a murder (*hit*) directed by a boss. This prevented infiltration by law enforcement and, because murder has no statute of limitations, the Mob had a lifetime guarantee that a member would not talk for fear of being prosecuted. To become a member today, you may just have to be a good source of income for the organization—be an earner. The prospective member also must have a sponsor who is a made man and obtain a unanimous vote by all family members.

Although there has never been a time in U.S. history when more Mafia leaders and members were in jail, there remains a large pool of potential members and leaders waiting to replace vacant positions. Even though additions to membership in most families are not always open, the opportunity for membership in the past has become available often enough to induct the most "worthy" gangsters. This may have changed today. According to Joe Pistone, an undercover FBI agent in the 1970s, the old values of the Mafia are fading as younger mobsters who are more about "my thing" than "our thing" replace the elder elite. The 25- to 35-year-old wiseguys do not have the same values as the older members and are more likely to engage in drug use and take greater risks.

Henry Hill: Wiseguy, and Goodfellas

Many Mafia members grow up in neighborhoods committing crimes as youngsters. This leads to associations with made men. Often their relatives are Mafia, exposing these young men to the culture of crime. Attraction to the Mafia lifestyle and crew operations is perhaps best illustrated by the Henry Hill story. Hill's mother was Italian and his father Irish (the reason he could not become a made man). Born in Brooklyn, New York in 1943, Hill became fascinated with the power and lifestyle of the wiseguys of the Lucchese family. His involvement in crime began at a young age with gambling and stealing. Caporegime Paul Vario took notice of Hill and began using him to run errands and do odd jobs. At age 16, after Hill was arrested for stolen credit cards, Vario arranged for Hill to get a union card and receive a paycheck without going to work except on payday. Hill was a good con man with charming ways.

After enlisting in the Army in 1960, he was arrested for bookmaking and loan sharking, and in 1963 was discharged. He then returned to the Vario crew and worked with Jimmy Burke, an Irishman and Mafia associate. As is often the case with crews, they specialized in highjacking at the John F. Kennedy Airport. Arrested in 1965 for untaxed cigarettes and later sentenced to ten years for collecting money by force for the Mob, Hill was a favorite associate. Hill found life in prison not much different from that on the streets and, much like other mobsters who go to jail, he continued to operate his criminal activities from prison. However, he broke the Lucchese rule of not selling dope. After he was paroled, Hill became an addict. He was responsible for providing the Mob information that resulted in the 1978 Lufthansa cargo robbery. Crewmembers began spending the money and were murdered on orders from the Mob boss, who feared drawing attention to the Lucchese crime family. In 1980, Hill was arrested for dealing dope. Certain that he would be killed for violating the rule against narcotics trafficking, Hill entered the witness protection program and testified against his role model Vario and fellow crewmember Burke. His testimony landed 30 mobsters in jail. After violating the rules of the protection program numerous times, he was kicked out of the program, but in 1999 seemed to beat his addiction and has since faded from the headlines.

Although recruitment into the Mafia has become more difficult today because of law enforcement pressure, there are still young men like Hill who are drawn to the seemingly glamorous lifestyle of mobsters. The 1990 book, *Wiseguy: Life Inside a Mafia Family* (by Nicholas Pileggi) and film entitled *GoodFellas* (by Martin Scorsese, Nicholas Pileggi, and Timothy Bricknell) are based on Hill's life.

Initiation

As stated earlier, some type of initiation ceremony is important for all crime organizations. It has real and symbolic consequences. The former prospect signifies that he is ready for membership and the members signify that he is now one of them forever with real consequences for betrayal of the group. Each crime organization, including biker gangs, has an initiation ritual that is a symbolic representation of this acceptance into the group complete with oaths and affirmations.

The Mafia initiation ritual has faded somewhat but some form of it remains. The initiation ceremony varies from family to family. It may include drawing of blood and repeating oaths of secrecy and obedience, or be as simple as a meeting where the new member is introduced and welcomed to the family and boss. The FBI recorded the initiation ceremony for the first time in 1989. This recording gave credibility to information provided by Mafia members who had cooperated with the FBI and established the existence of the American Mafia. Sammy "The Bull" Gravano, Joe Valachi, and Anthony Casso's court testimonies described the following initiation ceremony of a made man into the Mafia.

The initiate's trigger finger is pricked and made to bleed on a card with a picture of a Catholic Saint on it. This card is burned in his hand, and the initiate swears that he will never betray the Mafia or he will burn like the card. The boss and other members lock hands with the new member in the middle of the circle, and they welcome the new member, proclaiming his membership into the brotherhood. Usually a list of proposed members must be produced for approval by the Commission and other Mafia families. At least one list of proposed members seized by the FBI contained the man's full name and street address.

■ Activities and Methods of Operation

Provision of Illicit Services and Goods

The American Mafia is very open to any enterprises that make money; however, ever since the Prohibition era, the provision of illicit services and goods has been the mainstay of their illegal activities. Lyman and Potter (2006) define illicit services as "those that legitimate businesses do not provide and are proscribed by law." Illicit services include gambling, protection rackets (basically extortion where businesses pay for protection from unforeseen misfortune, such as fire or vandalism), loan-sharking (loaning money at exorbitant rates with violence as means of collecting), and prostitution.

The provision of illicit goods involves supplying items that are not available from legitimate sources. Organized crime groups in America, including the Mafia, became wealthy and powerful supplying alcohol during the Prohibition era, but today the largest money maker is illegal drugs. The market for illicit goods is always expanding and organized crime groups are quick to seize opportunities. One major market is for unregistered guns and stolen property that crime groups can supply at a lower price than legitimate businesses. Organized crime groups, including the Mafia, are the big suppliers of pornography, cultural objects, counterfeit or pirated goods, untaxed cigarettes, wild animals, intellectual property, human organs, and people for the sex trade and general labor.

Labor Racketeering

Labor racketeering is defined as the infiltration and/or control of a union or employee benefit plan through illegal, violent, or fraudulent means (U.S. Department of Labor, Office of Inspector General, 2006). Traditionally it has been one of the American Mafia's fundamental sources of profit, power, and influence. According to the FBI, one third of those arrested at the 1957 Apalachin Crime Conference listed their employment as "labor" or "labor management relations." U.S. Senate Investigations (the 1963 McClellan Committee and 1986 President's Council on Organized Crime) found extensive Mafia involvement in the International Brotherhood of Teamsters (Teamsters), the Hotel Employees and Restaurant Employees International Union (HEREIU), the Independent Laborers Association

(ILA; now the International Longshoremen's Union), and the Laborers International Union of North America (LIUNA). In 1978, Congress passed the Inspector General Act and placed the labor racketeering enforcement program in the Office of Inspector General–U.S. Department of Labor (Labor OIG). The Labor OIG reports that these international unions still make up a significant portion of their racketeering investigations (Office of Inspector General, 2004).

Industries most susceptible to labor racketeering are maritime, construction, surface transportation, garment manufacturing, motion picture production, legal gambling, and hotel services. Although nearly 50% of the OIG's racketeering investigations involve pensions and employee welfare benefit plans, the American Mafia also has been involved in loan sharking to employees and companies, gambling in the work setting, embezzlement, and extortion. Labor racketeering also includes the use of force or threats to obtain money for ensuring jobs or labor peace (Albanese, 2004:8). If the Mob is not paid, there will be no jobs available for laborers, or if the company does not pay, the gangsters there initiate violence, strikes, or vandalism.

The New York Lucchese crime family made millions soliciting labor-peace payoffs from freight-forwarding and trucking companies at the JFK Airport (Jacobs, 1999:58–59). The crime family controlled the unions' management, threatening to go on strike if payoffs were not paid. A five-month strike against Emery Worldwide (a freight forwarding company) cost the company $20 million in revenues and forced it into bankruptcy. Through the unions, the Lucchese crime family also controlled affiliated jobs such as truck drivers, warehouse workers, dispatchers, and clerical workers. Jobholders kicked back money to the crime family in order to continue in their employment.

Because of the Mob's labor racketeering activities, they have been able to control certain other businesses. In New York, the five families have controlled the Fulton Fish Market, the Javits Convention Center, and even air cargo at John F. Kennedy International Airport. At times, "legitimate" businessmen have willingly cooperated in order to derive benefits such as decreased labor costs, inflated prices, or increased business. However, the practice of "shaking hands with the devil" has consequences. The Mafia loans money to stockholders of companies in debt or who want to expand their businesses, and then they buy back the same stock cheap before it becomes available to investors on the stock market. Of course, the value of the stock is inflated so the Mafia can sell shares at excessive profits before the price of the stock falls. Corruption and political influence are employed in concert with violence to conduct business and control legal enterprises or protect illegal enterprises.

Other Mob businesses monopolies include pornography distribution, possible interest in Las Vegas and Atlantic City casinos, the garment industry, trucking firms, and other businesses. Twenty percent of the meat sold in the United States went through the New York meat market that was controlled by the Genovese, Gambino, and Lucchese families of New York. John Gotti, Jr. was president of Sampson Trucking Company. The Gambino family controlled ARC Plumbing Company that had contracts with New York City valued at $20 million. Controlling the unions, trucking, businesses, and other industries in addition to illegal enterprises allowed the Mafia to rise to unprecedented power.

New Partnerships

As the era of the political machine has faded, the political influence and corruption impact of organized crime has declined. Mayors in Kansas City, New York, Philadelphia, Chicago, and Boston were once associated with the Mafia. Competition from other organized crime groups has added to the alleged decline of Mafia activities and power. However, evidence exists that other organized crime groups are partnering with the Mafia in a variety of operations. The American Mafia has employed outlaw biker, Puerto Rican, Mexican, and Colombian gangs. Mob taxes have been collected from rackets and operations from black number operations in large cities as well as from Russians operating in Brighton Beach, New York. Many of the major organized crime groups pay *tribute* (taxes) to the Mafia because of their access to corrupt judges, politicians, and businessmen. While those other organized crime groups may be the peers of the Mafia and have much larger memberships, the Mafia maintains an ability to control many of the illegal markets.

The Russians were involved as partners in large fuel scams with the Mafia. Both Colombian and Mexican DTOs have major ties to the Mafia, so the United States is just one of the countries named in the global activity of these alliances. The political influence of the Mafia has been demonstrated by their attempts to pass legislation to widen avenues for illegal enterprises in states such as Louisiana. Although the goal of their activities is profit, political objectives are part of the overall plan to achieve power and control over both legal and criminal markets, which is attractive to other organized crime groups desiring to operate in the United States.

■ Investigative Strategies

From the 1980s to the present, the law enforcement response has had a tremendous impact on the Mafia. As early as 1990, as many as 1,400 Mafia members, representing all of the families throughout the United States, were sentenced to prison terms. Ranking Mafia members in Las Vegas, New Orleans, Chicago, Philadelphia, Cleveland, Boston, New Jersey, Las Vegas, Buffalo, and other cities have been convicted because of the work of task and strike forces, creative use of legislation, and strong prosecution.

Exposure: Informants and Witnesses

The acknowledgement of the existence of the Mafia was likely the beginning of its decline. The 1951 Kefauver Committee hearings exposed Mafia bosses Carlos Marcello and his friends, Santo Trafficante of Florida and Joe Savela of Dallas, Texas. This success brought a greater pressure from law enforcement and public demand for more effective legislation to deal with organized crime groups and the Mafia. The 1963 McClellan hearing was one of many that intensely investigated the Mafia. The 1972 House Select Committee hearings reported that Mafia boss Marcello was a menace to the U.S. government and its citizens. The 1979 House Assassination Committee concluded that Mafia members Carlos Marcello, Santo Trafficante, and their associate Jimmy Hoffa were probably responsible for the John

F. Kennedy assassination. This increased publicity and exposure led to increased efforts to "turn" members against each other and violate the code of omerta.

As stated earlier, the first Mafia member to break omerta and testify was Joseph "The Rat" Valachi, a soldier in New York who testified on national television during the McClellan hearings in 1963. His story is laid out in the 1968 book by Peter Maas, *The Valachi Papers*. Based on Valachi's testimony, Congress passed new laws, including the RICO statutes and the Title III, which included the federal authority to conduct electronic surveillance or wiretaps (see Chapter 12).

Since Valachi's conviction, a number of Mafia members have become government witnesses to avoid lengthy prison sentences after conviction. One tool of law enforcement is the federal Witness Security and Protection Program (WITSEC). Over 6,000 witnesses and over 14,000 dependents have been in the program. This valuable program has resulted in as many as 10,000 major criminals being convicted, in part on the testimony of protected witnesses (*rats*) who are given new identities and relocated.

Unlike Valachi, Jimmy "The Weasel" Fratianno was a ranking Mafia member. Fratianno's testimony resulted in the convictions of Mafia members and included the first reported Mafia boss, Frank Tieri, under RICO statutes (receiving income from the Mafia). This was an important milestone in the law enforcement strategy. After Tieri's trial, a number of Mafia members and bosses were indicted under RICO, including John Gotti, Jr., Nicky Scarfo, Paul Castellano, and many Gambino family members.

The Sammy "The Bull" Gravano saga illustrates the use of informants and Mafia members who turned into government witnesses. At the age of 16, Gravano dropped out of school and became a gang member. By age 25, he killed his friend Joey Colucci, whereby he "made his bones" (committed murder) and became a made member of the Colombo family. Later, he left the Colombo family and became a Gambino member. Gravano became close to Paul Castellano and began taking over a number of the gang's companies. As the underboss to John Gotti, Gravano knew everyone and many activities of the Mafia. In 1992, after being arrested on a variety of major criminal charges, he became a government witness and testified against his boss. His testimony resulted in the convictions of 4 bosses, 9 caporegimes, and 30 Mafia soldiers. The book, *Underboss* by Peter Maas (1997) describes Sammy Gravano's story. Gravano's testimony in 1997 was vital to the conviction of the Genovese boss, Vincent Gigante.

The strategy of developing informants and witnesses demonstrates the power of strong laws to force even powerful Mafia members to cooperate and convict their criminal peers.

Sting Operations

Sting operations are common police tactics designed to catch suspects committing a crime. They rely on deception, for example, when a police officer or an informant acting as a police agent purchases drugs while pretending to be a user or supplier. Stings are used in a variety of police operational strategies including auto thefts (using a bait car to catch a thief), prostitution (pretending to be johns or prostitutes), pornography (pretending to be seeking pornography), child molestation (pretending to be a child in an Internet chat room), and other crimes.

The nature of the sting depends on the crime and the actors involved. They have been used successfully by law enforcement authorities against organized crime, including the American Mafia.

One sting operation was used against the powerful New Orleans boss, Carlos Marcello. After the arrest of Joseph Hauser, a con man involved in scams and frauds, Hauser became another government informant and witness against the Mafia. Operation BRILAB (an acronym for bribery and labor) used Hauser in a 1979 FBI sting to develop a case on Marcello. It involved awarding insurance contracts using Marcello's corrupt contacts. Hauser and FBI agents acted undercover and used wiretaps and surveillance. This case resulted in Marcello, Larry Montague, and others being indicted on interstate travel of racketeering charges, RICO, and mail and wire fraud. Had the contracts been received, Marcello would have received around one million dollars a month.

Hours of audio tapes plus the sworn testimony of Hauser and two FBI agents during an 18-week trial in 1981 ended in a conviction and a 12-year sentence for 72-year-old Marcello; later Marcello was also found guilty of bribing a federal judge in Los Angles.

Government Oversight

To address the problem of corrupt unions and businesses, U.S. courts appoint monitors and trustees administer them to ensure there is no longer Mafia influence. Historically, the conviction of one or more Mafia union officials had little effect on the long-term operation of a corrupt union and business because they were merely replaced and "business as usual" continued. However, civil actions under RICO allow courts to use restraining orders, injunctions, and trusteeships to prevent racketeering and purge Mafia members and their associates from gaining a foothold in the defendant organization (Jacobs, 1999:223–233). The trustee appointed for a lengthy or indefinite term oversees the operation of the union or business to prevent the return of Mafia members, which signals to the membership that there will be no return to the status quo. Any interference with or ignoring of the monitor/trustee's orders can result in the union being held in contempt of the court's orders. Monitors/trustees have been appointed to oversee the operation of the Fulton Fish Market, the garment industry, waste hauling, and the trucking industry in New York City.

Grand Juries and Legislation

Grand juries are panels of citizens called together by state and federal courts to hear evidence and determine if criminal charges should be initiated. They also can be used in an investigative function with the extraordinary power of subpoena and immunity. A witness who lies to a grand jury can be charged with perjury, although one can invoke his Fifth Amendment right against self-incrimination. Investigative grand juries are one of the most effective tools a prosecutor can use against organized crime members. An organized crime member can be called before the grand jury, granted immunity, and then questioned about criminal activities, including the involvement of those higher up in the organization. If he lies, the charge is perjury. If he refuses to answer after being granted immunity, the charge is contempt of court.

Attacking the Mafia requires law enforcement to not only deal with individuals or the entire criminal organization, but also the subculture that produces continued Mafia membership. Eliminating the role models for potential new members is essential. RICO, conspiracy, and CCE statutes continue to be used successfully in prosecutions of the upper ranks of the Mafia and have impacted its subculture.

Regulatory initiatives are effective administrative tools that have helped reduce Mafia control over such entities as waste disposal, inspection services, the construction industries, and the transportation system. Licensing entities must be monitored to fight against bribery.

Conclusions

Although many Mafia bosses are in jail or dead, the threat of organized crime run by these families still exists. Promises to remove the Mafia were made in the past by powerful politicians and prosecutors such as Dewey and Kennedy, yet the Mafia remains. No other organized crime entity has so successfully bridged the gap between the everyday world and underworld. Though still a potent organized crime group in the United States, the Mafia is now less powerful, in part because of progressive investigation and prosecution strategies.

There will always be debate over structure, history, and method of operations of the Mafia. The successful investigator will discover the truth about these characteristics and activities of the Mafia in his or her jurisdiction, and develop effective strategies to deal with this criminal enterprise. Like other crime groups, the Mafia forms alliances with other organized crime groups and operates transnationally. The Mafia is learning from the mistakes of those killed or in prison and will evolve into a more complex and secretive organization that will become even more indistinguishable from legitimate enterprises. The phrase, "down but not out" best describes the current state of the Mafia. Their future will likely be a repeat of the past with the American Mafia adjusting and continuing to survive.

DISCUSSION QUESTIONS

1. Why has the Mafia been able to survive so long under intense pressure from law enforcement?
2. Why is the American Mafia considered unique from other organized crime groups?
3. Discuss the history of the Mafia in America.
4. Discuss the structure of the Mafia and how it is susceptible to law enforcement efforts.
5. What are the major activities of the Mafia? How has law enforcement been successful against Mafia operations?

REFERENCES

Albanese, J. S. (2004). *Organized Crime in Our Times*, (4th ed.). Cincinnati, OH: Anderson.

Anthony A. Graziano jailed for 11 years. Retrieved June 18, 2006 from http://www.mobmagazine.com

Asbury, H. (1928). *The Gangs of New York: An Informal History of the Underworld*. New York: Thunder's Mouth Press.

Blok, A. (1974). *The Mafia of a Sicilian Village, 1860–1960*. New York: Harper and Row.

Gambino, R. (2000). *Vendetta*, (2nd ed.). Toronto, Canada: Doubleday and Company, Inc.

Jacobs, J. (1999). *Gotham Unbound: How New York City was Liberated from the Grip of Organized Crime*. New York: New York University Press.

Lyman, M., & Potter, G. W. (2006). *Organized Crime*, (4th ed.). Upper Saddle River, New Jersey: Prentice Hall.

Maas, P. (1968). *The Valachi Papers*. New York: Putman.

Maas, P. (1997). *Under Boss: Sammy the Bull Gravano's Story of Life in the Mafia*. New York: Harper Collins.

Office of Inspector General. U.S. Department of Labor. (2004). The Evolution of Organized Crime and Labor Racketeering Corruption. Retrieved November 20, 2006 from http://www.oig.dol.gov/public/reports/laborracpaper.pdf

Report of the Commission of Police Integrity. *The History of Police Corruption in Chicago*. Retrieved from http://www.acsp.uic.edu/copi09.shtml

Roemer, W. F. (1995). *Accardo: The Genuine Godfather*. New York: Donald I. Fine.

Swearingen, G., & Lee, A. (1990, September 15). The Dixie Mafia: Sheriff Leroy Hobbs, Drugs and Murder. Retrieved June 20, 2006 from http://www.freerepublic.com/forum/a38a7958f0fa9.htm

Talese, G. (1971). *Honor Thy Father*. New York: World Publishing.

U.S. Department of Labor. Office of Inspector General. (2006). The OIG's Labor Racketeering Program. Retrieved November 20, 2006 from http://www.oig.dol.gov/laborracprogram.htm

Von Lampe, K. (2003). Criminally Exploitable Ties: A Network Approach to Organized Crime, E. Viano, et al. (Eds.). *Transnational Organized Crime: Myth, Power and Profit*. Durham, NC: Carolina Academic Press.

8 The Yakuza

"Just when you think you've graduated from the school of experience, someone thinks up a new course."

–Mary H. Waldrip, journalist

Chapter Objectives

After completing this chapter, readers should be able to:
- Discuss the origins of the Yakuza and why they are important to the investigation and prosecution of Yakuza members.
- Identify the major Yakuza clans and describe their structure.
- Discuss the activities of the Yakuza and how this group differs from other organized crime groups.
- Explain the six sacred oaths and how they contribute to the success of the Yakuza.

■ Introduction

The term *Yakuza* is derived from a Japanese card game, *Oicho-Kabu*, which is played similarly to the American card game of blackjack. The goal of Oicho-Kabu is to obtain a 19 score. Because the words *ya* (8), *ku* (9), *za* (3) sum to 20—a worthless hand in the game—the word Yakuza literally means "useless hands in society" (Haberman, 1985).

Believed to have originated in the early 1600s, the Yakuza group of organized crime now owns approximately $85 billion in assets and has about 150,000 members. Known for corporate extortion, gambling, prostitution, and drug trafficking, the Yakuza ranks among the most powerful and successful organized groups in the world. Like other organized crime groups, the Yakuza is considered a "shadow government" of Japan, and its alliances with other large organized crime groups makes it a threat to the global community. Although most of the 3,000 Yakuza organizations are based in Japan, it is well established in United States as well as most of Asia and other countries. Hawaii and California in particular have experienced the impact of the Yakuza. As with other organized crime groups, even more expansion of Yakuza activities in the United States is anticipated.

■ Historical Perspective

Early Criminal Groups

The origins of the Yakuza can be traced back to the early 15th century, when the *Kabuki-mono* (crazy ones), who wore odd clothing and carried swords, were terrorizing their communities. Once the servants of Shōgun (*hatamota-yakko*), these eccentric samuri became unemployed during the Tokugawa (peace) era of Japan. As *Ronin* (masterless *Samurai* fighters), many became criminals who robbed villages to survive. These bands of outlaws assumed various names and developed a slang language of their own. Yakuza has been described as "gangs or networks of adult male criminals who have structures of hierarchies and bosses similar to legitimate corporations and are involved in illegal, semi-illegal, and legal enterprises with strong ties to politicians" (Kersten, 1993).

The Yazuka, referred to by the Japanese government as *boryokudan* (violent group), deny their roots as Ronin or Kabuki-Mono. They believe that their ancestors were the *Machi-Yakko* (city servants), who were considered the people's heroes who defended them against the oppression of the Kabuki-Mono. To this day, many bosses and members believe they live the way of *Ninkyo-do*, the myth of the Yakuza opposing the strong to help the weak. These groups are not homogenous nor are they blood relatives.

Other suggested origins of these underworld groups are that they consisted of traditional gamblers (*Bakuto*), street peddlers (*Tekiya*), political right wing extremists (*Uyoku*), and common thugs (*Gurentai*). The common thread among these groups was a background of landless, poor misfits who where characterized as delinquents or worthless and violent. Although much of the history of the Yakuza is debatable, they did form "families," clans, or gangs with close relationships, where each member was the protector of all other members.

The Tekiya are believed to have come from the *Yashi* (peddlers), who were traveling merchants of patent medicines. They formed groups for protection as well as to control lucrative markets. Considered deceptive merchants who often misrepresented the quality and origins of their products, these groups or families formed relationships known as the *Oyabun-Kobun* (father-child role).

The Kobun (child) became servant and was loyal to the Oyabun (supreme boss). The Oyabun supervised the Kobun, controlling the goods and services that the family provided. These groups became influential in Japan's feudal system.

Tekiya were formed by the outlaw merchants who distanced themselves from the feudal caste system of Japan, preying on the poor and middle class by cheating them out of their money or goods.

The Bakuto originated during the Tokugawa era, also known as the Edo period (1603–1867). They were gamblers who were alleged to have been employed by the government to gamble with workers to get back much of the wages they were paid. The Bakuto sponsored gambling, which is illegal in Japan, and in addition to owning legitimate banks, also owned gambling houses and were involved in loan sharking and extortion. Both the Bakuto and Tekiya criminal groups survived because of economic and political events until 1945.

The Industrial Age through Post-World War II

Industrialization of Japan allowed these criminal groups to ally with the capitalists, providing cheap labor and controlling labor through violence and threat. Also employed as strike breakers, these groups provided similar services as the U.S. La Cosa Nostra. This affiliation with the ultraconservative party led to the formation of the political right wing.

The Uyoku are the nationalists or political right and are anticommunist. While targeting large corporations, the Uyoku also have strong ties to politicians. This group is believed to be pro-monarchist and anti-Western imperialistic. During the industrialization of Japan, the Yakuza began to create different secret organizations "that trained its members in warfare, languages, assassination, blackmail, etc." (Skold, retrieved 2006). Known as ultranationalists, their violence became more public. "They murdered two prime ministers, two finance ministers, attacked several politicians and industrialists" (Skold).

The Yakuza exploited Japan during the industrial and social changes of the late 19th and early 20th centuries. "They began recruiting heavily within the shipping and construction industry and also began to cooperate with authorities in return for more favorable treatment from police" (Murphy, 2001). Membership rose steadily until World War II. During the American occupation of Japan after the war, food was rationed, creating an enormous black market. A new kind of Yakuza known as the *Gurentai* (street hustlers or hoodlums) arose, whose members were mostly former Japanese militia. Patterning themselves after the American gangster Al Capone, these groups used intimidation and extortion to achieve their profits. Just like the Italian Mafia, the Gurentai began to dress in dark suits and wear sunglasses.

After the war, the Allied Command liberated the Chinese and Korean captives, who had been used as slave labor during the war. The gangsters among the former captives initially controlled the black markets, but after many turf battles, the Gurentai took over. Eventually, the Bakuto, Teriya, Uyoku, and the Gurentai merged and became more powerful and much more diverse in their criminal activities. Between 1958 and 1963, the Yakuza ranks rose to 184,000, which was larger than the Japanese army. Over 5,000 gangs in Japan were crowded against each other. Epidemic violence and turf wars over profits resulted in a situation similar to the LCN wars in the United States (Kaplan & Dubro, 1986).

The Yakuza crime group was formalized in the early 1960s through the negotiations of Yoshio Kodama, a thug who during the war had been recruited to establish a spy network in northern China and was titled rear admiral by a grateful Japanese government. During those years, he also dealt in supplies (nickel, copper, cobalt, and heroin) and parlayed his company (*Kodama-Kikan*) into a

$175 million-enterprise. Kodama was considered a war criminal and threat to the Allied-occupied post-war Japan, however, and was imprisoned only to be released later. Upset over the ever-increasing violence, the Allied Command later asked Kodama, known as the "Godfather" of the Japanese underworld, to negotiate peace between all of the rival gangs. It was this alliance between Kazuo-Taoka of the Yamaguchi-gumi, Tosei-Kai (Hisayuki Michii, Korean crime boss), the Kanto-Kai, and the Inagawa-Kai factions that formed the Yakuza, the coalition that created peace among Japan's organized crime groups.

Yamaguchi-Gumi Crime Group

The largest and most powerful Yakuza group is the Yamaguchi-gumi who, in 1902, had approximately over 23,000 members. The third Oyabun of the faction, Kazuo Taoka, was responsible for much of the faction's growth and power. This faction was formed in 1915 in the Kobe area. Taoka ruled as a violent dictator, developing strong ties to politicians, which increased the success of the organization. Kobe Harbor, a main port of Japan, was controlled by Taoka labor forces, and this led to the control of other harbors.

As with many organized crime groups, a split occurred, with Hiroshi Yamamoto creating the Ichiwa-Kai syndicate, which became the third largest organized crime group in Japan. The syndicate of Inagawa-Kai boss, Kakuji Inagawa, absorbed many of the old Bakuto.

Yoshinori Watanabe

Bosses became heroes in the public's eyes and were subjects of songs, movies, and media glamorization. The saga of Yoshinori Watanabe illustrates the rise of powerful bosses of the Yakuza.

The leader of the largest Yakuza clan (the Yamaguchi-gumi clan) is Yoshinori Watanabe. Born in 1941, Watanabe came from a huge family of farmers and a prosperous life. After finishing middle school, he worked in a Tokyo restaurant. He later moved to Kobe and became involved with the Yamaken-gumi gang, a subgroup of the Yamaguchi-gumi clan. When Watanabe joined the Yamaguchi-gumi sometime around 1960, they were embroiled in a series of deadly turf wars (Amoruso, 2002). During this time, he began to show leadership skills, and the bosses began to take notice of him. He rose quickly through the organization after the war.

When the Yamaguchi-gumi clan was having troubles during the early 1980s, law enforcement thought this could be the end of the group. "They had lost their third boss in 1981 due to a heart attack, his successor to liver failure, and his eventual successor to assassins" (Amoruso, 2002). Watanabe became the fifth boss of the Yamaguchi-gumi in 1988 when the Yamaguchi-gumi were the largest Yakuza clan in Japan. During the 1980s, however, they split into two rival factions and lost power during the war that followed. Twenty-six members were killed during this war (Amoruso).

During the 1990s, Watanabe began to drastically change the structure of the Yamaguchi-gumi. The original centralized power structure was split into seven semi-autonomous regional groups, simultaneously making it more difficult for the police to penetrate, and easier for the leaders of the clans to control internal and external friction (Amoruso, 2002). He focused on developing new alliances with rival clans while strengthening others. The clan's offices expanded from 39 to 43 of Japan's 47 prefectures. By 1999, the Yamaguchi-gumi had 165,000 full-time members, which is five times the size of the entire American Mafia at its peak in the 1950s (Amoruso).

Under Watanabe's leadership, the Yamaguchi-gumi survived the Japanese depression and the government's crackdown on organized crime. Other Yakuza clan bosses and members were jailed, and the police scrutiny and economic recession that followed caused many members to shift alliances. "The Yamaguchi-gumi grabbed what was left and managed to muscle in on the new economy" (Amoruso, 2002).

Because Watanabe was the most powerful Yakuza boss, police attempts to attack him met with little success. Distancing himself from the crimes of his group, he helped raise money and get out the vote for scores of politicians. Because of Watanabe's political power, it was believed that the police could do little to stop him unless they took on his political allies, too.

According to some sources, Watanabe is a simple man who lifts weights, avoids rich foods, and jogs. He likes to hike and ski and was an "avid student of Chinese history and Japanese's law" (Amoruso, 2002). He enjoys karaoke, and is especially fond of the music from the movie, *The Godfather*. Some say that he saw himself as a public servant who helped losers who could not hold down a regular job. "Since the Yakuza provides work for such people, and helps keep their frustration in check, or at least directed mainly at one another, he thinks of it as a pragmatic solution to an intractable problem" (Amoruso). Watanabe considered the alternative to the Yakuza solution of keeping these people in check was disorganized crime. Evidence shows that the organized crime crackdowns resulted in a 70% increase in serious crime, with the arrest rate falling from 90% to 70%. Corruption is rampant as scandals of cover-ups have plagued law enforcement agencies (Amoruso).

In the ever more successful struggle for police to control Yakuza's activities, by the mid-1960s smaller groups were absorbed by the large groups such as the Yamaguchi-gumi, Sumiyoshi-Kai, and the Ingawa-Kai to survive; over 60% of Yakuza members belonged to one of these three groups. *Koiki* (wide area) is the term police used to characterize their large criminal operations. These groups became extremely powerful because they operated both legal and illegal enterprises. By 1992, 16 groups were named by the police under a new law against Japanese organized crime to help target Yakuza members for arrest and prosecution (Act for the Prevention of Unlawful Activities by Boryukudan Members). Totaling 43,960 members, these groups are defined in **Table 8-1**.

Yakuza Today

Modern Yakuza members are more economically motivated and materialistic than the early Yakuza. Research on members indicates that most Yakuza are high school dropouts. Most join because of the perceived glamour and monetary success of Yakuza organizations. Many members were delinquents and involved in drug use (Uchiyama, 1989).

Table 8-1 Criminal Groups Operating as Yakuza in 1992	
Clan or Group	Approximate Membership
Yamaguchi-gumi	23,100
Sumiyoshi-Kai	8,000
Inagawa-Kai	7,400
Aizu Kotetsu	1,600
Kudo-rengo Kusano-ikka	600
Okinawa Kyokurya-kai	570
Dojin-kai	510
Kyokyryu-kai	430
Aida-ikka	370
Kyosei-kai	330
Kozakura-ikka	190
Asano-gumi	150
Yamano-kai	100
Ishikawa-ikka	100
Soai-kai	80
Shinwa-kai	80

Source: Data are from Keiza, N. (1993). "Anti-gang law wracks mob ranks." *The Nikkei Weekly*.

The Koiki-Boryokudan has made alliances with other global organized crime groups such as the Chinese Snake Head, South American drug cartels, and Russian organized crime groups. They have expanded into most of Asia, the United States, and Australia. Yakuza activity in the United States increased from the 1990s until the present because of the arms trade potential and lucrative investments in areas like real estate. One Yakuza entity, Rondlan Doyuki, is alleged to own stock in a number of U.S. corporations including Chase Manhattan, Citicorp, IBM, Dow Chemical, Bank of America, General Motors, Atlantic Richfield, and Sperry. Many believe that the major activity in the United States by the Yakuza is money laundering. These groups are extremely active in California, Hawaii, New York, and Nevada. There is good reason to believe that these enterprising groups will continue to expand their operations in the United States and other countries as they overcome the culture and language barriers. Intelligence reports indicate that meetings between major organized crime groups from many countries have occurred to discuss how to divide areas where more profits and less turmoil are possible. The Yakuza's history resulted in diversity in their criminal operations, which include prostitution, child pornography, gambling, entertainment, liquor distribution, drugs, arms, money laundering, and extortion (Tuohy, 2000).

The Yakuza has been active in the United States since the mid-1950s. It is likely that the Yakuza will operate in the United States in a similar fashion as they have in Japan. However, the groups are fluid and dynamic, and continue to evolve both in their legal and illegal enterprises.

Structure and Organization

Membership

Each group consists of a highly structured leadership that is pyramidal and stratified. This boss and his henchmen structure is based on the Oyabun-Kobun (father-child) relationship where the Kumicho or Oyabun is head of the clan (parent) and his followers are the Kobun (children). These clans consist of quasi-blood relationships similar to the old Japanese feudal system. There are subgroups under each boss. The *Saiko-Komon* is a senior advisor who has advocates, accountants, bookkeepers, and his own gang of "children." The *Waka-Gashira* is the number two man of the clan in authority and carries out orders from the Oyabun. The *Kyodai* (older brother) has a boss referred to as the *Shatei-Gashira* who has a higher rank than the Waka-Gashira but less authority. Younger brothers are called *Shatei* and junior leaders are known as *Wakashu*. The children can be a leader over their own gang. The clan becomes a large group with many subfamilies. **Figure 8-1** shows the ranking system.

All must obey their leader under threat of punishment (Yakuza, retrieved 2006). The structure of the Sumiyoshi-Kai differs from the other Koiki-Boryokudan in that it has a conglomerate structure where several bosses of the top Yakuza groups are a federation with an elected president.

Code of Conduct and Oaths

All groups are very traditional and must abide by a code of conduct, which demands loyalty to bosses and honored nondisclosure of the secrets of the Yakuza. There are four types of sanctions. The most severe is lynching for serious offenses as viewed by the boss. *Yubitsume* is the amputation of the fingers at the joints, formerly a bakuto custom that signifies a weakening of the hand, which at one time meant that his ability to handle a sword was diminished. Yubitsume is per-

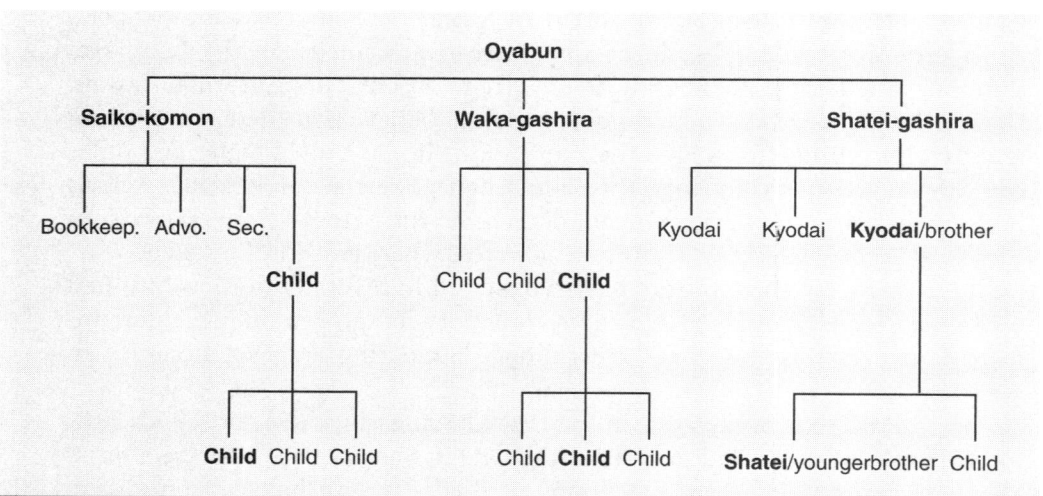

Figure 8-1 Organizational Chart for Some Clans of the Yakuza

formed as an act of apology to the boss, and the amputated finger is presented to the boss as a constant reminder of the error of the offending member. Currently, yubitsume is rarely practiced. The third form of sanction is *zetsuem*, which is the severing of the relationship between the boss and the offender. The offender may return to his former Yakuza gang after a period of time. The last sanction, *hamon*, is where the offender is removed from all Yakuza membership forever. The Yakuza have members (*Kumin*) and associates (*jun-Kumin*).

The Kumin are initiated into the clan by a ritual involving the exchange of sake (rice wine) cups to symbolize entry into the family and the father–child relationship. The ritual takes on a religious appearance and often is performed at a Shinto shrine or altar (Kaplan, 1986). In the Yakuza initiation ceremony, the sake symbolizes blood. The Oyabun and the initiate sit face-to-face as their sake is prepared by *azukarinin* (guarantors). Mixed with salt and fish scales, the sake is then carefully poured into cups and the Oyabun's cup is filled to the brim, befitting his status while the initiate gets much less. They drink a bit and then exchange cups, and each drinks from the other's cup, sealing the kobun's commitment to the family. From that moment on, even the kobun's wife and children must take a backseat to his obligations to his Yakuza family.

New members are required to abide by six sacred oaths:
- Never reveal the secrets of the organization.
- Never violate the wife or children of another member.
- Do not withhold money from the clan.
- Do not fail to obey supervisors.
- Do not become involved with narcotics.
- Do not appeal to the law or the police.

The similarity to the LCN's culture of omerta/oaths and rules for members and associates is obvious. Like other organized crime groups, the Yakuza began as protection from government or landowners and communities that was later corrupted by greed and power. The image of the Yakuza as outlaw hero remains with many members and the public, who see little wrong in who they are and what they do.

The older Yakuza system was an apprenticeship where the Kobun (child) would be trained by a member in the techniques of the occupation and criminal subculture of service to the clan. The clan is bound together by the traditions, rituals, and the concepts of *Ikka* (whole family; Kaplan & Dubro, 1986). The Yakuza display both *Otoki* (masculinity) and respect or *Kao* (face). The Bakuto also use the body suit style of tattooing the body. Criminals were marked by a tattoo around an arm for each offence. Illegal until 1948 and still considered shameful by most Japanese, the tattoo became a symbol of strength and masculinity, and identified the Yakuza as a misfit. (Again, this is similar to the tattoos of U.S. outlaw motorcycle gang members.) The tattooing of the entire body and missing finger joints can easily identify some Yakuza members.

The Yakuza have numerous ceremonies that are required under the concept or ethics of *Giri*, which requires them to honor and proclaim their clan name. These ceremonies are held to celebrate or mourn an event. All Yakuza are required to attend and contribute money. The ethics of Ninkyo-do were practiced more by the older Yakuza than the now materialistic Yakuza or Keizal Yakuza, who have done away with many of the old rituals and traditions (French, 2001). Japanese youth have become much like their Western counterparts who are individualistic and materialistic as well as opposed to the degree of service demanded of apprenticeship.

All members are required to pay a membership fee and contribute money during ceremonies. The huge amount of money going to the boss may allow him to prosper without having to be involved in criminal activity, which insulates him from arrest and prosecution while assuring him control over his group. Much of the recruiting of members is from martial arts clubs, boxing clubs, and misguided youth seeking avenues for success. The young Yakuza are more street thugs than their warrior ancestors. Yakuza are promoted based on the amount of money they contribute to the bosses and organization. Once a younger member reaches a certain rank (usually Shatei), he can establish his own "children" (gang). By this method, the clan can grow into the thousands in membership. All members obey their gang leaders and everyone obeys the Oyabun.

The group that most mirrors the origin of criminal groups like LCN is the Gurentai, who took economic advantage of the chaos and confusion in Japan after World War II. These thugs excelled by using threats, violence, and corruption to control the black markets, labor, and gambling.

Unlike other organized crime groups, the Yakuza do have ultranationalistic, conservative, and anti-communist political ideologies. Their long-term, rather peaceful relationship with the police is beginning to crumble because of the changing laws of Japan and public opinion. Unlike other organized crime groups, the Yakuza maintain a very public image and presence. The headquarters of the clans are well marked with the symbol of the clan. Each clan has a distinct symbol that is worn as a label on the black suits that have become their uniform. Displayed as power symbols, the pin and tattoos are signals for rivals and victims to give them respect and fear. Investigators of Yakuza clans should become familiar with the symbols of Yakuza members to identify and trace their movements and activities.

Most clan headquarters are very elaborate and are technologically advanced, as both physical and electronic security are prominently displayed. Well-armed guards are obvious to the public and police.

Concerned with their image and that of their cities and country, the Yakuza often contribute to good causes and offer or provide assistance in times of disaster. By ingratiating themselves with the public, the Yakuza hope to hamper enforcement of the new laws of Japan. However, they also have used violence to maintain their image when portrayed in an unfavorable manner in a movie. Yakuza still portray themselves as protectors of society's weaker members by maintaining a code of honor and exhibiting chivalry. Many in law enforcement believe that Yakuza associates—whose numbers may be 10 times that of Yakuza members—are the most serious threat posed by the clans because they maintain a low profile and are more difficult to identify. Given the diversity, history of survival, their extensive blending into legitimate businesses, and their ability to adjust to change, the structure of the Yakuza will likely survive and continue to expand globally.

■ Activities and Methods of Operation

The Yakuza traditionally operated wherever a Japanese population was found. They followed the Japanese immigrants to establish operations in places such as Hawaii, California, and Australia's Gold Coast. An estimated 80% of their revenue comes from illegal activities. However, they are rapidly becoming developers as they amass vast real estate holdings. Their objective appears to become more legitimate by investing their illegal profits into legal businesses, a plan that will result in an even more diminished ability of law enforcement to identity members and their operations. In addition to their traditional partnerships with Chinese Triads, the Yakuza have formed alliances with both Korean and Vietnamese gangs in California and possibly other U.S. states.

Business Acquisition

A typical approach to taking over a business is to visit the owner of a Japanese business involved in tourism and offer to steer large numbers of people to the business in return for a percentage of the profits. If the owner refuses, they resort to threats or violence, which eventually concludes with the Yakuza owning the business.

Protection and Extortion

Another tradition of Yakuza is the protection and extortion racket. They provide so called "protection" for money as bouncers or security in bars, restaurants, gaming houses, etc. Most owners pay the money and do not report the extortion for fear of reprisal.

Gambling

Like LCN and other organized crime groups, the Yakuza has filled the public's demand for illegal services and products. Gambling is a long tradition of the Bakuto faction and continues to be a source of revenue. Horse racing, bicycle racing, and a variety of other sports betting along with loan sharking and booking offer the Yakuza a steady source of revenue.

An Oyabun who testified at the President's Commission on Organized Crime in 1984 described the structure and activities of the Yamaguchi-gumi and the Sumiyoshi-rengo. He told the Commission that the clans try to identify any company having financial difficulty and then develop elaborate plans to take it over. By employing threats and entering fraudulent contracts with the company, it eventually fails because of profits directed into the clan's coffers. Other methods of business takeover include the Sokaiya (thugs) who specialize in disrupting stock markets and stockholders' meetings.

One of the more powerful groups of Sokaiya is the Rondan Doyukai. They have been very successful in Japan, where most stockholders decide it is cheaper to pay them off rather than risk the negative impact these groups can have on a company's stability. These groups have operated in the United States by targeting large corporations such as Chase Manhattan, Bank of New York, Bank of

America, IBM, General Motors, and a number of Japanese-owned banks, investment firms, and other companies. They normally begin by attending a stockholder meeting and introducing themselves as "your Japanese stockholders" and offer their praise of the company, wish them luck, and then leave.

The United States is a viable target with over $80 billion in trade per year between the United States and Japan. The Yakuza may resort to using force to take over major stock positions in corporate entities within the United States and Japan. They make millions of dollars a year through corporate extortion, and the Sokaiya (shareholders' meeting men) are the masters of this enterprise. Sokaiya will buy a small number of shares in a company so that they can attend shareholders' meetings. In preparation for the meeting, the Sokaiya gather damaging information about the company and its officers. Secret mistresses, tax evasion, unsatisfactory working conditions, and pollution are all opportunities for the Sokaiya. They then contact the company's corporate management and threaten to disclose whatever embarrassing information they have at the shareholders' meeting unless they are "compensated." If management does not give into their demands, the Sokaiya go to the shareholders' meeting and raise hell, shouting down anyone who is to speak, making a boisterous display of their presence, and shouting out their damaging revelations. In Japan, where people fear embarrassment and shame far more than physical threat, executives usually give the Sokaiya whatever they want. While this practice has been outlawed by the Japanese government, it does not mean that the practice of using the Sokaiya does not exist. Verified reports demonstrate that this strategy is still prevalent and the activities of the Yakuza are well documented in American Fortune 500 corporations. This mastered craft is providing a lucrative entrance into the legitimate businesses of America to an extent that is unfathomable by U.S. law enforcement authorities.

Narcotics Trafficking

By far, the biggest revenue source of the Yakuza is drug trafficking. Stimulants such as amphetamines and methamphetamines are in high demand in Japan, and the Yakuza are the primary suppliers. Intelligence indicates that the Yakuza are involved in cocaine distribution as well. If this distribution is true, an alliance with the Colombian cartels as well as other groups such as Chinese organized crime may be a reality.

As early as the 1930s, Harry Anslinger, then Director of the Federal Bureau of Narcotics (now DEA), warned that the Japanese were major world suppliers of illicit "white drugs," referring to morphine and heroin. Japanese morphine was seized from Japanese violators in the 1930s in Hawaii, Washington, and Oregon. Although World War II interrupted the Japanese drug supply, it is not surprising that their drug trafficking operations in the United States have returned.

Pornography

Hard core pornography is prohibited in Japan, where it is illegal to sell photographs or films showing human genitalia. Like other prohibitions, a public demand creates huge profits. Women from the United States and other countries are often imported either willingly or by subterfuge. U.S. fronts were created using English-speaking Yakuza agents, who placed enticing advertisements for actors, singers, and dancers, offering auditions in Japan. Once the woman was in Japan, the job requirements changed to prostitution or servitude. Those who were trapped could not earn enough money to return to their home country and so became permanent employees of the Yakuza. Often these women act as hostesses (prostitutes) in the Yakuza clubs where Japanese men will pay large fees for sex with a Western woman. The Los Angeles Police Department reported that hundreds of women fall victim to this type of exploitation. Sex tours for Japanese men with nude dancing and prostitution are offered by Yakuza-owned facilities. These facilities are located in many countries, including the United States.

Weapons and Smuggling

Another enterprise of the Yakuza is the arms business. American-made firearms and ammunition are ten times more valuable in Japan than in the United States. Although firearms are not part of the Japanese tradition of swords and knives, many gangs and clans in Japan have become quite well armed. Clans often corrupt military personnel to supply weapons in addition to the purchase and smuggling of weapons by American civilians.

Like with the narcotics trade, the methods of smuggling are inventive and have a high success rate of reaching Japan, where the weapons are sold to gangs. The United States is not the sole supplier; other countries are becoming involved. With the fall of the Soviet Union and the globalization of Russian organized crime groups, it may be that alliances between the Russians and Yakuza have formed based on the drug and weapons markets. Intelligence indicates that the Yakuza are becoming more involved in the global transportation industry, which certainly will impact their ability to move illicit goods from country to country.

Money Laundering

Money laundering goes hand-in-hand with profits from their diverse legal and illegal operations. Some methods involve washing the money through high volume cash businesses such as bars, construction companies, trucking or transportation companies, restaurants, and tourist gift shops. Japanese bankers are reluctant to cooperate with law enforcement because of threat and intimidation. Many bank executives are either employed by the Yakuza or recruited to become members of the organization. By owning their own financial institutions, concealing the source and existence of illegal funds is not difficult. Money can be transferred anywhere, anytime.

The Yakuza continues to explore new avenues of revenue as well as ways to improve their image, while simultaneously expanding operations. Insider stock trading and attempts to purchase or develop casinos in the United States have been documented. Japanese businessman, Ryo̅ichi Sasakawa, who is alleged to have ties to the Yakuza, and his son, Takashi, have been involved in investments in the United States. The father has contributed money to U.S. universities, institutes, and even the presidential library of Jimmy Carter, who has publicly praised the work of Sasakawa. Internationally, Sasakawa has financed the United States-Japan Foundation with a $48 million endowment, the Nippon Foundation, World Health Organization, among others, and been generous to disaster relief agencies and environmental causes. Some believe this has been done to enhance his image, which is a typical ploy of those who live the lifestyle of the upper echelon Yakuza.

In still another effort to expand a Tokyo real estate firm, West Tsusho, led by Ishii Susumu, boss of the Inagawa-Kai clan, purchased two American companies. In 1991, *Time Magazine* reported that West Tsusho purchased Quantum Access and Asset Management International Financing and Settlement with the help of Prescott Bush, Jr., brother of President Bush. Prescott Bush received a $250,000 fee, but reportedly was unaware of the connection of West Tsusho to the Yakuza.

Investigative Strategies

Many members of the Yakuza have been arrested during their criminal careers in Japan, and some members and associates have been arrested in the United States and other countries. The paid Sokaiya (discussed earlier) is now an illegal practice in Japan; however, there is evidence that the Yakuza are still employing this method of extortion. In the late 1990s, the banking industry of Japan suffered a major financial disaster due to bad loans to Yakuza members and bosses who refuse to repay. Efforts to collect these loans resulted in the death of at least one banker and an executive of another financial institution (Kaplan, 1998). These bad investments hurt the Yakuza in their wallets as well as their image. Companies are now reluctant to deal with the Yakuza because of their financial history and the violence associated with the groups. It appears that the financial difficulties due to their loss of face and the new anti-Boryokudan law have resulted in a more desperate and violent Yakuza.

Laws and Statutes

The Boryokudan Countermeasures Law of 1992 defined the Yakuza as an organization that uses violence to commit illegal acts (National Criminal Justice Reference Center, 2000). It provides for strict restrictions upon Yakuza activity. The law actually designated clans as targeted for law enforcement arrest for their style of extortion. The following acts of the clans are prohibited under the law:

- Demanding gifts
- Demanding subcontract jobs
- Demanding *mikajime* (muscle fee)
- Demanding protection money
- Collecting of high-interest loans
- Demanding exemption from loans or financial obligations
- Demanding loans
- Demanding that security brokers conduct credit transactions
- Demanding companies and others to purchase certain stock
- Demanding payment for return of evacuated land and buildings that are subject to public auction
- Illegally assembling on property
- Extortion by taking advantage of a person's weak points

- Demanding money on fraudulent facts
- Intervening in court cases or out-of-court case settlements

These laws provide an insight to the activities of the Yakuza and should be part of the investigative strategy. The law also restricts recruiting juveniles to join by coercing, threatening, or enticing.

The United States can expect the Yakuza to employ similar tactics and must be prepared for expanded operations within our borders. Task forces such as the LAPD Asian Task Force must be trained and established throughout the country, especially in large populations of Japanese Americans. Although the Yakuza in America may be difficult to distinguish from legitimate enterprise, the law enforcement community must be trained, educated, staffed, and equipped to investigate corporate America. The current successful investigations of Enron, WorldCom, and others are indicative of the ability to take on this type of criminal activity. Changes in the statutes and laws in many countries are needed to ensure U.S. cooperation with other countries. Money laundering violations, RICO, drug laws, and conspiracy statutes must be created to address the nature of criminal organizations such as the Yakuza.

Special Task Forces

On numerous occasions, Peter Lamb of the National Crime Authority of Australia has stated that law enforcement is playing catch up and must form teams capable of dealing with the economic and complex crimes of the Yakuza. Task forces need forensic accountants, attorneys, experts, analysis, and innovative techniques to address this crime organization. Like many other organized crime groups, their new tool is the Internet for moving money. Law enforcement must develop expertise in dealing with transnational crime.

Because the Yakuza quickly adapt to pressure from law enforcement and can develop new modes of operation, simply taking out the leaders is not enough. There is always a replacement who lusts for the power and money offered by being boss of a clan, and willing to do anything to get to that position. Centuries of Yakuza history attest to their ability to survive. Global cooperation is needed to deal successfully with this confederation of gangsters. Law enforcement must be able to cross national boundaries and attack the groups where they live. The new criminal alliances between Colombian, Chinese, Russian, Yakuza, and others must be broken.

Follow the Money

Yakuza are now investing in real estate and corporate America. The economic benefits of U.S. investments are close to what the Yakuza enjoyed in Japan, until bad loans and the economic slump seriously damaged their profit margin. The United States cannot afford to allow these investments to continue. Members and leaders along with their assets must be identified, targeted for investigation, and prosecuted to the fullest extent of the law. Following the money from illegal enterprises such as arms trafficking, sex-related enterprises, and drug trafficking to the legal enterprises must be a priority of American police and their foreign law enforcement counterparts. Sting operations or reverse undercover operations that have been successful against other organized crime groups, such as the Medellín and Cali Cartels of Colombia and the Mafia in Italy and the United States, also may be effective against the Yakuza.

More international agreements such as the Council of Europe's *Convention on Laundering, Search, Seizure, and Confiscation of the Proceeds of Crime* (also known as the Strasburg Convention) signed in 1990 that went into effect in 2001 are necessary (reported by the *Brama News* and *Community Press*, December 1, 2002; NCJR, 2000) . These agreements require that each nation adopt legislation creating the criminal offense of money laundering of funds from serious crime. Attacking the assets of the Yakuza is a proven strategy that must be developed further. Financial institutions and banks that assist organized crime groups such as the Yakuza are known to law enforcement (Hong Kong, Swiss, Cayman Islands, etc.) and must become targets of investigations. These semi-legal enterprises collect up to 20% fees for laundering millions with very little risk of prosecution. The Yakuza process their profits through layers of complex financial transactions to conceal the source of illicit income. The use of net worth, source, and application financial analysis can identify unexplained income of members of the Yakuza. Reconstruction of expenditures versus income allow investigators to form plans to legally pursue charges for money laundering, income tax violations, and reporting violations.

■ Conclusions

The Yakuza may be the most effective organized crime group that invests its illicit profits into legitimate business. Corrupting legitimate business is probably the most serious threat posed by groups such as the Yakuza. American law enforcement must overcome the language and cultural barriers to develop intelligence that is credible, accurate, and timely.

Past performance is a predictor of future activity of the Yakuza. Although the players change, the activities, structure, and patterns of these gangsters remain fairly constant. The dual goals of intelligence are both tactical and strategic. Intelligence leads to effective plans, actions, and decisions. Investigators must identify the Yakuza goals, methods of operation, and structure as they operate in the United States. This intelligence can provide an assessment of the level of threat and the nature of expansions, violence, and aggressiveness of the Yakuza. A proactive approach needs to be developed using solid tactical and strategic intelligence. Investigators must increase their understanding of the relationships between the many global organized crime groups to determine how they communicate, where they meet, how they operate, and how and where the money flows.

Physical surveillance, undercover operations, electronic surveillance, and informants are the major tools of investigations of organized crime. The properly managed and developed informant is perhaps the ultimate source of information regarding organized crime. Charts produced by analysis of this information are invaluable to both plan and develop courtroom presentations. Financial analysis is particularly effective in money laundering investigations. Both commodity and event flow analysis give an instant understanding of how the organization operates. Communication analysis offers strategies for capturing and providing evidence to obtain court orders for electronic surveillance. Electronic surveillance provides evidence of violations that can be prosecuted under RICO and CCE statutes, conspiracy, money laundering, and many other criminal acts. Experts are often needed to break codes or ciphers and explain conversations captured or recorded during electronic surveillance.

Major laws and statutes such as the Organized Crime Act of 1970, Money Laundering Act of 1986, various controlled substance acts, and conspiracy statutes such as RICO must be understood by the criminal investigator who takes on the Yakuza. Standardized and innovative training and education must be utilized by law enforcement to catch up to the complex operations of the Yakuza. Language fluency and a deep knowledge of the Japanese culture and history are crucial.

The Yakuza will continue to evolve into a more complex and sophisticated organization to maintain its level of profit and success. This Japanese criminal organization will continue to form and strengthen alliances with other organized crime groups, and employ corruption and violence to protect its operations. International drug trafficking, gambling, and the sex trade will always be part of the illicit operations of the Yakuza, but the infiltration of legitimate business may be an even more serious threat to the United States. Determining how the Yakuza launder their money may be more difficult than developing other types of criminal cases. The money trail is complex, and requires team efforts of well-trained and equipped law enforcement. Complex infrastructures of large numbers of people comprise the structure of the Yakuza. The successful investigation of this organization will require a dynamic law enforcement response by well-trained, globally cooperative, and highly technical investigators.

The Yakuza may well prove to be more threatening to the United States than the American Mafia and drug cartels. Their ability to infiltrate legitimate business and governments is well documented, and their money laundering operations and real estate investments can grow to be a serious threat to the economic stability of United States and other nations. The Yakuza also will continue to form alliances with other organized crime groups, which will make them even more of a challenge. As early as 1988, the Yakuza grossed over $10 billion (Skold, 2002). In the near future, members probably will operate more like underground or "shadow figures" while expanding their operations to move more into economic crime and appear less like the traditional Yakuza. Because of the lack of verifiable intelligence and penetration by law enforcement, much is unknown about the current state of Yakuza organized crime. The challenge for law enforcement is to develop current and accurate information about the structure and activities of today's Yakuza.

DISCUSSION QUESTIONS

1. Discuss the origins of the Yakuza. Why are they important to the investigation and prosecution of Yakuza members?
2. Who are the major Yakuza clans? What is their structure?
3. Why do you think the Yakuza has been so resilient to efforts to arrest and prosecute them? What does the future hold for the Yakuza?
4. Discuss the activities of the Yakuza. How does this organized crime group differ from other organized crime groups such as the DTOs or the LCN?
5. What are the six sacred oaths and how do they contribute to the success of the Yakuza? How are these oaths similar to rules of other organized crime groups?
6. What do you believe are the most effective enforcement tools against the Yakuza?

REFERENCES

Amoruso, D. A. (2002). *Yoshinori Watanabe.* Gangsters, Incorporated. Retrieved June 20, 2006 from http://gangstersinc.tripod.com/Watanabe.html

French, J. W. (2001, Oct 4). "Even in Ginza, Honor Among Thieves Crumbles." *New York Times.*

Haberman, C. (1985, Feb 6). "TV Funeral for Japan's Slain Godfather." *New York Times.*

Kaplan, D. (1986). *Yakuza: The Explosive Account of Japan's Criminal Underworld.* Reading, MA: Addison-Wesley Publishing.

Kaplan, D. (1998, April 13). "Yakuza Inc." *U.S. News and World Report.* Retrieved November 14, 2006 from http://www.usnews.com/usnews/biztech/articles/980413/archive_003691.htm

Kaplan, D. E., & Dubro, A. (1986). *Yakuza.* Reading, MA: Addison-Wesley Publishing.

Kersten, J. (1993). Street youth, bosozokoy and yakuza: subculture formation and societal reactions in Japan. *Crime and Delinquency, 39,* 277–295.

Murphy, D. (2001). *Things Japanese: Yakuza.* Yamasa, Japan: Achi Center for Japanese Culture. Retrieved June 20, 2006 from http://www.Yamasa.org/acjs/network/english/newsletter/ThingsJapanese12.html

National Criminal Justice Reference Center. (2000). "Present Situation of Organized Crime in Japan and Countermeasures Against It" (abstract). Washington, DC: Department of Justice. Retrieved November 14, 2006 from http://www.ncjrs.gov/app/publications/Abstract.aspx?id=197906

Nihon Keiza: Shimbun, Inc. (1993, March). "Anti-gang law wracks mob ranks." *The Nikkei Weekly.*

Skold, D. (2002). Yakuza. Oldman's homepage. Retrieved November 24, 2006, from http://w1.313.telia.com/~U31302275/yakuza.html

Uchiyama, A. (1989). "Economic life of member of organized crime gangs." Reports of NRIPS, 30(1).
Yakuza. (2000). Gangland.net. Retrieved June 20, 2006 from http://www.gangland.net/yakuza.htm

9 Triads and Tongs

"Opportunity is a moving target, the bigger the target, the faster it moves."
—Richard Gaylord Briley

Chapter Objectives
After completing this chapter, readers should be able to:
- Explain the difference between a tong and triad.
- Discuss the structure of the triads and its importance to investigators.
- Discuss the triad culture and its importance to tactical and strategic planning and operations.

■ Introduction

Hong Kong triads began the same way as many organized crime groups. They formed naturally as benevolent societies or guilds for protection of the community or to represent the interest of their community. In 1994, the Serious Crimes Ordinance of Hong Kong defined a triad as "any society which uses rituals that are common to triad societies, or uses any ritual similar to that used by triad societies and adopts triad title or nomenclature." This Ordinance also defines organized crime as, "a schedule offense connected to activities of a triad with extensive planning and organization by two or more persons to commit two or more schedule acts."

■ Historical Perspective

In the United States, the presence of Chinese organized crime is complex and consists of triads, tongs, secret societies, and gangs.

Triads are secret societies that, like the Yakuza, date back to the 17th century. Today, an estimated 57 triad societies operate in Hong Kong, which is the base for all triad societies worldwide. Only about 20 of these triads are involved in criminal activity. Membership ranges from a small 20 to 50 to over 30,000 members in each triad group. The recognized expert on Chinese organized crime, Ko-lin Chin, believes that these groups are not structured or coordinated like U.S. LCN, and that there is no single Chinese Mafia (Chin, 1996). However, substantial evidence exists of alliances between many Chinese street gangs and adult organizations such as the triads and tongs.

While most triads are based in Hong Kong, Macau, or Taiwan, *tongs* are American phenomena like the outlaw motorcycle gangs (OMGs). Developed around the 1850s in San Francisco during the Gold Rush era, these family associations were created among those having common surnames, such as "Long." Tongs were organized by persons (some were triad members in their home countries) of less common surnames to ensure representation in negotiations within their communities. The Chinese Consolidated Benevolent Association, comprising six companies, was formed as a political entity of the Chinese community.

Most tongs are respectable fraternal organizations, but some tong members became active in criminal activities and thus their group can be characterized as organized crime organizations. Known as *fighting tongs*, these groups soon controlled gambling, prostitution, and narcotics distribution by forming monopolies. They were linked to gangs and triads in Hong King, Taiwan, and Macau that exist today. For example, the Wah Ching tong originated from a 1960s street gang that, through extortion, violence, and other typical criminal activities, established a monopoly on Chinese entertainment in the United States.

Chinese organized crime activity exists in most major U.S. cities. Law enforcement intelligence reports agree that the triads, tongs, and their street gang associates prey mainly on the Chinese community. Although there are alliances between the three groups, they are separate entities that control their own activities. Some Chinese organized crime groups, such as the United Bamboo Crime Syndicate, began as a street gang in Taipei, Taiwan in the 1950s. Today, this group is international with over 40,000 members. This group is no longer only active in predominantly Chinese communities known as *Chinatowns*, but do operate networks that supply narcotics and human smuggling worldwide. The Chinese are a major supplier of heroin to the United States.

The reported alliances between the Yakuza, triads, LCN, and others present a major threat to law enforcement efforts, which is compounded by cultural and language barriers. Loyalty, secrecy, brotherhood, righteousness, and nationalism among these groups result in enterprises that are difficult to penetrate. These organizations can form networks rapidly when opportunities arise, and then dissolve just as fast upon completion of the criminal activity. The dynamic nature of the triads, tongs, and street gangs allow them to be fluid and mobile to take advantage of market opportunities.

Chinese culture emphasizes intergenerational family loyalty. *Guanxi*, a phenomenon where individuals are bound to others with mutual obligations (much like the American Mafia's omerta), is the basis for the strong loyalty displayed by triad or tong members. Family and mutual reciprocity (*qinqing*) allow all resources to be shared with each member, who in turn is obligated to contribute to the family, the heart of Chinese culture. Most Chinese in the United States are reluctant to provide information to law enforcement as a result of corruption and harsh treatment in their homeland by police and government.

In addition to the triads, tongs and street gangs, there is evidence that mainland Chinese syndicates have established operations in the United States. These new groups tend to be more aggressive and loosely organized than the traditional triads. All of these organizations are becoming more diverse in their criminal activity than the old triads, and have moved into committing Internet crimes, product counterfeiting, and fraud (Robinson, 1999).

With a world membership of over 100,000, these Chinese organized crime groups are an obvious threat to the United States. Alliances among Chinese and others may be a turning point in how their organized crime groups function. Chinese criminals are increasingly more competitive with other organized crime groups, and are penetrating legitimate business in ways much like the American LCN. The United States has become a major market for Chinese organized crime goods and services. It is important to realize that not all triads, tongs, and their members are involved in criminal activity, however.

Triads, tongs, Chinese gangs, and the new mainland societies/groups are separate entities but occasionally do form alliances to achieve specific criminal goals. Steve Macko (1997), a crime analyst, reported that the Chinese triads are more dangerous than the Italian and the Russian groups for two reasons. First, the Chinese triads are not a tightly unified crime organization. A triad may exist anywhere there is a Chinese community and operate a number of legal enterprises. Second, while the Russians are considered a very violent organized crime group, Macko believes the Chinese are less violent and much more subtle in their organizations' workings. Most Chinese triads will try to avoid committing violent acts that might draw attention to themselves, while other organized crime groups will commit frequent violent acts in the struggle to establish dominance over the marketplace. Triads commonly employ well-placed corrupt political contacts to control their enemies.

Because the triads in mainland China are the forerunners to the U.S. tongs and street gangs, knowing some of their history is helpful in understanding Chinese organized crime.

The Fighting Shaolin Monks

Many experts trace the origins of triad societies to the 17th century. Legend has it that the foundation for these societies began when the second Manchu emperor, Kiang Hsi, asked for help from the Siu Lam monastery, which trained monks in the martial arts. Facing a rebellion in Fukien, the emperor believed that, with their assistance, he would be able to quell any disturbance that should ever arise.

The fighting Shaolin monks agreed to aid the emperor and began their mission. After they helped to successfully end the revolt, emperor Kiang Hsi rewarded them with vast imperial power for their efforts. The monks returned to their Shaolin Temple and continued their monastic lifestyle as they had known it before. However, the emperor began to fear that the monks—who had easily defeated the rebellion in Fukien—could one day turn against him. With this in mind, he searched for a way to end the potential threat the monks presented. In order to prevent them from ever having the chance to overthrow his power, the emperor decided to destroy the monks and their temple, and soon afterwards sent his army to murder the monks. Knowing that the monks maintained stringent security over their temple, the emperor bribed one of them to assist his army to break in. Because this bribed monk was considered the number seven monk in the temple's hierarchy, he had the ability to sneak the army past security (Black, 1991).

Once inside the temple, the emperor's army caught the monks off guard and quickly murdered most of them. Only eighteen monks managed to escape from the carnage. After fierce battles against the army's hot pursuit and, despite their attempts to hide by splitting up, all but five monks were eventually murdered. These five escapees later formed their own monasteries in the areas in which they settled (Raamsdonk, 2001). Deeply angered by the emperor's betrayal, they also founded secret societies within their monasteries. These secret societies had one purpose: to destroy the Manchu (also known as the Ching dynasty) and restore the previous rulers, who were the Ming. The Ming family had ruled over China during what would become known as the country's finest era of peace and culture. The monks believed that by restoring the Ming to power, they would not only have fitting revenge upon the emperor for his treachery, but their country would benefit from their actions (Black, 1991).

The Ming family name was "Hung," and the family's color was red; Hung and red are both closely associated with the triad societies of today. Nearly all societies pay homage to the original five monks by displaying the triangular symbol from which the term *triad* (heaven, earth, and man) was derived, and the color red is prominent. These secret societies began to use the motto, "Crush the Ching, establish the Ming." To avoid detection by the emperor and his spies, each society developed secret handshakes and gestures to identify themselves (Black, 1991).

It is interesting to note that currently around the world there is a martial art practiced by several thousand individuals known as Hung Gar Kung Fu. While few realize it, the foundation for this martial art may be one of the secret societies of the original monks. The martial arts association's red flag shows a hand with outstretched palm and all fingers bent except for the pointer finger. One of the original slogans during the attempts to overthrow the emperor was that, "if every Chinese will lift but one finger, we can bring down the Ching and restore the Ming." The training forms of this martial art begin with this hand signal. Individuals who practice this school of martial art may be using one of the original secret hand signs of the ancient rebellion.

Chinese Rebellions Through the Revolution

Because of the secrecy these societies maintained, the constant martial arts training that occurred in these monasteries, and economic pressures, these societies eventually evolved from being political organizations to criminal organizations. Regardless of their reputation for criminal acts, these societies are still viewed by the public as protectors of the people from an oppressive ruler, much in the same way that the Italian Mafia and Japanese Yakuza were perceived in the their early years, and members see themselves and their organizations as being protectors of society rather than themselves in the role of common criminals.

The organizations did play important roles in several rebellions throughout China, most notably, the Boxer Rebellion (1896–1900), which involved the White Lotus Society, one of the original five societies. From 1910 to 1918, Chinese warlords, foreign commercial concerns maintaining their own governments along the coast, and Chinese intellectuals who were bitter over foreign imperialism fought for power and control. China was not unified. Oddly enough, the China dynasty tottered to its grave after being overthrown in 1911 by the Nationalist government, but by that time there were no longer any Mings to restore to the throne (Black, 1991).

Sadly, while the societies were fighting to overthrow their emperor, countries from the west—most notably Japan—took advantage of the Chinese. These countries imported Chinese citizens as menial labor, enforcing the sale of opium through war, and stole countless gold artifacts from the Chinese.

By 1927, the Nationalist government was established in China. Its leader, Chiang Kai Shek, was a known killer and member of a triad named Shang Hai Green Gang. The new China government and other Western countries used this gang to control the communists and to quell any unrest among laborers.

Global Dispersal of the Triads

With the 1947 attack by the Japanese during World War II, the Chinese triads began to work for the Japanese, running their criminal enterprises out of Hong Kong. During this time, the only complete unification of the triads took place. The Japanese organized the triads into one organization known as the *Hing Ah Kee Kwan* (Asia Flowering Association). The triads were entrusted with policing responsibilities as well as handling any anti-Japanese sentiment. After the war, their focus shifted once again to attempting to control the rising power of the communists. Membership in the triads had grown to an estimated 300,000 members by 1947. During this time, the 14K triad was organized by the Nationalist army lieutenant general, Kot Siu Wong, who headquartered in Canton. When the communists finally overtook China, triad members fled around the world, appearing in Hong Kong; Macao, Thailand; San Francisco, United States; Vancouver, Canada; and Perth, Australia (Black, 1991).

Since the Communist era, the United States has experienced a significant immigration of Chinese. During the 1990s, triads increased their presence by investing in legitimate U.S. businesses. The Big Circle gang and the Fukching gang became very active in the United States during the 1980s and the 1990s, and currently are engaged in drug trafficking, high tech crimes, and fraud. The Big Circle has been made part of the gang of Tranquil Happiness Triad, and the Fukching are associated with the Fukien American Association Tongs.

The criminal culture, relationships, and structure of the triads, tongs, gangs, and their associates are complex. This complexity requires investigators to invest time and effort into understanding these criminal organizations to develop effective strategies to attack the structure and operation of these groups. Drug trafficking does appear to involve more groups among the various components of Chinese organized crime.

Structure

The structure of the triads, tongs, and gangs varies somewhat between groups. The most commonly reported structure is for the triads. The British coined the term *triad* based on the triangle symbol that these societies maintained in their Hong Kong headquarters.

Membership

Ancient numerology (a system based on the I-Ching that has mystical associations between words and numbers) determines the positions in the triads. Each element is assigned a number in Chinese criminal societies. These numbers are always multiples of 3, where the number 36 means heaven, 108 is the number for man, and the number 72 is assigned to Earth. Numerology plays an important role in determining the amount of money a new member must pay to join the triad. Also of importance is the number seven. Because the Manchus (who destroyed the original Shaolin Temple) were aided by the number seven monk in the Shoalin hierarchy, the number seven is never used in the initiation ceremony. Failure to abide by this could result in various punishments including death (Raamsdonk, 2001).

As with initiates of the LCN, those wanting to join the organization need a triad sponsor who has rank to vouch for them. During the initiation, initiates swear to all of the oaths to the leaders of the triad they are attempting to join. To show respect for the original five founders of the five original triads, everyone drinks from a cup of blood drawn from each of the new recruits. Ceremonies of the past have lasted from hours to three days; however, today initiation ceremonies vary between triads, tongs, and gangs.

It is important to note that the control structure of the triads is not the same as in other organized crime groups. While the headquarters of every triad is based in Hong Kong, those in the headquarters do not always supervise or control its subgroups' activities. The headquarters is responsible for maintaining the image of the rituals and the triad as a whole. Each of the major leadership roles in the triads is assigned both an alphabetical name or rank and a numeral designation for that position.

Within each triad is a head figure who is the leader. This individual, named the *Shan Chu* (Dragon head or Hill Chief), is denoted by the number 489. This title is extended to all heads, so the main leader at the headquarters will bear this title as will the heads throughout the world. Directly under the Shan Chu is his assistant, the *Fu Shan Chu*, who is denoted by the number 438. The *Lungtau* is an advisor or counselor. Interestingly, the leader and his assistant may also be called by the title *Tai-Lo* (elder brother) and *I-Lo* (second elder brother), respectively. Regardless of which title is applied, these are the top two men and they are responsible for major decisions. One of the decisions reserved for these two individuals is the issuing of death sentences to members or outsiders.

Equal in rank but not decision-making are the *Heung Chu* (incense master) and the *Sing Fung* (vanguard), both denoted by the number 438. Carrying the spiritual responsibility of the triad, the Heung Chu is responsible for overseeing the rituals and oaths of new members. The Sing Fung may assist the Heung Chu in his duties, but the Sing Fung is charged with establishing subgroups of the triad. In essence, he has been compared to a franchise officer. The grass slipper, number 432, is the liaison for communications and interactions between units.

Next in the administrative hierarchy is the *Hung Kwan* (military commander), who is denoted by the number 426. Also called the Red Pole, the responsibility of this individual is to ensure the protection of all gang territory as well as overtaking properties of rival gangs, and supervision of the soldiers.

The next level is the *Pak Tsz Sin*, denoted by the number 415. This individual is also known as the White Paper Fan and is responsible for providing all financial and business advice to the triad.

The lowest level of triad membership is the *Sze Kau*, denoted by the number 49. These are the common gang members or soldiers.

Figures 9-1, **9-2**, and **9-3** depict the structure and associations of Chinese organized crime in the United States.

All members communicate through secret hand symbols. However, a new method of secret communication may involve the tea ceremony and organization of teacups and the teapot. To date, there has been nothing published that indicates what the various positions mean to triad members.

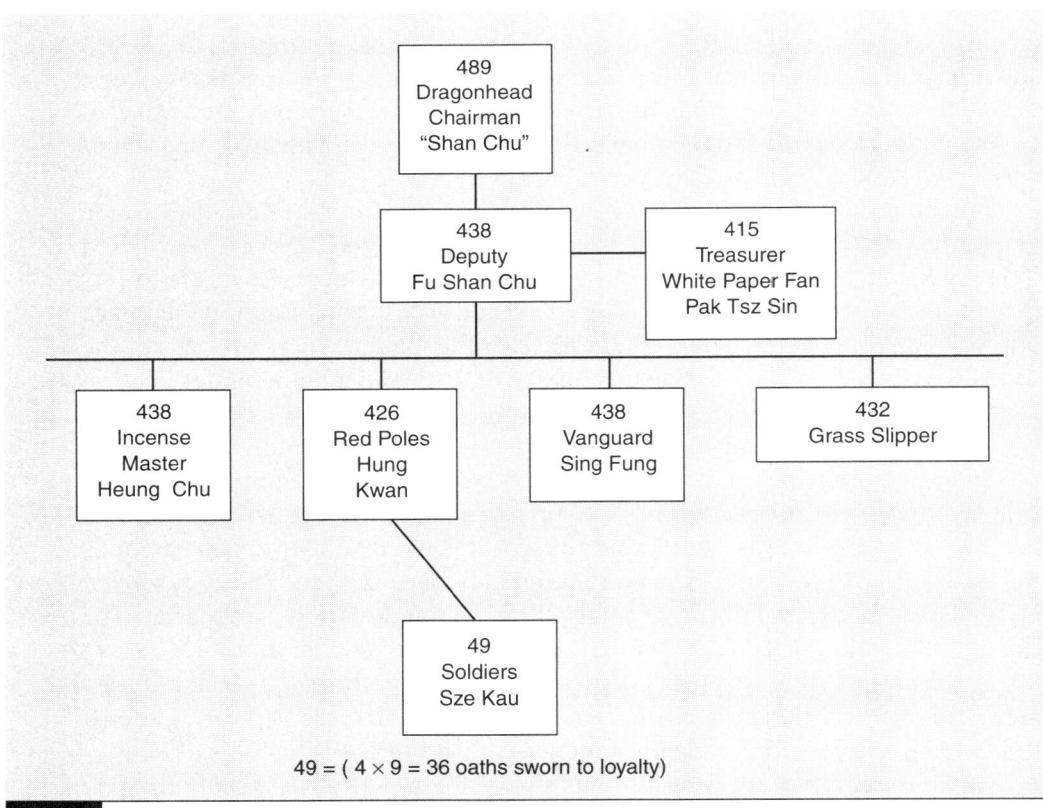

Figure 9-1 Structure of a Triad

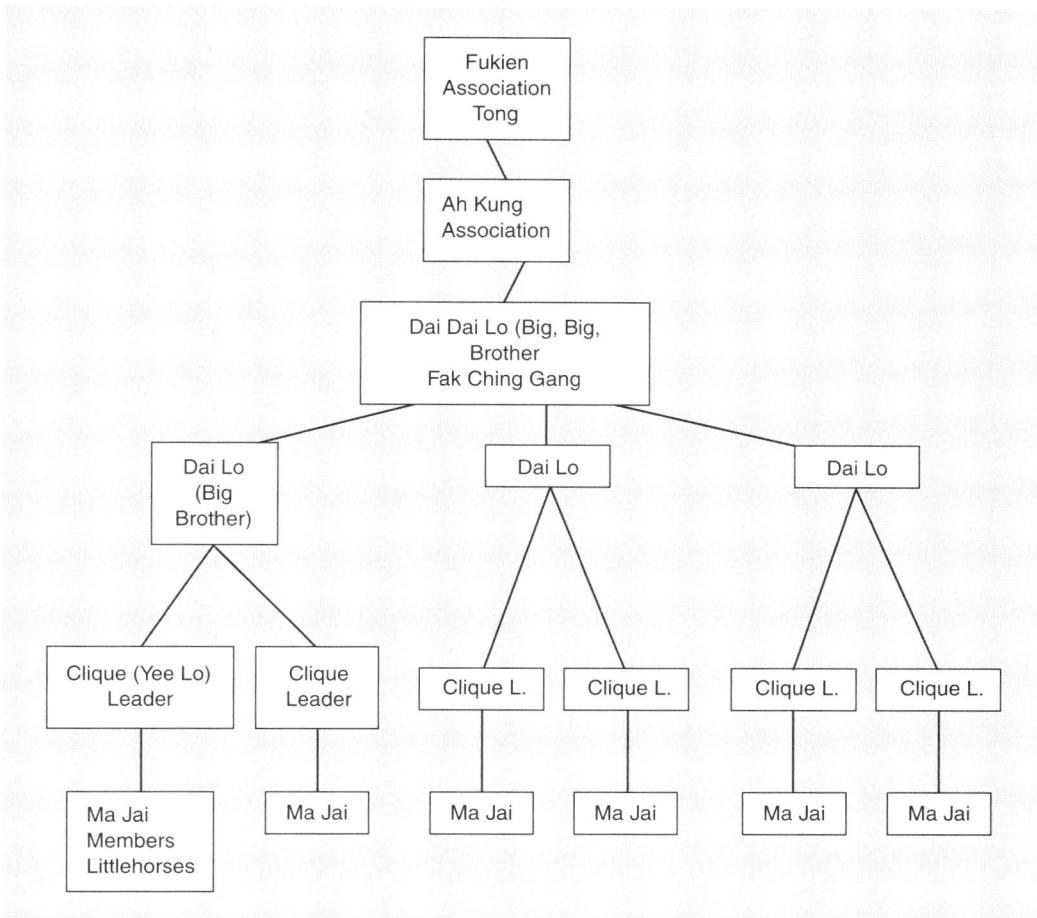

Figure 9-2 Structure and Association of a Tong-Affiliated Gang

Triad members also work in a variety of departments that are not denoted by a number. These include:

- *Accounting*—responsible for the various financial activities of the triad; money laundering is also their responsibility.
- *Recruiting*—Responsible for arranging social activities, developing spies for the triad, and finding new members (some of whom are forced to join the organization).
- *Operations*—Responsible for the drug trafficking and prostitution businesses.
- *Communications*—Responsible for maintaining ties to the other triads and the main lodge in Hong Kong.
- *Training and Welfare*—responsible for ensuring quality martial arts and weapons training. This department also ensures that families of jailed triad members are provided with adequate income for survival, and provides the medical coverage these families may need (Black, 1991). (Note: LCN sometimes practiced this policy for their members who were jailed.)

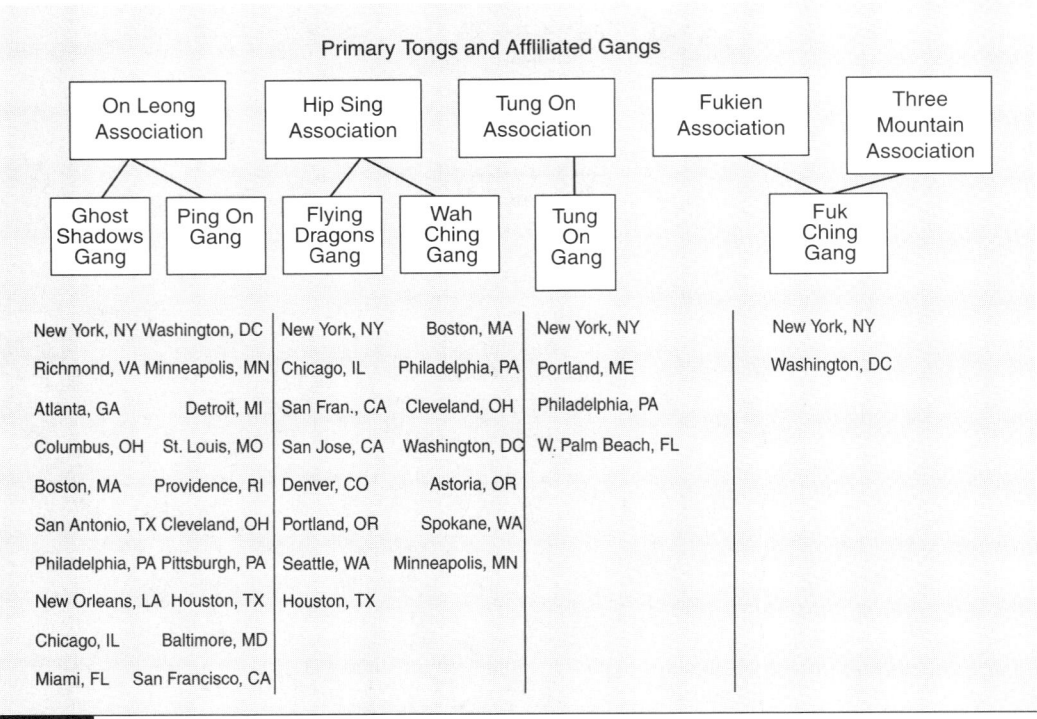

Figure 9-3 Chinese Organized Crime Groups Operating in the United States

The Shan Chu (supreme leader; dragonhead) is usually elected at an annual or biannual meeting; at the same time, the treasurer is also elected. The leader controls promotions along with a committee, supervises internal discipline, and settles disputes. The leader does not control or dictate to members in which criminal activities they will or will not engage.

Tongs

Tongs are structured much like political action groups, as they represent their constituents. The tongs that are involved in criminal activity often use street gangs to provide security for their gambling operations or other criminal activity. A *Dai Dai Lo* may be a tong member and the *Ah Kung* (grandpa) or *Skuk foo* (uncle) will direct operations through the Dai Dai Lo. However, tongs do not have direct control of the gangs, despite that the gangs act out many of the traditions of the triads. The gangs do have the connections to import large quantities of Southeast Asian heroin (also known as *China White*).

The top position in the gang is the *Dai Dai Lo*. Below the Dai Dai Lo is the *Dai Lo*, the *Yee Lo* and the *Ma Jai*. The tongs communicate through the grandfather or uncle. The tongs provide the gangs with meeting places and places to hang out and allow the gangs to operate in their territories, providing opportunities for making money from their criminal enterprises. The major triads do have subgroups. Hong Kong expert on Chinese organized crime, Peter Chong, illustrates the major triads with their subgroups in **Figure 9-4**.

This structure is similar to the OMGs and their puppet clubs. Linking these Chinese subgroups to their triad or tong groups allows the investigator to better understand the operations of triads as well as to employ the strategy of vicarious liability in conspiracy cases (described below).

Using appropriate methods to gather intelligence, the investigator must determine which triads, tongs, and gangs impact his or her jurisdiction. The identity and structure of the organization can serve as a starting point for tactical and strategic planning, but sharing this information with the (presumably secure) officials in the country of origin is also important. Many leaders of these organizations who profit by the criminal activity reside outside the United States. The leaders can be indicted in the United States and in the country where they reside through international cooperation and by employing conspiracy statutes. All triads must have the approval of their headquarters in Hong Kong, Taiwan, or other source countries to establish territory in the United States. These triads operate independently until disputes or major problems occur, which is when the boss at the headquarters will become involved. These subgroups and cell leaders are involved in a variety of complex criminal activities.

■ Activities and Methods of Operations

In many parts of the world, more money is spent on drugs than is spent on food. The heroin market is a major source of revenue for Chinese organized crime, but among other activities of triads, tongs, and gangs are debt collection, prostitution, human smuggling ($30 to $50K per person), loan sharking, gambling, and other narcotics trafficking.

Triad	14K	Chiu Chau	Wo Group	Luan group	Tung group	Chuen Group
Sub Group	Hau	Shing Ye On	Shing Wo	Kung Lok	Kwan Ying	Yat Chee
	Yan	Fukye Hing	On Lok	Lok Tong	Luen She	Chui Ying
	Chun	King Yee	Sing Yee	Ying She	San Wo	Hing Yee
	Tak	Tai Ho Choi	Lee Kwan			
	Mui	Yee Kwan	Lee Wo			
	Tung		Kwan Lok			

Figure 9-4 Major Triads and Their Subgroups

Like other organized crime groups, triads and tongs are moving into legitimate businesses such as banks, the music and entertainment industries, tourists markets, and software, among many others. With their estimated 1.5 million members in China, the triads are dynamic and are expanding rapidly despite the fact that it is a crime in China to be a member of a triad. Many have alliances with both the new government of Hong Kong and illicit organizations such as the Yakuza. It is said that the triads kill their enemies and only maim or injure their victims. They abide by their code of silence and are bonded to their organizations. Often referred to as *dragon syndicates*, their organizations are a serious threat to the United States.

Triads have become transnational and for many reasons it is difficult to determine which is the strongest of the triads. The three reported largest and most powerful are the 14K, the Wo Sing Wo, and the Sun Yee On (Macko, 1997). Major triads in Taiwan include the Sung Lian, Tian Dao, Four Seas, and the United Bamboo. Each of these is considered dangerous to the future of society, but the Sun Yee On is the one Macko fears the most. Citing the triad's adoption of business tactics, he believes that the Sun Yee On are following in the tradition of the Japanese Yakuza, and are currently becoming more and more involved in corrupting the activities of legitimate businesses.

The triad societies still follow a rather unique code of ethics. As an example, Graham (1997) cites the *United Bamboo's Code of Ethics*, which became available when the Los Angeles County Sheriff's Department seized it as a member was attempting to enter the United States. The United Bamboo, considered the strongest triad in Taiwan with over 10,000 members, has expanded internationally and is already established in California and other U.S. states. This code of ethics serves as one example of triad culture and activity.

1. Harmony with the people is the first priority. We have to establish good social and personal connections so as not to create enemies.
2. We have to seek special favors and help from uncommitted gang members by emphasizing our relationship with outside people. Let them publicize us.
3. Gambling is our main financial source. We must be careful how we handle it.
4. Do not take it upon yourself to start things and make decisions you are not authorized to make. You are to discuss and plan all matters with the group and the elder brother first.
5. Everyone has their assigned responsibility. Do not create confusion!
6. We must not divulge our plans and affairs to outsiders, for example to our wives and girlfriends. This is for our own safety.
7. We have to be united with all our brothers and obey our elder brother's orders.
8. All money earned outside the group must be turned over to the group. You must not keep any of it for yourself. Let the elder brother decide.
9. When targeting wealthy prospects do not act hastily. Furthermore, do not harass or threaten them. Act to prevent suspicion and fear upon their part.

10. If anything unexpected happens, do not abandon your brothers. If arrested, shoulder all responsibility and blame. Do not involve your brothers.

Clearly, the above code of ethics indicates that, despite the lack of a single leader as with other organized criminal groups, these triads do have a strict hierarchy. As mentioned earlier, this hierarchical structure gives the investigator the potential to apply vicarious liability for conspiracy cases. Several times in these codes, the individual is instructed to seek the guidance or the permission of the elder brother. Investigators must be aware of this vulnerability.

Secrecy is also paramount to the triads. However, the triad does not appear to be concerned with keeping themselves out of the spotlight, as the rules mention that they must let others publicize them. The code does require the vow of secrecy. Failure to abide by this most likely would end in death for the offender, because the code states that this rule is for the safety of all members.

Currently, the triads are experiencing growth due to a relaxation of state control over many activities of the Chinese people. However, it would be wrong to believe that the Chinese triads are only growing in China. These criminal groups focus on growth wherever there is a chance for financial growth, regardless of the geographic location. Stephen Vickers, head of the Hong Kong police criminal intelligence bureau, writes that the West would be wasting time preparing for the onslaught of Chinese triads in places such as the United States. Vicker is certain that the Chinese criminals who are going to come are already here (Macko, 1997).

There is documented growth of triad activity in other countries such as South Africa. The triads are involved in the illegal growth and export of abalone. Considered a delicacy and an aphrodisiac, this industry is not necessarily illegal, but it is highly regulated in China because of its effects. The triads are secretly exporting the abalone to China, reaping extraordinary prices for their product on the streets. It is likely that this activity in South Africa will result in alliances with organized crime groups in that country. Again, the trend for global alliances is a major challenge for U.S. and other nations' law enforcement. In addition to the abalone trade, triads are focusing worldwide on smuggling, drug trafficking, control of the fish and produce markets, and interestingly enough, control of karaoke bars.

Tongs exist along with triads and other societies or gangs, and contribute to the organized criminal activity in all major cities that have a significant Asian or Chinese population. Chicago has the On Leong and Hip Sing tongs that are major players in heroin trafficking to the United States from the Golden Triangle (Laos, Burma, and Thailand).

The U.S. tongs trafficked in opium and other drugs as well as operated gambling and prostitution rings in New York, San Francisco, and Chicago in the 19th century, and continue these activities to this day. The tongs are also involved in cocaine distribution. The fact that these are secret ethnic societies has limited infiltration and research, so there is a great lack of verifiable intelligence and the precise operations and extent of activity are difficult to determine. There is evidence that extortion, protection rackets, alien smuggling, murder, assault, money laundering, bribery, and corruption are their criminal activities in addition to their tradition of controlling prostitution, drug trafficking, and gambling.

Tongs, like the triads, engage in initiation rituals and have codes, symbols, and rules with punishment for their organization and members. They are well integrated into the culture of the Chinese community and have survived over a hundred years in America because of their method of operations, secrecy, loyalty, and by providing needed services to the community. For a number of reasons, including physical and cultural barriers like racism that separated Chinese immigrants from other settlers, Chinatowns only began to become part of the whole American community after antidiscrimination laws were passed in the 1960s.

But while tongs provided services to the Chinese community, they victimized them as well. Tongs became the unofficial government that provided arbitrary services including a credit and banking structure, schools, and providing for the needy. Tongs are very powerful and influential because of their legal and illegal services to the community (Booth, 2000).

Violence and Intimidation

Violence is part of the power that tongs employ to gain compliance. So-called *hatchet men* use a meat cleaver to chop up and injure their victims, and are feared by the Chinese community. Wounds produced by chopping are a symbol of both the tongs' and triads' retribution for noncompliance.

Because of U.S. restrictions on female immigration in the 1800s, early Chinatowns were predominately male. The tongs and triads (Snakeheads) smuggled young women from China who were deceived into thinking they would have good jobs in America. Known as *sing-song girls*, they were forced into prostitution and produced profits for the tongs.

Tongs are connected to Chinese gangs (Figure 9.3) that formed by the mid-1960s during the wave of large numbers of youths emigrating from Hong Kong. These Chinese gangs became predatory businesses. Tongs employed the gangs to do their dirty work and as security forces for their operations. Often classified as a young form of organized crime (Danner, 1992), gang affiliations produce profits for the tongs through protection fees collected from nearly all of the businesses in U.S. Chinatowns. Tongs do not control the gangs and most alliances are temporary or job-specific.

Turf Wars

Conflicts between tongs, between triads, and between gangs left a wake of violence in the Chinese community. In 1909, On Leong and Hip Sing (New York tongs) were at war over turf and the drug trade. Similar wars occurred in both Chicago and California (Abadinsky, 2003). Chinese gangs have formed against other Asian gangs such as the Vietamese, Viet Ching, and Cambodians. The Chinese Green Dragons' gang and the Vietnamese gang Born To Kill (BTK) are bitter enemies who murder each other, bringing violence to the community. The Big Circle Gang members, who sometimes wear a red arm band symbolizing their history as communist Red Guard militia, have cells in the United States and are involved in a variety of high tech crimes such as credit card fraud, financial crime, and complex theft operations. This gang is also involved in drug trafficking, gambling operations, prostitution, and extortion of the Chinese business community. New York gangs such as the Fuk Ching Tung On, Ghost Shadows, and Flying

Dragons have a capacity for violence that is a defining characteristic. However, these gangs are also involved in legitimate businesses, often owning retail stores, restaurants, video stores, fish markets, and even banks.

Chin (1996) and Finckenauer (2003) found that most Chinese gangs lack the professionalism and sophistication of the triads and tongs. However, Chin and others believe that the gangs are capable of corrupting government officials and police. California's dominate Chinese gangs or groups are the Wah Ching and the Wo Hop To. The triad-affiliated Chinese gangs appear to be expanding their criminal activities into such areas as human smuggling and are becoming more structured in similar ways as that of the triads and tongs. Like other American street gangs (i.e., Bloods, Crips, Vicelords, etc.), Asian gang members have initiations and rituals and wear tattoos that represent their membership in a particular gang. In addition to gang wars, there are gang alliances that evolve around drug distribution or other criminal activity. Asian, Black, Latino, and other youth gangs are often in collusion to make profits from criminal activity. Chinese organized crime is involved in illegal arms, and deal weapons to many gangs; tongs may employ gang members to do contract murders. Armed robberies and auto theft are common activities of Chinese gangs.

Business Investments

Perhaps the tongs' greatest criminal asset is their ability to invest profits from criminal activity into legitimate businesses. Their ability to corrupt both business and government officials makes Chinese organized crime a national threat comparable to other organized crime groups such as the Yakuza and LCN.

Human Smuggling

Zhang and Chin (2002) found in their research that nontraditional criminals are responsible for the majority of human smuggling of Chinese nationals. These groups are not associated with tongs, triads, or street gangs. Chin (1999) found two categories of snakeheads in his research: big snakeheads only invest money and oversee smuggling operations; little snakeheads are the recruiters and middlemen of the operation. These studies indicate that human smuggling is different from the traditional operations of the traditional tongs and triads.

Similar to other organized crime groups, Chinese organized crime is a result of social, economic, and legal conditions. As an ethnic organized group, the "Chinese Mafia" is not a single organization, but a number of groups operating independently but effectively. Although allied, they are often at war.

The centuries-long history of Chinese crime offers the investigator an opportunity to examine the methods of operation and activities to develop a better understanding of these criminals and create strategies for dealing with yet another formidable adversary. Like other organized crime groups, the triads and tongs are driven by profit and power. Alliances between triads to divide tasks between groups are common and efficient. Activities and methods of operation are dynamic. They need to be monitored and their activities and membership updated through effective and continuous intelligence-gathering efforts to ensure intervention by law enforcement. Chinese groups have formed alliances with the Dominican, Mexican, Colombian, and Italian crime groups, and also maintain connections with their origin groups in Mainland China. The ever-expanding nature of Chinese organized crime is a factor that must be considered when examining the trend of transnational organized crime.

Investigative Strategies

Cultural and Language Barriers

One of the biggest problems U.S. law enforcement encounters is the lack of understanding of the Chinese culture. U.S. history has trained the Chinese community to be distrustful of law enforcement and that, combined with intimidation from the crime groups, often deter them from providing information needed for successful investigations. Ambivalence towards the organized criminal activities of the triads, tongs, and gangs exists as well. The investigator must become familiar with the Chinatowns' informal economy, and note which criminal groups serve as providers and protectors while victimizing this economy and culture. Learning one or more Chinese languages will prove greatly beneficial. Factors that must be addressed by U.S. law enforcement include the cultural and language barriers, the community's lack of understanding of the U.S. justice system, and the fear of retaliation by members of the Chinese criminal groups. Gangs have often been successful in intimidating the community not to report, testify, or cooperate in criminal cases. The challenge for American law enforcement is to build the respect and trust among those in the Chinese community by addressing their problems and providing adequate protection for those who do provide assistance. Separation of the criminal element from the culture will require innovative strategies and constant positive contact with the Chinese community.

Criminal tongs, triads, and gang members must be removed from the community and replaced with officers who can provide the security and stability greater than what is now provided by the criminal element. This has proven to be a difficult task. Understanding the complex nature and structure of the tongs and triads, the dynamics of Chinese communities, and the complex nature and history of Chinatown is essential for successful intervention and investigation.

Surveillance and Sting Operations

The law enforcement response to Chinese organized crime includes electronic and physical surveillance, undercover operations, and undercover sting operations. Although the development and recruiting of informants is difficult, many members have cooperated and became witnesses for the government. Similar to LCN members who have violated omerta, Chinese organized crime members face severe penalties (including execution) from statutes such as RICO, CCE, conspiracy, and traditional statues of murder, extortion, and assault among others. The FBI has developed cases on the On Leong gang in Chicago, and the New York, San Francisco, and Los Angeles police departments have developed cases on many individuals in their areas. Although most members failed to cooperate, some did become informants for law enforcement. Insufficient intelligence remains a big problem when investigating triads and tongs. The Chinese organized crime methods of operation and activities are complex and differ from that of LCN, with whom American law enforcement agencies are most familiar. The tongs and triads have not suffered the prosecutions and setbacks like LCN and the OMGs.

Often a member who is under investigation or indictment will flee to China. International cooperation is crucial for not only intelligence sharing, but also extradition and joint investigations between countries. Each agency and individual investigator, in addition to the U.S. government, must develop contacts (including personal contacts) and networks to ensure cooperation with foreign law enforcement.

■ Conclusions

Creation of the international law enforcement academy in Bangkok, Thailand and the International Asian Organized Crime conferences are excellent avenues to develop contacts and networks for cooperation. The FBI Academy and other federal training must continue to be offered to foreign law enforcement to continue to develop understanding and cooperation. China, Macau, and other countries have made progress in addressing organized crime, but there is still much room for improvement. Lack of resources, training, intelligence, and adequate statutes and laws hamper the efforts of many countries. International or transnational task forces are an idea whose time has come in the face of the global organized crime alliances, networks, and cooperation. Interpol was created for data gathering, sharing information, and tracking criminal activity. The next step to creating an international investigative agency seems possible and is certainly needed. The corruption issue would be the major obstacle to the efficacy of such an agency. The U.S. effort itself is fragmented with turf wars and lack of cooperation. An international agency would certainly face the same problem.

Some organizations such as the Big Circle Gang have become so sophisticated that both physical and electronic surveillance are compromised. Perhaps financial investigative strategies will remain effective if the underground financial system used by the Chinese can be identified. Investigators must become more familiar with computer technologies and emerging telecommunications systems where money is moved. The monitoring and interception of communication and money transfer is essential to investigation of organized crime. Information systems must continue to improve to track and monitor organized crime activity of groups such as the triads and tongs. Traditional practices of asset forfeiture, witness protection programs, intelligence collection, and informant development all must be improved in the Chinese community to demonstrate that law enforcement can be effective, to serve and protect the Chinese community. Much of what occurs in the local Chinese community is shaped by events occurring in other countries, states, or jurisdictions within the United States. In the Chinese community, there is an inseparable merging of organized crime, business, and culture.

Understanding the phenomenon of *guanxi* and the concept of *quinqing* is essential to understanding Chinese culture. Because Chinese secret societies have existed for hundreds of years, they have replicated themselves in many parts of the world (including the United States) with great efficiency and efficacy. Like other organized crime groups, they employ violence, long-range planning, and corruption to ensure continuity and effective recruitment. The investigator must understand that each group is formed in the local community, protected by corruption, and engages in providing illegal services and goods to the local market. The networks of Chinese organized crime groups are extensive and global. Identifying their networks and their membership is instrumental to effective intervention and enforcement efforts. Improvements in global communication, transportation, and technology have provided groups like Chinese organized crime the means to become more effective. Law enforcement must take advantage of global networks and improved technology to address the triads, tongs, and others involved in complex criminal activity.

DISCUSSION QUESTIONS

1. Discuss the history of Chinese organized crime. Why is this important?
2. What is the difference between a tong and triad?
3. Discuss the structure of the triads and its importance to investigators.
4. What action would you as an investigator take to address Chinese crime?
5. Discuss the triad culture and its importance to tactical and strategic planning and operations.
6. What are the profitable activities of Chinese organized crime in the United States?

REFERENCES

Abadinsky, H. (2003). *Organized Crime*. Belmont, CA: Wadsworth/Thompson Learning.

Black, D. (1991). *Triad Takeover*. London, UK: Sidgwick and Jackson.

Booth, M. (2000). *The Dragon Syndicates: The Global Phenomenon of the Triads*. New York: Carroll and Graft.

Chin, K. (1996). *Chinatown Gangs*. Oxford, UK: Oxford University Press.

Chin, K. (1999). *Smuggled Chinese: Clandestine Immigration to the United States*. Philadelphia, PA: Temple University Press.

Danner, F. (1992, November). Revenge of the Green Dragons. *New Yorker*.

Finckenauer, J. O. (2003). *Chinese Transnational Organized Crime: The Fuk Ching*. Retrieved December 1, 2006 from: http://www.ojp.gov/nij/international/chinese.html

Graham, J. (1997, April). Taiwan's Triads. *Asia, Inc*. Retrieved December 1, 2006 from: http://orgcrime.tripod.com/taiwanstriads.htm

Macko, S. (1997, December 23). *Chinese Triads: An Update*. Chicago: ERRI EmergencyNet News Service. Retrieved December 1, 2006 from http://www.emergency.com/chi-tria.htm

Raamsdonk, R. V. (2001). *The Triads*. Wing Chun Viewpoint. Retrieved from http://www.wingchun.org/~danlucas.wcw.html

Robinson, J. (1999). *The Merger: How Organized Crime is Taking Over Canada and the World*. Toronto, Canada: McClelland and Stewart Inc.

Zhang, S, & Chin, K. (2002). Enter the dragon: Inside Chinese human smuggling organizations. *Criminology*, 40, 737–809.

10 American Outlaw Motorcycle Gangs

"What we see depends mainly on what we look for."
–John Lubbock

> **Chapter Objectives**
>
> **After completing this chapter, readers should be able to:**
> - Name the major OMGs in the United States and describe how they evolved.
> - Explain the typical structure of an OMG and how this structure is important to law enforcement.
> - Discuss the investigative strategies that are most effective against OMGs.
> - Describe the current trends of activity and method of operation of OMGs.

■ Introduction

Unlike the American Mafia and other organized crime groups, outlaw biker gangs are an American phenomenon. They were not formed for power and profit or greed, but were World War II (WWII) veterans who rejected society's norms as boring and restrictive. Outlaw biker gangs were glamorized in such films as *The Wild Ones*, *Easy Rider*, and *Angels on Wheels* as rebellious groups that wanted to create their own rules and lifestyle. This image has changed to one of gangs oriented toward the profit motive through crime, including regional, national, and international organized crime (Barker, 2004).

Historical Perspective

There is no accurate count of the number of outlaw biker clubs in the United States today; however, the great majority of clubs are not believed to be criminal or organized crime groups (Barker, 2005). Nevertheless, a few have evolved into complex groups that are classified as organized crime. According to the National Alliance of Gang Investigators Association (2005), an estimated 300 active outlaw motorcycle gangs (OMGs) use the motorcycle club as a conduit for criminal enterprises. They vary in membership from fewer than a dozen members in a single chapter to a large number of chapters with thousands of members (Barker, 2005). OMGs are major distributors of illegal drugs and are considered extremely violent in their efforts to control and expand their criminal activities. They are allied with international drug trafficking organizations (DTOs) and may operate through chapters in foreign countries (Barker, 2004).

OMGs conduct much of their criminal activity through puppet clubs, which are groups that are allied with the larger clubs but are not members of the larger club (Barker, 2005). The National Drug Intelligence Center (NDIC) reports that 11.5% of state and local law enforcement agencies indicate OMG involvement in drug distribution is moderate to high in their areas of jurisdiction (HIDTA, 2006). Foreign-produced drugs and precursor chemicals are smuggled from Mexico and Canada by OMGs. The OMGs purchase multi-pound quantities from Mexican DTOs and smuggle the drugs into the United States. OMGs, particularly the *Bandidos*, maintain close relations with prison gangs such as the *Texas Syndicate* to distribute methamphetamine (meth). *Hells Angels Motorcycle Club* (HAMC) members allied with Asian criminal groups were indicted in March 2004 for operating a drug distribution network involving $20 million in high-grade marijuana, known as BC Bud or Quebec Gold to customers in Southern Indiana (Intelligence Bulletin, May 2004). Many OMGs are considered organized crime because of their complex organization, ability to penetrate legitimate business, and launder money through businesses and casinos. The *Pagans* obtain large quantities of illicit drugs from both Colombian and Dominican criminal groups. Most OMGs are including smaller OMGs in their organization ("patching over") and using puppet clubs to carry out much of the diverse criminal activity of OMGs. They are considered organized crime and a considerable challenge to U.S. law enforcement. (Intelligence Bulletin, May 2004).

Post-World War II

The Hells Angels are considered to be the first and most powerful of the groups that were classified as organized crime (Barker, 2005). The Hells Angels begin as a group of California WWII veterans, who named themselves the *Pissed Off Bastards of Bloomington* (POBOB). Early activities of POBOB were acts of vandalism, public drunkenness, fighting, and traffic violations. They considered themselves to be tough guys who had their own rules of behavior. The term "outlaw" was first used by law enforcement officers in California to distinguish lawbreakers such as the POBOB from other law-abiding members of the American Motorcycle Association (AMA).

Rallies and Runs

The outlaw biker image was created at the 1947 Hollister, California motorcycle rally. Yates (1999) wrote that it was at Hollister that outlaw motorcycle gangs (OMGs) made their national debut. Approximately a thousand motorcyclists attended the event, including the clubs formed by the WWII veterans such as the Market Street Commandos, the Pissed Off Bastards of Bloomington, the Galloping Gooses, and the Boozefighters. The rally resulted in the drunken veterans driving the town's six police officers crazy and filling the jails. For some unknown reason, a photographer for the *San Francisco Chronicle* staged a photograph of a drunken motorcyclist that subsequently was printed in *Life Magazine* along with a distorted account of the incident, and the so-called "Hollister Riot" became national headlines (Reynolds, 2000).

Again in 1948, a Labor Day motorcycle rally was held in Riverside, California. Over a thousand motorcyclists attended and the events of Hollister were repeated with tragic results. The rally turned into a riot with one person dead. The violence was blamed on "outlaw" bikers visiting the city, cementing the outlaw motorcycle gang image in the public's eyes.

During the 1950s and 1960s, the OMGs became a symbol of rebellion, freedom, and outrageous deviant behavior. Unlike the American Mafia, their goal was uninhibited behavior and good times rather than profit and power. The earlier events gave rise to a tradition of *runs* by these OMG groups. A run occurs when a group of bikers from one or more clubs travel together on a club-sanctioned road trip by motorcycle to a specific location for some special reason. Some club members will travel up to 20,000 miles per year on different runs. One traditional run, until 2006, occurred on Labor Day weekend to Hollister, California, the site for the Independence Day Rally. The run was cancelled in 2006 for security reasons and its future status is in doubt.

In August each year, the Sturgis Rally occurs with thousands of bikers from many groups attending. This event lasts up to ten days and is the largest run or rally in the United States for OMGs and other motorcyclists. The runs are highly organized into a formation of two motorcycles traveling abreast. Those members belonging to a particular OMG ride in a specific order that includes club officers, members, prospective members, and the club's associates (**Figure 10-1**). Bikers generally are not allowed to carry firearms, drugs, or alcohol on their motorcycles during a run, and usually travel within speed limits. Crash trucks, vans, or cars associated with the club travel a distance in front of or behind the bikes, and those riding in the vehicles may be carrying firearms and drugs as well as sleeping bags, motorcycle parts, alcohol, and police scanners. Women and/or probates (members who are on probation before becoming a full member) usually drive the vans.

Most gangs own their own buildings (clubhouses) as part of the OMG culture that are used for business meetings, motorcycle repair, and partying. Most OMGs disallow drugs, weapons, or stolen goods in the clubhouses, which are

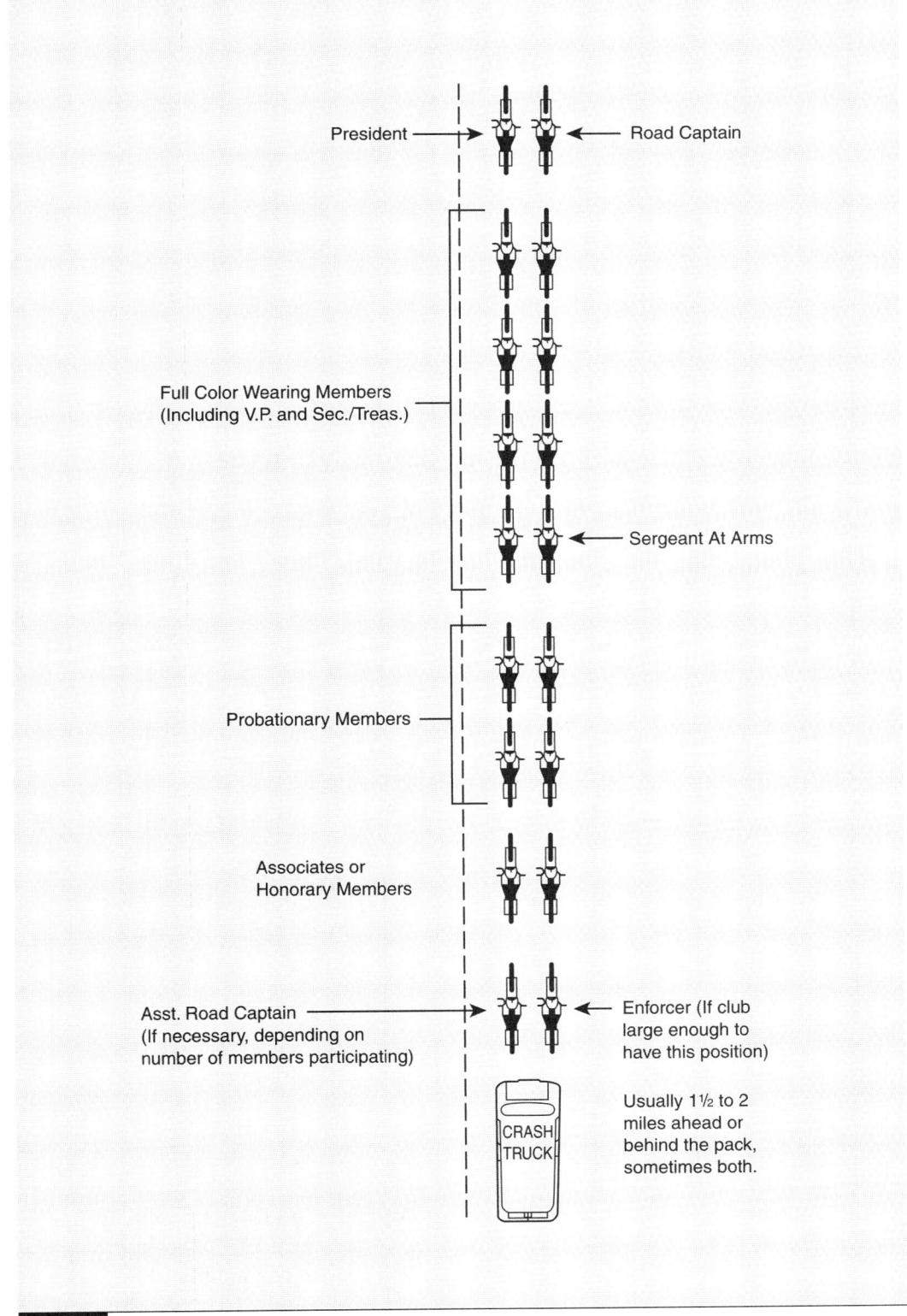

Figure 10-1 Formation and Line Up of a Typical OMG During a Run

guarded by members because of attacks by rival gangs. There are strict rules for behavior in the clubhouses.

Outlaw motorcycle gangs are also known as *one percenters*. AMA president William Berry coined the phrase *one percenter* by declaring that only one percent of motorcyclists in the United States were involved in lawlessness such as the outlaw clubs. This term became a symbol and now appears on the stitched appliqué patches (*colors*) worn by OMG members.

The growing years for OMGs were from 1947 to 1970. During this period, the early outlaw motorcycle clubs patched over other clubs, expanded their territory in the United States and overseas, and moved into drug trafficking, becoming gangs oriented toward profit from crime (Barker, 2004, 2005).

1970 to Today

Nomads, which are roaming members of various chapters, formed alliances with smaller groups and recruited new members throughout California and other areas of the United States in the 1950s and '60s. By the 1970s, the OMGs were structured and had an established leadership. During the 1970s and 1980s, the American drug culture had expanded and the OMGs became a major player in drug trafficking. These groups became more complex and diversified in their criminal activities.

Most biker gangs remain strong white supremacy groups, allowing only white males to become members. Today, there are black and other ethnic OMG members, but the majority of the gangs remain white males only. The goals of OMGs today are profit and power. They remain opposed to society and its laws and wear patches with the *FTW* ("F**k The World") logo. The motorcycle is a symbol of pride, freedom, and power. Most groups require a U.S.-made motorcycle of at least 900cc engines, usually a Harley-Davidson. They've developed their own rules and dress codes. Each member's identity is displayed on his sleeveless denim shirt, leather jacket, or vest. This patch is referred to as *colors*. Each club has a patch design that identifies the club, and each club has very strict rules about wearing, respecting, and placing patches on the clothing. The colors have three sections or *rockers*. The top rocker is usually the club name, the center rocker is the club emblem, and the bottom rocker is the geographic location of the club. Only authorized patches are allowed on the jackets, and loss of colors is a serious offense for members. Some members have the emblem tattooed (mandatory for Hells Angels and some others) on their bodies. Each club demands uniformity with regards to dress, colors, and type of motorcycles.

■ The Big Four

Although there are many OMGs that continue to grow and expand with alliances to other OMGs, law enforcement in the early 1970s recognized the Big Four as the OMGs that most typically exhibit the characteristics of organized crime: Hells Angels, Outlaws, Pagans, and the Bandidos. These groups evolved as paramilitary organizations with a bureaucratic structure (**Figure 10-2**).

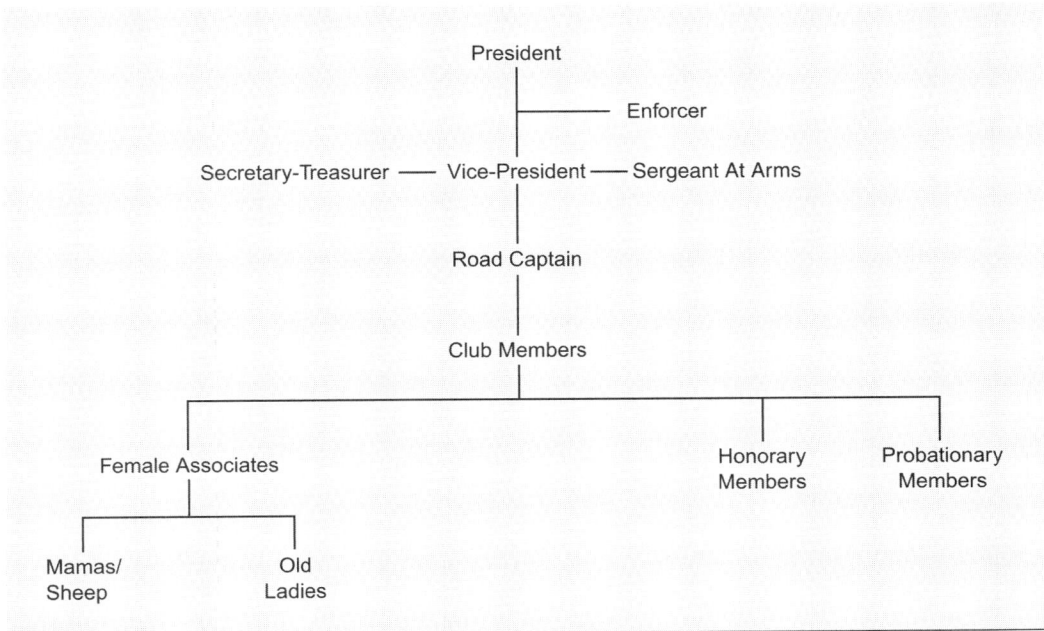

Figure 10-2 Bureaucratic Structure of a Typical OMG

Hells Angels

Members of the POBOBS formed a new gang on March 17, 1948 in San Bernardino, California. The name *Hells Angels* (HAMC) was taken from a WWII bomber plane, which can be seen in their crest that shows a skull with wings. The original chapter was named the "Berdoo" chapter and the Mother Chapter (headquarters and home of the national president) was in San Bernardino, California. In the 1960s, Ralph Hubert (Sonny) Barger, who was then president of the Oakland chapter, became the national president and the Mother Chapter moved to Oakland, California.

Hells Angels expanded during the 1960s and '70s because of national coverage, movies, and even the Vietnam War. Bored veterans returning home became members of biker groups like the Angels. The actual number of HAMC chapters is unknown and probably unknowable by outsiders (Barker, 2005). The club has an estimated 4000 colors-wearing members, with over 100 HAMC chapters, with 65 in North America and 35 in countries outside the United States, including Denmark, Brazil, New Zealand, Canada, Great Britain, Australia, Europe, Japan, and others (Veno, 2002). HAMC is estimated to have over 700 members in the United States (Barker, 2005). Although the number of chapters and members fluctuate, the Hells Angels are considered to be the largest, wealthiest, and most powerful of the Big Four. The Angels serve as a model for other OMGs and have puppet clubs such as the Red Devils Motorcycle Club, whose members assist them in their criminal activities such as drug trafficking.

Canadian law enforcement believes that the Hells Angel motorcycle gang is the most powerful and well-structured criminal organization in Canada (Criminal Intelligence Service, Canada, 2004). A two-year sting operation ended in January

2006 with the arrest of 27 people associated with the HAMC near Thunder Bay. Five of those arrested were patched members.

Outlaws

The *Outlaws* motorcycle club was formed in Chicago, Illinois, in 1935 by John Davis. At that time they were known as the McCook Outlaws Motorcycle Club "out of Matilda's Bar on Route 66 in McCook Illinois outside Chicago" (Barker, 2005). According to their official Web site, the club's name was changed to the Chicago Outlaws in 1950 and in 1965, the club became the Outlaws Motorcycle Club Nation. Their Mother Club was located in Chicago and then moved to Detroit. Since their beginning in 1935, the Outlaws have grown into one of the largest motorcycle clubs worldwide (Barker, 2005). The Outlaws Web site lists 80 chapters in 20 states; it also lists 116 chapters in 14 countries outside the United States. Barker (2005) offers an estimate of membership at 3,900 worldwide.

The Outlaws and Hells Angels have been at war since the late 1960s. Battles over territory and drug markets have escalated to blowing up each other's clubhouses, murders and assaults on members, and the theft of each other's stolen property. The Outlaws frequently have allied with the Bandidos, who are also enemies of the Hells Angels. The Outlaws' colors are a skull over crossed pistols, a graphic known as "Charlie." (Note: This emblem design was from *The Wild Ones* movie, staring Marlon Brando.) Chapters continue to be centered in the Great Lakes, Midwest, Northeast, and Southeast regions including Florida, Wisconsin, Illinois, Kentucky, and Indiana. The club motto is, "God forgives, Outlaws don't." In April 2003, the U.S. District Court of the Northern District of Ohio indicted 38 members of the Outlaws motorcycle gang with charges ranging from murder, drug distribution, firearms violations, to stolen property. The case involved large quantities of illicit drugs confiscated: 800 pounds of cocaine, 500 pounds of marijuana, 100 pounds of meth, 900,000 units of valium, and over 100,000 doses of LSD.

Bandidos

Donald Eugene Chambers in Houston, Texas founded this club in March 1966. Chambers expanded the club in Texas until he was arrested for murder in 1972. In 1974, Ronald Jerome Hodge was elected national president to replace Chambers. However, as with many organized crime leaders, Chambers continued to exert considerable influence from his jail cell.

Power is pluralistic in that it is divided among their elected officers. Like other OMGs, they are a law unto themselves. The club is referred to as the *Bandit Nation*, and they consider themselves separate and independent of the U.S. government. The club motto is: "Bandido by profession, biker by trade, lover by choice," and they describe themselves as "the people our parents warned us about." The colors of the club are yellow, gold, and red. In the center of the colors is the *Mexican Bandido* logo, a pot-bellied cartoon figure wearing a sombrero and brandishing pistols. If a member has been in the group for five years, he is a charter member and is allowed to wear this patch.

Incorporated in Texas in 1978 as a non-profit organization, the club's stated purpose is to provide social activity for its members who have a common interest in large motorcycles. This club has incorporated in other states such as Washington and Alabama, as well. Bandido members must abide by specific rules and by-laws (a sample of which is in the *Club Organization and Rules* section).

The history of the Bandidos is one of escalating violence and criminal activity, and its members have been convicted of almost all serious offenses. Clubs are located in the south, the state of Washington, other regions of the western United States as well as France, Scandinavia, and Australia. Membership is estimated at a total of 3,000 worldwide, with a large number of associates; there are over 80 chapters in 12 countries. Within the United States, the Bandidos have over 700 members and approximately 70 chapters in 14 states. There is evidence of the expansion of chapters with the Utah chapter established in 2003; the president of this chapter has been arrested for suspicion of murder.

In 2006, five members of the Canadian Bandidos were arrested with charges stemming from an in-group massacre. Eight murdered Bandito members were found in their vehicles on a remote farm near London, Ontario, Canada. At first, the Hells Angels were suspected, but later the Royal Canadian Mounted Police (RCMP) implicated fellow Bandidos in an apparent power struggle. In-group killings are not uncommon among OMG groups. As with all organized crime groups, the sense of brotherhood breaks down when power or profit get in the way.

Pagans

Established in 1959 in Prince George County, Maryland by then president Lou Dobkin, Pagan chapters are now located along the eastern U.S. seaboard as well as (New Orleans) Louisiana, Florida, Texas, California, and West Virginia, but is primarily centered in Pennsylvania, New Jersey, and New York. They were a fairly benign group until 1965, when the Pagans evolved into a fierce biker gang with ties to organized crime groups such as the American Mafia (Barker, 2005). Their violence grew under the leadership of John "Satan" Marron in the early 1970s (Lavigne, 1987). There is no evidence of international clubs and their Mother Club is not in a fixed location, but has been generally located in the northeast. Pagan leaders comprise 13 to 18 members who are chapter presidents, with the largest chapter located in Philadelphia. The Pagan membership has been dropping in recent years form law enforcement pressure, competition from other biker gangs (particularly the Hells Angels), and internal dissension (Barker, 2005). The estimated membership is between 600 and 900 patch-wearing members. Their colors show a Norse Fire God.

The Pagans have grown through merging with other smaller OMGs. Considered by law enforcement to be almost as complex and diversified as the Hells Angels, the discipline and structure of the Pagans is the most rigid of the Big Four OMGs. The following is the Pagan Outlaw Motorcycle Clubs' constitution, which explains much of the culture of OMGs.

Pagan Club Organization and Rules

The Pagan motorcycle club is run by the Mother Club. The Mother Club has last and final authority over all club matters. Any violation of the constitution will be dealt with by the Mother Club.

Six (6) members needed to start a chapter. No new chapter may be started without approval of the Mother Club.

President—Runs chapter under the direction of the Mother Club. Keeps chapter organized, makes sure chapter business is carried out, inspects all bikes before runs and makes President meetings.

Sergeant-at-Arms—Makes sure President's orders are carried out.

Vice-President—Takes over all Presidents' duties when the President is not there.

Secretary-Treasurer—In charge of minutes of meetings and treasury. No members may change chapters without the Mother Club members' permission in his area. All present chapter debts are paid and are approved by the president of the new chapter he wishes to change to. If a member has a "snival," he must use chain of command, in other words,

(1) His Chapter President,
(2) Mother Club member in area,
(3) President Club.

Meetings

1. Chapters must have one organized meeting per week.
2. Chapter meetings are attended by members only.
3. Members must be of sound mind (straight) when attending meetings.
4. If a Mother Club member attends a meeting and a member is fouled-up, he will be fined by the Mother Club member.
5. Miss three (3) meetings in a row, and you're out of the club.
6. Members must attend meeting to leave club and turn in his colors and everything that has the name PAGANS on it. (T-shirts, Wrist Bands, Mugs, Etc.).
7. If a member is thrown out of the club or quits without attending a meeting, he loses his colors, motorcycle, and anything that says PAGANS on it, and probably an ass kicking.
8. When a member is traveling, he must attend meeting of the area he is traveling in.
9. If a vote is taken at a meeting and member is not there, his vote is void.
10. Member must have colors with him when attending meeting.

Bikes

1. All members must have a Harley Davidson 750-1200cc.
2. If a member is not of sound mind or to fouled up to ride his motorcycle in the opinion of another member, his riding privilege may be pulled by said member until he has his head together.

3. All bikes must be on the road April 30th, or otherwise directed by the Mother Club.
4. All members must have a motorcycle license.

Mandatories

Two (2) mandatories, July 4, and Labor Day; Mother Club may call additional mandatories if need be.

Funerals

1. If a member dies in a chapter, it is necessary for all members in his chapter to attend his funeral.
2. Chapter is in charge of taking care of all funeral arrangements, parties, police, procession, etc.

Parties

Pagan parties are Pagan parties only. Each chapter must throw (1) party or run a year.

Respect

1. Respect is to be shown to all Mother Club members, officer members, member's personal property, Bike, Old Lady, House, Job, etc. In other words, if it's not yours, "Don't Mess With It."
2. No fighting among each other is allowed, any punches to be thrown will be done by the Sgt.-at-Arms or a Mother Club Member.
3. No stealing from members.
4. Respect your Colors.

Colors

1. President gets colors from Mother Club member in area when new member is voted in.
2. When a member leaves club, the president of his chapter turns over his colors to the Mother Club member in his area.
3. Respect your Colors, don't let anyone take them from you except the president of your chapter or a Mother Club member.
4. No colors are worn in a cage, except during funerals and loading or unloading a bike from a truck.
5. Nothing will be worn on the back of your jacket except your colors, Diamond, 13 Patch.
6. No Hippie s--t on the front.
7. Colors are to be put on cut off denim jackets only.
8. The only member who may keep his colors if he leaves the club is a Mother Club Member.

Old Ladies
1. Members are responsible for their Old Ladies.
2. Members may have more than one (1) Old Lady.
3. Members may not discuss club business with their Old Lady.
4. No Old Ladies allowed at meetings.
5. No property patch is worn on an Old Lady. So if you see a chick you better ask before you leap.

Prospects
1. Prospect must be at least 18 years old.
2. Prospect must be sponsored by one member who has known him at least one year.
3. Sponsor is responsible for prospect.
4. Prospect must have motorcycle.
5. Prospect must ride his bike to meeting at time of being voted into club.
6. Prospect cannot do any drugs.
7. Prospects cannot carry weapons at meetings and Pagan functions, unless otherwise directed by the president.
8. No stealing from Prospects.
9. Prospects must attend all meetings and club functions.
10. Prospect must do anything another member tells him to, that a member has done or would be willing to do himself.
11. Prospect must be voted in by all members of the chapter and Three (3) Mother Club Members.
12. Prospect must pay for his colors before receiving them.
13. Prospects period is determined by the Mother Club Member.
14. Pagans M.C. is a motorcycle club and a non-profit organization.

■ Other OMGs

Although the Big Four are considered the most formable threats, many smaller OMGs are involved in what can be classified as organized crime activity. The structure, method of operation, activities, and culture of these smaller OMGs are very similar to those of the Big Four. Many of these smaller OMGs act as puppet clubs for the Big Four or as their co-conspirators in illegal activities. A partial list of other independent clubs/gangs includes the Pistorellos, Warlocks, Vagos, Sons of Silence, Iron Horseman, Mongols, Grim Reapers, Kingsman, Red Devils, Ghost Riders, Diablos, Devils Disciples, Galloping Goose, and El Forastero.

These smaller OMGs are often involved in significant criminal activity. For example, the former national president of Diablos OMG was given a life sentence in U.S. court in 2002 for his role in the distribution of 40 pounds of meth in Indiana. In December 2005, several members were arrested on drug and weapon trafficking violations in Connecticut.

Grim Reapers

The Grim Reapers OMG is typical of an independent OMG, with a 44-year history and chapters in Tennessee, Iowa, Illinois, Kentucky, and Indiana. Considered an ally of the Outlaw OMG, the Grim Reapers (GRMC) has ties to the KKK (Ku Klux Klan) and state militia groups. This OMG is an advocate of white supremacist beliefs and is considered extremely violent. Grim Reapers OMGs in Canada are independent of the U.S. club and are allied with Hells Angels, with some chapters becoming Hells Angels' chapters.

The origin of Grim Reapers is believed to have begun in 1959 in Louisville, Kentucky. Like other OMGs, the Grim Reapers are involved in distribution of large quantities of illicit drugs, stolen motorcycles and other vehicles, money laundering, mail fraud, and firearms violations. Much like the Big Four, the GRMC has national rules that govern conduct, membership, and operations.

Officials in the club are national and located in the northern and southern regions; their national president is elected to a two-year term. Clubhouses, normally a residence, serve as meeting locations and are most often found in remote and well-fortified areas. There are two mandatory national runs and two regional runs each year. High-level meetings are called *presidentials*, where each chapter and regional president has one vote.

The structure of the GRMC is depicted in **Figure 10-3**. Membership has varied from 70 to 200 with the Mother Chapter located in Louisville. Similar to the Pagan rules (above), GRMC members must be 18-years-old, not be African American, and must own a 1000cc American-made motorcycle. During the clubs' probationary period, prospects are subjected to intense physical and mental abuse. As part of the proof they are not law enforcement, prospects often must commit crimes and provide an address for the next of kin.

GRMC colors are highly regarded (as with all OMGs), and the logo shows a red-shrouded Grim Reaper holding a red scythe. Club tattoos are required for members and are located on an arm after three years and on their back after eight years of membership. Members cannot be drug addicts, and must pay 10% of profits of drug sales and any profits from criminal activities to the treasurer of the club as a *road tax*; this money is split between the national, regional, and chapter treasuries.

It is probable that the GRMC will be absorbed into one of the larger OMGs, such as the Hells Angels, and continue to be involved in criminal activities, primarily drug distribution, smuggling, and theft. Law enforcement lacks information; such as expansion of chapters. Although not the same threat as the Big Four, clubs such as the GRMC are a concern for law enforcement and should be a focus for intelligence and law enforcement efforts (Intelligence Bulletin, April 2004).

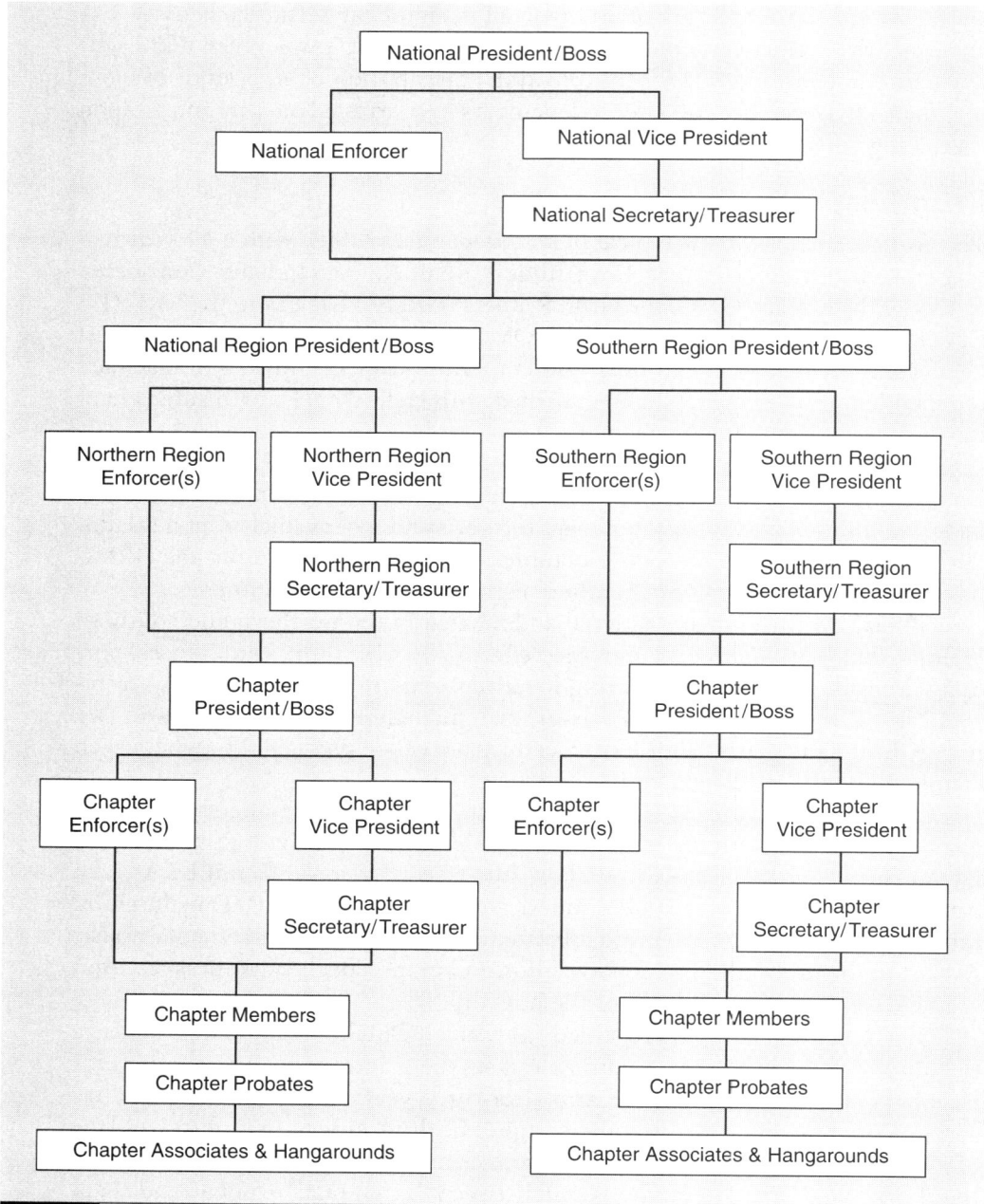

Figure 10-3 Organizational Structure of the Grim Reapers Outlaw Motorcycle Gang

■ Structure

Membership

OMGs are paramilitary organizations with a bureaucratic structure. **Figure 10-4** shows the chain of command within a typical OMG. An ecological map of the

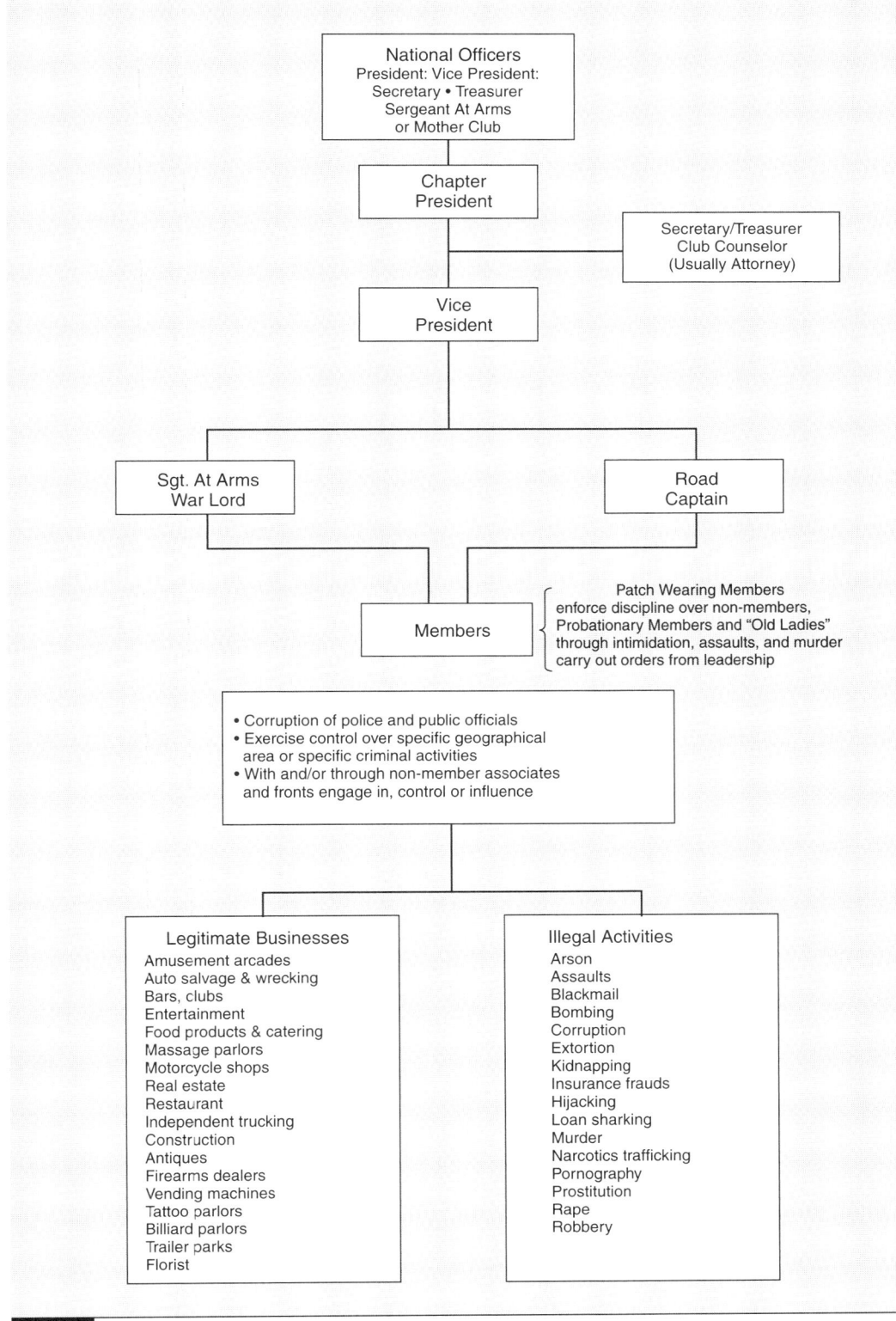

Figure 10-4 Typical Structure of a Major Outlaw Motorcycle Gang Chapter

social structure among members is illustrated in **Figure 10-5**. The leader (national president) rules from the Mother Club (national headquarters). Chapters and regional representatives are selected in each geographic territory of the club. These OMGs insulate the leaders from criminal activity through layers of members, puppet club members, probates, associates, and biker women. All major problems are submitted to the Mother Club or national leaders. Each club has its own elite enforcement unit: The "SS" for the Outlaws, The "Filthy Few" or "Death Squad" for the Hells Angles, The "Black T-Shirt Squad" for the Pagans, and the "Nomad Chapter" for the Bandidos. These elite enforcement groups operate from chapter to chapter and serve as the "hit men" and "fixers" for the club.

Biker women are treated as property and wear colors with the inscription "Property of (club name)." There seems to be no shortage of available women to become *old ladies*, *mamas*, or *sheep*. Often forced to work as prostitutes, dancers, or masseuses to support biker or OMG members, biker women are abused frequently and are considered property of the club. Most are initiated into the OMG by undergoing a "gang bang" (rape by most members). Mamas or sheep belong to the entire club and are expected to submit to sexual activity at any time with any member. Although they do not attend club meetings, they do work at the clubhouse as needed. Women referred to as old ladies belong to only one club member and cannot be touched by another member without reprisal; they do not attend club meetings. Biker women frequently provide housing for club members and work regular jobs for the member(s) to provide income. These women often drive the crash truck during runs. Because they often carry guns or drugs for the members, these women present a danger to anyone including law enforcement.

Biker women often are used to gather intelligence. One way to provide this service is their employment in strategic locations such as utility companies, telephone companies, and police departments. Operating in places such as court houses, law offices, and licensing agencies provide these women with opportunities to falsify documents and create new identities as well as monitor law enforcement and task force efforts.

During the 1970s, the attempt at legitimacy by the four major OMGs in their home communities resulted in formal charters with rules and by-laws. Each club now has a constitution and by-laws (the Hells Angels' by-laws are listed in this chapter).

As seen in Figure 10-5, each chapter president makes decisions about all club business and can overrule any decision voted on by chapter members. The vice president fills in when the president is absent. Bandido, Pagan, and Outlaw OMGs have a national president and four regional vice presidents. The Pagan's Mother Club is comprised of 13 to 18 former chapter presidents, who wear the number 13 on black T-shirts with their colors to signify their leadership position. Currently, the Hells Angels are divided into the east and west coast divisions. Presidents of the chapters meet to discuss runs, club business, and admitting new chapters. Criminal activity is not discussed at these sanctioned club meetings.

Each club has a secretary/treasurer who keeps minutes of club meetings, collects dues and fines, and keeps all business records for the club. The national secretary answers to the national president, handles national violations, and keeps business records. He also may serve as a bodyguard to the president. Order is kept by the sergeant-at-arms and he often doubles as the enforcer and "hit man" for

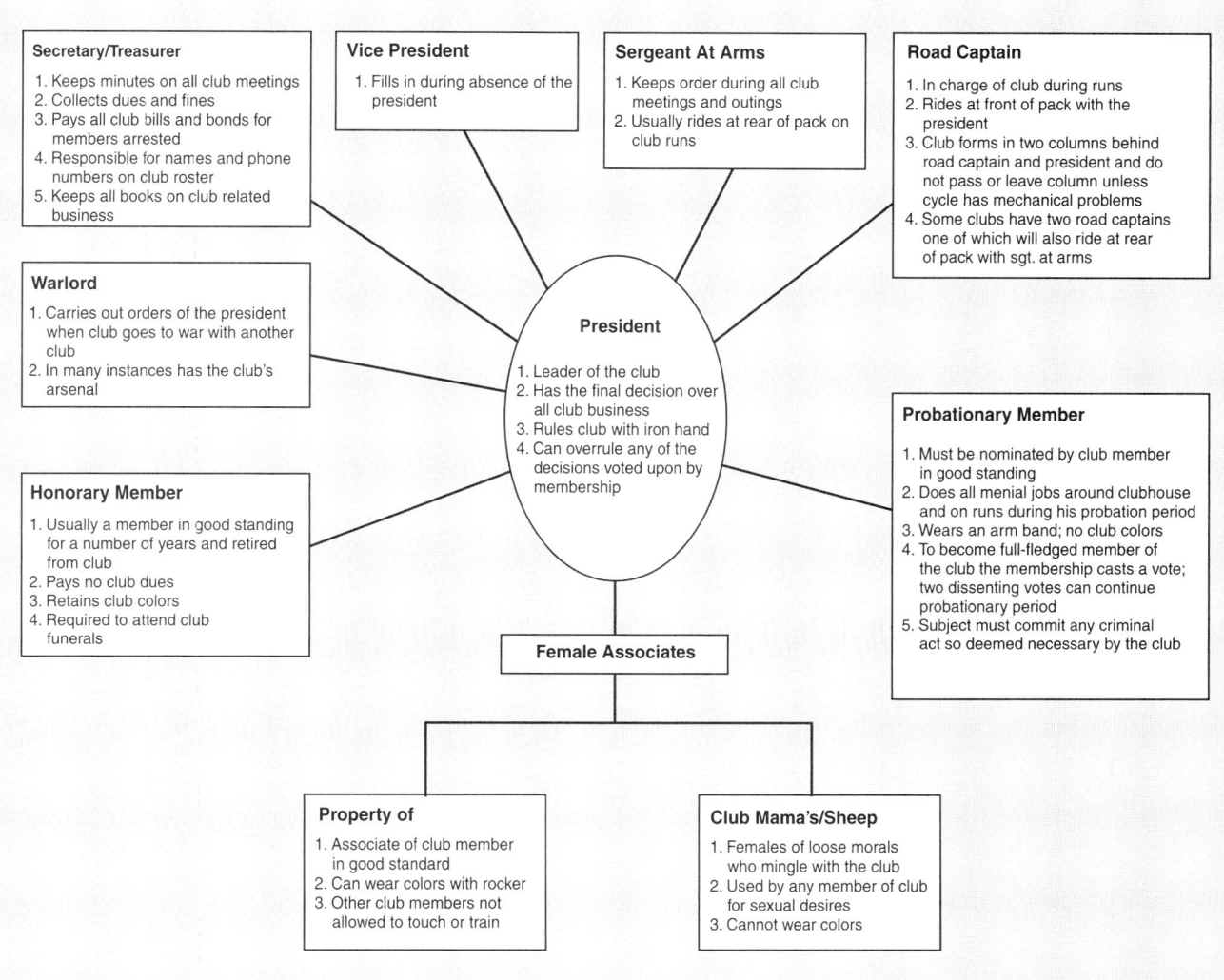

Figure 10-5 Social Interrelationships and Responsibilities among Typical Outlaw Motorcycle Gang Members

the chapter. The warlord keeps the weapons for the chapter and works directly for the chapter president. The road captain plans the runs, which includes security, logistics, and supplies.

Each chapter may have a clubhouse where club business is discussed and parties are held. Some have referred to the meetings in clubhouses as "church" (Tretheway and Katz, 1998). The Hells Angels have a "Church of Angels" with ministers, which allows them to visit incarcerated members as well as providing the club with tax exemptions. Clubhouses are frequently secured by both interior and exterior security, steel doors, special locks, safes, barbed wire, chain-link fences, guard dogs, armored plating, burglar alarms, surveillance cameras, police scanners, booby traps, and a variety of high-tech anti-intrusion devices. Turf wars against rival gangs as well as infiltration by law enforcement keeps them alert for intrusion.

Hells Angels' California By-Laws

1. All patches will be the same on the back, nothing will show on the back except the HELL ANGELS PATCH. City patch is optional for each chapter. 1 patch and 1 membership card per member. Member may keep original patch if made into a banner. Prospects will wear California rocker on back and prospect patch left from where top of pocket is on a Levi jacket.
   FINE: $100 for breaking above by-law.

2. No hypes. No use of Heroin in any form. Anyone using a needle for any reason other than having a doctor use it on you will be considered a hype.
   FINE: Automatic kick-out from club.

3. No explosives of any kind will be thrown into the fire where there is one or more HELLS ANGELS in this area.
   FINE: Ass-whipping and/or subject to California President's decision.

4. Guns on CA runs will not be displayed after 6 pm. They will be fired from dawn until 6 pm in a predetermined area only. Rule does not apply to anyone with a gun in a shoulder holster or belt that is seen by another member if it is not being shot or displayed.
   FINE: $100 for breaking above by-law.

5. Brothers shall not fight with each other with weapons; when any HELLS ANGELS fights another HELLS ANGELS, it is one on one; prospects same as members. If members are from different chapters, fine goes to CA Treasurer.
   FINE: $100 for breaking above by-law or possible loss of patch.

6. No narcotics burns. When making deals, persons get what they are promised or the deal is called off.
   FINE: Automatic kick-out from club.

7. All HELLS ANGELS fines will be paid within 30 days. Fines will be paid to that chapter's treasurer to be held for the next CA run.

8. One vote per chapter at CA officer's meetings. For CA 2 no votes instead of a majority to kill a new charter and a charter goes below 6 they must freeze or dissolve on the decision of CA Officers' Meeting.

9. If kicked out, must stay out 1 year then back to original chapter. HELLS ANGEL tattoo will have an in-date and out-date when the member quits. If kicked out HELLS ANGELS tattoo will be completely covered with a ½ X through the tattoo.

10. Runs are on the holidays; 3 mandatory runs are Memorial Day, July 4th, and Labor Day.
11. No leave period except hospital, medical or jail.

OMGs have restricted membership, with members paying dues. A probationary member or prospect must be nominated by a club member in good standing who has known the prospect for at least a year. Prospective members perform menial jobs at the clubhouse and on runs. The prospect must commit whatever criminal act is deemed necessary by the club. Once a period of time has passed, and he has completed all requirements and demands by the club, the prospect is voted in by the members. Rituals for initiation are disgusting and often involve humiliating acts. These rituals or initiation rites vary from club to club. The prospect may be allowed to wear an armband with the club's colors during the probationary period.

Honorary members are those who have retired and are usually in good standing (see below).

All members, prospects, and honorary members are required to attend runs, funerals, and sanctioned meetings. The larger clubs or OMGs invest a portion of their profits into legitimate business, which then become club assets. Many members are employed, some as lawyers, famous entertainers, and a variety of white collar professions. Membership has evolved from mostly war veterans to a variety of backgrounds, but most are from the criminal element of society. For every colors-wearing member, there are approximately ten associates who serve the club's interests.

Retirement By-Laws

Very little is known about aging OMG members, but it is clear that most of the Vietnam veteran era members are facing retirement. Those who have survived the gang's brutality and escaped prosecution must follow a set of rules, just as regular members.

The following list of regulations applies to OMG retirees:

1. You cannot change a by-law at anytime. (No ands –ifs or buts, no exceptions).
2. After five years of active duty, you automatically keep your rag. Plus, you still must serve two and a half years on mandatory runs and other mandatory get-togethers.
3. You have to make four runs a year. (This is mandatory).
    A. Steve Jamail is one run that you must be there or you will be fined $50.00.
    B. Also, you can pick any other three mandatory runs of your choice.
    C. If any mandatory runs are missed, you will automatically be fined $50.00 for every run that you do miss.
4. If any mandatory runs are missed, you are fined for it. Also, if you are unable to pay the money you owe, the club can take your color and keep it until you can pay up.

5. After seven and a half years, you are automatically retired; or you have an option of staying in the club.

6. After retirement, you do not have to be at any meetings but you still must pay your dues.

7. After five years, you still have to pay whatever dues the club may have in effect at that time.

■ Activities and Methods of Operation

As stated earlier, OMGs are very sophisticated in their counter-surveillance techniques and security employed to protect their criminal activity against rival gangs and law enforcement. Although drug trafficking is their most common and profitable criminal activity, their other criminal activities include: robbery, extortion, murder, arson, receiving stolen goods, white slavery, prostitution, rape, weapons trafficking, and assaults.

■ Networks

OMGs have a history of criminal relationships with LCN. The Hells Angels have done work for the Gambino crime family of New York and Cleveland. The Pagans have been associated with LCN families on the east coast, and have been used as enforcers for groups such as the Bruno crime family and Philadelphia Mafia crime boss, Joey Merlino.

Cocaine, methamphetamine, and marijuana were the original drugs trafficked by OMGs; however, today the OMGs will venture into any market that has the potential for profit. In 1986, the President's Commission on Organized Crime estimated that OMGs earned over $1 billion a year from drug trafficking and other criminal activities. OMGs have supported Mafia strip clubs by supplying women as dancers. OMGs also have taken on legitimate businesses that act as fronts for criminal activity and avenues for money laundering, much like that of the traditional Mafia groups.

OMGs control their networks by violence and intimidation of members, rivals, and potential witnesses. A current trend among OMGs is the employment of puppet clubs to conduct the criminal activity for the sponsor club. In Mississippi, the Pistorellos have seven chapters that are associated with the Bandidos' criminal activities. These puppet clubs take most of the risk and return most of the profits to the more powerful OMG members. This trend, along with the trend of Mafia associations, has allowed the OMG to expand their influence and become more diverse in both their legal and illegal enterprises.

Many of the associates act as a layer of security from prosecution and provide such services as clandestine laboratory operators, chemists for illicit drug labs, contract murderers, money launderers, and suppliers of weapons, chemicals, and high tech equipment. Attorneys who represent OMG members often help secure information regarding witnesses, who are then threatened with violence, injured, or killed. Like the Mafia, OMG have used methods of bribery and corruption by means of money, surveillance, drugs, or sex to obtain information or favors for the enterprise. Today, OMG members are much more sophisticated than those of the original clubs. More educated and manipulative, they are adept at using the criminal justice system and technology to their advantage.

Angie Wagner (2002) reported on the April 2002 fight between the Hells Angels and Mongols at Harrah's Casino in Laughlin, where three men were killed. The investigation revealed that the Hells Angels were using high tech equipment (such as night vision and quality weapons) to aid in their retaliation for the killing of Hells Angels member, Christian Tate. A large amount of ammunition and a number of weapons were confiscated in a raid connected to this investigation. Although OMGs have become more educated and sophisticated, events such as this are indicators that violence, revenge, and the outlaw behavior remain an integral part of OMG culture.

Similar to the Colombian DTOs, street gangs, and the American Mafia, OMGs sometimes change their public image from one of outlaw group to that of a service type of organization that assists the community in good causes and charities. Like Al Capone feeding the hungry in Chicago, the OMGs have taken on behavior that makes them popular with the public. This garners favorable public support and decreases law enforcement attention.

Although OMGs have diversified their criminal activities, drug trafficking remains their primary source of income. The use of counterintelligence and infiltration of government and business has allowed some OMGs to rival such groups as the American Mafia in power and wealth in a particular region.

■ Investigative Strategies

Intelligence

The most important aspect of investigating OMGs is gathering intelligence to prove that these groups are actually a criminal enterprise engaged in a pattern of racketeering. The collection, analysis, and dissemination of accurate and timely information are keys to developing strategies to address OMG criminal activity. It takes a team effort to gather the right information and then implement a strategy for effective enforcement.

The first step is to identify the structure of the OMG and the members who occupy positions in the structure. Intelligence must identify this structure as a criminal enterprise. Because OMGs are considered a group involved in conspiracy to commit criminal activity, RICO, conspiracy, and money laundering statutes can bring the entire membership to trial as well as capture their assets.

The investigator must identify the associates, women, and puppet clubs who are an integral part of the club's criminal activities. During the intelligence gathering activity, investigators also must identify all connections with white supremacy groups, prison gangs, Mafia associates, street gangs, and any groups or individuals who are receiving services or goods or providing them to OMGs. This amount of information can only be gathered with interagency cooperation and by task/force or strike/force operations.

The creation of joint task forces and the Organized Crime Drug Enforcement Task Forces (OCDETF) in 1982 has proven to be the most effective approach to successful investigations of OMGs. Such organizations as the National Alliance of Gang Investigators Associations is a tremendous asset to investigators for networking, developing contacts for assistance, and remaining current on OMG trends and activities. Information and identity of OMG members is much less difficult to obtain than the Mafia because of their public persona. OMGs exhibit themselves openly during their mandatory runs, established clubhouses, and frequent parties or meetings. Numerous investigator organizations hold frequent conferences where training, education, and networking occurs. These working conferences should be part of any investigator's schedule.

Intelligence gathering is not without enormous risks to the agents as well as the informants. A few club members have agreed to divulge club activities after being faced with jail terms and/or committing a particularly heinous crime. Deep undercover agents often must participate in crimes to preserve their subterfuge, and some obfuscate or outright lie to their handlers, which can result in an operation going out of control. One Arizona sting ("Black Biscuit") in 2003 found that the informer, Solo Angeles biker president Rudy Kramer, also continued to operate a meth lab and deal in weapons; he also brought a woman to a club party where she was subsequently murdered (Sher and Marsden, 2006). Despite that the Hells Angel's organization was shaken in many western states, the tangle of court cases for Black Biscuit is still unraveling.

Laws and Statutes

Two of the more common criminal violations of OMGs are firearms violations and illicit drug trafficking. Federal statutes provide mandatory sentences for carrying or using a firearm during the commission of a felony (Title 18 U.S.C. Section 924). The Continuing Criminal Enterprise (CCE) statute (Title 21 U.S.C. 848) is very potent against supervisors, financiers, organizers, or managers of drug trafficking organizations such as the OMGs. Combine these with RICO (18 U.S.C. 1961-68) and investigators have an effective arsenal to use against OMGs. Both criminal and civil RICO can be used against members and assets of the OMGs. Add the federal money laundering laws, (CTR, CMIR violations, the Money Laundering Act of 1986, The Money Laundering Prosecution Improvement Act of 1988, etc.), and the investigators have no excuse not to prosecute OMGs members, both individually and as an enterprise. These statutes are discussed in Chapter 12.

The Financial Crimes Enforcement (FinCen), created in 1990 under the Department of Treasury, is an excellent resource to use during money laundering investigations. The El Paso Intelligence Center is another excellent resource for following the money when conducting investigations of OMGs. The U.S. Treasury Department's TECSII System is an additional resource for tracking the criminal activities of OMGs. Currently, the Patriot Act is the broadest money laundering statute and has expanded the scope of money laundering investigations; the definition of illegal money-transmitting business was expanded as has the concept of specified unlawful activity.

In addition to becoming members of task forces and networking with other entities, the development and proper management of informants can provide the evidence of structure and criminal activity for an OMG to be classified as a criminal enterprise. Informants are very difficult to develop in OMGs because of the expectation of violent reprisals (including murder of themselves and their families) as punishment for anyone who provides information to law enforcement. Although Confidential Informants (CIs) have been very effective on occasions, they are difficult to control, protect, and develop. Often the CI can only provide limited information about the enterprise.

Both electronic and physical surveillance can be extremely valuable to the investigation. However, placing a listening device in the right location at the right time can be problematic because the area is often secured by both physical and electronic security and counter-surveillance measures. Identifying the proper location where valuable information can be intercepted (which phone, vehicle, business, clubhouse, or home) can be time consuming and dangerous. Undercover operations also have been successful (Hells Angels, Bandidos, Outlaw, and other U/C operations) but are long-term, expensive, and require a great deal of risk by highly trained officers (Sher & Marsden, 2006).

Developing intelligence for prosecution requires enormous resources and time. In the case of OMGs, external and international cooperation is a frequent requirement. Other programs not previously mentioned, such as the Regional Information Sharing System (RISS) and the High Intensity Drug Trafficking Areas (HIDTA), can be additional valuable resources against OMGs.

Grand Juries

As the investigation is certain to be long term, the use of the investigative grand juries can be extremely beneficial. The subpoena power and grant of immunity are useful during the investigation. Educating a jury gradually empowers them to synthesize the complex information and allows for a higher probability of an indictment. The intelligence analyst's role is critical so the enormous amount of data can be organized and summarized in a fashion that clearly defines the enterprise, provides a logical chronology of events, and details the illegal scheme/scam and money laundering activities. The adage, "follow the money" remains one of the best investigative strategies for proving the existence of a criminal enterprise. A flow chart of conversations and dates/times of phone calls is very enlightening to juries, because it can demonstrate correlations of criminal activity when combined with electronic surveillance videotapes.

There are dozens of statutes concerning drug trafficking at the state and federal levels that can be used to investigate OMGs (see Chapter 12). Any criminal violation discovered must be noted as a possible avenue for prosecution. However, taking all the assets, members, and associates to court is the only possible means to completely destroy the enterprise. RICO, money laundering, and conspiracy charges are the best avenues for near total destruction of OMGs.

The traditional Uniform Crime Reporting (UCR) Index Crimes of arson, assault, murder, theft, and robbery are additional avenues for developing prosecutable cases or proving a pattern of racketeering activity of a criminal enterprise. Crime scene investigations must be complete, using all available means to collect and analyze evidence to prove these traditional crimes by connecting violators, crime scene, and victims.

Because drug distribution and production will continue to be a major source of income for OMGs, there is a trend to ally with smaller OMGs and major criminal enterprises such as the Mexican DTO, the profits from which will strengthen these organizations both domestically and internationally. Larger and more powerful OMGs are likely the trend for the near future. Lack of intelligence remains a concern, including the extent of alliances among OMGs, their U.S. and foreign chapters as well as between other organized crime groups, and sources of weapons that OMGs are stockpiling.

■ Conclusions

In the end, it is the ability, perseverance, and fortitude of the investigators and their teams that brings about a successful prosecution of the OMG. They will find a way to address such a national threat as the OMG. The work of the team collects, develops, and presents evidence to juries, who will make their decisions based on the evidence and competency of the investigators.

Outlaw biker gangs will continue to expand with consolidation of many smaller gangs into the major groups. The trend of puppet clubs will continue, with some of these clubs becoming a major player and breaking away from their sponsoring club. Outlaw biker clubs will expand more into legitimate businesses and, like the Yakuza, abandon many of the traditions of the past. These trends will make the outlaw bikers more of an enterprise that, while criminally oriented, will be more difficult for law enforcement to address.

Rivalries will continue between the major clubs, but alliances will also occur between clubs and other organized crime groups. OMGs will expand their use of technology to increase their efficacy. Their growth is likely to expand to more groups than the Big Four for law enforcement to target. The future of OMGs will depend on their ability to evolve into a more complex structure, adding more layers between members and their criminal activities, and using Hollywood-type glamour to recruit new members as well as infiltrate legitimate business, as the Yakuza and Mafia have done, especially in the last two decades. If the OMGs become more diverse and form alliances with other organized crime groups, they will continue to grow both in membership and power.

DISCUSSION QUESTIONS

1. List and discuss the major OMGs in the United States. How did they evolve?
2. What is the typical structure of an OMG? Why and how is this structure important to law enforcement?
3. What criminal activities do the OMGs commit? What are the most profitable for these groups?
4. What investigative strategies are most effective against OMGs?
5. Which parts of the Patriot Act are most effective against organized crime such as OMGs? How can they be applied?
6. What are the current trends of activity and method of operation of OMGs?

REFERENCES

Barker, T. (2004). Exporting American Organized Crime—Outlaw Motorcycle Gangs. *Journal of Gang Research*, 11(2) 37–50.

Barker, T. (2005). One-Percent Bikers Clubs: A Description. *Trends in Organized Crime*, 9(1) 101–112.

Criminal Intelligence Service Canada. (2004). *Organized Crime in Canada: Annual Report.*

High Intensity Drug Trafficking Areas (HIDTA). Rockville, MD: Office of National Drug Policy. Retrieved December 3, 2006 from http://www.whitehousedrugpolicy.gov/hidta/index.html

Intelligence Bulletin. (2004, April). "Grim Reapers Motorcycle Club."

Intelligence Bulletin. (2004, May). "Outlaw Motorcycle Gangs and Drugs in the United States."

Lavigne, Y. (1987). *Hells Angels: Taking Care of Business.* Toronto: Ballantine.

National Alliance of Gang Investigators' Association. (2005). *National Gang Threat Assessment.* Bureau of Justice Assistance: GPO.

Reynolds, T. (2000). *Wild Ride: How the Outlaw Motorcycle Myth Conquered America.* New York: TV Books.

Sher, J., & Marsden, W. (2006). *Angels of Death: Inside the Biker Gangs' Crime Empire.* New York: Carroll & Graf.

Tretheway, S., & Katz, T. (1998). "Motorcycle Gangs or Motorcycle Mafia?" *Police Chief*, 66(4) 53–60.

Veno, A. (2002). *The Brotherhoods: Inside the Outlaw Motorcycle Clubs.* Crows Nest, NSW: Allen & Urwin.

Wagner, A. (April 27, 2002). "Three dead in Nevada's worst casino shooting as bikers clash." *Reno Gazette Journal.* Retrieved October 9, 2006 from http://rgj.com/news/printstory.php?id=13147

Yates, B. (1999). *Outlaw Machine: Harley-Davidson and the Search for the American Soul.* New York: Broadway Books.

11 Hispanic and African-American Gangs

"The critical responsibility for the generation you are in is to help provide the shoulders, the direction, and the support for those generations who come behind."

–Gloria Dean Randle Scott, educator and president, Beaumont College (1938–)

Chapter Objectives

After completing this chapter, readers should be able to:
- Discuss the history of black organized crime in the United States.
- Describe gang culture and explain why it evolved.
- Explain how and why some gangs evolve into organized crime.
- Discuss the different structures of gangs in the United States.

■ Introduction

The definition of a gang varies according to perspective. Gang definitions are found in state statutes (such as those for California) as well as academia and a variety of law enforcement agencies. Curry and Spengel (1988) define gang activity as, "law violating behavior by juveniles or adults in a group that can be complexly organized or unorganized and that is often cohesive with leadership and rules. They have a tradition of symbols, colors, turf, signs, and language, and engage in a wide variety of crimes frequently involving violence."

Gangs, particularly street gangs, have been of interest to academics, community groups, and law enforcement officials since Frederick Thrasher's classic study of 1,313 Chicago juvenile gangs in the early 1920s (Thrasher, 1968). These early gangs were juvenile play groups that evolved into identifiable entities engaged in conflict with one another and petty crime. By the 1950s and 1960s social and economic conditions had changed in Chicago and other urban areas, and these early street gangs had become crime groups dominated by African-American and Hispanic gangs involved in serious criminal behavior, including drug trafficking. They had expanded outside their original communities and become regional and national crime threats, requiring new approaches by law enforcement.

Developing crime analysis and intelligence units are essential investigative strategies because the gang culture and language barriers are difficult to overcome. By understanding the group's history, culture, and methods of operations, investigators become more effective in their efforts to deal with gangs that have the potential to rise to the level of organized crime.

■ Historical Perspective

Gang crime and violence are not recent phenomena, but have been around for millennia. In America, such groups as the "Forty Thieves" of New York in the 1930s, the Jones Brothers gang of 1930s Chicago, and of course the Italian "Black Hand" and the Irish "White Hand" gangs operated in most major cities of early 20th century America (Ianni, 1974). During the decade of tremendous growth in the Sun Belt cities, many people from depressed urban centers in the north and west began to move to the south. Gangs and gang violence moved with them and became commonplace throughout Mississippi, Georgia, Tennessee, Arkansas, Louisiana, and Alabama. Social dissatisfaction, lack of education and/or opportunities to succeed, and rebellion were motivating factors of those who migrated south. Many of these newcomers brought their culture of crime with them, and new gangs began forming.

The 1980s were years of considerable expansion of gangs in America, primarily because of America's appetite for illegal drugs. Most discussions of organized crime (OC) in the United States focus on activities in the major cities. However, rural states, such as Mississippi, experienced a tremendous increase in violence and drug distribution associated with gang activity, too. The Crips, Bloods, Folk Nation, and the People Nation all had criminal groups in Mississippi by the 1980s and were involved in drug distribution. Other states experienced the same growth.

Today, groups such as The Gangster Disciples have members in over 70 cities in more than 35 states. With membership at an estimated 20,000 in Chicago alone (Knox & Fuller, 2004), the FBI has designated them as a major organized group. However, whether gangs can be considered organized crime is debatable because some but not all groups appear to have many of the characteristics of organized crime.

■ Hispanic/Latino Gangs

Hispanic gangs are rooted in 19th century U.S. history (1852 annexation of the Southeastern territories) and they continue to play a major role in current gang criminal activities. (African and other ethnic minority groups share this disturbed

American history). Many Latinos were left without a country and were removed from their homes and ranches after annexation; these families tended to gather in small towns known as *barrios*. The word *varrio* is used to reference a gang, and barrio and varrio are often used interchangeably. After economic and political events (similar to those experienced in the source countries of the Italian, Jewish, and Irish Americans), there was a significant migration of immigrants from Mexico into the United States. Rivalries developed among immigrants that led to what most believe to be the first U.S. gang.

Today, one in five immigrants is from Mexico. Hispanic gangs are predicted to continue to increase in number. Dress, language, graffiti, hand signs, and tattoos all must be understood by law enforcement to help identify members and predict activities of the gang.

Gang Communication: Language, Graffiti, Hand Signals, and Dress

Graffiti is an important part of gang tradition. Hispanic gangs call their inscriptions *plaquesos* or *placas*. This artwork and writing proclaims to the world the status of the gang, marks their turf, and offers a challenge to rivals. "Cross cuts" (mark outs or destruction) of these writings are territorial insults that may escalate to violence, including "shoot outs."

The street slang, known as *Caló* (which incorporates ancient Spanish Gypsy, Mexican, and English words; it is similar to "Tex-Mex" and "Spanglish" except that Caló is used in rhymes), is the dialect formed by the gang that often appears in their graffiti. Much of this dialect/regional slang is incorporated into the American lexicon, too. *Monikers*, which are the street names of gang members, appear in the graffiti and can be valuable in identifying an individual gang member and his level of activity.

Investigators must receive training and education in Spanish, Mexican/Latino culture, and local street language to be able to communicate with members, informants, the community, and to interpret graffiti correctly.

Hand signs and tattoos are the other two means of non-verbal communication of gangs. The language of Latino gangs is a combination of English and Spanish made to form new words or phrases.

The dress of gangs has changed over the years and, because of the popularity of gang-type dress among non-gang members, it is now more difficult to determine membership in a gang. Some Latinos still wear the Pendleton type wool shirt, khaki pants, watch or knit cap or a bandana (*moko rag*), and the popular highly-polished leather shoes, but sports clothing and athletic shoes have become more common.

Clicas

Divisions within the gang, known as cliques (*clicas*), are organized by age range. Seven- or eight-year-old gang members are referred to as *Inano* or *Tiny Locos*. *Veteranos* (veterans) are older and likely have spent time in prison. Role models (the veteranos) train the younger members in the ways and culture of the gang. Hand signs and tattoos are part of the intergenerational culture; one sign represents the initials of the gang and others are messages known to the members. Tattoos are cryptic symbols that express gang culture and are often crudely inked while the gang member is in jail. One common tattoo is three dots, which represents *Mi Vida Loca* ("My Crazy Life").

Gang Culture

Most in law enforcement believe that unrealistic and violent television and the brutal prison mentality have had powerful emotional impacts that have led to more violent gang activity. Other reasons for gang culture given by sociologists include:

1. *Identity*: most identify themselves as warriors or soldiers.
2. *Recognition*: achieve a level or status that they feel is impossible to achieve outside the gang.
3. *Belonging*: the gang is a substitute for a family and the gang becomes the family.
4. *Discipline*: needed to achieve; gang leaders provide this to members.
5. *Love*: the gang is the family and the only place they receive "love."
6. *Money*: the assumption that the gang will meet all of their needs and desires.

Just why young people are attracted to gang culture and remain involved with gangs are difficult questions. Lack of positive role models, jobs, adult supervision, peer pressure, the need to belong, and proliferation of working parents or single parent households are a few of the factors contributing to gang culture. Many gang members are unsuccessful students who are high school dropouts or were expelled.

Rules of gangs vary from gang to gang, and violation can result in assault and even death. Chief among gang values is loyalty. The gang becomes their god and members will do anything to defend the gang.

A common paradigm of gang behaviors are the *three Rs*:

1. *Reputation*: being "jumped in" or "beaten down" by members of the gang gives status to the new member. Afterwards, members often hug each other and say they love each other, thus psychologically linking violence and love. The status (rank) of the member and the gang's street reputation are very important to the culture of gangs.
2. *Respect*: sought for by the individual and the gang. Disrespect (*Dis*) demands retaliation.
3. *Retaliation/revenge*: no challenge (Dis) goes unanswered.

Gangs have their own rituals, languages, and so-called *prayers* that are part of the culture. I heard the following prayer from a gang member:

"When I die and go to rest,
Lay two shotguns across my chest,
Tell all my vice lord brothers that I did my best."

■ Gang Structure

Gang structure may range from a loose coalition of individuals to a formal organization with established leadership and ruling council of powerful members. The gang may have codified written rules or unwritten rules and procedures. When the gang develops leadership and rules, it becomes more powerful and displays more characteristics of organized crime. The gang will be unified in "peace times" (when the group is not in conflict with a rival gang) and will often display some type of unity in dress.

Members

Members are generally divided by types according to their level of involvement (Grennan & Britz, 2006):

- *Hard core:* need and thrive on gang activity. They determine the level of violence of the gang and are often the leaders or have the respect of all members. They are knowledgeable in legal matters, streetwise, and are the most violent.
- *Affiliate:* associate with the gang for status and recognition. They are active in gang activity and wear tattoos, gang colors, or jackets,
- *Peripheral:* in and out of the gang based on interest in the current gang activity.

Recruiting into a gang can begin as early as age 9 or 10 but the majority are between 12 and 25 years of age. More often than not, they are underachievers with poor self-esteem. But there are exceptions. Members join the gang by being "jumped in" and committing a crime. Fagan (1988) classified gangs into four types:

1. *Social gang:* low level of delinquent and drug use or sales.
2. *Party gang:* acts of vandalism, extensive drug use, and cohesive based on patterns of drug use.
3. *Serious delinquents:* involved in drug sales and serious violent crime. They have organization and may be classified as organized crime.
4. *Young organizations:* extensive drug sales, highly cohesive, and organized. They have the most potential to become a formal organized group.

Another early work by Huff (1989) divided gangs into three types according to their activities:

1. *Hedonistic gangs:* minor crimes, getting high, and having fun.
2. *Instrumental gangs:* high volume of property crimes and not organized.
3. *Predatory gangs:* crimes of opportunity including robbery and theft. Serious drug abuse and drug sales often used to purchase weapons. They are a target of exploitation by organized crime groups but are not considered organized crime.

Gang members may refer to themselves as *warriors* and have rules regarding their behavior. This is particularly true with white gangs, such as the Stoners, Cowboys, and Arkies (gangs identified in California).

On the other hand, Southeast Asian gangs are considered a serious problem by law enforcement. Laotian, Cambodian, Vietnamese, and Chinese gangs are common in major U.S. cities and along the coastal states, such as Louisiana, Texas, and Mississippi. Most of the previous information applies to these gangs because they are both organized in some groups and unorganized in others.

Major Gangs

Some of the major black gangs whose members extend into multiple U.S. states include the Bloods, Crips, Vice Lords, the Folks, Black Gangster Disciples, and the Latin Kings. Membership in some gangs is multi-ethnic where whites, Latino/Hispanics, blacks, and other U.S. minorities may run in a single gang. The Vice Lord Nation also may be known as *People* while the Disciple Nation is sometimes called the *Folks*. Both the Folks and Disciple Nation appeared in Chicago, Illinois by the 1970s.

The origin and histories of these gangs are confusing and debated not only among academia and law enforcement, but also among gang members themselves. Their histories vary from state to state and city to city. It has been reported that the Vice Lord Nation (the conservative Vice Lords) originated in 1958 in the Illinois State Training School for Boys known as "Charlie Town"; they were very active in the Lawndale area of Chicago. Known as a very violent gang, they believe that if you are fearless, you attack before you are attacked. The culture and pressures of inner cities causes a social bond to form between the gangs and their community that is a major factor in the continued existence of gangs.

Bloods and Crips

The Crips were probably first formed around 1967 in Los Angeles, California. They now operate in many major cities, such as New York, Kansas City, and Chicago as well as in rural areas along the Mississippi Gulf Coast and Jackson, Mississippi. The Bloods are comprised of African Americans as well as Afro-Latinos; smaller gangs banded together in the early 1970s to protect themselves from the Crips' violence. Over 30 states report the presence of these gangs. The 2005 National Gang Threat Assessment reports that Bloods are operating in all regions of the United States (National Alliance of Gang Investigators Associations, 2005).

Along with the anti-Crips, players, and mob gangs, the Bloods began as social groups (Piru Boys) with their own dress style; they were very "turf" oriented. Their minor crimes evolved into auto thefts, drive-by shootings, and drug distribution. The Piru Boys of Compton or Piru Street had their primary color as red, and the Crips (East Side of Los Angeles around Fremont High School) used blue as their primary color. The Crips used the word *Cuzz* to greet one another, while the Pirus used the term *Blood* to greet another member.

Confrontations between the two groups led to extreme violence. After entering the criminal justice system, many members were placed into institutions such as the California Youth Authority, which only fostered the gang culture. Many factions of different gangs began to form alliances with either the Bloods or Crips. Membership in the two gangs is estimated at over 100,000 and networks or subgroups across the United States exist.

Although the leadership is constantly changing due to incarceration, death, and takeovers, these gangs display many characteristics of organized crime.

When gang members of the Crips or Bloods are incarcerated, they present a major problem for correctional facilities much like the G.D.s or Vice Lords. Crips members join or align with the prison gang known as the *Black Guerilla Family* (BGF), which are aligned with the *Black Liberation Army* (BLA). BGF has a rigid structure inside the prison that includes a chairman, central committee, field general, captains, lieutenants, and soldiers. Most members of the BGF are African-American street gang members who are sent to prison. The BGF has a code of discipline. Although the gang was originally formed in San Quentin in 1966 for protection of African-American inmates, it quickly became involved in diverse criminal activities inside the prison, and its members are connected to drug trafficking and other crimes outside the prison.

Despite the attempt by some leaders to unite the factions and subgroups of the Bloods and Crips with the Disciple Nation or the Vice Lord Nation, there is not much evidence of a united national gang. In some areas, the membership includes Asians or Latino members. Members dress in designer clothing with baggy trousers that are worn on or have the appearance of riding low on the hips. Referred to as *Homeboys* (fellow gang members), many are third-generation (Triple OG or original gangster) gang members. Members often locate to other states to avoid arrest, where they are welcomed and protected by the local gang. Relocation to rural areas or other states also opens new drug markets for the gang, as they recruit boys and young men into their criminal culture.

Jeff Fort and the Black P. Stone Nation

Born in Mississippi and moving north with his family while still young, Jeff Fort's Black Power rhetoric ignited an already burning rage over 1960s and 1970s American social conditions among young black men. A high school dropout, after leading the Blackstone Rangers that he formed in 1966 (one of hundreds of rough and tumble neighborhood gangs in Chicago), Fort negotiated a coalition of 21 warring gangs that became the *Black P. Stone Nation* in 1969 (Knox, 2004). He was incarcerated in 1972 for embezzlement of federal funds from a federal grant of $1 million that had been awarded to the Black P. Stone Nation to help form a learning program. While in prison, he formed *El Rukins* allegedly as a quasi-Muslim religious organization. Fort maintained his contacts in Mississippi and later was arrested and convicted of conspiracy to distribute marijuana, based on a case by Mississippi Bureau of Narcotics (MBN) agents. Later, Fort was given money by the Democratic Party to campaign in the Chicago area and was invited to the 1969 inauguration of President Nixon.

The Black P. Stone Nation gang had considerable assets, including many businesses and real estate ventures, a few of which were huge commercial buildings in Chicago that later proved to have been purchased with illicit funds from criminal activity, including cocaine distribution. Fort and other gang members were convicted of terrorist acts against the United States in addition to conspiracy to distribute cocaine. During the 1980s, over 60 members and Fort were charged and convicted of numerous crimes, including murder of rival gang members. In 1996, other El Rukin gang members, including Fort's son (known as "Nateta" or "The Prince") were convicted of cocaine distribution.

This gang's range of criminal activity is an example of the level and complexity that some gangs achieve. From an influence over politics strong enough to have federal grants awarded and attention from the President of the United States, these gangs continue extensive criminal activity in remarkable fashion. Despite prosecutorial misconduct by the U.S. Attorney's Office in Chicago that resulted in the dismissal of the U.S. Prosecutor new trials and reduced sentences for members of the gang (Knox, 2004), by 1996, persistent local, state, and federal government resulted in the gang's demise and most of their assets forfeited. Although referred to as a "community group" by President Nixon and many Chicago area politicians, law enforcement never stopped their exhaustive pursuit of illegal activities of Fort and his gang.

Larry Hoover and the Gangster Disciples

Larry Hoover was born in Mississippi, He joined *The Gangster Disciple (G.D.s)* gang, a branch of which was active in Jackson. Like other gangs, the G.D.s were loosely linked with major gangs in Chicago. Hoover was one of two protégés of Black Gangster Disciple Nation leader, "King" David Barksdale. After Barksdale's death in 1974, the Gangster Disciple Nation split into two factions—the Black Disciples and Gangster Disciples—but the G.D.s became well known for their violence under Hoover's leadership. Most of their income stemmed from drug distribution, but they also were involved in petty crimes that included theft and prostitution. To strengthen bonds with the community, the G.D.s operated a political arm (21st Century V.O.T.E.) and "Save the Children" campaigns that essentially are free rock concerts for young people.

Operating in a number of states, the Gangster Disciples soon established a formal structure similar to many other organized crime groups (Knox & Fuller, 2004). They collected money from anyone who wished to sell drugs on their turf. Their rivals were other gangs including the Black P. Stone Nation. Like the Black P. Stone Nation, the G.D.s involved themselves with politics by supporting candidates for office and voter registration drives; there is also considerable intelligence in Mississippi and other states that this gang was involved or attempted to corrupt a number of law enforcement personnel. The gang has members—including Hoover—who are continuing to conduct criminal activity while in prison. **Figure 11-1** shows the believed structure of the G.D.s gang.

With over 50,000 members (including very young *pee wees* and female counterparts), extensive leadership, and codified rules or laws, the gang is very bureaucratic and able to operate on the outside as well as inside prisons (Knox & Fuller, 2004). The G.D.s present a challenge for wardens and correctional facilities because of their potential for security disruption. The leadership and management have kept detailed records of their structure and operations, including financial data, which helps to establish excellent cases against them. During the late 1990s, the gang and its leader (Hoover) suffered multiple indictments and convictions, which has made them much less of a current threat. A frequent subject of the *Chicago Tribune*, the G.D.s gang saga is also well documented in

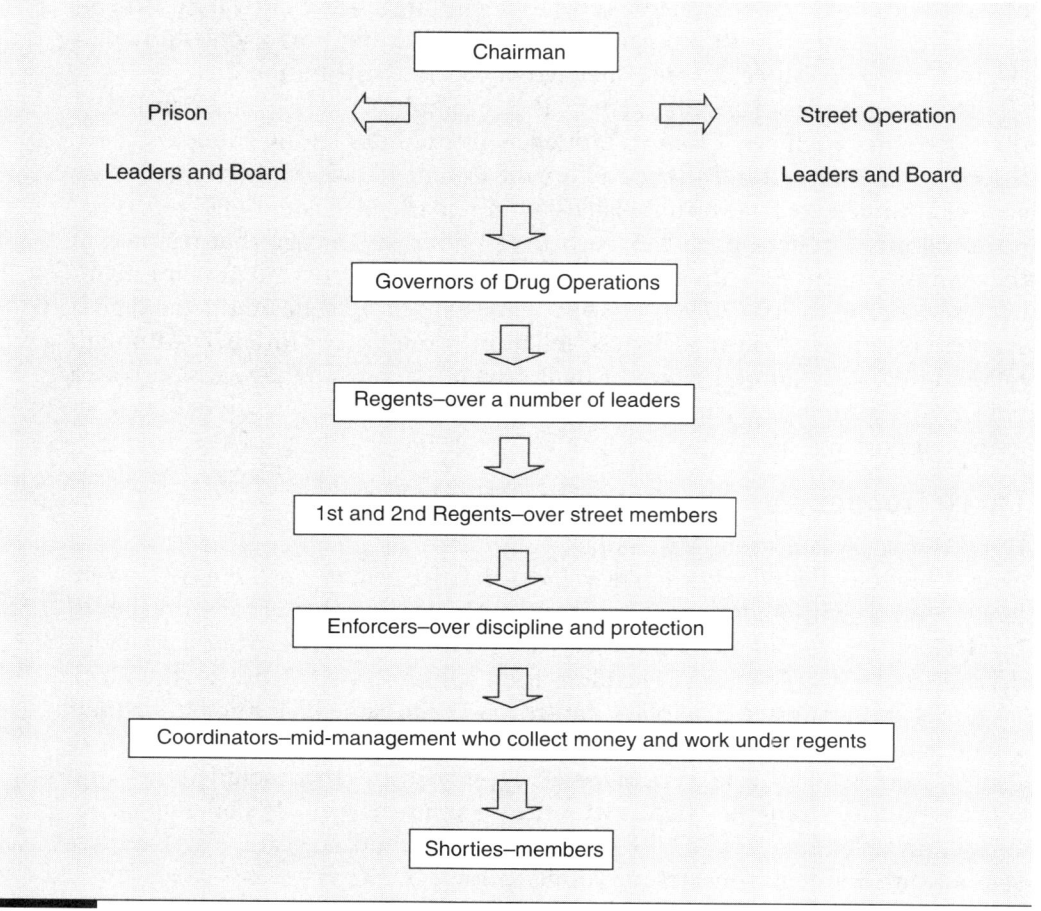

Figure 11-1 Structure of the Gangster Disciples (G.D.s) Gang

many city newspapers in Mississippi, Georgia, Missouri, and Illinois. The gang meets many of the criteria of organized crime, including corruption, violence, diverse criminal activities, hierarchy, money laundering, and profit sharing.

Historical Black Figures of Organized Crime

Frank Lucas

Until the 1970s, black criminals depended upon the Italian connection for their drug supplies. This changed with men such as Frank Lucas, who created an international heroin ring. Through a relative in Bangkok, Thailand, he established a direct source for the illegal drug. His organization's scam was smuggling heroin in what appeared to be military and government coffins to Fort Gordon, Georgia, and then on to New York City where it was distributed. Military personnel were bribed to ensure success. Known as the *Country Boys,* Lucas' organization expanded into Chicago, North Carolina, Los Angeles, and New Jersey. Profits of the organization allowed Lucas to become wealthy, and he owned numerous assets including several businesses in five states. Lucas was a high-profile drug trafficker who attracted the attention of law enforcement, becoming a major target of the DEA. He had connections to the LCN Genovese Family that provided him much information about organized crime in New York and other areas. By using military personnel and restricting membership in the Country Boys to his relatives, the Lucas organization prospered. Once convicted of drug trafficking, this information was parlayed into a lenient sentence for his cooperation with the government (Jacobson, 2000).

Frank Matthews

After his early start as a number's operator in North Carolina and later in Philadelphia, Frank Matthews became a major heroin trafficker in the 1960s. Matthews' claim to fame was his distribution network that included the infamous French connection. His organization operated in as many as 20 states (Goddard, 1978).

Leroy Barnes

In the 1970s, Leroy "Nicky" Barnes (known as the "King of Harlem") made a fortune in heroin trafficking. Like Matthews, Barnes had connections to LCN in New York. He grew up in Harlem and was involved in drug trafficking early in life. Eventually, Barnes was convicted of drug trafficking and sentenced to life in prison.

Charles Lucas

Charles Lucas is another African American considered to be an organized crime figure. He developed an international heroin smuggling and distribution network. He established contacts in Southeast Asia, using African American veterans of the Vietnam War (who were mostly relatives, much like Matthews' gang). His network included the New York Bronx, New Jersey, Los Angeles, and North Carolina regions. His organization had a division of labor with leadership management positions; they employed extensive technology that produced a very effective and efficient business.

The above three organizations certainly resemble many of the larger organized crime groups, but on a much smaller scale.

■ Other Black Criminal Organizations

Nigerian Organized Crime

A recent threat is the Nigerian criminal organizations that are involved in financial crimes such as fraud and drug trafficking. Members of these groups are organized along their home tribal cities. They have extensive smuggling operations routing Southeast Asia heroin and cocaine into Europe and the United States. The groups have developed connections to many street gangs. Although Nigeria is not a drug-producing country, it is a major transportation hub for heroin and cocaine.

Nigerian organized crime is also involved in major money-laundering operations.

Their elaborate fraud scams involved the promise of high profits for a small investment. The scam usually requests a bank number and access to a place to transfer a large amount of money. For allowing them this access, they promise a large profit. Instead, they ask the victim to pay the transaction fees and taxes, and then they clean out the victim's account.

Jamaican Organized Crime

Jamaican organized crime is another black organization that can be classified as organized crime. Individual criminal gangs adopted the name *posse* for their fondness of American Western genre movies. The Posses first grew out of the political turmoil in Kingston, Jamaica. They migrated to the United States to escape extreme poverty and politics. In 2001, violence in Jamaica again resulted in a new wave of gang members migrating

The Posses are most infamous for their level of violence, including over 2,000 drug-related murders between 1985 and 1990 (National Alliance of Gang Investigators' Associations, 2005). The Posses are now involved with Mexican DTOs and they are expanding into other countries. Because of their extreme violence and effective law enforcement, their activities have declined in the United States, but they continue to act as importers, wholesalers, and distributors here and in other countries. While the large Posses have experienced a demise, these groups remain a part of drug trafficking.

Two groups—the *Shower Posse* and the *Spangler Posse*—were rivals in the cocaine and marijuana distribution business. During the 1980s, they were very active and employed violence using state-of-the-art weaponry. Both Posses have a structured leadership. During the 1980s crack epidemic, there were 40 Posses in the United States with a membership estimated at over 20,000. Members are non-ideological. Using their profits, they have infiltrated legitimate businesses. In addition to links to their Colombian suppliers, they have many connections with black street gangs, such as the Crips. Leaders control the Posse; lieutenants transport drugs and guns, and carry money to the leaders; the members sell drugs to street gang members.

Jamaica continues to be a transshipment area for Colombian cocaine. These gangs are a problem in the United Kingdom because of their involvement in cocaine distribution as well as their use of violence. Both the DEA and U.S. law enforcement still view the Jamaicans as a problem.

Prison Gangs

Gangs exist in all ethnic communities. Although African-American and Latino/Hispanic gangs are more commonly found, the Asian and white gangs, and more recently female gangs, also exist.

Prison gangs are considered by some to be organized crime; however, these gangs do not meet the criteria established in Chapter 1. While these gangs normally have structure and a well-defined system of leadership, because of parole, transfers, and intervention by correctional officials, the leadership is unstable.

The objective of the gang is focused on controlling the prison environment and acquiring such items as drugs, money, and property inside the prison. Respect is obtained by any means necessary, including the use of violence.

One of the three most discussed prison gangs is the *Mexican Mafia* (EME), which was organized in 1957 in Deuel Vocational Institute in Tracy, California. They control homosexual prostitution, drug distribution, and gambling, and engage in extortion. Currently, they operate in a number of states and have networks outside of the prison. The EME has allied with the Arian Brotherhood against the Nuestra Familia, two other major prison gangs.

The *Nuestra Familia* (NF) was organized in 1967 in Soledad prison as a rival to the EME. Like other prison gangs, they have established their presence outside the prison system into communities. The gang has a constitution and membership includes ethnic groups other than of Latino or Hispanic origin. Their structure is rigid, with established positions including a general, captains, and lieutenants. NF has allied with the Black Guerilla Family (BGF) against the EME. Restricted membership and rules/creeds exist in the gang, with the death penalty for violations.

Other prison gangs include: the *Texas Syndicates*, founded in Folsom prison, Texas in 1974; the *Arian Brotherhood*, founded in the 1960s in San Quentin prison; and the *Black Guerilla Family*, founded in 1966 also in San Quentin. Prison gangs are defined as being close-knit disruptive groups of prison inmates, with a structure that ranges from informal rules to structured leadership with written creeds and regulations (Walker, 2006). The purposes of these groups range from protection of its members while in prison to large profit-producing enterprises.

One major problem in describing their activities as that of organized crime is that they are ideological. They have a political and often cultural agenda. For example, the Arian Brotherhood is associated with the Ku Klux Klan and other right wing hate groups. BGF goals are cultural unity and protection of black prison inmates. However, many prison gangs also have counterparts on the streets of our cities who do engage in diverse criminal activities.

■ Investigative Strategies and Laws

Investigation of black organized crime does not differ significantly from that of investigating other organized crime groups. Adult and juvenile gangs are addressed in the Violent Crime Control and Law Enforcement Act of 1994. The Act brings more types of cases under the federal judicial system. It includes enhanced penalties for using juveniles to distribute drugs and dealing drugs near schools, youth centers, playgrounds, and areas such as video arcades. The Anti-Gang Youth and Violence Act of 1997 provides for federal prosecution for serious and violent juveniles.

RICO, CCE, conspiracy, money laundering, electronic surveillance, undercover, and drug investigations are all strategies for dealing with black or gang organized crime activities (see Chapter 12). Bans on military or automatic weapons and gun law violations are used against the gangs. The youths in gangs know they are not normally subject to the same penalties as adults and often use this to their advantage.

Databanks and intelligence that identifies members, their activities, location, street names, vehicles, and gang affiliation are very important in developing investigative strategies. With gangs, such as the G.D.s, with membership that may be as large as 25,000 in 70 cities in the United States, developing a plan to deal with this type of organized crime is very difficult and requires extraordinary cooperation among law enforcement with support from federal agencies, such as the ATF, DEA, FBI, IRS, and U.S. Customs. Many major cities have gang units that are dedicated to investigations of street gangs, such as the Crips, Bloods, G.D.s, and Vice Lords.

Conclusions

African-American, Hispanic/Latino, and other gangs, which are expanding in number and violence, present a complex problem for law enforcement. While some gangs such as the Jamaican Posses have nearly disappeared, others like the brutally violent *MS13* are strong. Associated with the Mexican DTOs, MS13 is a loosely knit group of well armed youths striving to become more powerful. Competition between gangs will continue to produce violence, and many gangs will become classified as organized crime. The drug market will continue to be a major source of income for gangs. Gang alliances will form and dissipate. Their alliances will be with other street gangs, prison gangs, and in some cases, national and transnational organized crime.

How many gangs like MS13 will develop into major organized crime groups is uncertain, but history tells us at least some will do so. The complexity of the problem is not one for only law enforcement to address. A lack of positive role models, peer pressure, market demand, dysfunctional or unsupportive families, and the unsuccessful education and employment status of youth all contribute to the existence of gangs. These issues must be addressed in concert with sufficient and effective law enforcement. Some states have made it a crime to belong to a gang or be a gang member. Although much less is written about the histories and roles of groups, such as figures in African-American organized crime, there is evidence that gangs and all ethnic groups have played a major role in organized crime activity throughout history and will continue to contribute to organized crime activity in the future.

DISCUSSION QUESTIONS

1. Discuss the history of black organized crime in the United States.
2. Compare black organized crime to La Costa Nostra development and activities.
3. Discuss gang culture and explain why it evolved.
4. Discuss the different structures of gangs in the United States.
5. What are the law enforcement responses to gangs? What statutes or acts are specific to gang enforcement and why?
6. How and why do some gangs evolve into organized crime?

REFERENCES

Curry, G., & Spengel, I. (1988). Gang Homicide, Delinquency, and Community. *Criminology*, 26, 381–405.

Fagan, J. (1988). *The Social Organization of Drug Use and Drug Dealing Among Urban Gangs*. New York: John Jay College.

Goddard, D. (1978). *Easy Money*. New York: Farran, Straus, and Giroux.

Grennan, S., & Britz, M. (2006). *Organized Crime: A Worldwide Perspective*. Upper Saddle River, NJ: Prentice Hall.

Huff, C. (1989). Youth Gangs and Public Policy. *Crime and Delinquency*, 35, 524–537.

Ianni, F. A. J. (1974). *Black Mafia: Ethnic Succession in Organized Crime*. New York: Simon and Schuster.

Jacobson, M. (2000, August 14). The Return of Superfly. *New York Magazine*, pp. 36–45.

Knox, G. W. (2004). Gang Profile: Black P. Stone Nation. In: G. W. Knox & C. Robertson (Eds.). *Gang Profiles: An Anthology*. Chicago: National Gang Crime Research Center.

Knox, G. W., & Fuller, L. L. (2004). The Gangster Disciples: A Gang Profile. In: G. W. Knox & C. Robertson (Eds.). *Gang Profiles: An Anthology*. Chicago: National Gang Crime Research Center.

National Alliance of Gang Investigators' Associations. (2005). 2005 National Gang Threat Assessment. GPO: BJA. Retrieved December 4, 2006 from http://www.nagia.org

Thrasher, F. M. (1968). *The Gang: A Study of 1,313 Gangs in Chicago*, abridged. Chicago: University of Chicago Press (originally published in 1927).

Walker, R. (2006). *Gangs OR Us*. Retrieved December 4, 2006 from http://www.gangsorus.com

12 Major Statutes, Legislation, and Methods of Organized Crime Investigations

"Knowledge is the only instrument of production that is not subject to diminishing returns."

–John Bates Clark, neoclassical economist (1847–1938)

Chapter Objectives

After completing this chapter, readers should be able to:
- Compare the RICO statutes and investigation to conspiracy investigation.
- Recognize the elements of CCE.
- Discuss the issue of money laundering, including the definition, the 1958 and 1957 sections, and methods of laundering along with how to detect it.
- Discuss civil and criminal forfeiture and their impact on organized crime.
- Understand the controversies surrounding the statutes presented in this chapter.

■ Introduction

Numerous presidential commissions on crime and the U.S. Congress concluded in the late 1960s that existing laws were not adequate to address the complex criminal organizations that were operating similarly to legitimate businesses, but insulating their leaders and assets from traditional law enforcement methods. Major legislative actions increased the ability of law enforcement to address the complex and dynamic nature of organized crime.

The Omnibus Crime Control Act of 1968 allowed authorities to conduct electronic surveillance at state and federal levels. In 1970, the Organized Crime Control Act enhanced grand jury powers and allowed more authority to protect and secure witnesses. The Racketeer Influenced and Corrupt Organization Statute (RICO) of 1970 addressed the racketeering activity and funds gained through such activity. The 1986 Money Laundering Act (18 U.S.C. 1956 and 18 U.S.C. 1957) made it a federal crime to launder money. The Money Laundering Prosecution Improvement Act of 1988 allowed financial institutions to readily identify persons purchasing checks and money orders, and added special reporting requirements for these institutions. Both state and federal governments created conspiracy statutes that enhanced the ability to prosecute leaders of organized crime. The Continuing Criminal Enterprise (CCE) Statute of 1970 was directed towards major drug traffickers, as was the Foreign Narcotics Kingpin Designation Act of 1999, which applied to major foreign drug trafficking and provided extraordinary sanctions to the involved individuals and their organizations worldwide. These Acts followed federal and state statutes regulating controlled substances passed in the 1970s.

The USA Patriot Act, passed shortly after the terrorist attacks of September 11, 2001, expanded the scope of many of the above Acts. It increased the ability of many governmental agencies to use surveillance in relation to terrorist and criminal activities, and broadened regulations concerning the interception of communications. Particularly relevant are: Sections 201 and 202, which address rules on what communications can be intercepted as well as sharing information about criminal investigations; Section 206 on roving surveillance authority; Section 209, about seizure of stored communications (such as voice mail); and Sections 210 to 213, which address subpoenas and search warrants.

Many other laws are constantly used by law enforcement to establish major cases against leaders of organized crime and their organizations and assets. This chapter examines the most important laws and the elements needed to establish a prosecutable case or seize assets of major criminal organizations. Chapter 13 discusses the application of the intelligence function and its contribution to provide essential information to prosecute under these statutes and laws. It is critical for the investigator to not only identify the "labeled" criminal element/enterprise and its activities, but also establish the role of the upper world (corrupt business, government, and law enforcement) and seize their assets as well as prosecute them for their role in making organized crime such a successful enterprise.

■ The Hobbs Act and Extortion

One of the earliest statutes to deal with activity associated with organized crime was the Hobbs Act (18 U.S.C. 1951-1955), enacted in 1946. This Act made it a federal crime to obstruct or interfere with interstate commerce. Examples of obstruction include extortion (payment of money or other reward to avoid harm or harassment; involves fear; usually requiring payment of a "street tax" to continue to operate a business) or robbery. The Act also makes it a crime to travel or use interstate facilities (telephones, computers, mail, etc.) to aid illegal activity. The Hobbs Act was used to prosecute union officials who obtained kickbacks (a reward for using or buying a particular service or product), fees, loans, or any money or other reward for using their influence on the unions or people they represent.

Property is *extorted* under law by the Hobbs Act when a public official agrees that his or her official conduct will be controlled as promised or paid by another person. Extortion (also referred to as *blackmail*) is a common practice used by organized crime members to infiltrate legitimate businesses. Extortion is a means to obtain property by way of threats or intimidation. It can be defined also as obtaining property from another, with his consent by use of force, fear, or under color of official right. Under the *color of official right* section, violation of the Hobbs Act is a fine of $10,000 and up to three years in prison.

While the Hobbs Act remains a useful tool against organized crime, it often is not used because RICO or conspiracy laws have proven more effective. La Cosa Nostra (LCN; American Mafia) has been indicted with more Hobb's violations than most other organized crime groups, but the Yakuza and Russian Mafia are also frequent violators of the Hobbs Act and its extortion statutes.

■ RICO

No other statutes used to address organized crime and white collar crime have caused as much controversy and discussion as the 1970 Racketeer and Corrupt Organization Statute (RICO, 18 U.S.C. 1961-1965). In 1986, Robert Blakey (known as the "father of RICO") expressed concerns that there was no applicable definition of organized crime, racket, or racketeering (Blakey, 1986). He believed that the then current legal attempts to define organized crime were constitutionally vague in that they may violate the constitutional right to associate or assemble as well as the rights of due process or equal protection. His concerns remain controversial issues for some in today's society. RICO legislation has been attacked for being too vague, double jeopardy, Eighth Amendment violations, and accused of interfering with the rights of due process, including the right to a speedy trial and to counsel of choice. Many applaud its use while others call for restriction or elimination of RICO. The Patriot Act of 2001 is perhaps the only other legislation to become more controversial.

Before RICO, prosecution of major crime bosses was difficult at best because of the bosses' strategy of employing underlings to carry out the criminal acts, thus insulating them from identification and prosecution. Rather than proving criminal agreement (conspiracy) or committing a specific crime, RICO allows for prosecution of a pattern of crimes that are committed through an organization, referred to in the statute as an *enterprise*. RICO makes it a crime to acquire, receive income from, or operate an enterprise through a pattern of racketeering. Patterns of criminal acts committed by direct and indirect participants in criminal enterprises allow them to be prosecuted. Some believe that this statute leads to the prosecution of criminals who are not members of an organized crime group (crime by association), and that the statute is vague or too broad. As part of the 1970 Organized Crime Control Act, RICO (or Title IX), defines 32 *predicate offenses* that can be classified as racketeering activities for profit by organized crime. Not only does the statute have a mandatory punishment of 20 years in prison and a fine of $20,000, it also has a civil section. Under both the civil and criminal sections, assets derived from racketeering activities can be seized and forfeited. The civil section allows anyone who has been injured in his property or business by racketeering activity to sue responsible parties for triple damages and attorney fees.

The RICO specifically prohibits the following activites:

1. Using income received from a pattern of racketeering activity or through collection of an unlawful debt to acquire an interest in an enterprise affecting interstate commerce.
2. Acquiring or maintaining, through a pattern of racketeering activity or through collection of an unlawful debt, an interest in an enterprise affecting interstate commerce.
3. Conducting or participating, through a pattern of racketeering, racketeering activity, or collection of an unlawful debt, the affairs of an enterprise affecting interstate commerce.
4. Conspiring to participate in any of these activities.

Racketeering activity may include any of the listed predicate acts in the statute. A *pattern of racketeering* activity includes any two acts of racketeering by a person within ten years of each other (this varies among state statutes, as some require a 5-year period). The acts do not have to be the same type of violation, but must be related by some criteria, such as motive or purpose, design, etc. The enterprise may be a corporation, association, or group who interact and are involved in the activities of the enterprise.

Predicate offenses include fraud, Hobbs Act violations, white slavery, drug trafficking, arson, extortion, obstruction of justice, kidnapping, loan sharking, and a number of other offenses. The offenses vary somewhat from state to state in state statutes, but most are very similar in the offenses and elements of the crime.

A growing problem with the Russian Mafia is the offense of white slavery. In 1910, the Mann Act (also known as the "White Slave Act") was passed to prohibit interstate transportation of women for the purpose of prostitution or any immoral purpose. Today, trafficking of humans, male and female, young and old, is common with the Chinese Snake Heads and other Asian organized crime groups as well as many Russian groups.

Cases (such as *United States v Teri* in 1980) against traditional organized crime have led to the expansion of federal RICO statutes to include publication of obscene materials, drug trafficking by street gangs, and police corruption, but it's use in violent anti-abortion protest group cases was overturned by the Supreme Court in February 2006. This expansion has caused concern among some in the legal community. Most states now have RICO statutes, which have also contributed to the increased number of RICO prosecutions.

Under RICO statutes, courts can enter restraining orders before conviction to prevent transfer of potentially forfeitable property or assets. A wide range of civil actions is possible under RICO, including divestiture, dissolution, and reorganization. These actions add to the complaints and controversy of RICO. Prosecutors report that RICO statutes have dismantled large operations (such as prostitution rings) that under local or traditional statutes would allow the offenders to be back in business after short sentences while keeping their assets.

However, RICO cases do require excessive resources and time to develop and prosecute. RICO does allow the prosecutor to present a complete picture of the organization's activity, and allows trials with multiple defendants where the activities of all are presented to the jury. For the investigator developing a RICO case, it is essential to prove a pattern of racketeering or long-term criminal activity, and to have the group classified as a criminal enterprise. According to Abadinsky (2003), RICO fails to define organized crime and racketeering, which could be problematic for the case. However, most prosecutors and law enforcement believe that RICO is not too complex and has been very successful in combating organized crime and white collar crime, despite that RICO has been applied inappropriately to cases by some prosecutors. The Colombian cartels, LCN families, and many other criminals have been prosecuted successfully under RICO.

Another advantage of RICO is that prosecution is allowed in any jurisdiction where overt acts were committed. More than 1200 major crime figures have been successfully prosecuted under RICO by state and federal guidelines. While critics view RICO as a threat to individual rights, it remains the law. It is used frequently as tool in the arsenal of many law enforcement agencies to combat organized crime. Forfeiture provisions allow the government to take away incentive of profit. Under civil forfeiture, the property can be frozen without charging the owner with a crime.

■ Property Forfeiture

Civil forfeiture is a legal proceeding against property that either is purchased with profits from illegal activity or used to facilitate a crime. Vehicles, sea vessels, and aircraft can be seized when used to transport illegal contraband, such as drugs like cocaine or marijuana, and stolen goods. Criminal forfeiture requires that the defendant be found guilty of a crime and is ordered to forfeit property or funds related to the crime.

The Federal Comprehensive Forfeiture Act of 1984 enhanced the government's ability to seize assets of drug traffickers, including organizations such as the Mexican and Colombian DTOs. The major advantage of civil forfeiture is that it allows a lesser burden of proof (preponderance of the evidence) than criminal forfeiture (beyond a reasonable doubt). Probable cause is necessary before assets or property can be seized, which is the same rule as with any seized evidence. Once the property is seized, the burden shifts to the owner to prove the money or property was obtained legally (or did not facilitate a crime).

One advantage for law enforcement is that hearsay evidence can be used to establish probable cause. However, the U.S. Supreme Court (*U.S. v Real Property*, 510 U.S. 43) ruled that real property cannot be seized without notification of the owner and opportunity for the owner to contest the seizure. Another advantage of civil forfeiture, which is in *rem* (a lawsuit or legal action against a thing or property) rather than in *personam* (a lawsuit or legal action against a person), is that it allows the forfeiture of assets even with the acquittal of the owner involved in criminal activity.

Not only can money and vehicles be seized, but also any assets that are proceeds of criminal activity or that have facilitated criminal activity. This includes aircraft, boats, houses, weapons, and real estate property as well as other tangible goods. Seized and forfeited assets are given to law enforcement, which either auctions or uses them to supplement the cost of their operations (such as overtime, equipment, training, and property purchases). Defense attorney fees are also subject to forfeiture, which is a hotly debated issue. Criticism of forfeiture surrounds the issues of innocent owners (who are protected by law), excessive punishment such as seizing a yacht for only marijuana traces, and taking vehicles, which are necessary for a person to travel to work. The identification of hidden assets and tracing assets to criminal activity most often is a long-term and complex task. However, under civil forfeiture, it is only necessary to link the owner to drug trafficking in some aspect, and then to make the owner prove how the assets were obtained.

Taking the profit out of crime by following the money is an excellent strategy for combating organized crime.

■ Violations of the Internal Revenue Code

During the 1960s, tax investigations by the Internal Revenue Service (IRS) produced most of the convictions of organized crime offenders. These investigations remain a useful strategy against organized crime because tax evasion (failing to pay taxes) is a common crime of these enterprises. Financial analysis is a major tool for developing cases against even the biggest violators. Many involved with organized crime fail to keep required records and do not file a tax return while spending large sums of money. LCN and Yakuza members often do not report gambling income and are guilty of evading income taxes. By examining the violators' spending habits and assets acquired, the investigator can establish a tax case.

A few of the methods employed by the criminal investigation division of the IRS include network and expenditure schedule, source and application of funds, and the bank deposit methods. The first two strategies are explained in Chapter 11. Both result in unexplained or unreported income. The bank deposit method examines bank deposits, cash expenditures, purchases, and any cash on hand. (Probably the most famous conviction for tax evasion was Chicago Mob boss, Al Capone.) Once the unexplained income is discovered by investigators, the burden of proof shifts to the suspect to ensure that it was legally obtained.

Money Laundering Laws

A key strategy in fighting organized crime organizations is attacking their assets. Investigators need to be trained in banking and financial procedures to better understand how money is laundered.

Money laundering is always present in organized crime activity. Money laundering can be defined as all activities designed to conceal the existence, nature, and final disposition of funds gained through illicit activities. Money laundering has been a common theme in organized crime since the Prohibition era. Crooks need to "clean" the illegal funds before they can spend it. The massive amounts of money made by organized crime activity present a challenge for those who want to keep it as they not only need to "clean" the money, but protect it from seizure by law enforcement. The process can be as simple as mailing or physically transporting the cash out of the country or as complex as a bank takeover. The methods are often the same as legal business transactions except that the money was obtained illegally.

The President's Commission on Organized Crime in 1984 observed that new methods were occurring to move organized crime funds. These strategies included: wire transfers, avoiding the Currency Transaction Report (CTR) and Currency and Monetary Instrument Report (CMIR), "fronts" and shell corporations, and bank transfers. The Bank Secrecy Act of 1970 (31 U.S.C. 5311-5326) was the first attempt to combat money laundering by organized crime. The Act requires financial institutions to file a CTR on all cash transactions of more than $10,000. This CTR must be filed with the IRS within 15 days of the transaction, and the bank or institution must keep copies for five years. Also, a CMIR exceeding $10,000 in value that leaves or enters the United States must be filed with the IRS. These records assist in tracking cash through the national banking system. In response to these laws, organized crime members make multiple smaller transactions (under $10,000) to avoid the reporting requirement. This practice, referred to as *smurfing*, is a violation of 31 U.S.C. 5324, known as the Anti-Drug Abuse Act of 1986. The penalty for smurfing (structuring for each transaction) is five years in prison unless the amount exceeds $100,000 during a 12-month period, which increases the penalty to a ten-year sentence. The Right to Privacy Act of 1978 was amended to allow the financial institution to give authorities the name of the suspect or organization, the account number, and the nature of the suspected illegal transaction.

Section 1956 of the Money Laundering Act of 1986 deals with violations in a domestic context and those that occur when monetary instruments or funds are transported between the United States and a foreign country. The violator must conduct or attempt to conduct a transaction *knowing* (or with "willful blindness") that the assets involved are proceeds of unlawful activity, even if the launderer does not know the precise activity. This action must promote *specified unlawful activity*, which means to conceal or disguise the source, origin, location, or ownership of the proceeds, or be designed to avoid federal or state reporting requirements.

It should be noted that before the 1986 Money Laundering Act, it was not a federal crime to launder money. The 18 U.S. 1957 law makes it a violation to engage in monetary transactions in excess of $10,000 with property derived from proceeds of specified unlawful activity. Both CTR and CMIR violations are predicate acts under RICO. Violations of 1956 incur up to a 20-year prison term and a fine of up to $500,000, or twice the value of the property involved. Violations of the Money Laundering Act may receive up to a ten-year prison term and a fine. Title 18 U.S.C. 981 and 982 provide for civil and criminal forfeiture, respectively. Other Acts that address money laundering include:

- **The Drug Abuse Act 1988.** This requires that offshore banks record any U.S. cash transfers in excess of $10,000. They must also allow government access to those records.
- **The Annunzio-Wylie Money Laundering Act of 1992 and the Money Laundering Suppression Act of 1994.** The Annunzio-Wylie Act makes it a crime to operate a money laundering business, but it also protects financial institutions from civil liability when reporting suspicious activity of their customers. The Act requires that all financial institutions and gambling enterprises report suspicious activity.
- **The Money Laundering Prosecution Improvement Act of 1988.** This requires financial institutions to verify the identity of persons who purchase bank checks, traveling checks, or money orders in amounts of $3,000 or more. The Act also allows the government to target certain institutions or geographic area for special reporting requirements (U.S.C. Sections 5325–5326).

More recently, the *USA Patriot Act* (United and Strengthening America by Providing Appropriate Tools Required to Intercept and Obstruct Terrorism Act of 2001) is considered by American Bar Association (ABA) National Institute's Center for Continuing Legal Education to be the broadest money laundering statute on the books. Unlike Sections 1956 and 1957, the statutes do not require a list of specific offenses or *specified unlawful activities* (SUAs). The foreign crimes list has expanded to include bribery of public official, embezzlement and misappropriation, and theft. Although transactions may not have any connection to terrorism, they are included in the Act. The Act is a complement to the United Nations Convention against Transnational Organized Crime (held in Palermo, Italy in 2000), which requires extradition of violators who are involved in transnational organized crime or "serious" crime, which may include corporate tax violations and fraud occurring in a foreign country, such as SUAs money laundering charges (this includes computer fraud). The Act expands the definition of the term *illegal money transmitting business* to include unlicensed businesses and those who transport or transmit illegal proceeds or money intended to promote or support unlawful activity. The Act allows IRS information (CTRs and CMIRs; Forms 4789, 4790, and Form 8300 Report of Cash Payment over $10,000 received in a trade or business) to be available to law enforcement. Anyone who transports or transmits money by any method is considered subject to this Act.

All types of organized crime activity require the need for money laundering to legitimize their income. Doing so allows the violator to spend money without suspicion of criminal involvement. To make transporting cash less demanding, large profits from illegal activities somehow need to be infused into the U.S. banking system and subsequently exchanged for smaller bulky transactions. Money from international or transnational organizations then can be delivered to the organizations' source countries in their own currency. Only then can this now-clean money be converted into tangible assets such as expensive homes, real estate, cars, marine vehicles, and operating/bribery expenses among other cash outlays.

The Money Laundering Cycle

In 1990, the *Financial Crimes Enforcement Network* (FinCEN) was formed under the Department of Treasury to function as an intelligence center for all financial crimes. FinCEN divides money laundering into three stages:

1. *Placement*: The illegal proceeds placed into the financial system unnoticed or transported outside the United States.
2. *Layering*: The funds go through a series of financial transactions in such frequency, volume, and complexity that they are difficult to trace and appear to be legitimate financial transactions.
3. *Integration:* the funds integrate into the economy in such a way that they appear to be derived from legitimate income. At this stage, the investigation is faced with a major problem of distinguishing illicit from licit funds.

Cash transactions between the suppliers, transportation cells, and users can be considered money-laundering violations. Transportation of cash out of the United States leaves no paper trail to follow and is a common means used by organized crime; however, in today's nearly cashless society, other means are becoming more frequent.

Financial institutions are common players in the business of organized crime activity. The Western Union and U.S. banking system are two examples. These businesses can be used as black market exchanges to launder money, much like the Casa de Cambio or money exchange houses that convert U.S. dollars to pesos or buy U.S. dollars at a black market rate.

Remittance corporations operating as fronts under the guise of an investment company, broker, financial service provider, or check-cashing operation receive and transmit illegal funds. The CTR or CMIR will often only reflect the name of the company and not the organized crime figure or organization. This money is transmitted through a number of "fronts" before being placed in the violator's account or company, so that it appears to be legal income. It is common for funds to go through 15 to 20 financial institutions or banks. Real estate transactions are an excellent way to launder illegal proceeds. Buying property for $2 million in visible cash and $1 million "under the table" allows the violator to launder $1 million of illegal proceeds.

Law enforcement must be properly staffed and equipped to find and fight money laundering. The El Paso Intelligence Center (EPIC) and FinCEN are staffed by experts from a variety of federal agencies who have access to the Treasury's computer system (TECS II). TECS II has a database of all CTR, CMIR, and 8300 transactions. The Multi-Agency Financial Investigative Center (MAFIC) was formed to identify, target, seize, and forfeit any significant assets of major organized crime figures. These agencies have been and continue to be an essential asset in combating money laundering.

Controlled Substances Acts

Because drug trafficking is still the major profit producer of organized crime worldwide, acts that address illegal drug distribution are often used to convict major organized crime bosses and members. The Controlled Substance Act is a statute that exists in all U.S. states. The Comprehensive Drug Abuse Prevention and Control Act of 1970, which has been amended nearly each year to add new substances, gives federal jurisdiction for investigating drug trafficking and provides substantial penalties for violation of the Act. The Act divides substances into five schedules according to their potential for addiction and harm. Procedures for controlling a substance are provided in the Act. Requirements for legal distribution of pharmaceuticals are part of most statutes regarding controlled substances, which includes security, records, and reporting loss by pharmacists and the medical profession. Other Acts that supplement this statute include:

- **The 1988 Chemical Diversion and Trafficking Act** controls substances known as precursor chemicals needed to produce certain drugs. Records of purchases and transactions of these precursors are required by the Act to allow investigators to trace these products to clandestine laboratories that produce or manufacture illegal drugs.
- **The Comprehensive Crime Control Act of 1984 and the Anti-Drug Abuse Act of 1986** increased prison sentences for specific drug offenses.

Other drug abuse legislation and amendments have been directed at the demand side of the equation, which include penalties for using drugs and loss of license to drive, etc.

Conspiracy Statutes

The term *conspiracy* is the essence of organized crime activity. The success of the conspiracy is not necessary for conviction of the charge, and the conspiracy charge is distinct and separate from the substantive crime that was the goal of the conspiracy. Conspiracy laws originated in England in 1305 AD. Most states and the federal government have conspiracy laws with substantial penalties. Most prosecutors require proof of *overt acts* (any act that furthers the objective of the conspiracy, which may be a lawful or unlawful act). All participants do not need to know of the overt acts. The conspiracy or agreement may be established by any contrivance (either implied or tacit) for two or more persons to come to a common understanding to violate a law. Conspiracy laws have many advantages for case development and include the following:

1. Conspirators do not have to know each other.
2. Each is responsible for the actions of the others (Pinkerton Theory).
3. All are agents for each other.
4. Conspirators do not have to be aware of the actions of others.
5. Anything done to carry out the objective of the conspiracy is an overt act.
6. Overt acts need not be criminal in nature.

7. Overt acts need not be known by all participants.
8. Any act or statement by one conspirator can be used in court against all other conspirators.
9. All conspirators may be responsible for the substantive crimes of their co-conspirators provided,
   a. they were in the conspiracy at the time the offense was committed;
   b. the offense was committed in furtherance of the conspiracy; and,
   c. the offense was a foreseeable consequence of the conspiracy.
10. Venue lies in any jurisdiction in which an overt act occurred or where the agreement was made.
11. The conspirator must do something affirmative to withdraw from the conspiracy, such as inform the police about the conspiracy and inform known co-conspirators of their intention to withdraw.
12. The statute of limitations normally runs five years from the last overt act or when the conspiracy ends. (This number varies between states.)
13. The case can eliminate the entire criminal organization.
14. Evidence against one defendant is evidence against all.
15. Exception to the hearsay rule, where a defendant can testify concerning statements, deeds, or actions of the co-conspirators.
16. Asset forfeiture laws apply to drug conspiracy cases.

The disadvantage of a conspiracy includes the long-term commitment to gather evidence, which is likely to be manpower-intensive. In major investigations, extensive surveillance is conducted and testimony of witnesses needs to be verified and corroborated, which often requires overtime and manpower. Multiple venues often pose political and logistical problems.

Although conspiracy investigations are complex, they are much simpler to develop and understand than RICO offenses and money laundering cases. Conspiracy cases allow prosecution of leaders of organized crime groups even when they attempt to insulate themselves with subordinates, or when they remain in a foreign country, never entering the United States where the objective of the conspiracy is reached. Statutes usually incorporate an offense of conspiracy to violate the RICO Act. It should be noted that mere association or knowledge of the existence of the conspiracy does not constitute joining.

The types of conspiracies developed by organized crime activity include:

1. *Historical:* The object of the conspiracy has already been met. Investigators must locate witnesses, conduct warrants for physical evidence, including documents, and use informants to produce a case of this nature. Again, the goal is to prove that the agreement to violate the law existed.
2. *Ongoing:* Conspiracy still exists while it is being investigated.
3. *Chain:* All members are connected, yet only some members interact with the others:

$$A \leftrightarrow B \leftrightarrow C \leftrightarrow D \leftrightarrow E$$

In the chain type of conspiracy, not all of the members know each other and no single member knows all of the members. In the above diagram, persons A and B make the agreement to violate the laws and C, D, and E carry out overt acts. Persons E and D do not interact with persons A and B, and C only interacts with B and D; person E only interacts with person D.

4. *Wheel*: Like the spokes of a wagon wheel, the area between the spokes interacts with certain members. Although all are connected, only some of the links or members interact with others.

    Wheel conspiracies, also called *cell structures* or *compartmentalization*, are common structures found in terrorist and organized crime groups. A terrorist group may be referred to as a *sleeper cell* when they are dormant, waiting for instructions to carry out their mission or objective.

5. *Combination Wheel and Chain Conspiracies:* These occur when members of the wheel and chain frequently interact for operational purposes and are part of the same operations (cons) in the overall conspiracy. The structure contains a combination of smaller conspiracies that form a larger, more complex, interaction.

Opponents of conspiracy statutes argue that, too often, large numbers of people are forced to trial with people who were only distantly associated with a criminal operation (*guilty by association*).

Conspiracy Case Development

The development of a conspiracy case involves a wide variety of investigative techniques and methods. The investigator must be well trained in these methods and also be allowed time and resources to conduct such complex and long-term cases. The following are some of the methods frequently used to develop conspiracy cases:

1. Management and development of informants
2. Title III investigations and electronic surveillance
3. Mail covers
4. Photo spreads and line ups or show ups
5. Use of grand jury testimony and immunity of witnesses
6. Physical surveillance
7. Asset or financial investigations
8. Undercover operations
9. Trash runs
10. Search warrants for documents
11. Grand jury subpoenas or investigative grand juries
12. Analytical and intelligence support
13. Testimony of co-conspirators

Federal and state prosecutors and investigators have praised conspiracy cases as a valuable tool against organized crime activity. The penalty for violations is normally the same as if the object of the conspiracy was completed.

Continuing Criminal Enterprise Statute

The Continuing Criminal Enterprise (CCE) statute (21 U.S.C. 848) was enacted as part of the Comprehensive Drug Abuse Prevention and Control Act of 1970. Nothing puts fear in a violator or defense council like the possibility of a CCE conviction. Most often the violator is willing to cooperate and provide information in exchange for a lesser charge. The statute is directed at any person who occupies a position of organizer, supervisor, or in a position of management in a narcotic producing and distribution enterprise. The minimum sentence under CCE is 20 years in prison with no possibility of parole, but the court also may impose additional years up to a life sentence and fines up to $2 million dollars ($5 million dollars if it is an organization; a second conviction is a mandatory 30 year sentence). Additionally, all profits and assets of the operation are subject to forfeiture as prescribed in 21 U.S.C. 853.

Elements of the statute are the following:

1. A person who violates any federal drug offense law.
2. This violation is part of a continuing series of violations (three related transactions).
3. This person operates in concert with five or more persons and occupies a position of organizer, supervisor, or is in a management position.
4. This person receives substantial income or resources from the violations.

Proof of a CCE usually involves both direct and circumstantial evidence. This may include evidence of defendant's position in the organization, quantity of drugs involved, and the amount of money that changed hands, or lavish personal expenditures without any legitimate source of income. The investigator must demonstrate specific illegal acts that were committed by a defendant to prove CCE.

The Kingpin Act

The Foreign Narcotics Kingpin Designation Act signed into law in December 1999 as an Amendment to Public Law 106-120, Intelligence Authorization Act of FY2000. Modeled after the Specially Designated Narcotics Trafficker (SDNT) program, it seeks to expose, isolate, and incapacitate the financial infrastructure of major drug trafficking organizations (DTOs). Sanctions such as denying major traffickers and their businesses access to the U.S. financial system and prohibiting U.S. citizens and companies from conducting business with them are major parts of this Act.

Regulation and Monitoring of Business and Labor

Labor racketeering has been a major profit producer for such entities as LCN. According to numerous government investigative committees and subcommittees, four major international unions were dominated by organized crime: the International Brotherhood of Teamsters (IBT), Hotel and Restaurant Employees Union (HRE), Laborers International Union of North America, and the International LongShoreman's Association (ILA). Men such as Jimmy Hoffa, Jackie Presser, and Allan Dorfman are legends in the analysis of LCN history. By controlling the unions, LCN can control a number of associated businesses, such as labor, trucking, shipping, etc. Domination of a business or component of a business allows organized crime venues to launder money while paying taxes to appear to be legitimate, and is another venue for profit through diversification and legitimate employment for associates, friends, family, and members of the organization. Organized crime's major activities include extortion (*strike insurance*) and so-called *sweetheart contracts* that garner profits at the expense of workers and misuse of union benefit funds.

Using union power for personal profit began with LCN bosses such as Rothstein in the 1930s (see Chapter 7). A few of the business owners' benefits provided by organized crime range from harassment of competitors, controlling union labor, and increased profits. Although money laundering statutes, RICO, and conspiracy statutes combat business and labor racketeering, it is the cooperation among law enforcement, financial institutions, businesses, and the judiciary that can be extremely valuable in reducing organized crime's impact in the business world. Increased funding for regulatory agencies and partnering with these agencies will enhance the ability to monitor organized crime activity in an area that is not familiar to most law enforcement investigators.

The 1967 President's Commission on Crime reported a number of businesses vulnerable to organized crime:
- Construction
- Waste removal
- Real estate
- Garment industry
- Financial institutions
- Restaurants, bars, hotels, and legal gambling

This list continues to grow. Organized crime activities result in limiting competition, higher prices, lower wages, a reduction of legitimate employment, and enormous loss in taxes.

Electronic Surveillance

The federal government and states have authorized law enforcement to intercept telephone conversations and electronic communications, and record them for presentation as evidence during trials. Title III of the 1968 Omnibus Crime Control Act (18 U.S.C. 2510-2520) authorized federal law enforcement to eavesdrop on suspects when authorized by a warrant; most states have similar statutes. The Electronic Communications Privacy Act of 1986 expanded electronic surveillance to include cellular and electronic mail. To help establish probable cause that the communication device is being used to conduct criminal business, computerized *pen registers* (records of numbers of outgoing calls) and the *trap and trace records* (number of incoming calls) are placed on communication devices before a *wiretap* is started. The pen register and trap and trace capability is now a single computerized device that prints out the results of a link analysis of the calls, e-mails, or communication exchanges (location, time and length of call, and identification of callers). The Patriot Act of 2001 has enhanced the ability of federal agencies to share criminal information obtained by electronic surveillance. This includes contents of foreign intelligence and counterintelligence obtained by National Security Agency (NSA), Central Intelligence Agency (CIA), and any federal agency.

Prior to the 2001 Patriot Act, federal law enforcement had very limited authority to delay notification of "sneak and peak" searches. The Patriot Act expanded this to "reasonable cause" showing of adverse impact on the investigation. Title III authorizes covert entry to install interception devices (such as *bugs*, a transmitter that picks up conversations in a room or area). Without court approval or an extension, the target of the intercept must be notified of the wire tape within 90 days after the termination of the court-ordered intercept. Most orders for electronic surveillance are for 30 days unless they are extended.

The Patriot Act clarified that law enforcement can use Title III trap and trace and pen registers on computer networks. The Act also made possible a warrant that, once issued, is legal on any communication device a target used and in any jurisdiction the target travels (*roaming wiretap*). This type of warrant was used prior to the Patriot Act in major drug investigations.

Requirements to obtain an electronic intercept include:

1. Probable cause that a crime is being committed or about to be committed by the target, and that the crime is an offense under Title III.
2. All other investigative methods have failed or will not provide the evidence to meet the goals or objectives for a successful investigation.
3. Probable cause exists that the intercept will provide the communication evidence sought.
4. Probable cause that the area or device is being used or will be used by the target or targets to violate a particular law.

These types of investigations are extremely human- and time-intensive and, because they are complex, special equipment is often required. Most departments cannot support the financial or technical aspects of an intercept operation. Specialized training is also required for investigators to use equipment and gain knowledge of the rules and limitations. Equipment must be monitored 24 hours a day, and monitoring is discontinued when communication is privileged, not covered by the court order, or not related to an offense. There is also the possibility that no valuable evidence will be recorded despite the effort and expense. As communication becomes more "high tech," newer equipment and training become necessary to intercept communications (digital and cellular phones, e-mail, etc.). For these reasons, electronic surveillance can be problematic, even though it may produce evidence needed to develop a case and charge major organized crime members under RICO, money laundering, and conspiracy statutes.

Investigative Grand Juries

Federal and state prosecutors have experienced great success with the investigative grand jury concept. These juries have the authority to subpoena testimony and documents, grant immunity, and remain in session for six months or longer, which allows a complete investigation while maintaining secrecy. Refusal to honor a subpoena results in punishment of arrest and jail time. The testimony of reluctant persons can be compelled upon a grant of immunity from prosecution. Two types of immunity are possible:

1. *Derivative Use Immunity*: Prohibits the information provided by the witness from being used against them. However, if evidence of a crime is developed independently of the testimony, the witness can be prosecuted.

2. *Transactional Immunity*: This is broad and prohibits prosecution from the crime or criminal act they are testifying about.

The Witness Security Program (WITSEC) implemented in 1971 has benefited organized crime investigation and encouraged testimony without fear of retaliation. The program gives a new identity to witnesses and places them in a secure location with lifetime protection. The program has been successful in protecting essential organized crime witnesses.

Other Statutes Frequently Used During Organized Crime Investigations

The following list of statutes in the United States Code (U.S.C.) should be incorporated in the investigator's arsenal when coping with criminals.

1. 18 U.S.C. 4: Misprision of felony.
2. 18 U.S.C. 111: Assaulting, resisting, or impeding federal officers.
3. 18 U.S.C. 924 (c): Use or possession of a firearm during or in relation to drug trafficking offenses.
4. 18 U.S.C. 1071: Concealing a person from arrest.
5. 18 U.S.C. 1073: Flight to avoid prosecution or giving testimony.
6. 18 U.S.C. 1341: Frauds and swindles (includes mail fraud).
7. 18 U.S.C. 1503: Influencing or injuring an officer or juror generally.
8. 18 U.S.C. 1503(a): Influencing a juror by writing.
9. 18 U.S.C. 1510: Obstruction of criminal investigations.
10. 18 U.S.C. 1511: Obstruction of state or local law enforcement.
11. 18 U.S.C. 1512: Tampering with a witness, victim, or informant.
12. 18 U.S.C. 1513: Retaliating against a witness, victim, or informant.
13. 18 U.S.C. 1542: False statement in application of and use of a passport.
14. 18 U.S.C. 1543: Forgery or false use of a passport.
15. 18 U.S.C. 1621: Perjury generally.
16. 18 U.S.C. 1952: Interstate and foreign travel or transportation in aid of racketeering enterprises/ITAR.
17. 21 U.S.C. 843 (b): Use of a communication facility to facilitate a drug crime (also known as phone counts).

Most indictments include a number of these statutes and cases are fairly easy to develop. It is obvious that organized crime activity includes violations of all of these statutes.

Conclusions

Task forces, undercover operations, informant development, financial investigations, electronic surveillance, and technology are all useful tools that, when supported by powerful legislation and regulation, offer some hope of minimizing and even eliminating some organized crime groups. However, because of the political and economic relationships as well as public demand, organized crime refuses to go away. By creating policies that address market demand, the threat of organized crime can be controlled.

This law enforcement perspective is controversial, and some in academia and other organizations, such as the American Civil Liberties Union (ACLU), regularly produce position papers and lobby Congress to amend or outright appeal legal statutes. However, most of these statutes and methods have been applied to important cases against organized crime organizations and their membership for decades (with the exception of the Patriot Act), and they remain the most effective weapons for law enforcement.

DISCUSSION QUESTIONS

1. Compare the RICO statutes and investigation to conspiracy investigation.
2. Name and discuss the requirements for obtaining a Title III wiretap.
3. What are the advantages and disadvantages of electronic surveillance?
4. What are the elements of CCE?
5. Discuss the issue of money laundering, including the definition, the 1958 and 1957 sections, and methods of laundering along with how to detect it.
6. Discuss civil and criminal forfeiture and their impact on organized crime.
7. Explore and discuss controversies surrounding the statutes presented in this chapter. Why do you think these controversies continue after so many years of application?

REFERENCES

Abadinsky, H. (2003). *Organized Crime*, (7th ed.). Belmont, CA: Wadsworth/Thomson.

Anti-Drug Abuse Act of 1986. (Pub. L. 99-570).

Bank Secrecy Act of 1970. (31 U.S.C. 5311-5326). Regulatory: Overview. Washington, DC: Financial Crimes Network, Department of the Treasury. Accessed on December 4, 2006 from http://www.fincen.gov/reg_main.html

Blakey, G. (1986). Organized Crime in the United States: A Review of the Public Record. Bellevue, WA: Northwest Policy Studies Center.

Chemical Diversion and Trafficking Act of 1988. (Pub. L. 100-690). Diversion Control. Alexandria, VA: U.S. Drug Enforcement Administration. Accessed on December 4, 2006 from http://www.dea.gov/programs/diversion.htm

Comprehensive Drug Abuse Prevention and Control Act of 1970. (21 U.S.C. 881 (a) (7)) Controlled Substances Act. Everything2. Accessed December 4, 2006 from http://everything2.com/index.pl?node=Controlled%20Substances%20Act

Continuing Criminal Enterprise (CCE). (1970). (21 U.S.C. 848). Accessed December 4, 2006 from http://www.capdefnet.org/fdprc/contents/shared_files/titles/21_usc_848.htm

Electronic Communication Privacy Act of 1986. (Pub. L. 99-508). Accessed December 4, 2006 from http://www.cpsr.org/prevsite/cpsr/privacy/communications/wiretap/electronic_commun_privacy_act.txt

Federal Comprehensive Forfeiture Act of 1984. (21 U.S.C. 853).

Hobbs Act. (1970). (18 U.S.C. 1951-1955). U.S. Department of Justice. Accessed December 4, 2006 from http://www.usdoj.gov/usao/eousa/foia_reading_room/usam/title9/131mcrm.htm

Internal Revenue Service Code. (1986). (26 U.S.C. 7201, 7206). Accessed June 28, 2006 from http://www.geocities.com/CapitolHill/Senate/3616/TAXEVASION.html; and http://www.geocities.com/CapitolHill/Senate/3616/FALSEINCOMETAXRETURN.html

Mann Act of 1910. (18 U.S.C.A. 2421 et seq.).

Money Laundering Control Act of 1986. Bank Secrecy Act and Anti-Money Laundering. Washington, DC: Federal Deposit Insurance Corporation (FDIC). Accessed December 4, 2006 from http://www.fdic.gov/regulations/examinations/bsa/bsa_3.html

Money Laundering Prosecution Improvement Act of 1988. (21 U.S.C. 801) (also known as the Chemical Diversion and Trafficking Act of 1988). Vienna, Austria: United Nations Office on Drugs and Crime. Accessed December 4, 2006 from http://www.unodc.org/unodc/legal_library/us/legal_library_1990-06-21_1989-27.html

Omnibus Crime Control and Safe Streets Act of 1968. (18 U.S.C. 2510- 2520). Washington, DC: U.S. Department of Justice. Accessed December 4, 2006 from http://www.usdoj.gov/crt/split/42usc3789d.htm

Organized Crime Control Act of 1970. (18 U.S.C. 1956, 1957). Accessed December 4, 2006 from http://trac.syr.edu/laws/18USC1956.html and http://trac.syr.edu/laws/18USC1957.html

President's Commission on Law Enforcement and Administration of Justice (1967). *The Challenge of Crime in a Free Society.* Washington, DC: U.S. Government Printing Office.

President's Commission on Organized Crime, 1988. (Executive Order 12435). Harry S. Truman Library: The American Presidency Project. Accessed December 4, 2006 from http://www.presidency.ucsb.edu/ws/index.php?pid=41647&st=&st1=

Racketeer Influenced and Corrupt Organizations Act (RICO). (1970). (18 U.S.C. 1961-1965). Accessed December 4, 2006 from http://usinfo.state.gov/usa/infousa/laws/majorlaw/rico/rico.htm

The Foreign Narcotics Kingpin Designation Act. (1999). (21 U.S.C. 1901-1908, 8 U.S.C. 1182; Pub. L. 106-120). What You Need to Know About U.S. Sanctions About Drug Traffickers. Washington, DC: Office of Foreign Assets Control, U.S. Department of the Treasury. Accessed December 4, 2006 from http://www.ustreas.gov/offices/enforcement/ofac/programs/narco/drugs.pdf

Title V of the Organized Crime Control Act of 1970. (18 U.S.C. 1546). Accessed December 4, 2006 from http://trac.syr.edu/laws/18USC1546.html

United States Code (2006, November 6 update). Database. Available from GPO Access, Washington, DC. Retrieved December 4, 2006 from http://www.gpoaccess.gov/uscode/index.html

Uniting and Strengthening America by Providing Appropriate Tools to Intercept and Obstruct Terrorism Act (USA Patriot Act) of 2001. Washington, DC: Electronic Privacy Information Center. Accessed December 4, 2006 from http://www.epic.org/privacy/terrorism/hr3162.html

The Intelligence Function in Organized Crime

13

"People who see the big picture expand their experience because they expand their world."

—John Maxwell (1951–), author, pastor

Chapter Objectives

After completing this chapter, readers should be able to:
- Discuss the sources of intelligence involving organized crime.
- Recognize the problems encountered by intelligence units when gathering and disseminating information about organized crime.
- List and discuss the different products of the intelligence unit.
- Explain how the intelligence analyst evaluates information.

■ Introduction

This chapter examines the proactive process and application of strategic and tactical intelligence to the investigation of today's organized crime.

The development and application of criminal intelligence can pose a major threat to criminal organizations. Analytical models, association analysis, and event and commodity analyses are the most important processes used to identify the organization's structure, membership, activities, and methods of operation. This process results in the identification of patterns and trends, which are extremely valuable when developing strategic, tactical, and administrative law enforcement responses to organized crime activity. Since 2001, the emphasis on terrorism by federal agencies has negatively impacted the resources dedicated to organized crime intelligence, as state and local law enforcement are mandated to be more

Current Assessment of Organized Crime in the United States

Organized Crime's Connection to Terrorist Groups

Globalization and the technology and information age enable crime organizations like the Yakuza, the Red Mafia, Triads, Colombian and Mexican drug cartels, and terrorists to operate with no geographical boundaries. Former international threats have now become domestic threats for the U.S. public and American law enforcement.

As obvious from earlier chapters in this text, outlaw biker groups and La Costa Nostra (LCN) are not the only organized crime groups now operating within the United States. New organized crime groups and their partners are emerging, and alliances between these groups constitute an unprecedented threat to our country. Encryption, software, fiberoptic cables, digital cellular telephones, and satellite technologies allow these sophisticated enterprise criminals a new immunity from law enforcement efforts (McDowell, 1991).

Organized crime's connection to terrorism has intensified during the past decade, especially when considering that much funding of terrorist activity is derived form narcotics trafficking. In South America, the National Liberation Army (ELN), The Revolutionary Armed Forces of Colombia (FARC), and the United Self-Defense Groups of Colombia (AUC) all are classified as both terrorist and organized crime deriving much of their income from the drug trade. Hamas and Hizballah (violent Palestinian Islamist revolutionary groups) are operating in Paraguay, Brazil, and Argentina; both use drug trafficking to finance their activities in South America and the Middle East. The Taliban (former repressive quasi-Islamist ruling faction) has operated illicit opium production in Afghanistan with connections to political extremists in Uzbekistan and Pakistan. Money from this operation partially funded the Al-Qaeda terrorist organization. Drugs, geography, and money are common ground between terrorism and organized crime.

U.S. Drug Enforcement Agency intelligence has uncovered alliances between Russian organized crime, LCN, the Italian Mafia, Mexican and Colombian drug trafficking organizations, Japanese Yakuza, Chinese Triads, and Nigerian crime groups. Terrorist networks are linking with these organized crime groups and others to finance terrorist operations worldwide (Testimony of Casteel, 2003).

Whether state-sponsored or otherwise funded, these complex organizations have funneled illegal funds into the political and economic systems of many countries to influence these systems to support organized crime activity. They move their money and themselves from country to country with no regard of national boundaries, fleeing arrest and prosecution by means of corruption and influence. Rivalry, turf battles, or geographic and ethnic differences have not prevented these groups from working together.

Legislation

The National Security Act of 1947 prevented the Central Intelligence Agency from having law enforcement powers as well as gathering and sharing intelligence with the FBI and other U.S. law enforcement agencies (Holt, 1995). But investigation of today's organized crime groups in the country requires economic intelligence not only from the U.S. banking system, but also abroad, because U.S.-based groups' alliances with foreign criminal organizations are often classified as international or transnational organized crime groups. If accurate, complete, and timely intelligence is not collected and analyzed from within our own borders and abroad, these groups will become more secure, efficient, effective, and clandestine than ever before.

In 2001, the United States Congress passed the USA Patriot Act (discussed in Chapter 12). Although the purpose of this Act was to enhance law enforcement tools to deter and punish terrorists, it may well prove to be important in the battle against organized crime. Proven links between terrorism and organized crime as well as broadening rules for U.S. intelligence-gathering capabilities may open new avenues of resources and support of other agencies to combat these criminal enterprises. Opposed by the American Civil Liberties Union and other organizations as a violation of many U.S. constitutionally-granted freedoms, the Act allows major intelligence operations on American citizens. Expansion of financial investigations includes the use of information gathered under the Foreign Intelligence Surveillance Act (FISA, 1978l; amended 1994–2006), and opens new pathways of communication for the CIA and FBI to share information between themselves as well as state and local law enforcement. The Patriot Act amends the FISA to widen surveillance regulations for criminal investigations, including the ability to intercept any communications (computer, satellite, or any passive or active signal). Since 2003, additional legislation has been introduced by the House and Senate to temper the Act, and two sections (505 and 805) have been ruled as unconstitutional. This Act is temporary in that some sunset provisions exist (that is, the law will not exist after a date set by Congress; this has been extended twice at this writing).

Intelligence

Intelligence is not the same as information. It is a multi-step process that involves collecting, collating, integrating, analyzing, correctly interpreting and, finally, effectively disseminating the information. Crime incidents, criminal behaviors and characteristics, patterns, and trends are used in tactical, strategic, and administration functions and planning.

For example, one study of the Texas Law Enforcement Management and Administrative Statistics Program reported that 50% of information produced by crime analysis units in Texas were used for tactical, 27% for strategic, and 24% for administrative purposes (TLEMASP, 1995). Tactical analysis functions were divided into four categories: crime series pattern detection; suspect–crime correlations; target/suspect profiles; and crime-potential forecasts. Analyses of administrative program evaluations parlayed into cost/effectiveness reports and government support studies. Strategic analyses included the preparation of: exception reports; crime trend forecasts; resource allocation; and situation analyses. As revealed by this study, crime analysis units were viewed by Texas agencies as being very useful and their reports were frequently utilized by officers. However, the survey also revealed that the officers may lack understanding of the precise function of a crime analysis unit. Although this study was not directed specifically at intelligence used against organized crime, the functions reported are very similar to those used for enterprise/organized crime (TLEMASP).

Historical Perspective

Intelligence and crime analysis have a rich history that began with the need for effective criminal investigation. While criminal and intelligence investigations contain numerous distinctions, these law enforcement units do operate in similar manners. Criminal investigations are primarily reactive and intelligence is proactive. Intelligence is an ongoing process of information collection, analysis, and dissemination. It provides information about people, places, organizations, and businesses that are specific targets.

While criminal investigation case files are considered "open files" (the information could be known throughout law enforcement officers and agencies) with the goal of arrest and prosecution, intelligence files are "closed files" that often contain information about continuous activity that may not be corroborated or even factual. Information from intelligence files is never presented in courts and is protected from subpoena. Criminal investigation and intelligence files are filed in separate locations, with strictly limited access to the intelligence files.

Frequently, intelligence information is used to create a report (product) that may provide guidance to investigators. These products may be transferred to a criminal investigation file after the information is validated. Once released, it is used in court cases in the form of flow charts, graphs, analytical models, financial analysis, and link diagrams. Most agencies store intelligence files separately from the personnel of the intelligence unit, with a high-tech security system protecting the files because they contain extremely sensitive reports, including allegations of corruption and alleged illegal conduct by high profile people, locations, and/or businesses. This type of sensitive information is shared on a "need to know" basis with very few people.

Intelligence operation history arose from military operations, as scouts would assemble such things as terrain and the opposition's troop movements that could be reviewed and analyzed by the military command. Crime analysis in America became more codified in the early 1900s, when the innovative Berkeley police chief and educator, August Vollmer (and possibly others) developed *modus operandi* files. Vollmer's protégé, O.W. Wilson is credited with inventing the term *crime analysis* in his book entitled, *Police Administration*, which became the most influential text on administration for its era.

The Law Enforcement Assistance Administration created the Integrated Criminal Apprehension Program (ICAP), forerunner of the Violent Criminal Apprehension Program (VICAP) currently operated by the FBI. Police departments in most major cities, many state agencies, and federal agencies have developed crime analysis/intelligence units that are a distinct unit on the structural chart of the department; however, resources dedicated to intelligence by state and local law enforcement in the United States are often inadequate and unable to address major organized crime operations. Federal units include the El Paso Intelligence Center (EPIC), Narcotics and Dangerous Drug Information system (NADDIS) of the Drug Enforcement Agency (DEA), Regional Drug Intelligence Squads (RDIS), and the Financial Crimes Enforcement Network (FinCEN). The CIA and FBI have their own databases. Such entities as the National Drug Pointer Index and The Regional Information Sharing System (RISS) are also involved in supporting law enforcement in their efforts against organized crime.

It is interesting to note that there is a history of alliances between intelligence agencies and organized crime (Lyman & Potter, 2000). La Costra Nostra provided intelligence during World War II and conducted counter-intelligence operations for the U.S. government (see Chapter 7). The Air America operation of the CIA during the Vietnam War transported opium in return for support from the Hmong Tribe. As late as the 1980s, the Afghan Mujahideen (declared by Presidents Carter and Reagan as "freedom fighters" and trained by U.S. military; these men evolved into the rigid Islamic Taliban extremists) was financed by drug trafficking. The Iran-Contra political scandal during the 1980s, where U.S. weapons and training were secretly given to Nicaraguan guerrilla groups through America's avowed enemy (Iran) in a program funded by drug trafficking, is yet another example of alliances between organized crime and the intelligence community.

Sources who provide intelligence are often of questionable character and reputation. To what extreme our government should go to achieve goals and gather intelligence remains debatable.

Other problems faced by intelligence units include:
- Little or no information sharing (particularly on an international level) because of a lack of trust, communication, or corruption concerns.
- Threat that strategic intelligence will be compromised for tactical operations or intelligence functions.
- Laws regulating intelligence confidentially are different among countries (for example, Canadian courts allow sources to be revealed).
- No qualified analyst is located in source countries, which compromises effective and accurate intelligence functions.

Europol has developed a system with strict rules regarding dissemination of sources that may reverse the trend of non-sharing. Both strategic and tactical intelligence information are critical to long-term coordinated effort against organized crime (Schneider, Beare, and Hill, 2001).

Evaluation of Information

Information evaluation is an important function of any intelligence unit. The Mississippi Bureau of Narcotics (MBN) developed a system for evaluating information that is currently used by many intelligence units nationwide. This system varies somewhat among agencies, but most evaluate the source and the information separately. In short, letters are assigned to a particular source who is rated numerically according to the degree of validity of his/her information (or vice versa). An example of a system is the following:

Evaluation of Source

A = A reliable source who has a proven track record and is competent.

B = A source whose information is most often valid but has been wrong on occasion(s).

C = An unreliable source whose information is most often false.

D = A source whose accuracy of information cannot be determined.

Evaluation of Information

1 = Information is true and can be corroborated.

2 = Information is likely true and comes directly from a reliable source, but cannot be corroborated.

3 = Information is not of direct knowledge from source, but can be partially corroborated.

4 = Information cannot be corroborated and is not from source's direct knowledge (that is, it is hearsay).

When information from such a system is distributed to those outside of a select group within the law enforcement agency/department, the coded report replaces the source names with the assigned letter and number.

Analysis of intelligence involves collation, where specific information is compared to data from other sources. However, information does not become intelligence until after it is analyzed and interpreted. A combination of technology, human review, and interpretation produce the final product. Experienced senior supervisors review the analyst's work before the report (product) is delivered to the user. The number and type of reviews vary from agency to agency, but often this product will include suggested courses of action and/or alternatives in an effort to aid a criminal investigation (Price, 1991).

Sources of Intelligence

The enormous volume of information collected requires a major effort filtering and sorting. After sorting, the intelligence product is delivered to three levels: strategic (conduct and policy development), operational (plan effective deployment, tactics, and techniques), and tactical (execution of tasks).

Categories of intelligence sources are divided into human, open, and technical sources (that is, active/passive electronic transmissions). *Human sources* are common in organized crime investigations and include informants, business people, undercover officers, physical surveillance, friends of targets, associates of targets, relatives of targets, and professional workers. *Open sources* include any type of publications, business records, vital statistics, court records, tax records, and financial records. *Technical intelligence* involves imagery and/or signal intelligence. Imagery intelligence may be the result of sensors on the light spectrum, or from cameras and photography on satellites and aircraft. Signal sources include Title III electronic intercepts (bugs and wiretaps), computer fax transmissions, microwave transmissions, and satellite transmissions. Often the most credible intelligence is from technical intelligence (Graham & Kiras, 1995; O'Connell & Tomes, 2004). Informants and human sources are quite problematic in terms of control, protection, management, and determining reliability; however, most successful organized crime investigations involve human intelligence.

When combined, these intelligence sources allow the investigator to be inside the enemy's decision-making process. Intelligence must be a holistic approach with innovative leadership (backed with adequate resources) to remain at least one step ahead of organized crime activity. Development of technology capabilities, data transmission, and protection of sources are essential to this approach (Graham & Kiras, 1995). Edmund J. Pankau (1992), a former special agent with the IRS Organized Crime division, offers excellent practical guidance in his book entitled, *Check It Out*, which includes how to discover information about assets, people, and places. Data available without court orders include real estate records, bankruptcy records, voter registration, local permits, civil suits, and a large variety of other sources. Analyses of these data can provide valuable information and help to build profiles of organized crime groups and their members.

Application of Analytical Models to Organized Crime Investigations

With the current U.S. political emphasis on the terrorist threat, budget cuts, and fluid organized crime groups that are continuously becoming more complex and sophisticated, successful investigators require accurate, timely, and comprehensive information. Law enforcement must become more efficient with the available resources to address enterprise crime. State and local enforcement must develop effective intelligence functions and methods for both sharing and gathering intelligence from within the United States and abroad.

Good intelligence identifies the targets for effective police operations and provides direction for investigators. The focus expands from individuals to groups or organizations, with emphasis on establishing priorities for manpower, time, money, equipment, and other limited resources.

Although informants can be extremely valuable, their information should not be used when establishing priorities for police operations. As police supervisors or administrators develop priorities, intelligence and/or analytical product should be a vital step for them to gain a broad scope of the problem. (They can see the "big picture.") However, non-sharing of sensitive information between law enforcement entities remains an obstacle to effective decision making.

Computerized data banks are widely used as an investigative tool. However, law enforcement personnel must be better trained at using them.

Global criminal intelligence and threat analyses are becoming effective tools in dealing with transnational and international organized crime. As these criminal organizations adapt to global markets, identifying the money flow and new markets of interest to these crime groups requires strategic as well as tactical abilities. While tactical intelligence supports planning and execution of enforcement, strategic intelligence supports policy formulation and broad plans at the administrative level to develop long-term solutions to combating organized crime. This might involve analyzing drug trafficking, money laundering, and drug abuse trends in a specific geographical area when developing a threat assessment from both internal and external factors.

Coordination of enforcement activity between countries to include money-laundering operations should be a focal point of the intelligence unit (Price, 1991). Besides drug trafficking, other expanding markets include: small arms trafficking, cyber crime, nuclear weapons and explosive devices, other weapons of mass destruction (biological and chemical), human body parts (for transplantation), slave trafficking of women and children, and environmental crime. As the world moves toward a paperless, wireless, and cashless society, the intelligence unit must actively create methods for collecting, analyzing, and disseminating information by means of complex technology and data/information systems. With organized crime holding a lower priority in federal agencies, state and local divisions must fill the gap and become much more active.

Data Analysis

Discovering the source and funding strategies used by criminal organizations often results in the conviction of major players in organized crime groups. A number of sophisticated software programs are now being used in the intelligence development stages, which results in an improved intelligence product that may even be able to predict future events. The increased speed at which relationships and patterns are identified from huge amounts of data will enhance the ability to deliver timely information so necessary to deal with the dynamic and complex nature of organized crime.

Financial institutions are becoming an essential part of an organized criminal's method of operation. Identification of criminal patterns and trends is now possible by collecting and analyzing criminal information. Correlation of elements of criminal activity and identifying members of a criminal organization establish links that give law enforcement administrators direction when planning strategies to address these activities. A good threat assessment provides a broad overview of the impact and vulnerability of organized crime in a specific area. Analyzing historical and current data can help to determine future impact. When an intelligence product produces the historical evolution of organized crime groups, including their structure, activities, goals and objectives, and method of operation, often the investigative strategies become obvious. The product also may suggest the best use of resources, including personnel, equipment, and funding (McDowell, 1991).

Structure and Responsibilities of Agency Personnel

Within every agency is a chain of command. The intelligence/crime analyst supervisor (normally a sworn, ranking officer who supervises both sworn and non-sworn personnel), reports directly to the agency head/director on a daily basis to keep the director informed on sensitive or critical issues and events. This report and who is permitted to receive it must be approved by the director of the intelligence unit. With very sensitive information (for example, corruption or criminal activity done by a public official), it is easy to see why this dissemination must be approved by the agency head. Some intelligence/crime analyst units employ a few sworn officers whose primary responsibilities are to gather intelligence from human, open, and technical sources on targeted places, individuals, or organizations. Their goal is to gather valuable information rather than to develop a prosecutable case.

Agencies/departments establish intelligence files under individual names, organizations or groups (such as the Bandido Outlaw Motorcycle Club, the national and New Orleans family of LCN), and locations, businesses, corporations, and places. Access to these files is strictly limited and they are placed in a secure location separate from criminal investigation files. The index of these data contains thousands of names, locations, and organizations. Parts of these files may be transferred to criminal case files only if its content is corroborated and contributes to the prosecution.

Financial Analysis

One of the most productive products of a crime analysis/intelligence unit is the financial analysis. The adage, "follow the money" has resulted in RICO, money laundering, and IRS cases against major violators and organizations. Two methods are the net worth expenditures schedule and the source and application of funds. Both illustrate an amount of expenditures in excess of known legal sources of income or unexplained income. Most defendants are reluctant to take the stand and explain the source of this excess income because it probably derives from illegal enterprises. Many organized crime members invest this illegal income in a variety of legitimate businesses such as real estate, trucking, waste management, restaurants, and other assets.

Commodity Flow Analysis

Related to financial analysis is the commodity flow analysis, which is a graphic chart of the direction(s) of sophisticated intergroup activities. With organized crime, this pictorial definition of their operations illustrates the group's services, goods, materials, and products. These charts often link illegal sources of income to legitimate businesses or corporations. The objective of a commodity flow analysis is to identify the network of money flow between the leaders of major crime groups and the source of their crimes, which may include an apparently legal enterprise. A second chart may reveal the routes of transfer or shipments of illegal substances from source countries to street distribution. Then an intelligence product can be produced that combines the commodity flow with operational structure (**Figure 13-1**).

Event Flow Analysis

Another product of the unit is the event flow analysis. This depicts the time and date of an event, such as tracking cocaine from the growing field to processing, to loading and transport, and from transport to distribution. Each step of the process can be detailed by location and people involved.

Crime by Association

A frequent product used in prosecutions of organized crime members is the association or link chart. These graphic displays show the relationships between members of complex organizations. This may include each person's position in the hierarchy, the connections of illegal activities to legitimate businesses, or the power, strength, and influence of the organization. A number of association matrices and link diagrams may be incorporated into this analysis. For example, Figure 10.4 is an example of the organizational chart of the Grim Reapers Motorcycle Club, which is classified as an organized crime entity, without the names of

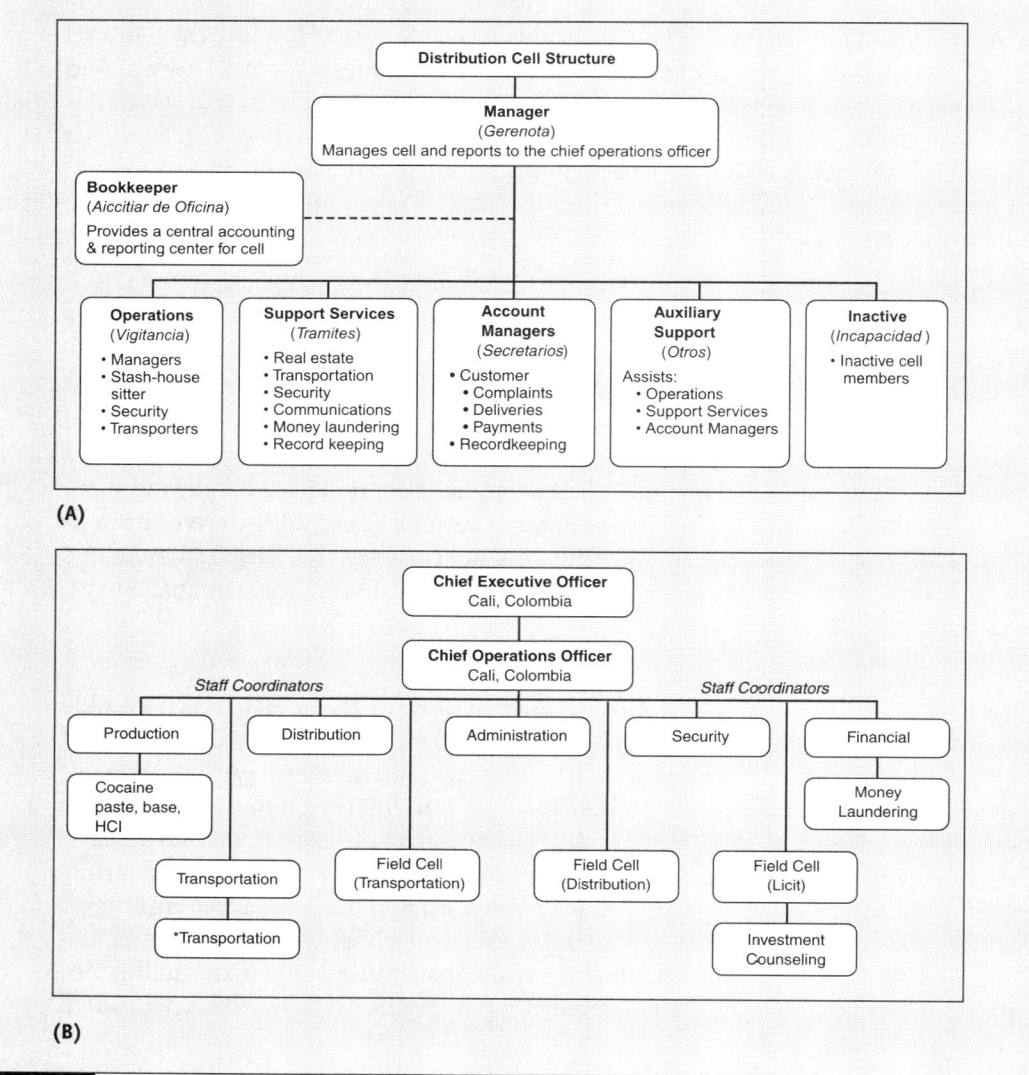

Figure 13-1 Sample of a Commodity Flow Analysis. (A) Distribution cell structure. (B) Operational structure.

members who currently occupy these positions of authority. With the names added, the prosecutor may prove that this is a criminal or continuing criminal enterprise. Conspiracy and RICO statutes allow for the leaders of these types of organizations to be prosecuted for the criminal acts of their subordinate members (vicarious criminal liability).

Other link analyses include those involving telephone/cellular records and wire transfers of money by such means as Western Union. These products are part of the preliminary steps to obtaining a court-ordered electronic intercept. Linking suspects by these records removes the possibility of a suspect's testimony that they did not know one another or never wired money to a known source of illegal goods or substances. Pen register and the technique of trap and trace link suspects in the matrix by detailing all incoming and outgoing calls.

Units within the Intelligence Division

The crime analyst in the intelligence unit can explore the overall scope of a criminal operation. An investigation may include the structure/hierarchy, gross income, quantities of illegal goods and services, identification of processes employed to launder money, and roles of members of an illegal enterprise. This unit may perform cryptanalysis for recorded conversations and racketeering documents that may contain encrypted information. Major violators often use codes or ciphers to disguise their criminal activities. Skilled analysts are able to graphically lay out an entire criminal enterprise (such as LCN or the Colombian North Valley Cartel) in a manner that the public serving on juries can easily understand. "A picture is worth a thousand words" is the prosecution's most satisfying adage when these materials are presented in court.

The importance of developing effective criminal intelligence is not limited to the U.S. government and law enforcement agencies. Intelligence opportunities in Canada are illustrated by the report of the Alberta Solicitor General and the Alberta Criminal Intelligence Service. Goals of their strategic plan include providing effective collection, analysis, and dissemination of criminal intelligence, developing intelligence-based analytical products, and participating in the preparation of provincial threat assessments on organized crime for the benefit of senior police managers and various levels of government (Criminal Intelligence Service Alberta, 2002).

U.S. agencies such as the FBI, DEA, ATF, Homeland Security, and state and local law enforcement depend on accurate, comprehensive, and timely intelligence products to successfully deal with organized/enterprise crime. Organized crime poses a threat to our political, economic, and social systems equal to that of terrorism. Our gaps in knowledge about these criminal organizations are filled by increasing the resources dedicated to producing effective intelligence products. State and local law enforcement must become more involved and knowledgeable about their intelligence functions to ensure that adequate resources are dedicated to this vital function.

■ Conclusions

The success of complex investigations of organized crime groups depends upon the ability to make sense out of massive amounts of information from a variety of sources. Skilled intelligence analysts are able to assemble a product from raw data that can assist administrators to develop the logistics for effective and efficient investigations as well as strategies to predict and/or deter future criminal activities. Accurate, comprehensive, and timely information is the goal of an intelligence unit. Agencies or departments that do not have this resource are unprepared to cope with organized crime and must depend on agencies with sufficient resources to take over this function.

Like many other professions, law enforcement is overwhelmed by the information age and new technologies. Law enforcement personnel must become more innovative and technologically advanced, applying the proactive approach of criminal and intelligence analysis. Computer and wireless technologies play major roles in organized crime activities and investigations of these activities. Law enforcement efficacy will depend on creative and proactive strategies to address the ever more complex technologies in conjunction with the growing phenomena of transnational organized crime.

By using intelligence gathering strategies and qualified personnel, gaps in knowledge and interagency communication problems encountered throughout the world can be bridged. Networks and consolidation of efforts must be established between worldwide law enforcement so that valuable information is protected and shared with the goal of producing proactive strategic enforcement. The professions of intelligence analyst and criminal analyst must continue to evolve into a variety of disciplines for it to remain effective. To staff these units, universities must develop quality programs that produce creative professionals capable of staying ahead of the criminals they will face on the street and in the justice system.

DISCUSSION QUESTIONS

1. Why are organized crime investigations vulnerable to the intelligence process?
2. Discuss the sources of intelligence involving organized crime.
3. Discuss the problems encountered by intelligence units when gathering and disseminating information about organized crime.
4. List and discuss the different products of the intelligence unit.
5. How does the intelligence analyst evaluate information?
6. What is the future of the intelligence function?

REFERENCES

Albanese, J. S. (2001). *The Prediction and Control of Organized Crime: A Risk Assessment Instrument for Targeting Law Enforcement Efforts Summary Report.* Virginia Commonwealth University: National Institute of Justice International.

Criminal Intelligence Service Alberta. (2002). Alberta Solicitor General and Criminal Intelligence Service Initiatives. Province of Alberta, Canada: Department of the Solicitor General.

Graham, C., & Kiras, J. D. (1995). Intelligence and peacekeeping: Definitions and limitations. *Peacekeeping and International Relations*, 24, 3–4.

Holt, P. M. (1995). Spying out new roles for Central Intelligence Agency. *Christian Science Monitor*, 87, 19.

Kitfield, J. (2000, September 16). Covert counterattack. *National Journal*, 32, 2858(8).

LeBeuf, M. E. (2001). Organized crime and cybercrime criminal investigations and intelligence on the cutting edge: Technical report-information technology series. Ottawa, Canada: Police Sciences School.

Lyman, M. D., & Potter, G. W. (2000). *Organized Crime*, (2nd ed). Upper Saddle River, NJ: Prentice-Hall, Inc.

McDowell, D. (1991). *Strategic intelligence in law enforcement: The development of a national capacity for production of strategic intelligence on the criminal environment of Australia.* Canberra, Australia: Attorney General's Department of Australia.

O'Connell, K., & Tomes, R. R. (2004). Keeping the information edge. *Policy Review*, 122, 19.

Pankau, E. J. (1992). *Check It Out.* Chicago: Contemporary Book, Inc.

Price, B. (1991). The use of intelligence in the fight against drugs. In S. Flood (Ed.). *Illicit Drugs and Organized Crime: Issues for a Unified Europe.* Chicago: Office of International Criminal Justice, pp. 131–141.

Schneider, S., Beare, M., & Hill, J. (2001, April). Alternative Approaches to Combating Transnational Crime. Rockville, MD: National Criminal Justice Reference Service. Retrieved December 4, 2006 from http://www.ncjrs.org/nathanson/etranscrime.html

Testimony of Steven W. Casteel, Assistant Administrator for Intelligence, Drug Enforcement Administration, Hearing of the Senate Judiciary Committee. (2003, May 13). Narco-Terrorism: International Drug Trafficking and Terrorism—A Dangerous Mix. Accessed December 4, 2006 from http://www.ciponline.org/colombia/030513cast.htm

Texas Law Enforcement Management and Administrative Statistics Program. (1995). *Crime Analysis: Administrative Aspects*. Huntsville, TX: Police Research Center.

SUGGESTED READING

Abadinsky, H. (2003). *Organized Crime*. Belmont, CA: Wadsworth/Thomson.

Baker, T. E. (2005). *Introductory Criminal Analysis: Crime Prevention and Intervention Strategies*. Upper Saddle River, NJ: Prentice-Hall, Inc.

Where Do We Go From Here?

14

"Personal excellence can be achieved by a visionary goal, thorough planning; dedicated execution and total follow through."

–Gerald R. Ford, 38th U. S. President

■ Law Enforcement Response

Law enforcement has accumulated a significant amount of information regarding the history, structure, activities, and methods of operation of these sophisticated criminal organizations.

Most disturbing about these groups is the lack of knowledge about the extent of current corruption and activities in the United States and abroad. Gaps in information concerning the extent of alliances among the many diverse organized crime groups also exist. If the past is any indication of what today and the future hold, we must assume that these groups will continue to become more efficient and effective in their ability to gain power and reap huge profits by means of both violence and corruption. With their history of successfully corrupting governments, businesses, and the community, why would we not assume that this is occurring on an unprecedented scale today and is certain to continue into the future?

Twenty-first century criminal enterprises will be more educated, high tech, and computer-literate organizations that will benefit from the growth of a global community and the information age. Certainly, one of the major targets of modern organized crime continues to be financial institutions, which will give rise to international conglomerates and corporations controlled by the wealth and power of organized crime groups. Major investments in legitimate avenues have been the trend since gangsters like Meyer Lansky first began to see their potential for profit. Profits from drug trafficking, theft of high tech information, systems, and equipment along with trafficking in human body parts and slave labor, global Internet sports betting, waste disposal, and other goods and services will contribute to an ever-increasing international market, both illicit and legitimate. Most of the providers of these revenue streams are the organized crime groups discussed in this book.

A variety of evolving groups such as MS-13 (Mara Salvatrucha 13) will rise and fall. MS-13's roots are in the revolution-torn countries of El Salvador and Honduras of the 1980s. This gang appeared in Los Angeles by the late 1980s and spread with Central American migrant workers and illegal aliens migrating throughout the United States. Now documented by the FBI in over 30 states with an estimated 20,000 members, over 200 members have been arrested by U.S. task forces established to develop cases on this gang. Known for their brutal ruthlessness, group members committed over 1,200 murders between 2000 and 2005, and they are involved in racketeering activity, which classifies them as an organized crime group. New groups such as MS-13 and transnational organized groups will continue to evolve.

Before money laundering and safe havens for the leaders of these complex criminal organizations can be eliminated, the entire global community must adopt more effective legislation and other strategies that can trace the money accurately. The power of regulatory agencies must be increased. Repealing bank security laws, establishing an international financial intelligence unit, criminalizing the act of money laundering, and developing RICO, conspiracy, CCE, and forfeiture laws in all nations is a must if any chance exists for significantly impacting these powerful organizations. If these organizations remain untouched until they reach the United States border, they will never be defeated.

Holding the thin line separating professional law enforcement from the ever more sophisticated organized crime alliances is a formidable task. The disparity between organized crime resources and those devoted to law enforcement must be addressed. Using satellites, telecommunications, and computers to compliment their effective use of violence and corruption, organized crime enjoys distinct advantages over today's law enforcement.

Organized crime's state-of-the-art equipment, the best experts in all professions that money can buy, and advanced communication systems put much of law enforcement resources to shame. These organizations may well operate in the future with more efficacy, efficiency, and impunity from arrest and prosecution.

Three factors have permitted organized crime greater opportunities to become even more powerful: the growth of new organized crime groups; U.S. resources diverted away from fighting organized crime and into Homeland Security; and the enforcement culture of not sharing information and resources. RICO statutes may have started the decline of some groups such as La Cosa Nostra, but others such as the Japanese Yakuza have increased their holdings in both stock and real estate in America and other countries worldwide. The questions remain: Who will manage multinational corporations and who will use any means to be successful?

With the fall of the Soviet Union, powerful nuclear, biological, and chemical weapons became available on the black market. Added to the level of danger are alliances of Russian organized crime with both Mexican and Colombian organized crime groups. Currently, foreign terrorist organizations such as FARC, ELN, the AUC, and others are engaging in organized crime activities, including narcotics trafficking with the DTOs of Colombia and Mexico. Hamas and Hizballah members located in Paraguay, Argentina, and Brazil generate income from drug and weapons trafficking as well as liquor that support their respective organizations in Lebanon, Palestine, and elsewhere in the Middle East. The Peruvian Shining Path group is yet another terrorist group engaged in drug trafficking. Additional groups in southwest Asia, including organizations in Afghanistan and Uzbekistan, are connected to al-Qaeda who derive significant income from heroin and opium trafficking. The Southeast Asian Tamil Tigers group also use drug trafficking to support their terrorist activities. Also located in Southeast Asia is The United Wa State Army, a major producer of both methamphetamines and heroin. The Philippines has the New People's Army, which supports its activity by cultivating and trafficking marijuana. Other Philippines groups that support terrorist activity by narcotics trafficking include the Moro National Front, the Moro Islamic Liberation Front, and Abu Sayyaf group. Financing terrorist networks and activities through drug trafficking has a decades-long history with narco-terrorist groups in Colombia, which have generated billions from their illicit trade.

Within the above examples are strong indications of the alliances between many organized crime and terrorist organizations. These alliances present problems for law enforcement that are likely to escalate in the future. Operations like the U.S. Attorney General's Money Laundering Operation (a 1999-initiated task force involving undercover sting operations designed to seize laundered drug proceeds) are necessary to legally capture and coerce organized crime groups to forfeit their assets and cash, and thus negatively impact the organization's major source of income for terrorist activity.

The link between terrorism and organized crime include state-sponsored entities such as Afghanistan opium and heroin operations (which have increased under U.S. occupation) or the narco-terrorist groups existing in Colombia. The war on drugs and the war on terrorism are linked. International effort and cooperation are needed now to prevent such events as the September 11 attacks.

Transnational organized crime is the most significant development of our time. The number of alliances that allowed these groups to collaborate and cooperate to deliver illicit goods and services are unprecedented. These enterprises have incorporated technological advancements and changes in the economic and political environments into their fluid schemes of operation. Globalization of organized crime has allowed these groups to deliver their goods and services anywhere, anytime, to anyone. They have no problem with violating international borders.

The basics of organized crime remain the same as have existed for centuries. These groups are still a local problem that depends upon corruption to continue to exist. However, crime organizations combined with terrorist groups add to the law enforcement problems of combating their crimes. The new face of organized crime is the alliance between traditional and nontraditional organized crime groups and international terrorists.

The historical evolution of a variety of organized crime groups and their leaders is sketchy and debatable, as is the structure of these groups. Much of what we think we know about organized crime comes from law enforcement or government sources. Media speculation, confessions of organized criminals, and other questionable sources contribute to our knowledge of organized crime. There is little sound research by academia into organized crime despite numerous publications and books. It is very difficult to conduct research into such secretive and dangerous organizations, which depend upon codes of conduct such as omerta and murderous retribution for their survival.

Many of these leaders began their criminal careers by committing petty crimes as they tried to imitate a criminal role model. Over time, they commit more serious crimes, become a gang member, and eventually are a member of an organized crime organization. Leaders grow into legitimate businessmen late in their careers as the profits of illegal activities are invested into reputable legal enterprises. By examining the rise and fall of these leaders, law enforcement can develop strategies for the future. Leaders and bosses of organized crime share many similarities, as demonstrated in this book. A pattern can be developed and used to help direct future law enforcement strategies.

It now seems that criminal leaders and their organizations will always be part of our future. They have proven to be a very dynamic phenomenon as they quickly adjust to new legislation and law enforcement strategies. To avoid arrest and prosecution, and continue to survive, their criminal organization will become more sophisticated, structured, and even more of a threat than in the past.

If America and other countries move toward being cashless and paperless societies, organized crime will be prepared with high tech electronics as well as financial and legal experts. This requires law enforcement and its investigators to be proactive in the training of their own experts on current technologies.

A different type of investigator trained in cutting-edge technology, computer, and financial investigations is necessary to meet this challenge. This will require substantial formal education in the areas of business, accounting, computer science, and market dynamics in addition to the criminal justice field. Task forces comprising highly specialized personnel are required, as is continuous training in both market dynamics and technology as they relate to organized crime activity. Investigators of the future may well be multilingual and possess advanced degrees in a variety of fields. In-service training involving case studies, and an ability to take advantage of technology to advance skills and knowledge are essential elements if investigators want to remain ahead of the dynamic nature of these criminal groups.

Governments will always have prohibitions on items such as drugs and alcohol, so the problem of corruption will continue to plague law enforcement efforts. While past efforts against organized crime members have been impressive, as explained in the preceding chapters, the war is far from won. Allegations of Mob influence at the U.S. presidential level spanning at least four presidents are certainly a major concern for the future. If these criminals have reached the presidential level in the past, what prevents this level of influence in the future?

Government efforts of the past are not sufficient to face an allied global organized crime community. With their ability to corrupt the U.S. government at the local, state, and the highest federal levels combined with mergers of these criminal syndicates with major corporations, we are seeing a new level of corporate crime.

Demands for illegal services and goods by the public are continuing and probably will increase in the future. If these global alliances between major organized crime groups are successful (that is, if they are not already established), then organized crime will become the largest business in the world, attracting large numbers of those who desire power and wealth no matter what the actual cost.

The early strategies of organized crime to neutralize law enforcement and politicians by bribery, control the source of supply by monopoly, and develop unity by structuring the organization and dividing the geographic areas among smaller affiliated groups will continue, only it will be on a global scale and not just for a single country. Theories, history, and definitions of organized crime are starting points for the investigator's understanding of this evolving phenomenon.

Concepts of organized crime and methods to address these complex groups will always be controversial. Because of the lack of accurate intelligence, one problem is that much of the information concerning organized crime is from journalistic sources. Many in academia disagree with or are suspicious of information from law enforcement sources. Informants and personal experiences form the remaining sources of information about these crime enterprises.

Controversies began with the variety of definitions for organized crime from country to country and among academia. If no comprehensive definition can be reached among experts, how can research be validated and meaningful discussions occur? How much organization and structure do these groups have? These questions are areas of discussion in academia, but are far less controversial among those in law enforcement who are coping with the destruction in the wake of these criminals.

Much debate surrounds U.S. statutes and legislation, such as the RICO Act, the Patriot Act, and narcotic laws. Invasion of privacy and individual rights are issues in the argument against the Patriot Act and RICO. Considered too broad and invasive, many believe them to violate constitutional freedoms and argue that they potentially could be used against individuals who do not belong to a criminal or terrorist group. RICO charges can lead to guilty pleas for executives whose business assets are frozen, even when the company is innocent of RICO violations. The threat of triple damages in civil suits, freezing personal assets, and being labeled a "racketeer" can be very intimidating.

Sunset clauses of The Patriot Act that expired in March 2006 are being debated in Congress as of this writing. Some arguments are over the following issues: whether such extreme measures are necessary to address terrorism; whether the broad money laundering statutes are effective, the involvement of the National Security Agency and CIA in domestic intelligence and surveillance collection; and the roving wire tap. Some abuse of forfeiture regulations has fueled controversy surrounding what is subject to forfeiture under what conditions. Policy such as "zero tolerance" (seizure of large assets when small amounts of drugs are discovered) has been a subject of concern and debate.

The idea of legalizing drugs and prostitution has been presented as a solution by some in law enforcement, who join the political left wing in this view. This concept also calls for spending more on prevention and education and less on law enforcement and corrections. Other proposals under debate include instituting relaxed legal hurdles for illegal workers to live in the United States, which include many families who have evaded deportment and paid taxes for a decade or more as well as criminal elements.

Another perspective proposed is that the U.S. government created the concept of organized crime to obtain support and funding for law enforcement and the bureaucracy. Those holding this view do not believe that organized crime groups have developed global alliances or are allied with terrorists. They consider this a plot to allow known government invasion of individual rights, and as an excuse to use the military and other government powers.

The vast majority of law enforcement—including me—does not support these extreme views.

Corruption is yet another subject of debate. How does corruption first occur? Do organized crime members corrupt people, businesses, and government, or are these criminals approached by those entities in their pursuit of power and profit? Has corruption become more frequent and underground, or have efforts against organized crime reduced corruption? Despite these and other questions, it remains that less coordination and sharing of information exists among international, national, state, and local law enforcement directly because of the threat of corruption.

Organized crime is controversial and will continue to generate much discussion. As it expands into our society, becoming more opaque, complex, and diverse, new issues will arise for those law enforcement and governments charged with developing new laws and strategies to combat their membership and crimes.

As is often said, if we fail to study and know the past, we are doomed to repeat our failures. The deeper the understanding and more accurate the concepts of organized crime the investigator develops, the more effective he or she becomes. As depicted throughout this book, the future of organized crime in America involves the increased diversity of groups such as Triads, drug cartels, the Red Mafia, and the Yakuza. All depend primarily on corruption and public demand for their services and goods. Just as the rising demand for drugs created an unprecedented number of sophisticated international and transnational criminal networks, the information age takeovers of financial institutions, and terrorist demands are an impetus for the continued growth of organized crime.

At this writing, an international commission may not be established among the many organized crime groups; however, doubtless there is increased cooperation among these groups. The market potential for such a new global crime community is unlimited. Despite numerous successes, all prior efforts have failed to stop the growth of organized crime. Investigators of the future must understand market dynamics to examine how these criminal enterprises have emerged, survived, and continue to profit by supplying the public demand for illegal services and goods. This calls for multiple strategies to address corruption, money laundering, and market demand, all of which require enormous improvements in developing intelligence on an international scale.

Organized crime's influence of politics and the business world must be targeted if we are to derail the growth of alliances, power, and wealth of these complex criminal organizations. Clearly, future investigators must view organized crime as a dynamic phenomenon and stay on top of these changes with accurate and timely intelligence. New strategies must be developed to ensure adequate resources to support the very best and brightest investigators America has to offer.

Index

A

Abadinsky, Howard, 8–9
Abalone trade, 143
Abu Sayyaf group, 223
Accardo, Tony, 21, 100, 101
ACLU (American Civil Liberties Union), 204, 209
Act for the Preservation of Unlawful Activities by Boryukudan Members, 118
Aerial eradication of coca leaves, 59
Afghan Mujahideen, 211
Afghanistan, drug trafficking operations, 223
African-American gangs. See Hispanic and African-American gangs
Ah Kung (grandpa), 140
Air America operation, 211
Aiuppa, Joseph, 25
Al-Qaeda, 208, 223
Albanese, J., 35–36, 38, 40
Alberta Criminal Intelligence Service, 217
Alberta Solicitor General, 217
Alcohol, crime associated with. See Prohibition of alcohol
Alien Conspiracy Theory, 34
Amalgamation, 9
American Civil Liberties Union (ACLU), 204, 209
American Mafia. See Italian-American Mafia
Amuso, Vittorio, 99
Anastasia, Albert, 21, 97
Annotated Codes of Maryland (2003), characteristics that defined organized crime, 7
Annunzio-Wylie Money Laundering Act (1992), 195
Anomie theory, 36–37, 43
Anslinger, Harry, 124
Anti-crime legislation, and the growth of organized criminal groups, 21–22
Anti-Drug Abuse Act (1986), 194, 197
Anti-Gang Youth and Violence Act (1997), 185
Appalachian region, illegal whiskey, 24
Appalachin Crime Conference, 100, 107
Arellano Felix Organization, 66–67
Arian Brotherhood, 185
Arizona Revised Statutes (2003), 7
Arkies, 178
Armenian criminal groups, 75, 79
Arnold Rothstein, 95–96
Art of War, The (Sun Tzu), 11
Associates (Giovane D'Honore), 104
ATF (Department of Alcohol, Tobacco, and Firearms), 25, 217
AUC (United Self-Defense Groups of Colombia), 60, 208

B

Baby cartels, Colombia, 58
Bagley, Bruce, 60, 65, 69, 70
Bakuto (gamblers), 115, 116, 121
Banana Wars, 99
Bandidos motorcycle gang, 151, 156–157
Bank Secrecy Act (1970), 194
Barger, Ralph Hubert (Sonny), 155
Barksdale, "King" David, 181
Barnes, Leroy "Nicky," 183
BC Bud, 151
Beccaria, Marches e de, 37
Bentham, Jeremy, 37
Big Circle Gang, 136, 144, 147
Biker gangs. See Outlaw motorcycle gangs (OMGs)
Biker women, 164
Bikes, OMGs, 158–159
Biological theory, 37
Black Belt, 100
"Black Biscuit" sting operation, 170
Black Guerilla Family (BGF), 180, 185
"Black Hand" gang, 92–94, 175
　cities they were established in, 93–94
　formation of criminal gangs, 93
　growth in power and income during the Prohibition Era, 93
　murder of David Hennessey, 92–93
Black Liberation Army (BLA), 180
Black market, in post-war Japan, 116
Black Market Peso Exchange, 56
Black P. Stone Nation, 180–181
Blakey, G. Robert, 6–7, 190
Blockaders, 24
Bloods, The, 5, 175, 179–180
Bonanno: Godfather's Story, 99
Bonanno, Joseph, 21, 25, 91, 97
　alliance with the Sicilian Mafia, 98
　the Banana Wars, 99
　contributions to the American Mafia's success, 99
　early life, 98
　makes peace with Lucciano, 98
Bonanno crime family, 98
Bootlegging, 20, 21
Borgata, 104
Born To Kill (BTK) gang, 144
Boryokudan, 115
Boryokudan Countermeasures Law (1992), 126–127
Boxer Rebellion, 136
Brazil, FARC drug trafficking network in, 60–61, 222
Brighton Beach ("Little Odessa"), 76, 83
Briley, Richard Gaylord, 132
Bruno, Angelo, 101
Bruno crime family, 168
Buchalter, Lepke, 95, 96
Bureaucratic/corporate model, 41
Burn company, 79
Bush, Prescott, Jr., 126
Business acquisitions, Yakuza, 123
Business and labor, regulation and monitoring of, 200–201

C

Calderon, Felipe, 71
Cali cartel, 26, 44, 53–56

Cali cartel (cont'd)
  decline of, 56–57
  major players in, 53
  operations
    extent of the cartel's control, 53–54
    factors in the success of, 54–55
    growth of into a multinational organization, 54
    money laundering, 55–56
    movement of cocaine inside U.S. borders, 55
    organizational chart, 55f
California, Russian criminal groups in, 78, 79
California Penal Code, definition of organized crime, 7
Caló street slang, 176
Camorra, 91, 92
Canada
  Hells Angels in, 155–156
  Russian Mafia in, 82
Cancun, 68
Capone, Al, 16, 19, 25, 100
  became boss of the "Outfit," 21
  conviction for tax evasion, 193
Caporegimes, 102, 104
Capro, Joe, 102
Caracas, Tomas Medina (Negro Acacio), 84
Cardenas, Osiel, 67
Caribbean countries
  as links in the drug trade, 54
  Russian Mafia and, 82
Carolla, Anthony, 102
Cartel, definition of, 4
Casa de Cambio, 196
Casso, Anthony, 107
Castellammarse Wars, 95, 98
Castellano, Paul, 110
Center for Strategic and International Studies on Russian Organized Crime, 75
Central Intelligence Agency (CIA), 225
Central Red Army Sports Club, 85
Chabat, Jorge, 69
Chain conspiracies, 198–199
"Charlie Town," 179
Chechens, 75
Check It Out, 213
Chemical Diversion and Trafficking Act (1988), 197
Chepesiuk, Ron, 50, 53–54
Chernobyl Nuclear Disaster charity, conspiracy to defraud, 85
Chiang Kai Shek, 136
Chicago Commission, 25
Chicago families, 25
Chicago Outfit, 21, 99–101, 104
Chicago tongs, 143
China White (heroin), 140
Chinatowns, 144
Chinese Consolidated Benevolent Association, 133
Chinese Snake Head, 119
Ching (Manchu) dynasty, 135
Choitner, Murray, 27
Chong, Peter, 141
"Church of Angels" (Hells Angels), 165

CIA, 225
Cirillo, Dominick "Quiet Don," 99
Clark, John Bates, 188
Classical theory, 37
Clicas, 176–177
CMIR (Currency and Monetary Instrument Report), 194, 196
Coca cultivation, 50, 59
Cocaine trafficking, 21
  in Colombia, 50
  Jamaican organized crime, 184
  Nigerian organized crime, 183–184
Colombo family, 110
Colors (patches), OMGs, 154, 159, 161
Colosimo, "Big Jim," 21, 100
Colucci, Joey, 110
Colombian cartels, 10, 26, 49–62
  Cali cartel, 53–56
    decline of, 56–57
    major players in, 53
    operations
      extent of the cartel's control, 53–54
      factors in the success of, 54–55
      growth of into a multinational organization, 54
      money laundering, 55–56
      movement of cocaine inside U.S. borders, 55
      organizational chart, 55f
  conclusions, 60–61
  current activities
    baby cartels, 58
    FARC, 58, 59, 60, 61, 222
    Norte del Valle cartel, 58, 59
    paramilitary groups, 58–59
    Plan Colombia, 50, 59–60
  decline of the major cartels, 56–57
  discussion questions, 62
  historical perspective
    affinity for smuggling, 50, 51f
    cocaine and coca leaf cultivation, 50, 59
    La Violenca, 50
    "Plan Colombia," 50, 59–60
    prominence of in the drug trade, 50
    role in the international proliferation of drugs, 49–50
    switch to heroin trafficking, 51–52
    U.S. move to stem the flow of drugs into the country, 50–51
  introduction, 49
  Medellín Cartel, 52–53
Colombian DTOs, 21, 25
Columbo, Joseph, 91
Columbo crime family, 98
Com pagnediarm, 91
Commissions and task forces. *See* Task and strike forces
The Commission, 96–98, 104, 105
Commodity flow analysis, 215, 216f
Comprehensive Crime Control Act (1984), 197
Confidential Informants (CI), 171
Consigliere, 104
Consortium, definition of, 4
Conspiracy, 42–43, 44
  definition of, 5

Continuing Criminal Enterprise (CCE) statute (1970), 6, 28, 170, 200
Controlled Substance Act, 21, 39
Corallo, Anthony "Ducks," 99
Corporate crime (white collar crime), 15
Corruption, 28
   corporate and political, 26–27
   corruption, law enforcement, and the government, 224–226
   growth of corruption and establishment of organized crime families (Dixie Mafia), 23–24
   and increase in serious crime, Yakuza, 118
   in Russia, investigation of, 27, 86
Costello, Frank, 21, 25, 95, 97, 101
Council of Europe, 128
Country Boys, The, 182–183
Cowboys, 178
Cressey, Donald, 8
Crime by association, 215–216
Crime families, rise of in the United States, 18f
Criminal-community relationship, 43
Criminal environment issues, 39
Crips, The, 175, 179–180
CTR (Currency Transaction Report), 194, 196
Cuban Marielitos, 26
Cultural transmission, 36
Culture conflict, 36
Currency and Foreign Transactions Reporting Acts, 86
Currency and Monetary Instrument Report (CMIR), 194, 196
Currency Transaction Report (CTR), 194, 196
Cybercrime, Russian Mafia, 79–80

D

Dai Dai Lo, 140
Daisy chain, 79
D'Alfonso, Frank "Flowers," 101
Daly, Richard, 100
Dannemora prison, 97
Data analysis, 214
Deering's California Codes Annotated (2003), 7
DeFede, Joe, 99
Delaware Code Annotated (2003), 7
Department of Alcohol, Tobacco, and Firearms (ATF), 25, 217
Derivative Use Immunity, 202–203
Deterrence Theory, 40–41
Dewey, Thomas, 97
Diamond, Eddie, 95, 96
Diamond, Jack "Legs," 95, 96
Differential association theory, 36
Differential opportunity, 36
"Disciple Nation, 5
Dixie Mafia. *See* Southern organized crime (Dixie Mafia)
Dobkin, Lou, 157
Dobovšek, B., 8
Donovan, Raymond, 27
Dorfman, Allan, 200
Doyuki Rondlan, 119
Dragon syndicates, 142

Drug Abuse Act (1988), 195
Drug Enforcement Agency (DEA), 217
   narcotics unit massacred by Colombian soldiers, 60
   organized crime connections to terrorist groups, 208
   takedown of the Cali cartel, 57
Drug Lords: The Rise and Fall of the Cali Cartel, 53
Drug policies: impact and consequences
   Mexican DTOs, 70–71
   Mexico, 70–71
Drug trafficking, 26, 39
   growth of, 20, 21–23
   motorcycle gangs, 151, 169
   Nuevo Laredo, Mexico, 65–66
   Russian Mafia, 21–22, 80, 81
   terrorists groups, 222–223
   Yakuza, 124
Drug trafficking organizations (DTOS), 21. *See also* specific organizations
Drug use in the United States, statistics, 64
Durkheim, D., 36

E

Eastman gang, 19
Eaton, Tracey, 68
Edo period (1603-1867), 115
Eighteenth Amendment. *See* Prohibition of alcohol
El Paso Intelligence Center (EPIC), 170, 196, 211
El Rukins, 180, 181
Electronic Communications Privacy Act (1986), 201
Electronic surveillance, 201–202
ELN (National Liberation Army), 208
Enforcers (Kryshas), 77
Enron scandal, 15, 17, 26
Enterprise theory of investigation (ETI), 39–40
Environmental and role model influences, 43
EPIC (El Paso Intelligence Center), 170, 196, 211
Escobar, Pablo, 16, 52
   shot and killed, 56–57
   stay in "The Cathedral," 56
Ethnic groups, Russian Mafia, 75
Ethnicity, 43
European Union Bank, 82
Event flow analysis, 215
Evolution of organized crime. *See also* Southern organized crime (Dixie Mafia)
   commissions and task forces, 25–26
   corporate and political corruption, 26–27
   discussion questions, 30
   expansion of organized crime in the United States
      anti-crime legislation and, 21–22
      Chicago, 21
      drug trafficking, 20, 21–23
      Harrison Narcotics Act (1914), 20
      prohibition of alcohol era (1920-1930), 20, 21
   future impact on law enforcement efforts, 27–29
      corruption, 28
      creation of task and strike forces, 28
      crime control legislation, 28

Evolution of organized crime (cont'd)
   improved intelligence gathering, 28
   threat of terrorism, 27–28
   what needs to be done, 28–29
  introduction, 14–16
   alliances among major crime groups, 16
   efforts against terrorism, 15–16
   how American crime has become transnational, 15
   priorities of Congress and the President, 15
   United Nations Convention Against Transnational Organized Crime, 15
  modern development, 25
  origins of organized crime in the United States
   colonial piracy, 16–17
   historical evolution, 18f
   immigrant crime groups and political machines, 17–19
   rise of the Robber Barons and crime families, 17
Exner, Judith, 101
Exposure: informants and witnesses, 109–110
Extortion (blackmail), and the Hobbs Act, 189–190

F

Fainberg, Ludwig ("Tarzan"), 84
FARC (Revolutionary Armed Forces of Colombia), 58, 59, 60, 61, 208, 222
  alliance with Russian organized crime, 83–84
FBI, intelligence gathering and, 217
  groups designated as priority targets, 5
  recognition of the Mafia by, 94–95
FBI Academy, 147
Federal Comprehensive Forfeiture Act (1984), 192
Fein, "Dopey" Benny, 93
Felix, Javier Arellano, 66–67
Felix, Rafael Arellano, 67
Financial analysis, 215
Financial Crime Enforcement (FinCen), 170, 196, 211
FISA (Foreign Intelligence Surveillance Act), 209
Five Families of New York, 98–99
Five Points Gang, 19, 93, 96, 99
Flying Dragons gang, 144
Folk Nation, 175
Ford, Gerald R., 221
Foreign Intelligence Surveillance Act (FISA), 209
Foreign Narcotics Kingpin Designation Act (1999), 200
Fort, Jeff, 180–181
Forty Thieves, 93, 175
Four Seas, 142
14K, 142
Fox, Vincente, 64–65, 69, 70–71
Fratianno, Jimmy "The Weasel," 110
Fraud
  fuel fraud, United States, 79, 109
  Nigerian organized crime, 184
  Russian Mafia
   bank fraud schemes, 8
   fraud of Russian companies, 80
   medical and insurance fraud, 80
"French Connection," 63, 183
Freud, S., 38
Fu Shan Chu, 137
Fuel fraud, in the United States, 79, 109
Fuentes, Amando Carillo, 54, 67–68
Fuentes, Vincente Carillo, 68
Fuk Ching Tung On gang, 144
Fukching gang, 136
Fukien American Association of Tongs, 136
Fulton Fish Market, 108, 111

G

Gabelloti, 92
Gacha, Jose, 52
Gagliano, Thomas, 97
Galante, Carmine, 98
Gambino, Carlo, 25, 91, 97, 99
Gambino Family, 108, 110
  and Hells Angels, 168
Gambling, Yakuza, 123–124
Gang(s). *See also* Hispanic and African-American gangs
  and the beginning of criminal organizations, 19
  definition of, 4–5
  violence, in insuring the vote, 19
Gangster Disciples (GDs), 175, 181–182, 182f, 186
Genovese, Vito, 21, 25, 91, 99
Genovese family, 108
Georgians, 75
Ghost Shadows gang, 144
Giancana, Sam, 25
  assassination of, 101
  and Las Vegas, 100–101
Gigante, Vincent "The Chin," 99, 110
Gillich, Mike, Jr., 23
Giri, ethics of, 121–122
Global criminal intelligence and treat analyses, 213
Globalization, expansion of organized crime and, 42, 226
Golden Crescent, 21
Golden Triangle, 21
Gonzales, Alberto, 57
GoodFellas (film), 106
Gotti, John III, 99, 108, 110
Government oversight, 111
Graffiti, Hispanic gangs, 176
Grand juries, 111–112, 171–172, 202–203
Gravano, Sammy "the Bull," 107, 110
Great Meadow Prison, 97
Green Dragons' gang, 144
Grifazzi, Nick, 102
Grim Reapers (GRMC), 161, 162f
Guanxi, 34, 133, 147
Guilt by association, 199
Gulf cartel, 65, 67
Gurentai (common thugs), 115, 116, 122
Guzman, Joaquin (El Chapo), 67

H

Halat, Pete, 23
Hamas, 208

Hamon, Yakuza sanction, 121
Hand signals and dress, Hispanic gangs, 176
Harley Davidson bikes, 158–159
Harrison Narcotics Act (1914), 20, 21
Hatamota-yakko (Shogun), 115
Hatchet men, 144
Hauser, Joseph, 111
Hedonistic gangs, 178
Hells Angels (HAMC), 155–156
  by-laws, 167–169
  "Church of Angels," 165
  and Mongols, fight between (2002), 169
Hennessey, David, murder of, 92–93
HEREIU (Hotel Employees and Restaurant Employees International Union), 107
Heroin trafficking, 21, 50, 58, 223
  Charles Lucas, 183
  Chinese triads and tongs, 140, 142, 143
  the Country Boys, 182–183
  Frank Matthews, 183
  the "French Connection" and, 63
  Leroy Barnes, 183
  Nigerian organized crime, 183–184
Herrera, Pacho, 53
Herrera family, 63–64
Heung Chu (incense master), 137–138
Hierarchical and local-ethnic models, 40
Hierarchy of a Mafia family, 103–105, 103f
High Intensity Drug Trafficking Areas (HIDTA), 171
Hill, Henry, 105–106
Hill, Tracey, 81
Hing Ah Kee Kwan, 136
Hip Sing tong, 143, 144
Hispanic and African-American gangs, 174–187
  African-American gangs
    historical black figures
      Charles Lucas, 183
      Frank Lucas, 182–183
      Frank Matthews, 183
      Leroy Barnes, 183
    major black gangs, 179–182
      Bloods and Crips, 179–180
      Jeff Fort and the Black P. Stone Nation, 180–181
      Larry Hoover and the Gangster Disciples (GDs), 181–182, 182f, 186
    other black criminal organizations
      Jamaican organized crime, 184
      Nigerian organized crime, 183–184
  conclusions, 186
  discussion questions, 187
  gang culture, 177
  gang definitions, 174
  gang structure, 177–178
  Hispanic/Latino gangs, 175–177
    clicas, 176–177
    gang communication: language, graffiti, hand signals, and dress, 176
    tattoos, 177
  historical perspective, 175
  introduction, 174–175
  investigative strategies and laws, 185–186
  members, 177–178
  MS13 gang, 186
  prison gangs, 26, 184–185
  three Rs of gang behavior, 177
Historical conspiracies, 198
Hit man, 104
Hizballah, 208
Hobbs, Leroy, 102
Hobbs Act (1970), 189–190
Hoff, "Boo-Boo," 101
Hoffa, Jimmy, 109, 200
Hollister, CA motorcycle rallies, 152
Homeboys, 180
Homeland Security, 28, 217
Honor Thy Father (Talese), 99
Hoodlums ("Los Hampones"), 52
Hoover, J. Edgar, 1, 95
Hoover, Larry, 181–182, 182f
"Hot spot" theory, 36
Hotel Employees and Restaurant Employees International Union (HEREIU), 107
House Assassination Committee (1979), 109–110
House Select Committee (1972), 109
Human rights violations, Mexico, 70
Human smuggling, by triads and tongs, 144–146
Hung Gar Kung Fu, 135
Hung Kwan (military commander), 137

I

I-Ching, 137
ICAP (Integrated Criminal Apprehension Program), 210
Ikka, 121
Illegal enterprise, 7
Illegal money transmission mission business, defined, 195
Illicit goods and services, the provision of, 107
Illinois State Training School for Boys, 179
Immigration to the United States, criminals from Russia, 76, 83
Immunity
  Derivative Use Immunity, 202–203
  Transactional Immunity, 202–203
Inano, 176
Independent Laborer's Association, 107
Indianapolis, Greenwood, seizure of Mexican meth in, 69–70
Ingawa, Sumiyoshi-Kai group, 118
Initiation into a Mafia Family, 106–107
Innovation, 36
Inspector General Act, 108
Institutional crime, 25
Instrumental gangs, 178
Insulation and need-to-know principle, 2
Integrated Criminal Apprehension Program (ICAP), 210
Intelligence gathering, 28, 209–217
  application of analytical models to organized crime investigations, 213–217
    commodity flow analysis, 215, 216f
    coordination between countries, 214

Intelligence gathering (cont'd)
   crime by association, 215–216
   data analysis, 214
   event flow analysis, 215
   financial analysis, 215
   focus of good intelligence, 213
   global criminal intelligence and treat analyses, 213
   structure and responsibilities of agency personnel, 214–215
   units within the intelligence unit, 217
  conclusions, 217–218
  discussion questions, 219
  evaluation of information, 211–212
  historical perspective, 210–211
  introduction, 209–210
  open sources, 211
  organized crime connection to terrorism, 208–209
  sources of intelligence, 212–213
  technical intelligence, 211
Internal Revenue Service (IRS) tax investigations, 193, 213
International Asian Organized Crime conferences, 147
International cooperation, 42
International Crime Control strategy, 86
International Enforcement Academy (Budapest), 86
Iran-Contra scandal, 211
Irish immigrants and political machines, 19, 34
Italian-American Mafia, 1, 90–113
  activities and methods of operation
   labor racketeering, 107–108
   new partnerships, 109
   provision of illicit goods and services, 107
  American Mafia today, 102–103
  Chicago, 99–100
  conclusions, 112
  discussion questions, 113
  historical perspective
   the FBI and the Mafia, 94–95
   immigration years: the Black Hand, 92–94
    cities they were established in, 93–94
    formation of criminal gangs, 93
    growth in power and income during the Prohibition Era, 93
    murder of David Hennessey, 92–93
   overview, 91–92
  introduction, 90–91
  investigative strategies
   exposure: informants and witnesses, 109–110
   government oversight, 111
   grand juries and legislation, 111–112
   sting operations, 110–111
  and the Kennedys, 100–101
  Las Vegas and Sam Giancana, 100–101
  New Orleans, 101–102
  New York
   Arnold Rothstein, 95–96
   Charles "Lucky" Luciano, 96
   the Commission, 96–98
   the Five Families, 98–99
  Philadelphia and Atlantic City, 101
  rise of, 25
  structure and organization
   hierarchy of a Mafia family, 103–105, 103f
   initiation, 106–107
   membership, 105–106
Ivanov, Vyacheslav K., 82–83

J

Jackson-Vanik Amendment, 76
Jamaican organized crime, 184
Jamail, Steve, 167
James Street Boys, 99
Jamundi, Colombia, 60
Javits Convention Center, 108
Jewish influence, 20, 34, 87
Johnson, Junior, 24
Johnson, Lyndon, 25–26, 50, 90
Jones Brothers gang, 100, 175
Juárez cartel, 67–68

K

Kabuki-mono (crazy groups), 115
Kao (respect or face), 121
Kazuo-Taoka, 117
Kefauver Committee, 8, 25, 26, 91, 109
Keizal-Yakuza, 121–122
Kelly, Paul, 99
Kennedy, John F., 50
  assassination of, 100, 102, 109–110
  the Chicago Mob and the election of, 100
Kennedy, Joseph, 100
Kennedy, Robert, 100, 102
Kharabadze, Nikolai, 79
Kiang Hsi, 134
Kidd, Captain William, 16
King, Martin Luther, Jr., assassination of, 102
"Kingpin Strategy," 56
Kirillov, Oleg, 22
Klebnikov, Paul, 86
Kobun, 121
Kodama-Kikan, 116–117
Kodama Yoshio, 116–117
Koiki (wide area), 118
Koiki-Boryokudan, 119
Konanykhine, Alexander, 82
Kot Siu Wong, 136
Kryshas (enforcers), 77
Ku Klux Klan (KKK)
  associated with the Arian Brotherhood, 185
  ties to outlaw motorcycle gangs, 161

L

La Cosa Nostra (LCN), 10, 34. *See also* Italian-American Mafia
  alliances with the Medellín Cartel, 52
  bosses, 19
  intelligence during WWII, 211
  labor racketeering, 200–201
  as most powerful in the U.S., 26
  rise of, 25
  term first used, 91

La Violenca, 50
Labor OIG, 108
Labor racketeering, 107–108, 200–201
Laborer's International Union of North America (LIUNA), 108
Lamb, Peter, 127
Lambardino, Frank, 102
Lansky, Meyer, 21, 27, 96, 97, 101, 221
LAPD Asian Task Force, 127
Las Vegas and Sam Giancana, 100–101
Latin Kings, 179
Law Enforcement Assistance Administration, 210
Law enforcement response, 221–226, 224–225
   concepts of organized crime and methods, controversies about, 225
   corruption, law enforcement, and the government, 224–226
   debate around U.S. statutes and legislation, 225
   evolving groups, 222
   future of organized crime in America, 226
   gaps in information about extent of alliances among crime groups, 221
   idea about legalizing drugs and prostitution, 225
   market potential for a global crime community, 226
   need for more effective legislation, 222
   organized crime alliances with terrorist groups, 222–223
   organized crime resources vs. law enforcement's, 222
   21st century criminal enterprises, 221
   training on current technologies, 224
Laws and statutes, 170–171
Laxalt, Paul, 27
Lehder, Carlos, 52
LIUNA (Laborer's International Union of North America), 108
Lombardo, Joseph "the Clown," 101
Lombroso, Cesare, 37
Long, Huey P., 25, 101
"Los Pepes," 56
LSD (lysergic acid diethylamide), 21
Lucas, Charles, 183
Lucas, Frank, 182–183
Luchesse Crime Family, 25, 91, 98, 99, 108
Luciano, Charles "Lucky," 21, 25, 95, 96
   activities in Cuba and expulsion to Palermo, 97–98
   and the Commission, 96–98
   convicted and sentenced to Dannemora prison, 97
   death in 1962, 98
   pardoned and extradited to Italy, 97
   U.S. Naval Intelligence visits him in prison, 97
Lufthansa cargo robbery, 106
Lungtau, 137
Lynching, Yakuza sanction, 120

M

Ma Jai, 140
Machi-Yakko (city servants), 115
Macko, Steve, 134
Mafia
   defined by Santino, 9
   described by the Kefauver Committee, 8
Mafia-Cali alliance, 54
Mafia Commission (1931), 98
Maggaddino, Stephano, 97, 98
Mann Act (1910), 191
Mara Salvatrucha 13 (MS13) gang, 186, 222
Maranzano, Salvatore, 96
Marcello, Carlos, 25, 27, 101, 102, 109, 111
Marcello brothers, 102
Margano, Vincent, 97
Marijuana Tax (1937), 21
Marijuana trafficking, 21, 50
Marron, John, 157
Masseria, "Joe the Boss," 96
Massina, Joseph, 99
Matranga, Anthony, 92, 101
Matranga, Charles, 92, 101
Matthews, Frank, 183
Maxwell, John, 207
McClellan Committee, 25, 26, 107, 109–110
McDonald, Big Michael, 21, 93, 99
McGuire, Phyllis, association with Giancana, 101
Medellín Cartel, 44, 52–53
Medina, Carlos, 58
Membership in a Mafia Family, 105–106
Merlino, Joey, 168
Merton, R., 36
Methamphetamines (ecstacy), 21, 223
   distribution by OMGs, 151
   Mexico, 69–70
   Russian organized crime groups, 84
Mexican DTOs, 21, 27, 63–72
   alliance with Russian organized crime groups, 84
   Colombian-Mexican partnerships, 58, 67–68
   conclusions, 71
   current activity
      meth labs, 69–70
      Mexican control over the U.S. drug market, 69
      Russian Mafia and, 70
   development and expansion, 64–65
   discussion questions, 72
   drug policies: impact and consequences, 70–71
   historical perspective, 63–64
   increased involvement in cocaine trade, 51
   introduction, 63
   involvement with the Cali cartel, 54
   major drug cartels, 66–69, 66f
      Gulf cartel, 65, 67
      Juárez cartel, 67–68
      Sinaloa cartel, 65, 67
      Tijuana cartel (Arellano Felix Organization), 66–67
   Mexican drug highway, 51
   Negros, 67
   subsidiary groups, 68–69
   violence and DTO competition, 65–66
   Zetas, 67
Mexican Mafia (EME), 185
Mi Vida Loca, 177
Mikaelian Organization, 79
Militant Groups, 10
Miller, Henry, 49
Ming family, 135, 136

Mississippi Bureau of Narcotics (MBM), 211
Mogilevich, Semion, 81–82
Money laundering, 6, 33
 Cali cartel, 55–56
 Nigerian organized crime, 184
 Russian Mafia, 80, 81
 Yakuza, 119, 125–126
Money Laundering Acts (1986, 1994), 6, 86, 129, 170, 194–195
Money laundering laws, 194–196
Money Laundering Prosecution Improvement Act (1988), 195
Money Laundering Suppression Act (1994), 195
Mongols, and Hells Angels, fight between (2002), 169
Monikers, 176
Moonshiners, 23, 24, 25
Moro Islamic Liberation Front, 223
Moro National Front, 223
Moscow Sporteak, 85
Mother Club, OMGs, 157–160, 164
Motorcycle gangs. *See* Outlaw motorcycle gangs (OMGs)
MS-13 (Mara Salvatrucha 13), 186, 222
Mules, 51
Multi-Agency Financial Investigative Center (MAFIC), 196
Murder, Inc., 97
"Muscle and murder," 25
Music piracy, Russian Mafia, 80
Muskalel, Meyer, 79

N

Narcotics and Dangerous Drug Information system (NADDIS), 211
Narcotics trafficking. *See* Drug trafficking
Natale, Ralph, 102
National Alliance of Gang Investigators Association, 151, 170
National Association for Stock Car Auto Racing, 24
National Crime Authority of Australia, 127
National FBI Academy, 86
National Gang Threat Assessment report (2005), 179
National Liberation Army (ELN), 208
National Narcotics Directorate, 58
National Security Act (1947), 209
National Security Agency, 225
National Task Force of Organized Crime, 26
Ndragheta (Society of Men of Honor), 91, 92
Negros, 67
New Mexico Statutes Annotated (2003), 7
New Orleans family, 25, 101–102
New York, organized crime in, 25
 Arnold Rothstein, 95–96
 Charles "Lucky" Lucciano, 96
 the Commission, 96–98
 the Five Families, 25, 98–99
New York tongs, 144
Nigerian organized crime, 183–184
Ninkyo-do, 115, 121
Nippon Foundation, 125
Nitti, Frank, 97, 100
Nixon, Richard, 27

Noel, Joey, 96
Nomads, 154
Nomenklatura, 75, 77
Norte del Valle cartel, 58, 59
North American Free Trade Agreement (NAFTA), 42, 51
Nuestra Family (NF), 185
Nuevo Laredo, Mexico, violence and drug trafficking in, 65–66
Nuova Sacra Corona Unita, 91, 92

O

Obstruct Terrorism Act (2001), 195
OCDETF (Organized Crime Drug Enforcement Task Forces), 170
Ochoa brothers, 52, 56
Odessa Mafia, 76, 79
"Office," 104
Office of Drug Control Policy, 39–40
Office of Foreign Assets Control (OFAC), 57
Office of National Drug Control Policy, 58
Oicho-Kabu, 114
Omerta, 2, 34
OMGs. *See* Outlaw motorcycle gangs (OMGs)
Omnibus Crime Control Act (1968), 201
On Leong tong, 143, 144, 146
One percenters, 154
Ongoing conspiracies, 198
Operation BRILAB, 111
"Operation Green Ice," 56
Opium trafficking, 143, 223
Opportunity factors, 38
Organized crime, introduction to. *See also* Evolution of organized crime
 conclusions, 10–11
 connections to terrorist groups, 208, 222–223
  legislation, 209
 criteria of being defined as organized crime, 7–8
 as defined by laws, agencies, and governments, 5–10
  conclusions, 10–11
  FBI description, 5
  international perspective, 6
  other approaches to defining organized crime, 9–10
  a synthesis of definitions, 8–9
  United States Federal definitions, 6–8
 defining organized crime, 1–4
  definitions of, 3–4
  elements of an organization, 2
  incorporating principles of legitimate organizations, 2
  working definition for, 2–3
 discussion questions, 12
 investigation definitions, 4–5
Organized Crime Act (1970), 129
Organized Crime Control Act, New York, 7
Organized Crime Drug Enforcement Task Forces (OCDETF), 170
Organized Crime Strike Force Unit, 86
Organizing crime, concept of, 9
Orgen, "Little Augie," 95, 96

Otoki (masculinity), 121
Outfit, 21, 99–100
Outlaw motorcycle gangs (OMGs), 10, 25, 26, 150–173
  activities and methods of operation, 168
    bikes, 158–159
    bureaucratic structure, 154, 155f
    colors (patches), 154, 159, 161
  conclusions, 172
  discussion questions, 173
  historical perspective
    1970 to today, 154
    drug smuggling and trafficking, 151
    number of active grous, 151
    post-WWII, 151–152
    rallies and runs, 152, 153f, 154
  introduction, 150
  investigative strategies
    grand juries, 171–172
    intelligence, 169
    laws and statutes, 170–171
  the Mother Club, 157–160, 164
  networks, 168–169
  one percenters, 154
  puppet clubs, 151
  specific large groups
    Bandidos, 156–157
    Hells Angels (HAMC), 155–156
      by-laws, 167–169
      "Church of Angels," 165
      and Mongols, fight between (2002), 169
    Nomads, 154
    the Outlaws, 156
    the Pagans, 151
      organization and rules, 157–160
    the Pissed Off Bastards of Bloomington (POBOB), 151–152
    Red Devils Motorcycle Club, 155
  specific small groups, 160–162, 162f
    the Grim Reapers (GRMC), 161, 162f
  structure
    biker women, 164
    chain of command, 162, 163f
    club house, 165
    constitution and bylaws, 164
    enforcement units, 164
    Hells Angels' California By-laws, 166–167
    membership, 167
    ministers, 165
    retirement by-laws, 167
    security, 165
    social structure, 164, 165f
  tattoos, 154
  ties to the KKK, 161
Outlaws, the, 156
Overt acts, defined, 197
Oyabun An, 123
Oyabun-Kobun (father-child role), 115
Oyster Bay Conferences, 25

P

Pagans, 151
  organization and rules, 157–160
    bikes, 158–159
    colors, 159
    funerals, 159
    mandatories, 159
    meetings, 158
    officers, 158
    old ladies, 160
    parties, 159
    prospects, 160
    respect, 159
Pak Tsz Sin, 137
Pakhan, 76
Palestine Islamist revolutionary groups, 208
Pankau, Edmund J., 213
Paramilitary groups, Colombia, 58–59
Partnerships with the Mafia, 109
Party gang, 178
Patrimonial/patron-client model, 41
Patriot Act. *See* USA Patriot Act
PCP (phencyclidine), 21
Peckler, Margarita, 79
Pecora, Norfio, 102
Pendergrast Machine, 19
People Nation, 175
Pharmaceuticals, restricted and legal, 22
Philadelphia/Atlantic City family, 101
Picotto (hit man), 104
Piracy
  colonial, 16–17
  modern, 17
Piru boys, 179
Pissed Off Bastards of Bloomington (POBOB), 151–152
Plan Colombia, 50, 59–60
Plug Uglies, 93
Police Administration, 210
Political machines and immigrant crime groups, 17–19, 34
Poretto, Joe, 102
Pornography, Yakuza, 124–125
Positivism, 37
Posses, The, 184
Predatory gangs, 178
President's Commission on Crime (1967), 201
President's Commission on Law Enforcement and Administration of Justice (1965), 26
President's Commission on Organized Crime, 2, 5, 9
  essential components of organized crime, 10
  groups that meet the definition of organized crime, 10
  methods to move organized crime funds, 194
  OMGs earnings from criminal activities, 168
  testimony about the Yamaguchi-gumi, 123
President's Council on Organized Crime, 107
President's Task Force on Organized Crime (1967, 1976, 1986), 8
Presser, Jackie, 27, 200

Principle of definition, 2
Principle of specialization, 2
Prison gangs, 26, 184–185
Profaci, Joseph, 97
Professional sports fixing, 84–85
Profiling, 37–38
Prohibition of alcohol, 20, 21, 23–24, 39
  repeal of (1933), 21, 24–25
  and the rise of the Mafia, 93
Property forfeiture, 192–193
Protection and extortion, Yakuza, 123
Provenzano crime family, 92
Puppet clubs, OMGs, 151
Purple Gang, 19
Pyramidal structure, organizations, 2

Q

Qinqing, 133–134, 147
Quebec Gold, 151
"Queer ladder of mobility," 34

R

Racketeering Influenced and Corrupt Organizations. *See* RICO
Rallies and runs, outlaw motorcycle gangs, 152, 153f, 154
Rational choice, 37
Reagan, Ronald, 26, 27
Red Command, 61
Red Devils Motorcycle Club, 155
Red Guard militia, 144
Red Pole, 137
Regional criminal groups, Russian Mafia, 75
Regional Drug Intelligence Squads (RDIS), 211
Regional Information Sharing System (RISS), 171, 211
Revenuers, 24
Revolutionary Armed Forces of Colombia (FARC). *See* FARC
Ricca, Paul, 100
RICO, 6, 28, 86, 110, 112, 190–192
  activities prohibited by, 191
  civil actions under, 192
  controversial issues, 190–191
  Organized Crime Control and Safe Streets Act, 5
  successful prosecutions under, 192
Ridge runners, 24
Rizzuto, Tom, 101
Robber Barons, 17
Roberts, Bartholomew ("Black Bart"), 16
Rodríguez, Gilberto, 53, 57
Rodríguez, Miguel, 53, 57
Rondan Doyukai, 123–124
Ronin, 115
Rosen, Nig, 101
Rothstein, Arnold, 20, 21, 95–96
Rules
  omerta, 2, 34
  Pagans, organization and rules, 157–160
  "Thieves Code," 74
  Triads and Tongs, initiation rituals, codes, symbols, and rules, 144
Russian Mafia, 10, 26, 34, 73–88
  activities and methods of organization
    cybercrime, 79–80
    extending their reach, 80–85
      bank fraud schemes, 8
      drugs and money laundering, 80, 81
      illegal weapons' trafficking, 80–81
      links with other organized crime groups, 83–85
      medical and insurance fraud, 80
      pirated music and computer crime, 80
      Semion Mogilevich, 81–82
      Vyacheslav K. Ivanov, 82–83
    theft, kidnapping, and murder, 78–79
  conclusions, 87
  corruption and, 27, 86
  discussion questions, 88
  drug trafficking, 21–22
  historical perspective
    after World War II, 74
    black market, 75
    centers of criminality
      ethnic groups, 75
      the nomenklatura, 75
      regional criminal groups, 75
      the Vory, 74–75
    criminal gangs operating in 1991, 73–74
    Russian Mafia (Red Mafia) takes over, 75–76
  introduction, 73
  investigative strategies, 85–87
    cooperation with the source country, 85
    dealing with non-cooperation and the corruption potential, 86
    International Crime Control strategy, 86
    legislation, 86
    Organized Crime Strike Force Unit, 86
    task forces dedicated to Russian organized crime, 85
    training for U.S. and foreign law enforcement, 86
    undercover operations and informants, 86–87
  and Mexican cartels, 70
  structure and organization
    enforcers (Kryshas), 77
    groups in the United States, 77–78
    levels of criminal groups, 76, 78f
    the nomenklatura, 77
    parallel structure, 76, 77f
  white slavery, 191
Russo, Andrew, 99

S

Sabella, Salvatore, 101
Safe havens for organized crime members, 33
Safiev, Georgy, 79
Samper, Ernesto, 26
Santacruz, Jose, 53
Santino, U., 9
Santoro, Salvatore, 99

Sasakawa Ryoichi, 125–126
Sasakawa Takashi, 125
Savela, Joe, 109
Scarfo, "Little Nicky," 101, 102, 110
Schultz, Dutch, 95, 96
Scott, Gloria Dean Randle, 174
Self-control, criminal activity and, 35
Seneca, 14
Serious Crimes Ordinance of Hong Kong, 132
Serious delinquents in gangs, 178
Sex trade industry, 84
"Shadow governments," 42, 104, 115
Shan Chu (Dragon Head or Hill Chief), 137, 140
Shang Hai Green Gang, 136
Shaolin monks, 134–135
Shapiro, Jacob "Gurrah," 95
Shatei, 122
Shelley, Louise, 6
Sherry, Judge Vincent, 23
Sherry, Margaret, 23
Shining Path (Peru), 223
Shogun (hatamota-yakko), 115
Shower Posse, 184
Sicilian Mafia, 34, 91
  Bonanno's alliance with, 98
Siegel, Benjamin "Bugsy," 96, 101
Sinaloa cartel, 65, 67
Sinatra, Frank, association with Giancana, 101
Sing Fung (vanguard), 137–138
Sing-song girls, 144
Skuk foo (uncle), 140
Smuggling
  Colombian cartels, 50, 51f
  Yakuza, 15, 125
"Smurfs," 55–56
Snakeheads. See Triads and tongs
Social Control Theory, 35
Social gang, 178
Sokaiya (shareholders' meeting men), 123, 124
South Africa, triad activity in, 143
Southeast Asia Tamil Tigers, 223
Southeast Asian gangs, 179
Southern organized crime (Dixie Mafia), 22–25, 102
  illegal whiskey
    during the colonial period, 23
    growth of corruption and establishment of organized crime families, 23–24
    prohibition of, 23–24
    prohibition repeal and its aftermath, 24–25
    U.S. places tax on distilled spirits, 23
  murder of the Sherrys, 23
Span of control, organizations, 2
Spangler Posse, 184
Speakeasies, 23
Special skills of organized crime members, 38
Specially Designated Narcotics Trafficker (SNDT), 200
Specified unlawful activities (SUAs), 195
Stanfa, John, 101

Statutes, legislation, methods of organized crime investigations, 188–205. See also Intelligence gathering
  conclusions, 203–204
  conspiracy statutes, 197–203
    advantages of, 197–198
    case development, 199
    disadvantages of conspiracy investigations, 198
    electronic surveillance, 201–202
    guilt by association, 199
    investigative grand juries, 202–203
    regulation and monitoring of business and labor, 200–201
    term conspiracy, 197
    types of conspiracies, 198–199
  Continuing Criminal Enterprise (CCE) Statute (1970), 189, 200
  controlled substances acts
    Anti-Drug Abuse Act (1986), 197
    Chemical Diversion and Trafficking Act (1988), 197
    Comprehensive Crime Control Act (1984), 197
  discussion questions, 205
  Foreign Narcotics Kingpin Designation Act (1999), 189, 200
  internal revenue code violations, 193
  introduction, 188–189
  the money laundering cycle, 196
  money laundering laws, 194–196
    Annunzio-Wylie Money Laundering Act (1992), 195
    Drug Abuse Act (1988), 195
    Money Laundering Act (1986), 194–195
    Money Laundering Prosecution Improvement Act (1988), 195
    Money Laundering Suppression Act (1994), 195
    Patriot Act, 189, 195, 201–202, 204
  other statutes used during investigations, 203
  property forfeiture, 192–193
  RICO, 190–192
    activities prohibited by, 191
    civil actions under, 192
    controversial issues, 190–191
    successful prosecutions under, 192
Sting operations, 110–111
Stoners, 178
Strain theory and anomie, 36–37, 43
Strasburg convention, 128
Street gang mentality, 4
Strike insurance, 201
Structuralists, 35
Sturgis Rally, 152
Sullivan, "Big Tim," 19
Sumiyoshi-Kai group, 118
Sun Tzu, 11
Sun Yee On triad, 142
Sung Lian triad, 142
Susumu Ishii, 126
Sutherland, E., 36
Sweetheart contracts, 201
Syndicate, definition of, 4

T

Tai-Lo (elder brother), 137
Taiwan, major triads in, 142
Taliban, 208, 211
Tamil Tigers, 223
Tammany Hall Machine, 19
Task and strike forces
  commissions and task forces, 25–26
  creation of, 28
  dedicated to Russian organized crime, 85
  LAPD Asian Task Force, 127
  National Task Force of Organized Crime, 26
  President's Task Force on Organized Crime (1967, 1976, 1986), 8
  against the Yakuda, 127
Tate, Christian, 169
Tattoos
  Hispanic/Latino gangs, 177
  outlaw motorcycle gangs, 154
  on prisoners, 74
  Yakuza, 121
Taylor, Frederick W., 95
Teach, Edward ("Blackbeard"), 16
Teamsters, 107
Technology and organized crime, 208
TECS II, 196
Tekiya (street peddlers), 115, 116
Tennes, Mont, 21
Terrorist groups, 27–28
  efforts against, 15–16
  organized crime's connection to, 42, 208, 222–223
  legislation, 209
Testa, Philip, 101
Texas Law Enforcement Management and Administrative Statistics Program (TLEMASP), 209
Texas Statutes and Codes (2003), 7
Texas Syndicate, 151, 185
Theft, kidnapping, and murder, Russian Mafia, 78–79
Theories on the continued existence of organized crime, 32–47
  beyond theory, 41–42
  combining theory and other explanations
    anomie concept, 43
    conspiracy, 42–43, 44
    criminal-community relationship, 43
    environmental and role model influences, 43
    ethnicity, 43
    relevance of theories, 44–45
    why most people do not enter criminal organizations, 44
  conclusions, 45–46
  discussion questions, 47
  introduction, 32–34
  theories
    Albanese's theory of typologies, 35–36
    Alien Conspiracy Theory, 34
    Beccaria and Lombroso's classical theory, 37
    biological, 37
    Durkheim and Merton's strain theory and anomie, 36–37
    "hot spot" theory, 36
    Social Control Theory, 35
    summary of the theoretical approach, 37–38
    Sutherland's theory of differential association, 36
    "the queer ladder of mobility," 34
    why are most people not criminals?, 36
  theories related to law enforcement efforts, 38–41
    bureaucratic/corporate model, 41
    criminal environment issues, 39
    Deterrence Theory, 40–41
    enterprise theory, 39–40
    hierarchical and local-ethnic models, 40
    opportunity factors, 38
    patrimonial/patron-client model, 41
    special skills, 38
Theory of bureaucracy, 95
Theory of differential association, 36
Theory of efficient operations, 95
Theory of typologies, 35–36
"Thieves Code," 74
"Thieves World," 87
Thrasher, Federick, 174
"Three R's" characteristics, 4
Tian Dao triad, 142
Tieri, Frank, 110
Tijuana cartel (Arellano Felix Organization), 66–67
Tiny Locos, 176
TLEMASP (Texas Law Enforcement Management and Administrative Statistics Program), 209
Tokugawa (peace) era of Japan, 115, 116
Tolson, Clyde, 95
Tongs and Triads. See Triads and Tongs
Torrio, John, 21, 25, 99
Torrio-Capone vs. the Dion-O'Bannion Organizations, 99–100
Trafficante, Santo, 109
Training
  on current technologies, 224
  of Mexican soldiers by U.S., 67
  for U.S. and foreign law enforcement, 86
Tranquil Happiness Triad, 136
Transactional Immunity, 202–203
Transnational Crime and Corruption Center (TraCCC), 6
Trap and trace records, 201
Treaty of Mutual Assistance in Criminal Matters (1973), 6
Triads and Tongs, 10, 21, 132–149
  activities and methods of operation, 141–146
    business investments, 145–146
    code of ethics, 142–143
    dragon syndicates, 142
    human smuggling, 144, 145–146
    initiation rituals, codes, symbols, and rules, 144
    international growth, 143
    major activities, 141–142
    major triads, 142
    secrecy, 143
    turf wars, 144–145
    U.S. tongs, 143, 144
    violence and intimidation, 144

conclusions, 147–148
discussion questions, 149
historical perspective
  alliances with other crime organizations, 133
  Chinese Consolidated Benevolent Association, 133
  Chinese rebellions through the revolution, 135–136
  development of in 1850s San Francisco, 133
  the fighting Shaolin monks, 134–135
  fighting tongs, 133
  global dispersal of the triads, 136
  intergenerational family loyalty, 133–134
  number of triads in Hong Kong today, 132–133
  operations in the United States, 134
  United Bamboo Crime Syndicate, 133
  Wah Ching tong, 133
  world membership, 134
introduction, 132
investigative strategies
  cultural and language barriers, 146
  surveillance and sting operations, 146–147
structure
  Chinese groups operating in the United States, 140f
  departments not denoted by number, 139
  major triads and their subgoups, 141f
  membership, 137–140
  numerology system, 137
  structure of a triad, 137–138, 138f, 139f
  tongs, 140–141
triad defined, 132
Tweed, William March (Boss Tweed), 19, 93
Twenty-first Amendment. *See* Prohibition of alcohol

U

Umansky, Alexander, 79
Underboss (Maas), 110
Undercover operations and informants, against the Russian Mafia, 86–87
Uniform Crime Reporting (UCR) Index Crimes, 171–172
Uniform Narcotic Drug Act (1932), 21
Unions dominated by organized crime, 200
Unit of command, organizations, 2
United Bamboo Code of Ethics, 142–143
United Bamboo Crime Syndicate, 133
United Nations Convention Against Transnational Organized Crime, 15, 195
United Self-Defense Groups of Colombia (AUC), 60, 208
United States-Japan Foundation, 125
United States v. Real Property, 193
United States v. Teri, 191
United Wa State Army, 223
Uribe, Alvano, 60
U.S. Naval Intelligence, and Luciano, 97
U.S. Senate Appropriations Committee, funding for Plan Colombia, 60
U.S. tongs, 143
U.S. Treasury Dept. TECSII System, 170
U.S. War on Drugs, Mexican DTOS and, 64
USA Patriot Act, 28, 170, 189, 195, 201–202, 204
  debates about, 209, 225

Utilitarians, 37
Uyoku (right wing extremists), 115, 116

V

Valachi, Joseph "the Rat," 25, 91, 99, 107, 110
Valachi Papers, The (Maas), 110
Valdez, Edgar "La Barbie," 67
Vario, Paul, 106
Vendetta, 105
Veteranos, 176
Vice Lord Nation, 179
Vice Lords, 179
Vickers, Stephen, 142–143
Violent Crime Control and Law Enforcement Act (1994), 185
Violent Criminal Apprehension Program (VICAP), 210
Volkov, Alexander, 83
Vollmer, August, 210
Voloshin, Vladimir, 83
Voroskoy Zakon, 74–75
Vory, 74–75

W

Wagner, Angie, 169
Wah Ching tong, 133, 145
Waldrip, Mary H., 114
Walters, John, 58
Watanabe Yoshinori, 117–118
Weapons, illegal trafficking in
  Russian Mafia, 80–81
  Yakuza, 15, 125
Weber, Max, 2, 95
Weiss, Hymie, 100
West Tsusho, 126
Wheel and chain conspiracies, 199
Whiskey riots (1794), 23
White collar crime (corporate crime), 15
"White Hand" gang, 175
White Lotus Society, 136
"White Slave Act," 191
White slavery, 191
Wickersham Committee, 25
Wilson, O.W., 210
Wiretaps, 201, 202
Wiseguy: Life Inside a Mafia Family (Pileggi), 106
Witness Security and Protection Program (WITSEC), 110, 203
Wo Hop To gang, 145
Wo Sing Wo triad, 142
World Health Organization, 125
WorldCom scandal, 15, 17, 26

Y

Yakuza, 10, 26, 114–130
  Act for the Preservation of Unlawful Activities by Boryokudan Members, 118
  activities and methods of operation
    business acquisition, 123
    gambling, 123–124

Yakuza (cont'd)
   money laundering, 125–126
   narcotics trafficking, 124
   pornography, 124–125
   protection and extortion, 123
   weapons and smuggling, 15, 125
assets, 114
conclusion, 128–129
corruption and increase in serious crime, 118
derivation of term, 114
described, 115
discussion questions, 130
full-time members (1999), 118
historical perspective
   early criminal groups, 115–116
   the industrial age through post-World War II, 116–117
   Yamaguchi-gumi, 117–118
   Yoshinori Watanabe, 117–118
introduction, 114–115
investigative strategies, laws and statutes
   Boryokudan Countermeasures Law (1992), 126–127
   follow the money, 127–128
   LAPD Asian Task Force, 127
   special task forces, 127
Keizal-Yakuza, 121–122
a "shadow government" of Japan, 114–115
structure and organization
   code of conduct and oaths, 120–122, 121–122
      ceremonies under the concept of Giri, 121–122
      contributions to good causes, 122
      fees and contributions, 122
      initiation into the clan, 121
      maintaining the image, 122
      political ideologies, 122
      sanctions, 120–121
      six sacred oaths, 121
      tattooing the body, 121
   membership, 120, 120f
Sumiyoshi-Kai group, 118
today
   activity in the United States, 119
   alliances with other organized crime groups, 119
   criminal groups operating in 1992, 118–119, 119t
   criminal operations, 119
   Koiki-Boryokudan, 119
   money laundering, 119
Yamaguchi-gumi, 117–118, 123
Yashi (peddlers), 115
Yee Lo, 140
Young organized gangs, 178
Yubitsume, Yakuza sanction, 120–121
Yucatan, 68

Z

Zakone, Vory V. (thief-in-law), 74
Zetas, 67
Zetsuem, Yakuza sanction, 121